AN
IRRESISTIBLE
FORCE

AN IRRESISTIBLE FORCE

LIEUTENANT COLONEL BEN VANDERVOORT
AND THE
2ND BATTALION, 505TH PARACHUTE INFANTRY
IN WORLD WAR II

PHIL NORDYKE

PUBLISHED BY
HISTORIC VENTURES

First published in 2011 by Historic Ventures, LLC.
Copyright © 2011 by Phil Nordyke

Library of Congress Cataloging-in-Publication Data

Nordyke, Phil.
    An irresistible force: Lieutenant Colonel Ben Vandervoort and the 2nd Battalion, 505th Parachute Infantry in World War II / Phil Nordyke.
        p.cm.
    Includes biographical references and index.
    ISBN 978-0-9847151-0-7

1. United States. Army, Parachute Infantry Regiment, 505th. 2. World War, 1939—1945—Regimental histories—United States. 3. World War, 1939—1945—Campaigns—Western Front. I. Title

On the front cover: The 2nd Battalion, 505th Parachute Infantry Regiment moves through the rubble strewn streets of St.-Sauveur-le-Vicomte, June 16, 1944. Lieutenant Colonel Vandervoort is at the left center with his left leg in a cast and using a crutch. *U.S. Army photograph, National Archives*

CONTENTS

ACKNOWLEDGMENTS ....…....6

CHAPTER 1 "Tough and Intelligent ....…...8

CHAPTER 2 "He Was Pushing Everybody" 39

CHAPTER 3 "Well, Let's Go!" ....…....50

CHAPTER 4 "On One Leg And A Crutch" ....…....72

CHAPTER 5 "The Best Damn Soldiers In The War" 105

CHAPTER 6 "You Fired Fast And Straight" 124

CHAPTER 7 "No Quarter Combat" ....…...........152

CHAPTER 8 "We Had Never Retreated" 176

CHAPTER 9 "One Of The Most Fearless" ....…....199

EPILOGUE "He Was A True Warrior" 229

NOTES ....…............231

BIBLIOGRAPHY 248

INDEX TO MAPS 257

INDEX 258

ACKNOWLEDGMENTS

I am indebted to many individuals and groups for their contributions to the completion of this project. First, I want to thank my wife, Nancy, whose proof reading and suggestions to improve manuscript have been invaluable.

The research materials for the book came from several repositories and archives. I am indebted to a number of wonderful people who provided help in obtaining the information.

The Cornelius Ryan Collection at Ohio University in Athens, Ohio was a wealth of veterans' accounts and documents relating to the Normandy and Holland campaigns. I want to thank Doug McCabe, Curator of Manuscripts, Robert E. and Jean R. Mahn Center for Archives and Special Collections, the Alden Library, Ohio University for providing the large volume of materials referenced in this book.

I want to thank Martin K. A. Morgan, the outstanding author and historian for providing copies of veterans' oral history transcripts and written accounts of D-Day from the Eisenhower Center and National World War II Museum in New Orleans, Louisiana.

I want to extend my gratitude to Dr. John Duvall, Museums Chief, and Betty Rucker, Collections Manager, who opened up the Ridgway–Gavin Archives at The 82nd Airborne Division War Memorial Museum at Fort Bragg, North Carolina, a rich source of primary documents for this book.

Ericka L. Loze, Librarian, Donovan Research Library, Fort Benning, Georgia provided monographs of 505th Parachute Infantry Regiment veterans from the library's massive collection.

The dedicated people at the National Archives at College Park, Maryland provided much assistance with locating such primary source documents such as general orders, awards files, hospital interviews, after-action reports, and map overlays have been invaluable and their efforts are very much appreciated.

The book written by Michel De Trez about Colonel Vandervoort was a wealth of information about the colonel's early life and career and I want to thank Michel for his willingness to help me with my book.

My sincere appreciation is extended to Father G. Thuring and Frank van den Bergh with the Liberation Museum at Groesbeek, Holland. They provided much information about the campaign in Holland. Their books and expertise helped correct several errors in my understanding of the battle for the Nijmegen bridges.

Phil Schwartzberg, the cartographer at Meridian Mapping, Minneapolis, Minnesota produces the best maps in the business and I owe him my thanks for his superb work.

The veterans of the 505th RCT Association deserve the greatest credit and appreciation for making this book possible. I must begin by acknowledging the early support of the late Lieutenant General Jack Norton, Colonel Mark

Alexander, and Colonel Ed Sayre. They encouraged and inspired me to write this book.

There were individuals with each unit who helped me with contact information, who provided entrées to others in their units, and who provided information about the units. The names are too numerous to mention without invariably omitting to thank one or more. To the veterans, friends, and families of the 505th RCT who contributed to the book, I owe the greatest appreciation. This book would not have been possible without the first person accounts of the veterans.

In some cases, I have made minor changes to some of the personal accounts, correcting grammatical and spelling errors, rearranged sentences to put the action in chronological order, or to omit repetitive or irrelevant information in long quotes, and to have consistency in unit designations, equipment, and other items. However, the first person accounts are always true to the veterans' original words.

It is to all of the officers and men who served with the 2nd Battalion, 505th Parachute Infantry Regiment during World War II that this book is dedicated.

CHAPTER 1

"Tough and Intelligent"

Cottesmore airfield in England was a beehive of activity in the fading light. Paratroopers of the 2nd Battalion, 505th Parachute Infantry Regiment gathered near their assigned C-47 aircraft, helping one another tighten the straps fastening the ponderous combat loads to each man. The troopers went about the preparations in a business-like manner. Most were veterans of two night combat jumps—spearheading the invasion of Sicily and coming to the rescue of the amphibious landings at Salerno, Italy. Now, they were preparing for the largest airborne operation in history in support of Operation Overlord—the invasion of Normandy, France, which would begin in a few hours on June 6, 1944.

While waiting on the tarmac to board the lead aircraft, twenty-nine year old Major Ben Vandervoort received word of his promotion from major to lieutenant colonel. Although he had been the commanding officer of the 2nd Battalion a relatively short time—since October 1943—Vandervoort was not a newcomer to the regiment and the airborne.

Benjamin H. Vandervoort was born on March 3, 1915, at Gasport, New York, the son of an army officer. He was handsome, an athletic five feet ten inches tall, and one hundred sixty pounds. After graduating from high school at Columbus, Ohio, he attended Washington College at Chestertown, Maryland, where he participated in varsity football and track and was a member of the Titsworth Debate Club, the YMCA, the Varsity Club, and the Mount Vernon Literary Society. Vandervoort majored in Economics and Government, graduating in June 1938 with a Bachelor of Science degree. He received a U.S. Army Reserve commission as a second lieutenant resulting from his participation in the Citizen Military Training Corps.

Upon graduation, Lieutenant Vandervoort received orders to report to the 11th Infantry Regiment at Fort Benjamin Harrison, Indiana. The following year, in August of 1939, through competitive tests, he received a regular army commission. Vandervoort's next duty was with the 10th Infantry Regiment of the 5th Infantry Division at Fort Hayes, Ohio.

In 1940, the young officer volunteered for parachute training, graduating from the Parachute School at Fort Benning, Georgia on January 21, 1941 and was assigned to the U.S. Army's first parachute infantry unit—the 501st Parachute Infantry Battalion.

He served in Company B, under the command of Captain Robert F. Sink, who would later command the 506th Parachute Infantry Regiment of the famed 101st Airborne Division.

Next, Vandervoort received a promotion to the rank of captain and was assigned as the Operations and Training Officer at the Parachute School.

During the fall of 1941, Captain Vandervoort and Lieutenant Melvin Zais flew to Central America to conduct a clandestine mission. Dressed as civilians, Vandervoort and Zais scouted suitable drop zones in Costa Rica, Guatemala, Honduras, and Nicaragua in the event the countries' significant German populations attempted to overthrow the governments or if Germany invaded any of those countries. After the mission, Vandervoort rejoined the 501st Parachute Infantry Battalion, which had already been deployed to the Panama Canal Zone to defend it against potential seizure by Germany.

With the Japanese bombing of Pearl Harbor, the U.S. military mobilization accelerated. Experienced commissioned and non-commissioned officers were badly needed for training. In June 1942, Vandervoort returned to Fort Benning, where he became a member of the cadre of the newly forming 505th Parachute Infantry Regiment. His initial assignment was as the first commanding officer of Company F, which was part of Captain James A. Gray's 2nd Battalion.

The 505th was activated on June 25, 1942, and Lieutenant Colonel James M. Gavin took command of the regiment on July 6. Vandervoort knew that the regiment was receiving highly motivated and very physically fit young men, but much more was needed for them to be highly effective in combat. "All of the enlisted men were 'double volunteers'—not draftees. Called to arms by Pearl Harbor, they had volunteered for the army and again for the paratroops. Screened, tested, and jump qualified by the Parachute School, they were the top of the line of America's citizen soldiers. Many would have been in college except for the war. The goal of the regimental cadre was to train them into as tough and intelligent a group of fighting men as ever pulled on jump boots."[1]

As the Parachute School produced new jump classes each week, paratroopers joined the newly forming companies of the regiment in the Frying Pan area of Fort Benning during July and August. After the 505 reached full strength, it moved across the Chattahoochee River on August 29, 1942, to Camp Billy Mitchell, known to the troopers as the "Alabama Area."

The cadre drove the regiment hard with long marches with full field gear, grueling daily calisthenics, five-mile runs, hand-to-hand combat training, tactical problems, and weapons training. During this training, Private Russell W. Brown, an original member of Company F, described Vandervoort as "tough but fair."[2]

Gavin, promoted to full colonel in September, felt that the "training program was just about as tough and demanding as we could make it. The troopers responded well. However, despite the rigors of their training, they always seemed to have enough energy left to get into fights in Phenix City, Alabama, and its environs during time off."[3]

One evening, six 2nd Battalion paratroopers were drinking at Cotton's Fish Camp, a roadhouse in Phenix City, and got into a fistfight with a large number of the local citizens. The troopers more than held their own in the brawl. Unknown to the civilians, Sergeant Tommy Thompson, with Company D, was one of the regiment's boxing champions. He and the other troopers were getting the best of them when the locals pulled knives and straight razors. A slash from a straight razor left a laceration a foot long and three-quarters of an inch wide on the back of Company D trooper Private Gasper Lucero, whose wound required hospitalization. The other five troopers escaped back to the Alabama Area, telling their buddies what had transpired. A group of troopers went back to Cotton's Fish Camp that Friday night to tear the roadhouse apart. However, Alabama state troopers and military police had been tipped off and were waiting as the paratroopers approached. When the law enforcement officers attempted to arrest the paratroopers, a melee broke out as some troopers took on the billy club wielding police, while others bolted from the scene to avoid arrest. Twenty-seven troopers were arrested and delivered to the post guardhouse at Fort Benning, where they spent the night.

For Colonel Gavin, "that was a disastrous turn of events. I called on the provost marshal in person and assured him that if he would let me take the men out of the guardhouse I could handle them myself. At first he was somewhat reluctant to sanction such an irregular proposal, but I finally convinced him that the paratroopers were a special kind of soldier, just too full of imagination and ideas, and that I knew how to handle them. I marched them back to camp and that evening took the entire regiment on an all-night march down through the canebreaks in the bottoms of the Chattahoochee River. It was a Saturday night, and we maneuvered one battalion against two through the night. At daylight we were resupplied by parachute."[4]

When the forced march began, Lieutenant Frank P. Woosley, with Company E, had his doubts as to whether one of the other officers in the company was up to the task. "When I met Lieutenant Wray, he said to me, 'My name is Waverly W. Wray, but just call me Charlie.' He had a Mississippi drawl. We wondered a little about Charlie—he had a soft face, maybe a little heavy, read his Bible daily, and did not drink, smoke, or chase women. He was not quite our picture of a real paratroop hero. We were on a forced punishment march after the Cotton's Fish Camp incident and the light machine gunners were complaining. There was no way to carry a light machine gun that it did not hurt—heavy and all sharp edges. Charlie said, 'John Brown,' which was his harshest expletive. He took both guns from the gunners in the platoon he was in and carried one on each shoulder until the next break. This seemed impossible. Then he walked up and down the road where the platoon lay in the ditch during the break, with the guns still on his shoulders and carried them until the following break. We did not wonder about Charlie anymore. We all knew we had a man among us."[5]

On Sunday evening, Gavin marched the regiment back to the training area, completing a fifty-four mile trek in just twenty-four hours. "Later in the evening I noticed quite a few of them in dress uniforms, wearing polished boots, on their way to the bus stop to go to Phenix City."[6]

As the subsequent training progressed, Lieutenant Woosley knew that the regiment was tough, but not yet combat tested. "We were trained in all phases of infantry combat and were developing swiftly, if not always too happily, into combat soldiers. Before we sailed, our unit could start on a forced march early in the morning, walk all day and late into the night, then bivouac along the road, for enough time for everyone to get to sleep. Then, if we were ordered to move out under combat conditions, each man would wake when touched, wake the man behind him, assemble his equipment, and be ready to move out with no noise or light. After such a unit has had combat experience, the ones who are left can be called a combat unit."[7]

During the time in the Alabama Area, any officer or enlisted man who fell out during training for anything other than a bona fide injury was quickly transferred out of the regiment.

On February 7, 1943, the 505th moved by train to Camp Hoffman, North Carolina, near Fort Bragg, where on February 12, it joined the 82nd Airborne Division, commanded by General Matthew B. Ridgway. After seven months, the regiment was in superb physical condition. Gavin had developed the original airborne operational doctrine and had thoroughly schooled the regiment in all its aspects. The tough training had weeded most of the weak and had developed extremely tight bonds among the officers, non-commissioned officers, and the enlisted men. There was intense unit pride, which rose above even that of the other parachute regiments. It was arguably the best parachute regiment in the U.S. Army.

The intense training regimen continued at Fort Bragg. One day, Private David V. Bowman and the rest of Company D attended a lecture conducted by Captain Vandervoort, who stood in front of them on a platform. "He began the lecture about the mechanics of hand grenades and then drifted into their proper use. He had always impressed me as being a little spastic, and this was no more in evidence than now, as he carelessly bounced the grenade from one hand to the other. 'Now, in order to arm the grenade you must first pull the pin,' he began. 'After you pull the pin, however, it still will not go off as long as you hold this lever down.' He pointed to the lever. 'Just hold it down after you pull the pin. So, you see, if you pull the pin then realize for some reason or another that you don't need to throw the grenade, then you can reinsert it, like this.' Then he pulled the pin! This crazy, spastic ass pulled the pin of a hand grenade! He then clumsily shifted it to the other hand, almost dropping it; then reinserted the pin. What a relief. The pin is back in the grenade, and we relaxed. Then, unbelievably, he started through the sequence again! 'So you see how it works now? You can pull the pin and as long as you keep the lever compressed, it won't go off. Then he pulled the pin and again started to transfer the grenade to his other hand, but this time he dropped it. The lever flew off, and Vandervoort yelled. It became apparent that all of us in the audience had become tense and were fearful of this very thing happening, as we took to our heels in a near state of panic, only to see the grenade drop harmlessly to the ground several yards to our front while we were still on the run. We had been duped. It had been only a dummy grenade, and Vandervoort had played his role well. We were called back to the stage where the grinning captain promptly informed us that the only proper way to react to a live grenade in one's midst, whether inadvertently dropped by one of your own or thrown by the enemy, was to throw it as Private 'Doe' had just done. Embarrassing for us? Yes, but all except Private 'Doe' had fallen for it. I still have the suspicion, however, that the private, who coincidentally happened to be assigned to battalion headquarters, was a 'plant'—that he had been instructed beforehand what to do and performed accordingly."[8]

The 505th made history on March 30, 1943, when it made the U.S. Army's first regimental sized mass parachute jump at Fort Jackson, South Carolina. During the jump, his forty-sixth, Vandervoort broke his left ankle and was hospitalized at Fort Bragg.

On April 20, 1943, the 505th moved in strict secrecy by train from Fort Bragg to Camp Edwards, Massachusetts, to prepare for movement overseas. The regiment made final preparations and entrained for New York City on April 28. The following day as part of a convoy of warships and troop transports carrying the 82nd Airborne Division, the 505th embarked on the *U.S.S. Monterey* for the voyage to North Africa, docking at Casablanca, French Morocco, on May 10. Two days later, the regiment moved to its training base located some 300 miles away, outside the small town of Oujda, French Morocco. Units were transported by slow moving trains, riding in blazing hot passenger cars and "40 & 8s" (boxcars that held forty men or eight horses); by truck convoys over rough and dust choked roads; and if lucky, by C-47 aircraft.

Private Irvin W. "Turk" Seelye, with Company E, rode in a passenger car of one of the troop trains. "The ride was a hot and dirty one. We ate K-rations and tried to sleep on the hard wooden seats. There were no toilet facilities. On the way, the train passed other trains carrying German and Italian POWs. At various stops, we had our first glimpses of Arab towns—not impressive."[9]

Private Dave Bowman, with Company D, arrived at the bivouac site after a long train ride in a 40 & 8 boxcar. "Our company was assigned a particular area, which was further broken down into platoon and squad areas. The individual soldier had one-half of a pup tent, so we were paired, and two men lived in this pup tent. We were instructed to dig a trench around the tent to keep water out of the floor when it rained. Now, you can imagine how much good a trench would do on level ground when a torrential downpour came with an accompanying wind—and this occurred more than just a couple of times while we were there.

"We continued the training, very much as before—physical exercises, night problems, assaults, defense, and other such military exercises and maneuvers. When we started out in this desert or, I guess more precisely, semi-desert—in the morning, we had with us only one canteen of water, and this was to last us through our whole day of exertion in the heat. 'Water discipline,' they called it. Occasionally, they would bring a Lister bag full of water, well heated in the desert sun – but this was rare. Equally painful to me was the skimpy amount of food we were allowed while there. But this may have been of minor importance to most, considering that many contracted malaria and yellow jaundice, and I think we all got dysentery at some time or another."[10]

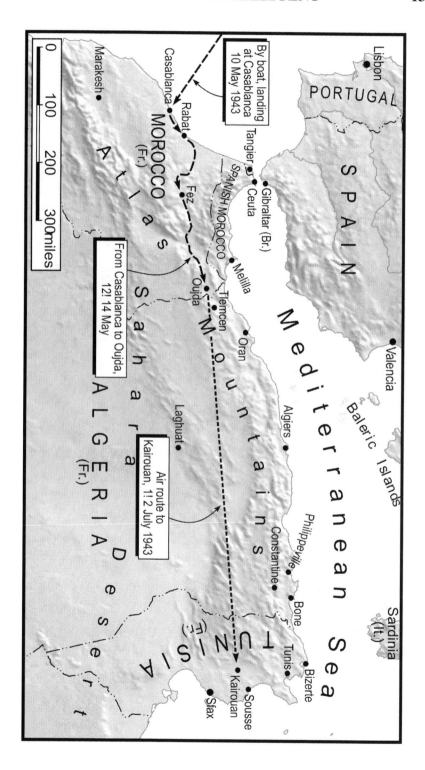

Shortly after getting settled in the division's new bivouac, Colonel Gavin was ordered to report to General Ridgway. "General Ridgway called myself and Colonel [Reuben H.] Tucker [commanding the 504th Parachute Infantry Regiment] up to orient us on our probable combat task. It had been directed by the G.H.Q., and was to be known as 'Husky' and was to be executed July 10th. It contemplated the seizure of Sicily. The 505th C.T. was to spearhead the amphibious landing of the 1st or 45th Divisions. Our jump was to take place in moonlight the night of July 9th, 11:30 p.m. The exact mission was yet an issue. From an analysis of the probable missions it was clear that the effort would be a very risky one and a costly one."[11]

The 505th Regimental Combat Team would be composed of the 505th P.I.R., commanded by Colonel Gavin and attached units. The 3rd Battalion, 504th P.I.R., commanded by Lieutenant Colonel Charles W. Kouns, was attached to provide additional infantry strength. The 456th Parachute Field Artillery Battalion, commanded by Lieutenant Colonel Harrison B. Harden, Jr., would provide the artillery support for the combat team. Demolition missions would be conducted by Company B, 307th Airborne Engineer Battalion, commanded by Captain William H. Johnson. A detachment of the 82nd Airborne Signal Company, commanded by Lieutenant Edward Kacyainski would assist the combat in establishing communications with the 1st and 45th Infantry Divisions, and a detachment of the 307th Airborne Medical Company, commanded by Staff Sergeant Jack M. Bartley would assist the 505th P.I.R. medical detachment with medical evacuations.

The 505's primary objective would be to capture and hold a key crossroads northeast of Gela, Sicily, to block enemy reinforcements from reaching the beach where the U.S. 1st Infantry Division would land. The 1st and 2nd Battalions, supported by two platoons of Company B, 307th Airborne Engineer Battalion had the objective of assaulting and capturing the fortifications defending the crossroads, which was code named Objective "Y".

With aerial reconnaissance photos of the objectives, Gavin had full-scale replicas constructed of the fortifications at each objective. Pillboxes, trenches, blockhouses, and barbed-wire obstacles were of the type and location of the same fortifications at each objective. Assaults were rehearsed repetitively against these fortifications using live ammunition.

While training in Oujda, the 82nd Airborne Division was under the command of the General Mark W. Clark's U.S. Fifth Army. However, during the invasion of Sicily, the division would fight as part of the U.S. Seventh Army, led by the already legendary General George S. Patton. On May 19, a division review was conducted for Clark.

The 52nd Troop Carrier Wing, assigned to carry the 505th Regimental Combat Team serials into Sicily, received very little training in night operations despite the efforts of the commander, Brigadier General Hal Clark. The C-47 flight crews had not received training in the U.S. in close-formation night flying prior to deployment to North Africa. The airfields around Oujda, from which the 52nd Troop Carrier Wing would conduct practice drops with the 82nd, were not completed until May 25, 1943. The 52nd was not ready for training operations with the 82nd Airborne Division until June 1. There just had not been enough time to conduct the training to prepare the troop carrier flight crews for the Sicily night jump. General Clark developed a combat formation for the Sicily drop of nine planes flying in a V-of-Vs configuration, which would become the standard formation for future parachute operations.

Nine planes would carry a company of paratroopers. Each V-of-V would fly one behind the next about a minute and a half apart. Four or five nine-plane formations would make up a serial. A serial would carry a parachute battalion. The serials would follow each other at 10-minute intervals. This formation would become standard in future airborne operations, although the intervals between serials would later be reduced.

On the night of June 14, a full dress rehearsal, code-named Operation "Pirate" began with a night jump by battalion staffs, company commanders, and platoon leaders. The drop was scattered. The following night, the ground portion of the operation—night organization of a defensive area was conducted. A critique of the operation was held the following evening at the Paris Theater in Oujda. The poor performance of Major James Gray's 2nd Battalion was emphasized. The following day, Major Gray flew to Kairouan, Tunisia to inspect the airfields. Gavin considered him AWOL (absent without leave) for not having informed him, although Gray would claim upon his return that he told Captain Alfred W. Ireland, the regimental adjutant of his plans.

On June 21, Gavin gave the regimental combat team's key personnel a big picture orientation of Operation Husky. The next day, Gavin relieved Gray as battalion commander, and replaced him with the 2nd Battalion executive officer, Major Mark J. Alexander. Gavin promoted the man he felt was one of his best company commanders, Capt. Vandervoort to major and assigned him to the regimental staff as the S-3 (plans and operations). Lieutenant Neal L. McRoberts was transferred on June 22, from 1st Battalion S-2 to commanding officer of Company F, replacing Vandervoort.

On June 24, 1943, General Ridgway ordered the 82nd Airborne Division to move to Kairouan, Tunisia, the staging area for Operation Husky.

On July 7 and 8, briefings were conducted to inform each trooper of his company or platoon's mission. Each trooper was issued a combat load, which was designed to allow the paratroopers to be self-sufficient for several days. The typical combat load carried by each paratrooper included a main parachute, plus a reserve parachute. Each carried his personal weapon, ammunition, and grenades; typically an M1 rifle, one hundred sixty-eight rounds of .30-caliber M1 ammunition, four fragmentation grenades, one smoke grenade, plus a bayonet, trench knife, and switchblade jump knife. Along with their jumpsuit, each wore a helmet, gloves, silk escape map and compass sown inside their jumpsuit, wristwatch, combat harness, and carried a handkerchief. Extra clothes included two pairs of socks and one pair of under shorts. Each had a musette bag that held a mess kit, one "K" and one "D" ration, tooth brush, tooth powder, safety razor with five blades, one bar of soap, pencil, paper, ten packs of Camel cigarettes, matches, cigarette lighter, and Halazone tablets (for water purification). And finally, each load included a 30-foot rope, blanket, shelter half, gas mask, entrenching tool, two first aid kits, and a canteen filled with water. Most carried extra .30-caliber machine gun ammunition or other special items. Officers and NCOs carried a .45-caliber pistol with ammunition. Including the main and reserve parachutes, the average load would weigh around eighty to ninety pounds.

The next day, July 9, the crew-served weapons (60mm and 81mm mortars, .30-caliber machine guns, bazookas, and 75mm pack howitzers) and ammunition, extra small arms ammunition, medical supplies, demolition materials (C2, fuses, blasting caps, detonators), and communications gear (radios, wire, switchboards) previously packed in equipment bundles, were attached underneath the fuselages of the C-47s and the release mechanisms tested.

As the bundles were being loaded underneath and into the planes, Private Dave Bowman, with Company D, saw one of his platoon leaders, Lieutenant Waverly Wray approaching. "Three men from the air corps were struggling on the tarmac to load one of our equipment bundles onto the plane. Wray was walking by at the time and observed them for a moment, then picked the [bundle] up and hefted it inside, much to the amazement of the men. As he walked away, one of the men exclaimed, 'Geez, all you paratroopers that strong!'

"Well, no—as much as we'd like that image, we're not. He was strong, even for a paratrooper. He was an unusually strong man. I suppose he could, without exaggeration, be called 'powerful.'"[12]

That evening, troopers began boarding their assigned aircraft. As Company E trooper, Private Turk Seelye, sat in his plane there was little conversation. "No one knew what to expect or what was about to happen. Each was nervous and frightened."[13]

Finally, after a long wait as the other serials took off, Private Berge Avadanian, with Headquarters Company, 2nd Battalion, could feel his plane taxi to the end of the runway, then turn, and begin powering up the engines. "The takeoff was without flaw—lots of dust, and it seemed all planes were soon airborne.

"There was a lot of chatter among troopers.

"'How the hell am I going to take a leak or a dump?'

"'What a relief to get out of A-rab country.'

"'I wonder what Axis Sally looks like.'"[14]

After takeoff, Sergeant Otis L. Sampson commanding the 60mm mortar squad of the 1st Platoon, Company E looked out of the door of his C-47. "The sunset was beautiful as we climbed in a wide circle to gain altitude; below the shadows had lengthened and turned to darkness. In flock formation of three, we had joined the long line of planes and disappeared into the night out over a darkening sea. The troopers had settled down and I supposed their thoughts were much the same as mine. There was much of my past life I wanted to think over and put in place; it would be a long four hours, the time we were told it took before crossing the Sicilian coast over our destination. 'Plenty of time to reminisce,' I thought."[15]

ON THE NIGHT OF JULY 9-10, the 505th Regimental Combat Team dropped by parachute into Sicily to spearhead Operation Husky. Major Vandervoort was a member of Colonel Gavin's stick. "The troop carrying C-47s scattered us sixty miles wide and forty miles deep. There had not been enough aircraft or time for sufficient night formation flying and navigation practice without electronic aids."[16]

About an hour after landing, Colonel Gavin, Major Vandervoort, Captain Alfred W. Ireland (regimental S-1), and about twenty troopers had assembled. Gavin and his small group moved out, not knowing their location. "I was leading and Vandervoort was alongside. I had been picking up troopers as I moved along through the shadows in the olive groves, over stone walls, darting across moonlit roads, going in what I hoped was the direction of our objective. There had been occasional bursts of small arms fire, sometimes quite close, but so far we had not seen an actual enemy."[17]

Then, in the distance, Gavin heard the sound of a man whistling what sounded to him like "*O Sole Mio.*" Gavin ordered his group to get down behind a stone wall bordering the road down which the man, an Italian soldier was walking.

As he came near, Gavin said, "Alto" and the man immediately stopped. "Vandervoort rushed through an opening in the wall with a .45 in one hand and a knife in the other.

"'I'll take care of him,' Van said. I wasn't sure what he meant, but I said, 'No, let's get the hell out of the middle of the road. Let's get over into the shadows and maybe we can get some information out of him.

"There was still some doubt as to whether we were in Sicily, Italy, or the Balkins, although the odds strongly favored the first.

"About a half a dozen of us surrounded him, and I tried the few Italian words I knew.

"'Dove Palermo?'

"No reply. He seemed too scared or too bewildered to answer.

"'Dove Siracusa?'

"I figured if he would point in the general direction of either or both of these two cities, which were at opposite ends of the island, we could get our first fix on where we were. Since he acted as if he had never heard of either, for a moment it seemed that perhaps we were not even in Sicily. But he was obviously very scared."[18]

When they couldn't even get the prisoner's name, Gavin realized that the Italian soldier was petrified and "reluctantly decided that we would have to take him along. Vandervoort had taken an intelligence course and knew how to handle a prisoner in a situation like this. The idea was to take the belt out of the prisoner's trousers and to cut the buttons off his fly so that he would have to hold up his trousers when he walked. Van put his .45 in its holster, pressed his knife against the Italian's chest, and said, 'I'll take care of the bastard.'

"The Italian was muttering, '*Mamma mia, Mamma mia*' over and over again. His concern was understandable. The moonlight was shining on the knife blade, and it looked as though it was a foot long. He took off his [the Italian's] belt and dropped it. Then Van went into phase two of the operation and reached for his fly with one hand, bringing the knife down with the other.

"A scream went up that could be heard all the way to Rome. The [German propaganda of] atrocities of the paratroopers and the stories the Italian heard about Ethiopia must have flashed through his mind; he was being castrated. He screamed louder, grabbing the knife blade with his right hand. The blood ran down his hand as we fell in a kicking, yelling, fighting mass, and he got away. I do not know how he did it, but one second he was with us and the next he was gone. I was madder than hell. I asked Vandervoort, 'What in the hell did you think you were doing?'

"Vandervoort didn't answer. I decided we had better get going. By now we had probably alerted any enemy for miles around."[19]

The group moved on through the night, toward the sound of gunfire in the distance. By morning, the group totaled just eight, including Vandervoort, Gavin, and Ireland, as others had become separated in the darkness.

As the group moved westward, Vandervoort saw the lead scout suddenly go down just in front of him. "Midmorning, we ran into an Italian thirty-five man anti-paratroop patrol. They were seventy yards in front of us. An intense firefight ensued. Two of our troopers were hit and lay very still. In the time it takes to fire two dozen well aimed shots with a carbine, the Italians were driven to cover behind a stone wall. In the lull, we disengaged straight back, one at a time, the others covering. The colonel was the last man to withdraw from the position. We took temporary cover in a cane break. We were dirty, sweaty, tired, and distressed at having to leave wounded behind. The colonel looked over his six-man command and said, 'This is a hell of a place for a regimental commander to be.'"[20]

THE 2ND BATTALION SERIAL WAS THE LAST ONE INTO SICILY. Major Mark Alexander, the commanding officer, was standing in the door looking at the beautiful blue water of the Mediterranean Sea below, which shone in the moonlight as the armada approached the coast of Sicily. "The red light came on—we hooked up and prepared to jump. The green light came on and I was still looking down at the Mediterranean. Of course, the men tried to push me out the door and after fighting them off; I went forward and cussed out [Lieutenant Colonel Tommy] Thompson. His reply was simply that the copilot was nervous and had gotten in too much of a hurry.

"We received considerable tracer fire as we finally crossed the coast. We were to have dropped on a ground elevation of one hundred twenty meters, but instead, were dropped on an elevation of two hundred to two hundred fifty meters."[21]

Private Berge Avadanian, and his stick of Headquarters Company, 2nd Battalion, troopers had a different experience. "When we approached the Sicily shoreline and [began receiving] antiaircraft fire, I believe the pilot rose way above the formation to evade ground fire. When the green light went on, I could see planes below and behind. When we exited and the chutes opened, I swore other planes would fly through our chutes. On landing in a hilly area, among olive trees, I was unhurt.

"The first person I met could not remember the countersign to my 'George!' He blurted out 'Washington!' It had to be one of ours—it was [Captain] Dr. Lester Stein, battalion surgeon. Next one, I believe was Private [Thomas J.] Michaud. Going toward a coastal pillbox, I ran into Lieutenant Eugene [A.] Doerfler [2nd Battalion S-2 officer] and others."[22]

Private Turk Seelye, with Company E, just wanted to get out his plane. "Some of the troopers became ill and vomited. The steel floor of the plane was slippery. We jumped at about four hundred feet."[23]

Private Dave Bowman, an assistant machine gunner with Company D, was carrying a box of machine gun ammunition, which an officer and an NCO had strapped to the front of his reserve chute shortly before takeoff from Kairouan. "When I left the door, my body was supposed to retain the upright position. But, because of the extra load on my chest, I began tipping over, headfirst. As the chute opened, the suspension lines grabbed my left ankle, and when the inevitable opening shock came, I thought my knee had been pulled from the socket. That was bad enough, but potentially worse was yet to come, as I was now going down headfirst. I frantically worked to untangle the lines from my foot and eventually managed to do so and assume the proper landing position, just as I hit one of the Siciliano's ubiquitous stone walls. After hitting that wall, I rolled over it and landed in a ditch by the side of a dirt road, where machine gun bullets were flying by.

"I have no idea what they were firing at, but apparently it was not me, since they could easily have scored a hit, had they seen me. After the passage of a long period of time struggling with my harness, I finally freed myself of it. Then, by hugging the low wall, reached its top and rolled over to the other side with the box of ammo still attached to my chest. Here, with greater leisure and less anxiety, I removed the box—and now, with this spectacular baptism of fire still in my mind, I prepared to join my unit."[24]

After landing, Private First Class Russ Brown, with Company F, found the other troopers with his mortar squad, but they were unable to locate the equipment bundle containing their 60mm mortar. "We were in an olive grove and a native Sicilian came and invited the squad to his home. He made spaghetti for the squad. He made the spaghetti in large black pots hung over a fire. It was good to get a hot meal."[25]

Lieutenant James J. Coyle, with the 1st Platoon, Company E, was Lieutenant Waverly Wray's assistant platoon leader. Coyle was making only his seventh jump. "The red light came on—I was barely able to get the men's static lines hooked up to the cable in the plane and get an equipment check before we crossed the coast of Sicily. The green light came on and we jumped into the dark.

"It seemed that my chute had only been deployed about ten seconds when I hit the ground. While it is difficult to judge altitude at night, I am certain that my planeload was jumped at no more than four hundred feet. No one in the 1st Platoon was injured, however, and we were able to assemble and locate our equipment bundles quickly.

"The mission of the 1st Platoon was to set out a roadblock about two miles north of the DZ to prevent the enemy forces from moving to the beach at Gela, where the 1st Division was to land in the morning. We moved out with Wray in the lead and myself bringing up the rear, which is where Wray always placed me. In this case it was fortunate that he did.

"We had observed antiaircraft beacon light, which we assumed was on an airfield indicated on our maps as north of Gela. This would be an aid in moving cross country, as there were no roads that would take us to our objective. The moon was now bright, but it was rough going at times, because we seemed to hit a stone wall, which we had to climb over, every two hundred yards or so. After an hour, the column halted and the men sat down for a break.

"After about fifteen minutes had passed and we had not moved out again, I went to the head of the column—or what was left of it! When Wray had moved out after the break, half of the platoon had moved out with him—but about half way back in the column, a couple of men had fallen asleep and never saw the front half of the column move on.

"I got the men awake and on their feet and started after the rest of the platoon. I led the men for another half hour over the stone walls and was finally becoming concerned about locating Wray and the rest of the platoon, when I was challenged and found them covering us with their weapons from behind a stone wall. Lieutenant Wray had reached a road which appeared to be the objective and we set up our roadblock and waited until dawn."[26]

Major Alexander and his "battalion headquarters company dropped on a concentration of five pillboxes and wire. Lieutenant (Dr.) [Kurt B.] Klee unfortunately landed in the wire to the east of the larger pillbox and was killed immediately. Corporal Fred [W.] Freeland [Company D] got hung up in the same area and played dead until we took the pillboxes later in the morning. My Battalion X.O., Captain John Norton had an interesting experience. 'George'-'Marshall' was our sign and countersign. In the dark of early D-Day, in trying to locate other members of the battalion, he approached what appeared to be a house, heard low voices, called out, 'George' and some Italian voice called back, 'George, hell!' and nearly shot his head off with a machine gun. Norton later learned that he had approached one of the pillboxes."[27]

Through the darkness and into the dawn's light, Major Mark Alexander and his 2nd Battalion worked to knock out the pillbox complex that he and his men had landed among. "We had a good fight in the early hours of the morning. The two large pillboxes gave us considerable resistance. With Lieutenant [William T.] Wilson directing the fire of his light machine guns into the apertures and Lieutenant [Ivey K.] Connell directing mortar fire, we attacked and cleared out the large domed pillbox of about forty feet in diameter. In the meantime, we were receiving heavy fire from the smaller, two story pillbox. Lieutenant [John D.] Sprinkle [the executive officer of Company D] led the gallant attack on this pillbox later in the morning."[28]

Captain John D. Rice, the commander of Company D, watched the assault as Lieutenant Sprinkle "went forward with a small patrol to knock out an enemy pillbox, which was preventing the advance of our troops to Marina di Ragusa. He succeeded in eliminating it, then drew fire from Postal Block House #452. He had his men cover him as he went forward to make a personal reconnaissance and got within grenade throwing range. He threw one grenade which effected sufficient damage to allow his men to advance and destroy the block house. In the encounter, Lieutenant Sprinkle was killed."[29]

Lieutenant Sprinkle's heroic actions opened the way for the 2nd Battalion to continue the advance, for which he was posthumously awarded the Distinguished Service Cross.

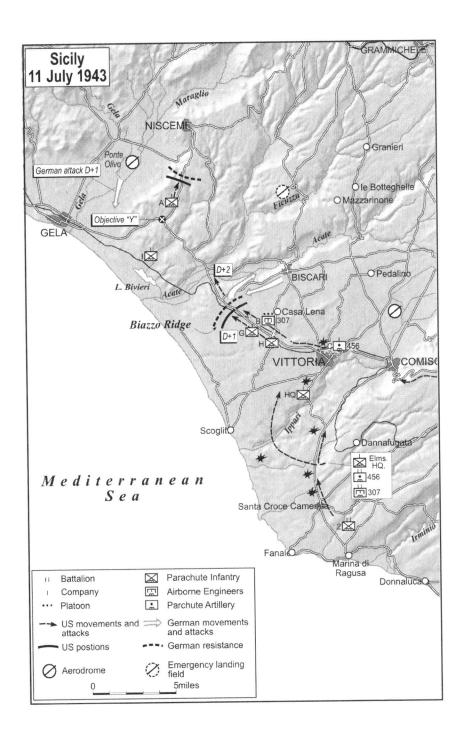

Sicily
11 July 1943

GRAMMICHELE

Maraglio

Gela

NISCEME

Ponte
Olivo

German attack D+1

Gela

Objective "Y"

GELA

L. Bivieri

Acate

Biazzo Ridge

Granieri

le Botteghelle

Mazzarinone

Ficuzza

Acate

D+2

BISCARI

Pedalino

Casa Lena

B 307

D+1 G

H C 456

VITTORIA

COMISO

HQ

Scoglit

Ippari

Dannafugata

Mediterranean
Sea

Elms.
HQ.
456
307

Santa Croce Camerina

2

Irminio

Fanal

Marina di
Ragusa

Donnaluca

	Battalion		Parachute Infantry
⌶	Company		Airborne Engineers
•••	Platoon		Parchute Artillery
→•	US movements and attacks	⇒	German movements and attacks
—	US postions	----	German resistance
⊘	Aerodrome		Emergency landing field

0   5miles

Major Alexander watched his troopers finish off the pillboxes "by throwing grenades through the fire ports and a door at ground level. By about 10:00 a.m. we had cleared out the five pillboxes and were pretty well organized. I could see some enemy armor and trucks on a road about one half mile north of us, but they chose not to attack. I was faced with the decision of whether to stay there and fight or move toward the regimental objective.

"In the early morning we had accounted for about four hundred men, by 10:00 a.m. we had assembled about four hundred seventy-five men. By 11:00 a.m. we had most of the battalion, plus twenty-one men from the 456th Parachute Field Artillery with Lieutenant Colonel Harrison Harden, Jr., and one 75mm howitzer and thirty rounds of ammunition. My adjutant, Lieutenant Clyde [R.] Russell, gave me a strength report at about 12:00 on D-Day, and our total strength was five hundred thirty-six men inclusive of the twenty-one from the 456th.

"On the coast and one half mile south of our landing area, we had spotted an extensive coastal artillery fortification, at the village of Marina di Ragusa. We attacked from the north and rear. We placed a few rounds of 75mm howitzer into the fortification and without much trouble, captured most of the artillery company defending the fortification. We disabled the guns by throwing the breach blocks and other weapons into the sea. By this time it was late in the day and we took a perimeter defense position to the north and west of Marina di Ragusa."[30]

As the sun rose, Lieutenant Jim Coyle, was at the Company E roadblock established earlier by Lieutenant Wray. "No Germans or Italian soldiers showed up. There were no houses or civilians around to question as to our exact location, but everything indicated that we were in the right spot or close to it. About 0900 hours, a runner from headquarters company arrived to inform us that we had dropped at Marina di Ragusa, about twenty miles east of Gela! Wray and I couldn't believe it, as everything looked so right. (I later learned that the beacon we had seen was at the Comiso airfield, not the airfield north of Gela as we had thought.) We rejoined the company outside of Marina di Ragusa."[31]

BY THE AFTERNOON OF JULY 10, Kampfgruppe Links (Left), the eastern force of the Hermann Göring Panzer Division moved south to attack the U.S. 45th Infantry Division's beachhead. This powerful armored force consisted of the 1st Hermann Göring Panzer Grenadier Regiment; the 2nd Company, 504th Schwere Panzer Abteilung, consisting of seventeen Mark VI Tiger I tanks, each weighing sixty tons and mounting an 88mm main gun; and two batteries of the Hermann Göring Artillery Regiment.

Meanwhile, Gavin, Vandervoort, Ireland, and the other three troopers in the group waited until dark and moved out again, marching to the sound of the guns. By dawn on July 11, they arrived at Vittoria after moving all night. There, Colonel Gavin, Major Vandervoort, and Captain Al Ireland borrowed a jeep and drove west looking for the regiment. A couple of miles west of town, they found

Major Edward C. "Cannonball" Krause and a couple of hundred of his 3rd Battalion troopers sitting on the edges of their foxholes in a tomato field beside the road. Krause explained to Gavin that he was getting the battalion reorganized. Gavin ordered him to get the 3rd Battalion moving west toward Gela to join elements of the 505th that he hoped had been dropped northeast of there, near the regimental objective.

Gavin, Vandervoort, and Ireland then left, driving west along the highway to Gela. About two miles down the road, Gavin found "a group of forty men of L Company, 180th Infantry, and twenty parachutists."[32]

Gavin ordered the paratroopers—Company B, 307th engineers, under the command of Lieutenant Ben L. Wechsler—to move west as well. Gavin drove a little less than a mile west "to the railroad station one mile east of Biazzo Ridge, where a point reconnaissance was made. At this point, a German officer and private suddenly came around the corner in a motorcycle and were captured. They made no effort to resist capture and appeared to be quite disgusted with the lack of resistance being offered by the Italian troops, but refused to give any information regarding their own troops."[33]

Gavin sent Vandervoort back down the road to expedite the arrival of Krause's troopers, then to find the 45th Division CP to get a message to the 1st Infantry and 82nd Airborne Divisions that he would advance west toward Gela. Meanwhile, Gavin awaited the arrival of the twenty paratroopers that he had found a couple of miles back. "Just ahead was a ridge [Biazzo Ridge], about half a mile away and perhaps a hundred feet high. The slope to the top was gradual. On both sides of the road were olive trees and beneath them tall brown and yellow grass, burnt by the hot Sicilian summer sun. The firing from the ridge increased. I told Lieutenant Wechsler to deploy his platoon on the right and to move on to seize the ridge.

"We moved forward. I was with Wechsler, and in a few hundred yards the fire became intense. As we neared the top of the ridge, there was a rain of leaves and branches as bullets tore through the trees, and there was a buzzing like the sound of swarms of bees. A few moments later Wechsler was hit and fell. Some troopers were hit; others continued to crawl forward. Soon we were pinned down by heavy small arms fire, but so far nothing else.

"I made my way back to the railroad crossing and in about twenty minutes Major [William J.] Hagan joined me. He was the battalion executive officer for the 3rd Battalion. He said the battalion was coming up. I asked where Cannonball [Krause] was, and he said that he had gone back to the 45th Division to tell them what was going on. I ordered Hagen [Hagan] to have the troops drop their packs and get ready to attack the Germans on the ridge as soon as they came up. By that time, we had picked up a platoon of the 45th Division that happened to be there, part of a company from the 180th Infantry. There was also a sailor or two who had come ashore in the amphibious landings. We grabbed them also."[34]

A short time later, some Company G troopers—the lead elements of Krause's battalion—arrived and were ordered to attack the ridge. As the company swept across the ground in front of the ridge, pinned-down engineers and headquarters troopers jumped to their feet and joined them in the assault up the eastern slope.

As the 3rd Battalion troopers coming up the road from the east reached the top of the ridge, Colonel Gavin directed their deployment. "The attack went off as planned, and the infantry reached the top of the ridge and continued to attack down the far side. As they went over the top of the ridge, the fire became intense. We were going to have a very serious situation on our hands. This was not a patrol or platoon action. Mortar and artillery fire began to fall on the ridge, and there was considerable machine gun fire."[35]

Immediately afterward, German infantry counterattacked and pushed the thin line of paratroopers back over the crest of the ridge. Just as the Germans reached the crest, Company H arrived. They were ordered to fix bayonets and then the company charged through the Company G troopers and over the top of the ridge, where they engaged the German infantry in a short, brutal, close-quarters hand-to-hand fight. The surviving enemy troops fled down the other side of the ridge with Company H followed by Company G and the engineers in pursuit.

As they reached the bottom of the ridge, more German infantry was preparing to launch another counterattack; this time with several huge Mark VI Tiger tanks. White phosphorous mortar shells soon began to rain down on the troopers.

Captain Al Ireland, the regimental S-1, and the other troopers "started digging slit trenches and foxholes. Everybody was trying to dig their foxholes deep enough so that the tanks would roll over us. Everybody was scraping with their helmets and trenching tools, but it was hard ground. We hardly had time to dig holes when they attacked and hit us hard. They drove up five or six tanks and infantry; they were coming at us. They looked like the biggest tanks ever invented. I thought we had it when the Germans got up within fifty or sixty yards of the CP, but we held them off with a lot of heavy firing, and we used 75mm howitzers [from two newly arrived crews of the 456th Parachute Field Artillery Battalion] to kind of slow them down.

"During the attack, they were pounding us with a lot of mortars. They had these Russian mortars that were like screaming meemies and when they came in and hit the ground, you shook; just bounced you out of the foxhole. I remember praying, 'Don't let one drop on me.' They were hitting all around."[36]

The fighting on Biazzo Ridge drew paratroopers like a magnet. Gavin fed them into the thin line as quickly as they arrived. However, that afternoon, Gavin sent Captain Ireland to the 45th Infantry Division to get some help. Ireland returned with forward observer parties to direct the fire of a 155mm artillery battalion and naval guns offshore. As the artillery pounded the Germans, turning the tide in favor of Gavin's small force, several Sherman tanks arrived. Gavin ordered a counterattack with every man he could get his hands on; and together with the tanks, a thin skirmish line of tired, dirty, thirsty troopers charged down the slope and drove the Germans from the battlefield.

Major Vandervoort's assessment of the battle was that "they had more than enough capabilities to wipe us off the ridge. Either their mission was to defend or their commander was lousy."[37]

The 2nd Battalion had largely missed major combat during the first days of the invasion due to being misdropped. On July 13, Colonel Gavin, with about twelve hundred men under his command, reported to General Ridgway at the division command post. The 505th RCT reorganized over the next few days and moved out at 6:00 a.m. on July 17, following the 504th RCT west, where the division relieved the U.S. 39th Infantry Division near Realmonte on July 18. The following morning at 3:00 a.m., with the 504th PIR in the lead, the division began an advance along the coast toward Trapani.

At 9:30 a.m. on July 21, the 505th took the lead, with the 2nd Battalion passing through the 504th at Tumminello, marched to Santa Margherita, occupying it by 11:40 a.m., then pushed on to capture Bellice by 3:00 p.m.—a total of twenty-three miles, without food or a resupply of water.

The drive up the west coast of Sicily by the 82nd Airborne Division culminated in the capture of Trapani on the northwestern tip of the island on July 23.

That same day, Major Mark Alexander received a promotion to lieutenant colonel. A few days later, Alexander and his 2nd Battalion were bivouacked in an olive orchard at a village near Trapani. "I had a battalion headquarters tent and an improvised desk of two boxes and some boards. Two of our demolition men came to my tent and asked the adjutant if they could speak to the colonel privately. I said O.K., and invited them into the tent.

"Their story was that they had gotten drunk on native wine the night before and had blown a small bank vault at the village. They took a box of jewelry and Italian money, which they sat on my desk. They asked if I would give it back and not let anyone know what they had done. I agreed, as I did not want the details of a court-martial anymore than they did. However, I fined each one a month's pay and restricted each to hard labor for a week, such as the company commander should provide. I told the company commander of the incident, and he agreed to my decision to keep the incident quiet, as we had a war on, and didn't want to waste time on a court marshal.

"Not two hours later, after I finished with the demolition men, two A.MGOT [Allied Military Government of the Occupied Territories] officers came to me and said a small bank had been blown in the village the night before. They had some leads that indicated the perpetrators probably came from my battalion. I asked them if I could get a return of the stolen articles, would they drop the hunt. They readily agreed. I pulled the box from under my desk and sat it in front of them. Their eyes opened wide, they checked the contents of the box, thanked me, and departed. For some time after, I checked the behavior of the two demolition men. They were both good soldiers."[38]

With the invasion of Sicily, the 505th RCT had conducted the first regimental-sized combat jump in U.S. Army history. Although the drops were badly scattered, the paratroopers had engaged elements of the Hermann Göring Division, 15th Panzer Grenadier Division, the Italian 4th Livorno Division, the Italian 54th Napoli Division, and the Italian 206th Coastal Division. The aggressive fighting by the 2nd Battalion had cleared defenders from the beach area around Marina di Ragusa, assisting the landing of the U.S. 45th Infantry Division.

ON JULY 29, General Ridgway received a warning order that the division would execute a jump on the Italian mainland in support of amphibious landings in the Bay of Salerno, scheduled to begin September 9. The regiment had little time to integrate replacements for casualties suffered in Sicily, work with the troop carrier forces to improve the accuracy of jumping on the drop zone, and rehearse for the planned parachute operation. Most of the replacements were unable to receive the benefit of much training and integration with their new units. To improve accuracy of the jumps, a pathfinder concept was developed, teams were trained, and successful tests were conducted. Because the paratroopers were conducting occupation duty in Sicily and the troop carrier forces remained stationed around Kairouan, there were no opportunities to conduct joint training. The 505th was unable to return to the Kairouan area until August 19-20.

Fortunately, several overly ambitious airborne operations were planned and subsequently cancelled, including jumps near Avellino as well as northwest of Naples and finally near Rome. Each of these planned jumps, far from the planned landings at Salerno, would have resulted in the likely destruction of the 504th and 505th Parachute Infantry Regiments before friendly forces could link up with them.

On September 5, the regiment flew to Sicily to prepare for a jump near Rome, which General Eisenhower's headquarters cancelled at the last minute. Four days later, Operation Avalanche, the amphibious landings in the Bay of Salerno, began at 3:30 a.m.

When the Germans launched a massive counterattack against the beach landed forces on September 12, and again the following day, breaking through and threatening to drive all the way to the beaches, the U.S. Fifth Army commander, General Mark Clark called on the 82nd Airborne Division for assistance. That night, the 504th Parachute Infantry Regiment parachuted inside of American lines near the beach near Paestum, followed by the 505th the next night, stabilizing the situation. The Fifth Army soon went over to the offensive and the 505th led the breakout on the northern flank of the beachhead through the Sorrento Mountains and across the plain, encountering primarily German rear guard delaying actions. The 505th liberated Naples on October 1, 1943—the first city on the continent of Europe liberated by Allied forces.

THE 82ND AIRBORNE DIVISION performed occupation duties in Naples for the next month and a half. During that time, Major Vandervoort heard about an incident that would become a cartoon by Bill Mauldin in *Stars and Stripes*. "When we jumped into Salerno in September 1943, our jump boots were wearing out. There were no replacements because the boots, issued exclusively to the airborne, were being short-stopped in the supply lines. In Naples the 3rd Battalion, 505, was billeted near the harbor docks. In those days, parachute boots were as sacred to the paratroopers as their wings. Quartermaster Corps longshoremen and Supply Corps officers showed up wearing shiny new jump boots. That did it! The 3rd Battalion troopers took the boots off their 'chairborne' feet and left them on pass, without any shoes. Outraged, officers in their stocking feet stormed into the battalion command post. The only sympathy they got there was an interrogation by the battalion duty officer. 'Where did you get your jump boots?' In the rear echelons, the word went around: If you weren't jump qualified, don't take your boots to town. The flow of parachute boots to the 82nd Airborne began immediately."[39]

ON THE MORNING OF OCTOBER 4, Colonel Gavin received an order attaching the regiment to the British 23rd Armoured Brigade for an operation near the Volturno River to the north. Leaving the 3rd Battalion to occupy the regiment's sector in Naples, Gavin dispatched the 2nd Battalion immediately and gave an order for the 1st Battalion to be ready to move out the following morning. Lieutenant Colonel Alexander moved his battalion to the Capuccini airfield, where it loaded onto British trucks and was driven to an area south of the town of Villa Literno. "We arrived at about 18:00 hours with the mission to drive to the Volturno River, about fifteen miles to the northwest, to save five canal bridges in route to the Volturno River and the village of Arnone on the southwest bank of the river. The bridges were essential to the movement of the armored brigade and eventual crossing of the Volturno River.

"Rather than wait until morning, I directed two platoons of about twenty-four men each to move out as fast as possible in the dark to take the first two bridges. Each platoon had a light machine gun and a bazooka team. The battalion followed in column on both sides of the road."[40]

Company F led the battalion as it approached the first canal bridge, which it took without incident. Private Spencer F. Wurst and his platoon were following the two lead platoons toward the second bridge. Wurst had been busted from sergeant to private in Sicily, when somebody tossed an empty wine bottle into his slit trench while he was away, and the commanding officer assumed Wurst had drunk the wine. "We approached the bridge, which was already partially destroyed, sometime towards midnight. At least two and maybe three German machine guns from across the canal took us under fire. Very fortunately for us, they were shooting high, but from the first slug that went over our heads, it wasn't a split second before everyone was in the ditch. I can still see the tracers whizzing two or three feet above us. I am thankful to this day that the Germans didn't have guns covering the ditches. The guns were positioned forward, from twenty-five to fifty yards off to the left and right of the road, and they really poured it onto us."[41]

Lieutenant Colonel Alexander was walking along the road with the battalion, just behind Company F. "The leading platoons had alerted the Germans as we heard fire fighting ahead of us. As we marched along on this very dark night the Germans let loose on the battalion, with tracer machine gun fire skipping down the concrete road ahead of us. Of course, both columns of men on both sides of the road took a dive into the ditches on the roadside. It was so dark that we did not know there was a five-foot concrete ditch on the right side of the road. First, I heard thuds and banging as the men on the right side of the road hit the concrete bottom; then moans and curses. When daylight came I could see cut and bruised faces from the dive to the bottom of the concrete-lined ditch on the right."[42]

Up ahead, Private Wurst just stayed down in the ditch while the German machine guns continued to fire in the darkness. "We didn't return much fire. We remained in the ditch waiting for orders, and the MGs finally stopped. The orders were that we would go into defensive positions and start attacking at first light. The 1st Platoon, the point, dug in on the south side of the bridge. The 2nd and 3rd Platoons went into all-around circular positions and dug in, the 2nd Platoon moving off to the left of the road, and the 3rd Platoon, which was mine, moving to the right. We had to string out and dig individual foxholes.

"We remained in these positions throughout the night in a high state of alert, because we were in such close contact with the enemy. Usually, we tried to pair up, two men to a fighting position, digging two-man holes whenever the situation allowed. People performed much better when they had someone with them. With two men to a hole, when we were not in battle, we could also take turns staying on the alert and sleeping or resting. That night, however, no one got any sleep. The unit's defense area was just too large to permit us to pair up. I remember it was very cold. With jaundice and malaria coming on, and a very empty stomach, I spent an entirely miserable night.

"At first break of light on October 5th, a tremendous firefight broke out in the 1st Platoon's area, a position close to the road, by the partially destroyed bridge. The canal was about twenty feet across, and the Germans were still in position on the other side, or had moved back in through the night undetected. The 1st Platoon lost a number of men, and so did the Germans, although they didn't hold us up too long."[43]

Early on October 5, the 1st Battalion was trucked from Naples to Villa Literno, where it dismounted and moved up to cover the flanks and rear of the 2nd Battalion. Up ahead, Sergeant Victor M. Schmidt moved with the Company E column north on the road toward Arnone. "The terrain ahead of us was flat farmland with a canal alongside the gravel road, and we were walking in a staggered column. About two miles in the distance, a ridge of hills rose up sharply from the plain. We could see a few buildings with our binoculars.

"When we came within about one and a half miles of these buildings, the Germans opened up at us in a steady crossfire with their machine guns. All of us immediately jumped down into the canal, which had a gentle slope, so we didn't have to wade in the water, and it made good cover.

"The Germans had placed barbed wire across this canal about every one hundred feet, so that we had to come out of the canal on the run, jump around the wire and back into the canal again to escape getting hit. In addition to this barbed wire, they had laid some tether mine booby traps along the canal.

"At the head of the column was the 1st Platoon, then 2nd Platoon, and then 3rd. I was with 2nd Platoon, with the mortar squad. When word was passed from the head of the column that I was wanted up front immediately, I assumed that they had captured some Germans and wanted me to question them. (I spoke a little German.)

"I was moving along at a fast trot, passing the guys coming up from the canal to get around the barbed wire, and word came back to watch for this booby trap across our path. I saw the wire across the path about twenty feet away, in front of a trooper named [Private First Class Louis H.] Garrett. I shouted out to him to look out for it. I don't know why, but he turned around and looked at me as I was running toward him—at the same time, he tripped over the wire—it was about six inches above the ground, stretched across our path.

"As he did this, I was about ten feet from him. I dived to my right, toward the canal, and I was in the water when the mine exploded. For some reason, I was watching him as I jumped, and it was like slow motion. It blasted him into the air and I saw a piece of shrapnel tear away about an inch and a half of his face—from behind his right ear, through his hair, and across his chest.

"He fell along the canal embankment on his face. By this time, I had landed headfirst down the embankment, too. I started to get up, but my left foot felt as if someone had run a red hot poker through it. I could see a hole in the top of my boot, with blood running from it.

"I got on my hands and knees to get to Garrett, but by this time our company medic, [Private First Class Clyde F.] Knox, had come up to help me. I told him to take care of Garrett first, as he was badly hurt. While he was occupied with Garrett, I pulled off my jump boot and found a clean hole in my foot. I wrapped a bandage around it and went to Garrett and the medic (Knox). I could see wounds all over Garrett, mostly on his back—he was really hurting.

"About an hour after Garrett and I were hit, a jeep with stretchers came and took us to first aid. From there, we went by ambulance to the hospital in Naples. Garrett died later [November 21, 1943]. His liver and other vital organs were saturated with shrapnel—he was about twenty years old."[44]

Private Berge Avadanian, with the 2nd Battalion S-2 section, caught a ride on a jeep driven by Lieutenant Richard M. Janney, with regimental Headquarters and Headquarters Company, to deliver intelligence information to the battalion command post. "There were three of us, including one wounded. Our communications corporal, Francis [J.] August of Worcester, Massachusetts, pleaded for a ride on the jeep—he needed more wire. I gave him my passenger side seat, while I mounted the rear spare tire.

"That jeep didn't get fifty feet—it was blown up by a Teller mine—all three were killed. I was the lucky one on the spare tire, who was uninjured. August lay ten feet from me—dead—he saved my life by hitching that ride."[45]

Lieutenant Colonel Alexander kept his battalion moving rapidly toward the third bridge. "The Germans had blown about half of the bridge, but other than for intermittent German machine gun fire from a farmhouse about one hundred yards to the right, we could cross between bursts of fire, and I led my men across. About this time D Company, which I had moving parallel to the road about one hundred yards to our right flank, took the farmhouse and silenced the machine gun.

"Ahead of us about one-third mile, I could see Germans retreating north on the road. I brought forward an 81mm mortar, and they had a good shoot, very accurate, as they could see their targets. The Germans moved out fast ahead of us and left a horse-drawn wagonload of ammunition and guns, plus a 35mm antitank gun. We drove forward rapidly, took the fourth and fifth canal bridges, and set down for the night to attacking the village of Arnone and the railroad yard the next morning.

"A Company of the 1st Battalion under command of Captain [Edwin M.] Ed Sayre had been attached to my 2nd Battalion in our advance. Captain Sayre had tripped a wired mine and was severely injured. A Company was still held back in reserve. The last three miles of our drive we had straddled the road, with the railroad running along parallel and about one hundred yards to our left; the railroad and road converging at Arnone. For the morning attack, Captain Talton [W. 'Woody'] Long led E Company in the railroad yard and Captain Neal [L.] McRoberts led F Company in the attack on the village of Arnone. D Company under Captain [John D.] Casey Rice was held in reserve on the right flank, A Company still not committed."[46]

Company F, together with the light machine gun platoon and 81mm mortar platoon of Headquarters Company, 2nd Battalion, moved into the town unopposed. Arnone was situated between two bends in the Volturno River, which prevented friendly forces from securing the flanks of any force occupying the village. To secure the flanks, Company F was ordered to put a platoon across the river to establish a bridgehead. The 1st Platoon, Company F, moved out of the village, crossed a levee, and prepared to cross the river. Private First Class Russ Brown was a member of the 1st Platoon's 60mm mortar squad. "The 1st Platoon was about to try to cross the Voluturno River, but was met with heavy machine gun and small arms fire."[47]

The 1st Platoon was ordered to withdraw over the dike and move back into the town. Just as they crossed the dike going back into the town, Private First Class Daryle E. Whitfield heard the unmistakable sound of a mortar firing in the distance. "We hit the ground and the shell landed up in town. We got up and starting moving a little further, and they fired again. We hit the ground again, and [the shell] hit down next to the river. After it went off, we got up and started to move again, and they fired another round. That time, when we hit the ground, the shell landed right in the middle of a boy's back, about ten or twelve feet behind me. It killed him [Private First Class Frank J. Nowinski] [and] wounded me, Sergeant [Arthur L.] Gregory, and another guy. It hit me in my right hip, my left leg, my neck had a big chunk of steel in it, and all up and down my back. My neck was burning so, that I hollered for the medic. When he got to me, I asked him to get that piece of metal out of my neck. I was lying on my stomach, and he had his knee on my shoulder and one on my hip. He grabbed that piece of metal and it burned his hand, so he got his handkerchief out and wrapped it up and tried to pull it out. He said, 'I can't get it out.'

"I said, 'Man, you've got to get it out—it's burning the hell out of me.' He finally managed to jerk it, and it came out."[48]

As they were getting shelled, Private First Class Brown and his mortar squad quickly set up and started returning fire. "For every round we fired, we got many [fired] back.

"I saw [Edward A.] Ed Slavin and three other troopers tear out a door [and] use it for a stretcher for [Private] Francis [L.] Malay, who later died."[49]

Private Spencer Wurst was outside of town with the 3rd Platoon. "We could tell by the amount of incoming artillery and small-arms fire that the 1st and 2nd Platoons were having quite a fight in town. Eventually, we received orders to move forward. We moved on the double to help our comrades, going from one covered position to the next. We got into town and deployed to the left of the company position, where it was reported that the Germans were attempting to counterattack. We had our hands full in our portion of town. We moved quickly through Arnone, passing the company CP. The scene sticks in my mind, because the CP area was like a shed with an open side—and this served as a collection point for the wounded and the dead. We saw them lying there as we passed through; I think most of the fatalities and wounds were caused by the heavy artillery fire we had been receiving. It turned out that after the artillery barrages, an enemy company had hit the 1st and 2nd Platoons from the west, and a German battalion from across the river had joined them in the attack."[50]

As Company F was being attacked, Company E moved into the railroad yard to clear the enemy company from F Company's flank, with the 1st Platoon led by Lieutenant David L. Packard at the point. Sergeant Julius D. Axman was the acting platoon sergeant. "The 1st Platoon advanced to the railroad yard on the right bank, climbing the twelve-foot elevation to the yard's level. We had scouts out—[Private First Class Ben N.] Popilsky, [Private First Class Thomas J.] Burke, and [Corporal Edward B.] Carpus; [Private Alvin E.] Hart was also a lead man. Lieutenant Packard led the main body up the right side. I was directly behind Lieutenant Packard. The 1st Platoon squad leader, Sergeant [Edward G.] Bartunek, was on the left flank, Corporal Carpus had the 1st Squad, but was also acting as scout.

"When we reached the rear of the second railroad car, the Krauts opened up on us from both sides and the front. We all hit the dirt, and when I looked up, Lieutenant Packard was in a standing position and firing his Thompson. I yelled for him to get down, which he did. He gave me an order to take five men and circle around to the left; the fire was intense as I moved to the rear."[51]

As the Germans hit the point of the platoon from three sides, Corporal Carpus glanced over as the two scouts, "Ben Popilsky and Tom Burke dashed to my right." Carpus then heard Packard say "something like, 'Let me get them!' He stepped out to the front of a car and took a burst of burp gun fire. As he fell he said to me, 'Put me under the car!' No luck, he was already dead."[52]

As the burst hit Lieutenant Packard, Private Earl W. Boling dove for cover between a set of tracks. "As I hit the dirt I called, 'Medic!' to try to get medical aid for the lieutenant. As I was lying between the rails of one set of tracks, I rolled over to get between two sets of tracks where I was not quite as exposed to enemy fire. Every time I attempted to move I was coming under automatic weapons fire, with tracers and other bullets hitting the rails a few inches from my face. I finally spotted the gunner on a railroad signal tower and returned fire until he fell from the tower."[53]

Once behind cover, Private John W. Keller tried to figure out what to do next. "[Corporal] Jack Francis was in a shell hole about twenty feet northeast of where I was positioned. I could hear him trying to raise E Company to our rear. He was saying, 'E Company, can you hear me?!' and repeated it several times, then commented, 'Damn, the batteries must be dead!'"[54]

As Sergeant Axman and five men began moving toward the rear to hit the flank of the Germans, he ran into the assistant platoon leader, who ordered him to cover the right flank instead. "We were quite fortunate to have a little cover, as railroad ties were piled up along the bank about twelve inches high in places. I crawled to a position where I could observe a bunker and alternate positions where heavy fire was coming from. Captain Long and the rest of the company [were] completely cut off from us."[55]

Sergeant Otis Sampson and his mortar squad were bringing up the rear of the 1st Platoon column, hauling their 60mm mortar and heavy load of ammunition. "The sound of machine gun and rifle fire broke out forward of us; freight cars obstructed our view. I brought the squad to a halt and gave the signal to 'Get down!'

"'Nothing unusual about running into opposition . . . knock it out and continue on,' were my thoughts as I lazily lay there taking advantage of the rest.

"[Private] Jack Hill, Captain Long's runner, came running around the back of a freight car that sat just to the left of us. There was a serious expression on his face as he said, 'Hey, Sarge, Lieutenant Packard has been killed and the platoon is pinned down! And nothing is being done!'

"My first thought, 'I've got to get to the front!'

"Turning to [Private First Class Harry G.] Pickels, I said, 'Take over!'

"'Let's get the hell up front. Jack, lead the way!'

"Hill took off at a run and I followed. We worked our way to the left of the yard and ended up at the left front of a freight car. Dense foliage was on our left. 'Jerry' was in control, and I knew something had to be done and fast.

"'Cover my back!' I quickly said to Hill, and I saw his long legs take off for the rear to position himself.

"'If I can only hold them up long enough for the platoon to get organized,' I thought, and dashed forward, well out in front along the tracks that were barren of cars, and went down firing at two helmeted Germans that were sighting in on me. The bullets were whizzing by. . . My helmet interfered with my sighting. With one sweep of my right hand I knocked it off.

"I tried my best to get one or two shots off at a time to save ammunition and to have more control of the Tommy [gun]. . .

"I know I wasn't short on targets as I silenced one gun after another. I was getting very tired; the sweat was rolling off of me."[56]

During a lull in the firing, Sampson quickly moved behind an embankment to his left, near a switch box. "A burst of burp gun fire shattered the branches just forward of my head. About a five-foot bank ran at left angle to the higher railroad yard and continued on out into the flat lands for a couple of hundred yards or more, starting just forward of me. I saw the heads and shoulders of two helmeted soldiers using the bank's top to support their machine pistols. I was zeroed in at a range of about fifty feet at eleven o'clock. Picking the one on the right, I figured he was the one that had missed me. I knew I wouldn't have a second chance, and I made sure of my first; his face just disappeared. On his right, the soldier had ducked down, but came right back up and got the first burst in, which again just cleared my head. A couple of quick shots and he too picked up some .45 slugs; his face just disappeared too. A third one appeared just to the right side of the last, [and] a quick burst sent him to the protection of the bank; I doubted if I had hit him."[57]

Sampson ducked behind the embankment and quickly did an ammo check. "I checked my inserted clip to see if I had enough rounds in it for another possible shoot-out. I counted eight, and reached for another [clip]. There wasn't any! Frantically, I searched, with the thought, 'I couldn't be out of them!' I scanned the area thinking, 'I must have lost them in the commotion I had gone through,' but I saw no full ones. A feeling of panic seized me. I had gone through most all of my ammunition; I must have been fighting longer than I thought. Time had stood still.

"I hadn't thought of myself. I just happened to be in the right place at the right time; the enemy's control over the front had to be stopped. How I accomplished the job is simple. I just wasn't hit. Now I had little to fight back with if more Jerries popped up. I was licked. . . . I needed help! 'Mortar fire!' I yelled, repeating the command and giving the short range and direction to get mortar fire behind that bank.

"A Jerry crawled the near bank and tried to take me out with a concussion grenade. It landed a little to my right rear. I glanced its way when it hit and saw a funnel-shaped form shoot upward from the explosion. Just glad it had not been a potato masher.

"Like a prayer answered from heaven, a mortar shell exploded about twenty feet back of the bank where the two Germans had been killed...a perfect round. I looked around, amazed at the short time it took to put the mortar in action. The sight that met my eyes will go to my grave with me, for there was [Corporal Harry G.] Pickels and [Private Roy L.] Watts right out in the open at about four o'clock from where I lay, facing north with the side of the freight car for a background. Pickels had a squinted face as he sighted in the M4 sights with a look of expecting to feel the impact of bullets. But it didn't interfere with the work cut out for him. Watts sat on the ground, his legs crossed under him to the right of the mortar, a shell in hand, ready to feed another to the tube as soon as he received the command. The mortar tube looked almost vertical; utility wires dominated the area above. It was a worry that some may be hit. I felt proud of those two men. I did not intend for them to come forward as they did, but to set up in a protected position. They knew there was only one way to get the job done quickly. My voice must have told them I was in trouble. They were willing to sacrifice their lives to help me and the rest of the platoon when help was so badly needed.

"A large German soldier, in a lumbering run, tried to escape to the rear of the five-foot bank to get away from the bursting shells. Carefully I took aim to be sure of preserving my precious last rounds. I let one off—as if hit in the head by a sledgehammer, he went down. I put another one into him to be sure. Another tried his luck, but with the same results. A third started, but changed his mind, knowing the fate of the first two. They were trying for the protective coverage of the foliage to their rear along the railroad bank.

"I had but a few rounds left when [Private] John [W.] Burdge came running up from the rear between a freight car and the foliage, his long BAR in his hands. 'Where are they?' he excitedly asked, ready to do battle.

"'Set up your rifle here,' I said, picking out a suitable spot forward of the switch box, 'one will be coming out at the end of that bank.'

"'Are you sure?' he asked, after a short wait.

"'Yes, I'm quite sure. He knows he will be picked off if he tries it from here, he will be coming out soon.' I encouraged him.

"I recalled the scared look in the eyes of the third man as they met mine when he returned to the safety of the bank. One more step or two before turning back and he too would have died with his buddies. I figured he would use the protection of the bank until he came to its end and then try again for the rear and seek the heavy brush farther back on the railroad bank.

"As I predicted, he came out at its end and started his run, only he had not figured on a BAR coming into the picture. (The small arms weapon most feared by the Germans, on account of its accuracy.)

"'Take your time and squeeze it off—no hurry,' I softly said. 'The first shot kicked up a little dirt [near] his heels.'

"I coached as if we were back on a firing range in the States. Burdge fired his second shot and the German lunged forward and down.

"'Good shot!' I commanded, 'Throw another shot into him just to be sure.'"[58]

Sergeant Sampson had been instrumental in knocking out several German positions on the left or west side of the railroad yard. Private First Class Tom Burke had crawled between the railroad tracks under intense automatic weapons fire and had killed a German machine gun crew with grenades. Individual acts such as these turned the tide. Finally, Corporal Jack L. Francis got the radio working again. "I was trying to get Captain Long on the radio to relay a range for the British artillery that was backing us up."[59]

Captain Long received the call for help from his 1st Platoon. "I was south of the railroad station and east of the railroad a bit. I double-timed the reserve platoon (2nd Platoon) up to the railroad station. I jumped a ditch, moving to the east a little to use the station building as cover. [Private David D.] Dave Comly, a runner, who was second behind me, was hit while in the air jumping the ditch;

his death was instant. I always thought the shot came from a sniper in the station building."[60]

Sergeant Sampson was still near the embankment west of the railroad tracks when the 2nd Platoon arrived. "I heard [Private Dennis G.] O'Loughlin's voice behind me.

"'Do you want some mortar fire up there?'

"Looking back down I saw him, loaded down with the mortar and a bag of ammunition, not counting the rest of his equipment.

"'Where in the hell did you come from?' I asked, wondering at the time what a 2nd Platoon man was doing up with the 1st.

"'Captain Long sent me up. I've lost my men and the lieutenant trying to get through, but I've got the mortar and some ammunition.'

"'Yes, let's give them a few rounds.'

"O'Loughlin's mortar fire itself helped to keep Jerry held down. He was set up at the bottom of the V-shaped ditch just to my rear. O'Loughlin was a good man to have around, cool and steady. It was the first time I had worked with him in action—it wouldn't be the last."[61]

After being pinned down for a short time, Captain Long arrived with the rest of the 2nd Platoon. "I next recall being up in the station area and to the left (west) of some railroad cars. There was some machine gun and rifle fire coming from the left front, [and] it seemed to be coming from a grown-up area of foliage just west of the railroad tracks. I recall calling for artillery fire and trying to adjust by reference to pre-designated concentrations. I don't think the salvo did much good except scare them off. I know I was pretty upset when I was told that we had used up our allocation."[62]

However, the short British artillery barrage had forced the German company in the railroad yard and west of Arnone to withdraw across the river over a footbridge that was still intact.

As darkness closed in, Lieutenant Colonel Alexander left a few outposts in Arnone and the rail yard and pulled Companies E and F back to better defensive positions, anticipating a possible counterattack by the German battalion across the river. Alexander moved up Company A on the left flank of Company E and had them dig in for the night.

Alexander called back to his command post to get medical treatment for the wounded who had been evacuated from Arnone and the railroad yard. "We had twenty-four or twenty-five wounded and sheltered under a culvert, but no doctor. I got on the field telephone and told one of our doctors that we needed him at the forward aid station. He insisted that I should take [the wounded] back to him at the rear CP. I told him we had no transportation and also that the road had not been cleared of mines. [The doctor] argued, and I told him to come forward or I would come back there and kick his ass all the way forward.

"He did not arrive, so I headed back to the rear to get him. I looked down the road and there he comes, medical bag across his shoulder, a white bandage around his head (helmet on top), and limping. I said, 'What happened to you?'

"He said, 'You go to hell!' and continued to walk toward the forward aid station and the wounded.

"I said, 'O.K.' He was going in the right direction, so what more could I say?

"I went down the road a little farther and met Dr. [Captain Robert] Franco [another of the battalion's doctors] and asked him what happened. [Franco] said he was watching the ambulance head toward our forward positions when it hit a mine and blew up in the air, coming down in a pile of junk. He then said he ran to the site. He was standing there looking at what was left of the ambulance when a voice called out, 'Don't just stand there you dummy! Get me out from under here!' Franco said he pulled [the doctor] out, bandaged his head, and off he went, headed for the front. The ambulance driver had been killed."[63]

When Captain Franco saw the ambulance hit the mine, he could hardly believe anyone survived. "The visual effect was stupendous. The whole vehicle rose ten or twelve feet, a wheel leaving every few feet, reached the top of its rise, slowly turned over, and landed flat on its top."[64]

Captain George B. Wood, the regiment's Protestant chaplain, took a few volunteers with him the next morning and recovered the bodies of Lieutenant Packard and the others killed the previous day in Arnone and the railroad yard. That same morning, Lieutenant Colonel Alexander reported to British Brigadier General H. R. Arkwright, commander of the British 23rd Armored Brigade, that the 505th had captured all five bridges, as ordered. "All Germans had withdrawn across the bridge to safety. E Company held the railroad zone and F Company controlled Arnone. D Company was still in reserve. A Company of the 1st Battalion was never committed. I set up a CP in a farmhouse back about 250 yards from the river. We had taken our final objective and I so reported to General Arkwright.

"We held our position on the Volturno River for three days and were relieved by an infantry regiment of the British brigade.

"I was promoted to regimental executive officer; Colonel Gavin having been promoted to brigadier general and assistant division commander [on October 7, 1943]; Lieutenant Colonel [Herbert F.] Batcheller to regimental commander; and Major Vandervoort to CO, 2nd Battalion."[65]

That night, the regiment was relieved from attachment and trucked the following day back to Naples.

After the return to Naples, Lieutenant Theodore L. "Pete" Peterson took command of the 1st Platoon, Company E, replacing Lieutenant Packard, who had been killed in action. Captain Long was transferred to command regimental Headquarters Company, and Captain Clyde Russell, the 2nd Battalion adjutant, took command of Company E.

THE 2ND BATTALION performed occupation duty in Naples during the remainder of October and first half of November. With little to do during that time, discipline began to slide as cases of venereal disease, incidents resulting from public intoxication, and troopers absent without leave (AWOL) began to rise. The transition of command of the battalion only exacerbated the problem.

It was during this period that Private Earl Boling heard about an incident involving another Company E trooper, who had made a particularly bad error in judgment. "It seems that someone asked one of the cooks why we were eating #10 cans of C-rations while in the rear area and he replied that he could only prepare what he got. So on the patrol near the dock area, certain troopers questioned truck drivers of what they were hauling and where it was going. If it was going to troops at the front or a hospital, it was not bothered, but if it was intended for a rear unit, etcetera, a requisitioned product might be obtained to take back to supplement our rations.

"We had received a new battalion commander to replace Colonel Alexander, and had not really gotten to know Major Benjamin Vandervoort, but on this particular night, Thomas Burke had decided that carrying rations back to the area was too tiring and borrowed the major's jeep without permission to haul the 'requisitioned rations.'

"As he entered the battalion area he was challenged. After giving the password, he was asked his identity and answered, 'P.F.C. Burke.'

"Then the answer came, 'I'm Major Vandervoort and that's my jeep you are driving.' Needless to say, this stopped the 'moonlight requisitions' of any more rations."[66]

CHAPTER 2

"He Was Pushing Everybody"

On November 18, the 82nd Airborne Division sailed from Naples for Northern Ireland and upon arriving at Belfast on December 9, the 505th moved to billets in Quonset huts near Cookstown.

Shortly afterward, new replacements like Private First Class Frank A. Bilich arrived and were assigned to their respective companies. Bilich would unexpectedly meet one of guys he knew from his old Croatian neighborhood in Chicago. "The first couple of days I was in Cookstown, none of us knew which company we were going to. A truck came in after we were there about two or three days, and we were riding in the back of the truck. None of us knew each other—we were all new replacements. We wondered where we were going and when we pulled into this area, as we got out of the truck, there was a guy standing there, and he said, 'Fall out over here. The rest of you guys stay in the trucks.' So, when he called my name out, I fell out to the right.

"There was another guy by the name of [Private] Carl [A.] Beck; there were about twelve of us. They dropped us off there. The other trucks kept on going. So Beck turned around and he said, 'What outfit is this?'

"The guy said, 'The 505.' He said, 'You go down to that Quonset hut. There's going to be a roll call there in about ten minutes.

"So we went down to the Quonset hut and he called off our names. He said, 'When I call off your name, you go to that first Quonset if you are in D Company; second Quonset hut, E Company; third Quonset hut, F Company.' He said, 'Bilich and Barnett, you guys take off.'

"So we took off; we had that big damned duffle bag with us. We get up to the first Quonset hut and we walk in. By this time, it was already dark. All the sudden the door opens and a fellow comes in and he says, 'When I call the roll, sound off like you've got a pair of balls.'

"And I thought to myself, 'Gee that voice sounds familiar.' So he called out my name and I said, 'Here!'

"He said, 'Where's Bilich?'

"I said, 'Here.'

"He said, 'I want to see you up at the orderly room after this formation.'

"So I figured, 'What the hell happened now?' So, I went up there and as I walked in the door, there was John Rabig standing there. I said, 'Hey, John.'

"He said, 'John, my ass! Ain't you got any brains?'

"I said, 'What do you mean?'

"He said, 'What the hell are you doing here?'

"I said, 'How about you?'

"He said, 'Shut up! I'm doing the talking! What am I going to tell your mother if something happens to you?'

"I said, John. . .'

"He said, 'Listen, you better pay attention to everything you learn here and hope you stay alive. I thought you had better sense than that.'

"I said, 'Well, how about you?'

"He said, 'I'm a lot older than you.'

"That was the first time I had seen him since he left for the CCC camp. He was then acting first sergeant. They were making changes in the company rosters. Our first sergeant, John [R.] Razumich, was being transferred to F Company and our company commander [Captain John D. Rice] went to another company."[1]

Major Vandervoort had clamped down and made changes in the Company D leadership because of discipline problems.

Officers like Lieutenant Jim Coyle, an assistant platoon leader with Company E, found it difficult to integrate the replacements while in Northern Ireland. "Training them and the veterans in the company was restricted to road marches and athletics, because all of the open areas were planted farmland.

"We did travel to a range at Strawberry Hill, near Lough Neagh, where the men had an opportunity to 'zero in' their rifles and fire the company weapons, including machine guns and mortars. While there, we ran obstacle courses and dug foxholes, which we occupied while tanks were driven over us to prove it was safe. This made a change from our normal routine.

"The men were given three-day passes and furloughs while in [Northern] Ireland, and there was a problem in connection with men staying 'absent without leave.' The AWOL rate took a sharp upward curve, due to the fact that the Irish girls were the first English speaking females the men had seen in almost a year. [Captain] Clyde R. Russell, who had a very good sense of humor, called it 'Belfast Fever' and told the men at one formation that they weren't 'fighters,' they were 'lovers.'"[2]

The number of cases of AWOL and venereal disease in Company D were the highest of any in the regiment. Private First Class Bilich had been a member of Company D for just a few days when Vandervoort addressed the assembled company. "He was chewing everybody's asses out and right while he was talking, three guys fell flat on their faces—drunk. We had about seven or eight VD cases and five guys over the hill [AWOL]. He was pissed off at D Company and rightfully so."[3]

The measures taken by Major Vandervoort to enforce discipline caused growing resentment among the combat veterans of the 2nd Battalion. Some of the troopers derisively nicknamed him "Shaky Jake" because of the tendency of his left leg to shake slightly when he stood at attention, caused by the weakness when he had broken his left ankle during the practice jump in the U.S.

ON FEBRUARY 3, 1944, the regiment moved by ship from Northern Ireland to Scotland, then by troop train to its pre-invasion staging base at Camp Quorn, in the village of Quorndon, Leicestershire, England, between the town of Loughborough and the city of Leicester. There, the 505th began training for the upcoming cross-channel invasion.

Major Vandervoort drove the 2nd Battalion relentlessly during training. Many of the combat veterans of the 2nd Battalion resented his iron-willed approach to training and discipline, believing they did not need the physical conditioning and repetitive training they already knew all too well. However, Vandervoort knew that the German opposition they would face would likely be far stronger than that encountered in Sicily and Italy. Further, he knew that the battalion had not been in combat since early October of 1943 and had really not had an opportunity to conduct practice parachute jumps as well as tactical and weapons training since. Additionally, the battalion had to integrate the replacements with their squads, platoons, and companies in order to count on them in the coming invasion.

Private First Class Bilich noticed growing resentment toward Major Vandervoort among his buddies in D Company. "He was pushing everybody—training, training, training—night jumps, practice, reassemble, combat conditions—and the guys were getting pissed off, because they wanted some time to go to town to drink and raise a little hell."[4]

For the veterans of Sicily and Italy, like Private First Class Turk Seelye, the training was boring; having done all of it more times than they cared to count. "Training consisted of the typical problems associated with preparing infantry soldiers for combat, plus dozens of forced marches, tactical problems, and several parachute jumps, some done at night."[5]

Some of the training, such as parachute landings at night and live fire at shooting ranges was inherently dangerous. Staff Sergeant Russell W. Brown was the squad leader of the 60mm Mortar Squad, 1st Platoon, Company F. "The mortar squad went to the Bradgate Park mortar range near Leicester to train. My squad and Lieutenant [John H.] Dodd were on a hillside observing fire on targets to our front. The 2nd Platoon mortar squad had their mortar set up behind us in a small depression and did the firing.

"It was during this firing, that a short round—I believe the fins may have come off [the shell], I don't know, but the round hit us and sent six plus myself to the hospital. I was hit in the left leg above the knee."[6]

Bilich found that Company D had its share of colorful personalities with colorful nicknames—Swamp Rat, Saddlebags, Red Dog, The Beast—and maybe more than its share of hell raisers. "When I joined D Company, I wrote a letter home to my teacher and what I put in the letter was 'I'm in a company of characters.' Everybody had something going or jokes they were pulling, and everybody had a nickname. You had Stanley W. Kotlarz, they called him 'Pockets,' because he had the jump pants and if you needed a piece of wire or pair of pliers, he had it. You had [Robert J. Niland] 'The Beast.' [Frank] Schneider, they called him 'Trigger.' He was blind as a bat; he had thick combat glasses. How he got that name, I don't know. They called [Leonard M.] Skolek,

'Big Joe.' [William R.] 'Rebel' Haynes' first name wasn't 'Rebel', but they called him 'Rebel' because of the way he acted."[7]

Even though the training was almost constant, the troopers still found ways to get into trouble. Two of the company's hell raisers in particular stood out, as Bilich soon learned after joining the company. "Tommy Thompson got into many fights in Leicester. One night he fought with the MPs and knocked a Provo Marshal on his back."[8] Thompson had been involved in the the infamous Cotton's Fish Camp incident back at Phenix City, Alabama.

The other man with that reputation was Melvin P. "M. P." Brown. Bilich heard the guys ask Brown from time to time, 'M. P., what does that stand for? More pain?'[9]

"He was a tough fist fighter who could take on four or five men at one time. He had huge hands and built like a tank.

"Brown was always in trouble. When he came out of a combat zone you knew he would be off AWOL, and you could not do much about it. He was the best combat soldier you ever saw, a sort of guy you would want next to you in a tough spot."[10]

The new Company D first sergeant, John H. Rabig, had the difficult responsibility of controlling troopers like Brown. "That guy was a playboy in garrison; he wanted wine, women and song. He was going to get that, [no matter] what the hell the circumstances were. Brown was once again in the camp stockade; a barbed wire enclosure with pup tents to sleep in.

"Brown was due out of the stockade after serving five weeks for something or other. One day I was sitting in the orderly room when the phone rang. It was the MPs to tell me that Brown's time was up and he was due out now. So I go down to the stockade and get the son-of-a-bitch.

"As we are walking back to the company, he says, 'Will I get a pass tonight?' Now this is the guy I've just got out of the stockade and he is asking me for a pass.

"My answer was 'No!'

"'Why not?' Brown asks.

"'Because you are on guard duty tonight. You happen to be on the roster. Brown was not very happy.

"I told him, 'You go on guard duty tonight and I'll see you get a pass for tomorrow.' He agreed. It was a combined company guard, with about six men from each company forming the guard to police the camp.

"So Brown stood guard that night. I'm sitting in the orderly room later and the phone rings.

"I answered, 'Company D, Sergeant Rabig.'

"'Is M. P. Brown in your company?'

"'Yes, he is on guard duty tonight.'

"The voice on the other end of the phone says, 'No he ain't, he's in the guard house.'

"Oh shit! I just got him out of there and now he is back in. So down I go to the duty officer and found out they put him in charge of the prisoners at the stockade; his friends who he had spent the last five weeks with. It appears that the prisoners were supposed to be clearing up the garbage around the perimeter of the camp. The duty officer had found Brown's rifle leaning up against the wall; Brown was holding a baby while his two charges were with two dames in the bushes.

"The duty officer throws all three in the guard house. I go and see Brown the next day. He says, 'Well, they were my friends.' What the hell can you do with a guy like that?"[11]

The discipline in the 505th had become so bad that Lieutenant Colonel Herbert Batcheller was relieved of command of the regiment and assigned to command the 1st Battalion, 508th Parachute Infantry Regiment. The executive officer of the 508th, Lieutenant Colonel William E. Ekman, became the new commanding officer of the 505th. Ekman addressed the assembled regiment shortly after taking command, in which he told them that he couldn't stop them from doing wrong, but he could make it damned hard on those who were caught. He took steps to make the camp more appealing, such as providing more entertainment like movies, a game room, and a reading room. Ekman promised to transfer troublemakers to "leg" outfits, which worked very effectively. The discipline of the regiment dramatically improved over the next few weeks as Ekman dealt with the few remaining troopers who refused to comply.

After arriving in England, each of the parachute regiments received its respective assigned mission. The 505th would drop just west of St.-Sauveur-le-Vicomte, capture the town and the bridges over the Douve River, and send patrols to the south of Prairies Marécageuses. The newly attached 507th Parachute Infantry Regiment would land to the north of Hill 110 near Hills 71 and 82 and defend against a German attack from the north. The other newly attached parachute regiment, the 508th, would drop astride Hill 110, consolidate its position, and move south and west to intercept German forces attempting to reinforce those on the Cotentin Peninsula. The division would hold the area until the forces landed at Utah Beach driving west would link up with it.

The battalion S-2 and S-3 sections worked in the 505th's war room to assist in preparing briefing materials, unit orders, etcetera. Technician Fourth Grade Berge Avadanian, with the 2nd Battalion S-2 section, was assigned to review aerial photos of the drop zone and construct a sand table of the area to be used for the briefings. "I worked on a large (sand table type) mockup of the drop zones. The table area contours were made of paper maché instead of sand. It was about a ten feet by five feet by ten inches deep box with little buildings, etc.

"When I needed supplies in the city of Leicester for the war room, I was accompanied by guards to prevent leaks."[12]

About a week before moving to the airfields for the upcoming invasion, the division's assignment changed due to the detection of the presence of elements of the recently arrived German 91st Air Landing Division, which had moved into the area around Hill 110 and St.-Sauveur-le-Vicomte. It was working to turn all fields large enough for glider landings into deathtraps. The 82nd Airborne had been just days away from parachuting directly on top of a German division specially trained to counter airborne operations.

The 82nd Airborne Division's new orders were to: "Land astride the Merderet River. Seize, clear, and secure the general area within its zone. Capture Ste.-Mère-Église, seize and secure crossings of the Merderet River at La Fiere and Chef-du-Pont, and establish a bridgehead covering these two crossings. Seize and destroy the crossings of the Douve River at Beuzeville-la-Bastille and Ètienville. Protect the northwest flank of the VII Corps within the division zone and be prepared to advance west on Corps order to the line of the Douve north of its junction with the Prairies Marécageuses."[13]

General Ridgway assigned the most critical objective to the 505th. "The 505 was the only parachute regiment in the division (or the whole Allied airborne effort for that matter) with combat experience, slated for the Normandy operation, and accordingly I assigned it the most important task—the capture and retention of Ste.-Mère-Église."[14]

The town sat astride the N-13 highway that ran from the port city of Cherbourg south to Paris. The town was a key crossroads and chokepoint in the road network for enemy forces counterattacking Utah Beach from the western and northern areas of the Cotentin Peninsula.

On May 29, the 505th moved to two airfields. Regimental Headquarters and Headquarters Company, the 1st Battalion, and one platoon of Company B, 307th Airborne Engineer Battalion were sealed in at Spanhoe airfield. The 2nd Battalion, 3rd Battalion, and a section with Battery C, 456th Parachute Field Artillery Battalion were staged at Cottesmore airfield.

Shortly after arrival, each unit conducted briefings of the operation. Captain Hubert S. Bass, now commanding Company F, attended the 2nd Battalion briefing. "[Major] Vandervoort called a company commanders' meeting to brief us on our mission – Lieutenant [William E.] Schmees, commanding Headquarters Company; Captain [Clyde] Russell, E Company; Lieutenant [Taylor G.] Smith, D Company; and Captain Bass, F Company. This was it—we had received our combat orders. We knew how and where we were going, but not sure when. Morale was better now that our missions and objectives were known—our men were trained fighters who desired to close with the enemy. Captain [William J.] Harris, the battalion S-3, issued plane assignments."[15]

After briefings by their respective battalion commanders and staffs, the company commanders conducted briefings for their platoon leaders and their assistants. During the Company E briefings, Lieutenant Jim Coyle learned that "E Company was to set up roadblocks at Neuville-au-Plain, a small town north of Ste.-Mère-Église. Ste.-Mère-Église was a main road junction which the German reserves would have to use in order to attack the 4th Division, which was landing on the beaches east of our objectives. Third Battalion was to take Ste.-Mère-Église. Second Battalion, including our company, was to protect Ste.-Mère-Église from attack from the north by holding Neuville-au-Plain. We were briefed on our mission on large, scale maps of the area and low level aerial photos of the town of Neuville-au-Plain."[16]

The platoon leaders then conducted briefings of their respective platoons, so that each trooper knew the mission of their platoon, company, battalion, and regiment.

Corporal Roy O. King, with Company D, felt that the sand tables were of great benefit. "I personally thought they were great. The briefings were concise and more clear with the tables."[17]

Company E veteran, Sergeant Cullen E. Clark, Jr., had confidence that the officers and men of the 505 would be successful in accomplishing the regiment's mission. "These men had been tested in combat and had proven that they were real paratroopers. Our company commander was Captain Clyde R. Russell, who was one of the old original officers and was one of the most capable and respected company commanders in the regiment. He had given us our briefing prior to departure from the marshalling area and all members of the platoon felt fully confident that our mission was going to be a success. I recall several men remarking that they sure were glad that our 'old man' was one of the old men and was one of us and not one of the new officers who were in some of the other companies at that time."[18]

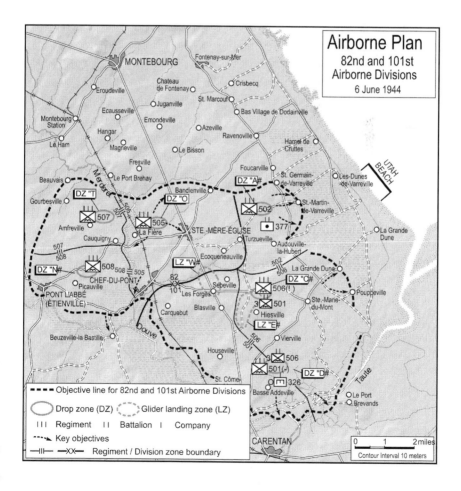

Major Vandervoort had watched the metamorphosis of the regiment through two campaigns. "When we left Italy the regiment was lean, mean, and battle smart. Through innumerable small unit actions, the junior officers became knowledgeable, combat-wise leaders. Whatever job the 505 was given, the lieutenants and NCOs made it work. They led like respected older brothers in a fraternity. Their emphasis was on self-discipline, rather than discipline applied from above. With never a doubt as to who was in charge, they shared foxholes, rations, hazards, and hopes with their troopers."[19]

Yet, some of the 2nd Battalion troopers didn't have confidence or faith in Vandervoort and many didn't like him. He had come down hard on the battalion to enforce discipline and had driven them hard during the training for the invasion. Major Vandervoort's tough, hardnosed style had not convinced some of the veteran troopers that he could lead them in combat. Because Vandervoort have been a staff officer in Sicily and Italy, some believed he was not suited for a combat command or Gavin would have used him in that capacity.

Captain Lyle B. Putnam was the 2nd Battalion surgeon. "My battalion commanding officer, then Major Benjamin Vandervoort, was an unusual man. A very proud individual, with ambition to do a good job, he was regarded in Sicily and Italy as over anxious, indecisive, and with too much desire to gain personally, with no regard to cost of trouble to others. The man knew this—he was determined to rectify the general opinion, but not to lose efficiency of his unit in doing so."[20]

On the evening of June 4, over 13,000 paratroopers of the 82nd and 101st Airborne Divisions prepared for the jump. The U.S. Army Air Corps fed them a great meal. The battalion, regimental, and division commanders gave them final pep talks. They fastened the enormous loads that each would carry into combat—main and reserve parachutes, helmets, gloves, Griswold cases containing individual weapons, bandoliers of small arms and boxes of machine gun ammunition, fragmentation grenades, smoke grenades, Gammon grenades, Hawkins antitank mines, canteens, bayonets, entrenching tools, blankets, and shelter-halves. They strapped on musette bags containing changes of clothes, toiletry items, and first aid kits. They stuffed their jumpsuits pockets with K-rations, D-rations, candy bars, cigarettes, matches, and other items.

However, as the troopers gathered around their assigned planes, they received word of the postponement of the jump because of high winds, high tides, and rain in Normandy. Most spent a restless, sleepless night as a result of the adrenaline their bodies had generated in anticipation of the jump.

The following morning, the weather improved enough for the operation to commence on the night of June 5-6. That evening, they repeated the process of getting ready for the operation. Again, the air corps treated the troopers to a great meal. After reaching the end of the serving line with his plate of food piled high, Private Kenneth E. Russell, a new replacement with Company F, looked for a place to sit. "The air force always had good food, and they gave us what you might say was the 'Last Supper.' I recall at that 'Last Supper,' a fellow by the name of [Lee G.] Graves, who was in the company, who was a very devout, religious man. He'd always sit down at the end of the table by himself, you know. I do recall at the dinner that evening that there was something within me that wanted to be close to Graves, because he had something I didn't have. He was a devout, religious man, and I got my tray of food, and I went down, and I asked him, 'Graves, may I sit here with you?'

"He said, 'Yes.'

"I said, 'Well, may I share in your blessing?' He was aghast, because I had never done that before. None of us had. Of course, we kind of looked at him as a weirdo. I guess it was something that we sensed—danger. I didn't want to press it. But that was the first time I ever wanted to even sit close to Graves, because he would always pray."[21]

Another man in Russell's platoon who was deeply religious was Private First Class Charles P. Blankenship. Young Ken Russell admired him. "He was a devout religious fellow, nineteen years old at the time. His father was a Baptist minister. He was the only man that went to regimental headquarters and asked to take his tithe out of his meager army earnings. Blankenship, he was a nice guy. I guess he knew I was nervous. He was nervous too, but he made me feel good.

"He said to me, 'Well Russell, I'm the tough guy in the unit. I'll be around a long time. In fact, Russell, I'll tell you what I'm going to do. I'm going to raise the chickens to pick the grass off of your grave.'

"He was trying to cheer me up, I guess."[22]

THAT EVENING AT THE AIRFIELD AT NORTH WITHAM, where the pathfinder teams of the two American airborne divisions had trained in secrecy, Private First Class Dennis G. O'Loughlin, a Company E trooper and member of the 2nd Battalion team, readied himself for the jump, even though he had a broken hand. "Whether to make the jump or not with my broken hand was left up to me. They knew damned well I would jump. Told 'em if I could get that cast cut off my hand and a tight bandage put on it so I could use my fingers a little, I thought I could make it. We were hauled to a shop where they sprayed us all we wanted with green paint and handed us burnt cork to rub on our faces and hands. Then we were taken to the plane that was to take us in and lined up and had our picture taken along with the plane crew. We all got copies later."[23]

With nine planes carrying the division's pathfinder teams leading the way, 378 transport aircraft took off from Cottesmore and Spanhoe airfields carrying the parachute element of the 82nd Airborne Division. The gigantic sky-train swept over the darkening English countryside in mile upon mile of nine plane waves arrayed in V-of-V formation. Each nine plane wave transported a company and were grouped in thirty-six to forty-five plane serials carrying a battalion. The 2nd Battalion serial was in the lead, followed by the 3rd Battalion, and then the 1st Battalion serial, which included regimental Headquarters and Headquarters Company.

Private John W. Keller, with E Company, was a veteran of the Sicily and Salerno, Italy combat jumps. "Upon becoming airborne we could smoke. I lit a cigarette and do remember feeling very uncomfortable. My mind was full of many thoughts, but I was mainly concerned with what it would be like when we reached our goal, for I anticipated the worst. My harness was a tight one and pinched at my crotch, so I gave it an upward pull at the buckles, was relieved and shortly thereafter I dozed."[24]

Technical Sergeant Buffalo Boy Canoe, making his third combat jump, looking at the other Company D troopers in his plane saw "some of the group in deep thought, some praying, some trying to hold a conversation, others reading old letters, a few with big tears of fear—which we all had. My thought was what will it feel like to be hit in the sky and if I would ever see my dear ones."[25]

Captain Hubert Bass, commanding Company F, looked at his watch; it was almost midnight. "At 23:49 hours, 5 June 1944, our flight was to rendezvous in the vicinity of Coventry, England. My thoughts while I was sitting near the plane's door were about our mission, our plans, wondering what kind of reception we would get from the Germans during the drop."[26]

Looking out the door for checkpoints, Captain Bass glanced at his watch once again. "Just forty-nine minutes have passed since we left Coventry; seems like an eternity. I kept thinking of a saying I once heard. 'A coward dies many times before his death, but the valiant tastes the sting of death only once.'

"Some of the troopers in the plane had their eyes closed as if they were sleeping, others were just staring, someone would look at his watch occasionally, loosen or tighten a harness buckle. Those were brave men and [it was] a wonderful comfort to be on their team. There were several checkpoints between Coventry and the English coast. However, I was watching for the coastline, checkpoint 'Flatbush.' Then a destroyer in the Channel...a submarine, at which point we change our flight direction towards the Cherbourg Peninsula, Guernsey Island would be on our right.

"Lieutenant [James J.] Smith was on detached service to division headquarters. He was in command of our pathfinder group. Our success of hitting our drop zone depended on his group."[27]

THE 82ND AIRBORNE PATHFINDER TEAMS jumped on time at 1:21 a.m. The three 505th pathfinder teams were the only ones dropped together on the proper drop zone. The thirty-six C-47s carrying the 2nd Battalion serial were only thirty minutes away from Drop Zone "O," when the pathfinders jumped.

Upon landing, Private First Class Anthony J. "Tony" DeMayo, a Company E pathfinder, quickly assembled his rifle and looked around in the moonlight for familiar landmarks to determine if he had landed in the correct field. "Back in England in the war room, when we were briefed, we were told that the DZ consisted of three fields surrounded by hedgerows. On the edge of the center field, we were told to look for a barn and a haystack. As I got up to get out of my harness, lo and behold, off to the edge of the field was the haystack and the barn – I was surprised.

"Our mission was to get a set of seven lights to form a 'T' and a radar, to send out a code for the 2nd Battalion planes to beam in on. After this equipment was set up, the radar man was to start sending out his code, immediately. The light men, of which I was one of, were to leave the lights off and take cover until we heard the sound of the first planes. The rest of the men set up a defense of the DZ."[28]

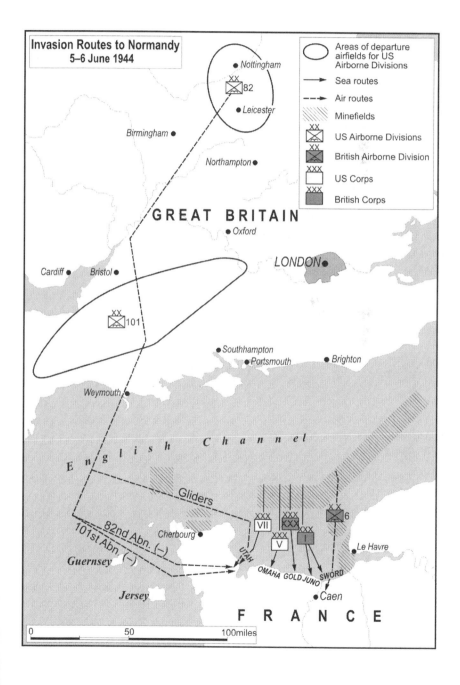

CHAPTER 3

"Well, Let's Go!"

Lieutenant Colonel Ben Vandervoort was the jumpmaster in the lead plane of the 2nd Battalion, 505th serial, which was the lead element of the main force of the 82nd Airborne Division. "On leaving England in our flight across the channel we flew over elements of the seaborne invasion fleet. There, stretched out as far as the eye could see were hundreds of vessels—all without lights—their wakes gleaming in the moonlight as they zigged and zagged in unison—all moving toward the French coast. The mass and magnitude of the coordinated motion gave one the sensation of being part of an irresistible force that nothing could stop. As we came in over the Normandy coast we stood up and hooked up, ready to jump. Isolated fires were blazing on the ground below. Imagination told us they were aircraft already shot down. We ran into a cloudbank."[1]

The troop carrier pilots, veterans of the Sicily and Salerno jumps, climbed and went over the cloudbank on the western side of the Cotentin Peninsula, keeping the 505th serials together to a much greater degree than the troop carrier units transporting other airborne units. As the pilots did so, Private First Class Daryle E. Whitfield, with Company F, felt the plane climb "straight up in the air, seems like we went no telling how high."[2]

IN THREE ADJACENT FIELDS just west of Ste.-Mère-Église, the three 505th pathfinder teams were set up and waiting for the division to arrive. At the edge of one of the moonlit fields, Company E pathfinder Private First Class Anthony J. DeMayo and the other 2nd Battalion light team waited by a hedgerow as the Eureka operator tapped out the Morse code to guide the pathfinder plane to the drop zone. "At this point the only sound was an occasional rattle of the equipment. We were told that it would be about thirty minutes from our drop to the drop of the main body. It felt like thirty hours. Then, off in the distance we heard the sound of the first plane motors.

"At this point, the other light men and I went out and turned on the lights and headed back for cover, because we surely thought this would be it, with the field lit up. But still, no sound except for the sound of the planes, which were getting louder all the time."[3]

As the 2nd Battalion serial emerged from the clouds, the sky erupted with German antiaircraft and small arms fire. Multicolored tracers from 20mm antiaircraft guns and machine guns crisscrossed, rising up to meet the oncoming planes, as flak bursts from 88mm antiaircraft guns lit up the sky. Large spotlights searched the sky to illuminate targets for the antiaircraft guns.

In one of the nine Company F planes, Captain Hubert Bass was watching for the landmarks and the lights marking the drop zone as he called out the commands they all knew by heart. "'Stand up and hook up! . . . Check equipment! . . . Stand in the door!' I don't believe I could be heard—maybe they read my lips. Every man tightened up, pushing towards the door.

"Where were Smith's lights? I began to get worried. It was dark; clouds kept flying past, blocking vision of the ground. Our coded light was color green.

"We could pass beyond our DZ without knowing. The following planes would see us jump. We had to hit our DZ. I was determined [to jump] when we crossed the second river, which was the Merderet and last reference point. To hesitate would put us within seconds of the coast. Where in the hell are those pathfinder lights?"[4]

As he looked out the door of the lead plane, Vandervoort could see that "flak in large volumes was coming up from Ste.-Mère-Église. Our planes were flying too high and too fast. I was standing in the open door ready to go—checking off the landmarks (highways, railroads, bodies of water) we had memorized during our pre-invasion briefings and studies. Suddenly the green light was turned on. I knew where we were, and the signal was premature. The crew chief standing by me could communicate with the pilot over the intercom. I told him to tell them to turn 'the G.D. thing off' and wait and come down to the proper altitude and speed. The green light went out. We continued to fly as before."[5]

Unfortunately, the troopers in three planes carrying Lieutenant William J. Meddaugh and his 2nd Platoon of Company E, jumped when the green lights were prematurely turned on in their planes. "I was in the lead plane of the three-plane group to the right. In this position, I was able to see the lead three-plane group and the group to its left, very clearly. Suddenly, the three-plane group at the point of the V banked sharply to the left—so sharply that the group to its left had to pull up sharply to avoid a midair collision. In doing so, the three planes scattered. I knew at that instant that our company formation was destroyed.

"With a quick flash, I recalled the jump I made in the Sicilian invasion, where I landed sixty miles away from my DZ. 'Here we go again,' I said to myself. At that instant, I saw the equipment bundles sweep by underneath the plane. The pilot had salvoed the load too early. I swore to myself and saw the green light flash on. No time to think—automatically—'Let's go!' I stepped out and waited for the opening shock. It came—hard. Our jumping speed was too fast. I hung on and hit hard. I was in France and alive. My platoon was dropped about three miles from the planned drop zone. We were isolated with various other scattered elements of the 507 and 508 Regiments."[6]

As Captain Bass watched the last landmark, the Merderet River, pass beneath his plane, he could see a fire burning in Ste.-Mère-Église. "Suddenly, as if in answer to thousands of prayers, the clouds opened up and I saw lights on the ground formed in a 'T' with a green light at the bottom of the stem. Good old Smith."[7]

As the first nine planes of the thirty-six plane 2nd Battalion serial approached the lights of the drop zone, Lieutenant Colonel Vandervoort "told the crew chief to tell the pilot to pass the jump signal back to the trailing aircraft. The green light came on again and out we went. The opening shock (due to our speed) was such that it tore off my musette bag and snapped blinding flashes in front of my eyes. We were too high (perhaps three thousand feet) and drifted away from our drop zone. As I came down, I selected a small field with a clump of brush in the center and slipped my chute toward the shadows of the brush to be able to conceal myself while getting out of my harness.

"I landed on about a forty-five degree slope—hit hard and felt my ankle snap and knew at once it was broken. I got out of my chute in the shadows. I was alone—and crawled over to one corner of the hedgerows surrounding the field. The ankle hurt and I shot myself in the leg with a morphine syrette carried in our paratrooper's first-aid kit."[8]

Only Easy Company's headquarters and 1st Platoon sticks were dropped on the drop zone. Lieutenant Jim Coyle was the assistant platoon leader of the 1st Platoon. "The plane's engines slowed down and I knew we would receive the green light to go soon, but I still could not see the lights to be set up by the pathfinders who had jumped earlier to mark the DZ. Suddenly, we made a sharp left turn, and I picked out the blue-green lights in a 'T' formation directly in front of us. Just at that moment, the green light beside the door went on, and giving the order to 'Go,' I jumped.

"I had no trouble on landing, despite all the equipment we carried. As soon as I got out of my parachute and stood up, I saw the green light, which was our battalion assembly signal, a short distance away. The first man I encountered was our battalion commander, Lieutenant Colonel Benjamin Vandervoort. He asked me if I had found my medical aid man, but I told him I was alone. At the time, he did not mention that he was injured, but he had broken his ankle on the jump. He ordered me to continue to locate my men."[9]

Company E trooper, Private John Keller had loosened his harness during the flight, then fallen asleep, and awoke just before his stick hooked up their static lines—went out the door of his plane. "Then I remember feeling something under my feet—as if I was for a minute walking on a very thick and spongy mattress. I was on somebody's chute! Suddenly my reserve gave me a good belt under the chin; I had forgotten to retighten the buckles on my harness and it had me wedged for the rest of the way down. There were a hell of a lot of tracers—red, white, and green—as I remember, and the next thing I knew, I landed in a small field bordered by six or seven foot tall hedges."[10]

A German searchlight locked on to the lead plane of the three-plane "Vee" carrying Lieutenant Roper R. Peddicord and a stick of his 3rd Platoon of Company E. The third man in the stick, Sergeant Cullen E. Clark, Jr., could see out the door. "As soon as the searchlight picked us up and then went ahead of us, we could see the lines of tracers coming up from the ground. They looked like they were coming right in the door, but curved like a thin line of fire and hit the tail of the airplane. We were all hooked up and ready to jump, but the pilot started zigzagging, and the plane engines sounded like they were going to tear off from the plane. We got away from the searchlight, and Lieutenant Peddicord jumped, then we all followed him.

"Lieutenant Peddicord and I landed quite close together, and I recall [him] saying, 'Clark, this makes three times we have jumped in combat, and all three times we have landed close together. Now, let's start killing Germans.'

"Lieutenant Peddicord informed the planeload of men who had jumped with us 'that the pilot apparently dropped us in the wrong spot. And all I know is that we are in France some place with German soldiers all around us, but we must find Ste.-Mère-Église and join the rest of our platoon and E Company.'"[11] Peddicord's platoon landed about two miles southeast of Ste.-Mère-Église, just east of Les Forges.

The combination of heavy equipment loads and some C-47s traveling faster as a result of the descent after going over the cloudbank on the western coast of the Cotentin Peninsula, resulted in some troopers experiencing a violent opening shock as their chutes deployed, with blown-out panels in their canopies, equipment torn off, and rough landings. One of them was Company E trooper, Private George R. Jacobus, who landed northeast of Ste.-Mère-Église. "Out the door—the worst opening shock ever. I looked at the canopy—I had blown three panels and was dropping fast. We were high—at least fifteen hundred to eighteen hundred feet. As the ground began to come into focus, so did a German machine gun nest on my right. There appeared to be a small building to my left. With all my strength, I pulled on the risers to go left away from the machine gun nest. I did, and slammed into the building like a ton of bricks, and on the ground, on my back. Something had hit my left eye.

"I knew in an instant that I had broken my left leg. It was eerie, as I lay amidst the tangled shroud lines and wriggled out of my chute. Then the pain in the left leg became a reality. It hurt like hell. Suddenly, after quite some time, there was another trooper from another airborne unit. He was big enough to pick me up by the armpits and drag me over to be propped up against a tree."[12]

After landing, Sergeant Otis Sampson found another Company E trooper, Sergeant George A. Clark, the 1st Platoon's radio operator. As they were discussing in which direction the plane's equipment bundles were likely located; Sampson heard an explosion at the other end of the field. "Thinking it to be mortar fire, our first reaction was to seek cover, as we expected a barrage; but a fire started to light up the area. We both ran forward as quickly as possible to extinguish it before it brought in artillery fire against us. It was a chute on fire. We quickly put it out and darkness closed in around us again. The trooper, on landing, had tripped a mine; one he carried or one in the field, we never knew. He was lying on his back, unconscious. On checking him out for broken bones, I found his legs felt like jelly. I gave him a shot of morphine as Clark made sure the fire wouldn't start up again. We left him there in the open field near a hedgerow; time was vital and we moved on. We had at least saved him from being burned.

"In the next field we saw the green 'T' light. We had landed not far from it. It was a small light, but enough to guide us in."[13]

Watching the spectacle above him, Company D pathfinder, Private First Class Julius "Ike" Eisner, "looked up—it was 1:51. They were coming in; I could see chutes coming down, the antiaircraft going up. It was a once in a lifetime to see that—never again will there be a scene like that again."[14]

It was an equally exhilarating experience for the commander of Company E, Captain Clyde Russell. "I jumped in the same plane with Ben. . . Our plane hit the DZ and since we were leading the division it was a wonderful show as the balance of the troops and equipment came in."[15]

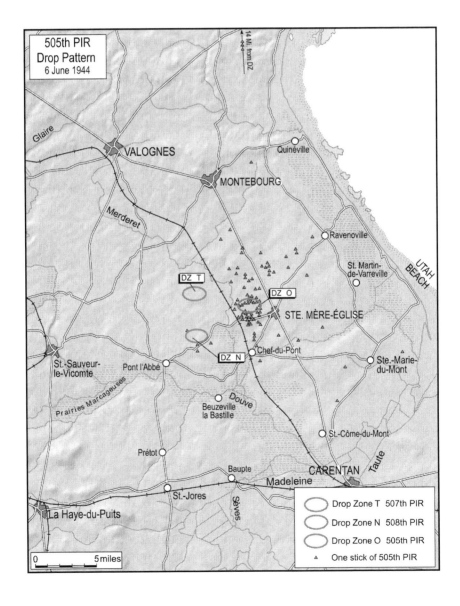

JUST TO THE EAST IN STE.-MÈRE-ÉGLISE, twenty year old Raymond Paris along with sixty to seventy other citizens were fighting a fire at a building on the southeastern side of the town square as Germans with the Infantry Gun Company, 3rd Battalion, 1058th Grenadier Regiment, 91st Air Landing Division stood by, fully armed and alerted. Paris and the other civilians were passing buckets from person to person when they heard planes approaching. "It was still not quite dark and there was a full moon that night and we were able to see that the side doors of the airplanes were open. We suddenly saw men jumping out of all the airplanes and their parachutes opening. I was standing on the edge of the square shouting, 'That's it, it's the invasion!'"[16]

A planeload of troopers containing a stick that included the 60mm Mortar Squad, 2nd Platoon, Company F overshot the drop zone. Private Ken Russell, an assistant bazooka gunner, was jumping in that stick. "As we left the plane we had flak, machine gun fire, and everything else all the way down, because we were sitting targets."[17]

Private First Class Daryle Whitfield, the pusher of that stick and the last man out of the plane, jumped at "about 2,500 feet. On the way down, I heard a bunch of racket on the ground. I looked up and saw red tracers going through my canopy."[18]

After his parachute deployed, Russell became a part of a terrifying spectacle. "I saw something I never want to see in my life. I looked to my right, I saw a guy, and instantaneously, there was just an empty parachute coming down. A shell of some kind must have hit one of his Gammon grenades—he was blown away.

"I was trying to hide behind my reserve chute, because you could hear the shells hitting. We were all sitting ducks coming down.

"One guy landed in the fire. I heard him scream one time before he hit the fire. . . . I saw him land in the fire. It was heat from the fire that was drawing all these parachutes in towards the fire.

"I could feel shells hitting the parachute. When I hit the roof [of the church], a couple of my suspension lines, or maybe more, went around the church steeple and I slid off the roof. I was hanging on the edge of the roof on the right side of the church."[19]

Another Company F trooper, Private John M. Steele also landed on the roof. "I was trying to dodge the burning building and didn't see the steeple. I actually hit the roof of the church and then my chute caught on the steeple.

"There was furious fighting going on all around the church."[20]

Raymond Paris watched in horror as "all the Germans who were there on the spot with us, it goes without saying, began to fire at the boys who were coming down. There was a parachutist who fell directly into the lime trees just by the pump, and some of us helped him down and out of his harness.

"At that moment I found myself in the street, ten or fifteen meters from the pump, when a nearby German soldier suddenly lifted his machine gun to fire on a parachutist. I tapped him on the shoulder, saying, 'Don't shoot, civilian,' to distract him. The parachutist was very lucky, as the German soldier did not fire. However, a few seconds later, the very opposite occurred. I saw a parachutist fall into the trees, where he remained hanging helplessly, and before he could make the slightest movement, he was shot by some German soldiers. Almost immediately afterward, another parachutist became tangled up in the trees and, once again, the Germans shot him.

"It was getting too dangerous for us, because the Germans were firing all around our ears; they were panic stricken. Those who experienced the *parachutage* will never forget it, because there was the sound of the bell, which was still tolling and sounded very lugubrious, the noise of the airplanes, the bursts of automatic gunfire, the shouts and cries of the German soldiers, the cries of the French and screams of the women, who obviously were terrified. It was Dante-esque."[21]

Just as he slid over the edge of the roof and his risers caught him, Private Russell saw the 2nd Platoon mortar squad leader, Sergeant John P. Ray, land. "He missed the edge of the church, he hit in front of the church. Sergeant Ray landed after we did, a split second, I would say.

"I'll never forget, a red haired German soldier came around from behind the church to shoot Steele and me, who were still hanging there. As he came around, he shot Ray in the stomach. Sergeant Ray, while dying in agony, got his .45 out, and as this German soldier started turning around to us, he shot the German soldier in the back of the head and killed him. It was an agonizing death that Ray went through.

"I was scared to death. I finally got to my trench knife. It was carried down on your right jump boot. I cut my risers, threw my knife away, and fell to the ground. I looked up and I knew I couldn't do anything. I thought he [Private Steele] was dead. The only Americans that I saw there were dead, and it was our [Company F] men, you know. Most our stick were killed. Lieutenant [Harold O.] Cadish, [Private] H. T. Bryant, and [Private Ladislaw] Laddie Tlapa landed on telephone poles down the street—it was like they were crucified there. [Private First Class] Charles Blankenship was in a tree. [Ernest R.] Blanchard landed in a tree, and he got so excited, he got his trench knife out to cut his risers and cut one of his fingers off and didn't know it until he was down.

"I didn't see anyone else around, so I dashed across the street, and the machine gun fire was knocking up pieces of earth all around me. I ran over into a grove of trees. I wasn't completely out of town. I was the loneliest man in the world—strange country—just a boy, really. I should have been in high school rather than in a strange country. I think my class was graduating that night.

"There were planes still coming over bringing jumpers in. I almost ran into a flak gun in the grove of trees, shooting our men. I was scared to death. I got my Gammon grenade out, and I threw the grenade in on it. There was a huge explosion. The gun stopped firing. I ran up this field a little ways, and I saw a bicycle come down the road. I knew it couldn't have been an American. I had to take care of the guy on the bicycle. I went two hundred or three hundred yards back to my left in the area where I was at, because I didn't know what else would be coming down this road. I found a guy from the 101st Airborne Division. So, we went down the hedgerow and we found another guy from the

82nd. He was from the 507th, I believe. He had a broken leg. Well, we finally found several guys there.

"One of the guys said, 'Well, what are we going to do?'

"I said, 'Well, we've got to get back into Ste.-Mère-Église.' So we came back into Ste.-Mère-Église and there was [gun] fire all around the area."[22]

The last man in Russell's stick, Private First Class Daryle Whitfield, was fortunate. "I landed on the other side of Ste.-Mère-Église in a pasture out behind a house. I got up and started looking for someone I knew."[23]

Landing on the drop zone, the commanding officer of Company F, Captain Hubert Bass got out of his parachute harness "as fast as I could, made several contacts with company troopers, and started in the direction of [Lieutenant J. J.] Smith's Keller lights."[24]

As he was making his way to the lights on the drop zone, Captain Bass mentally reviewed his company, battalion, and regiment's missions. "First Platoon, Company F was to provide security on the march to our position, 3rd Platoon to provide connecting groups, 2nd Platoon to protect our rear. Roadblocks were to be established, minefields to be put out to protect our battalion area. F Company code-named 'Snake'. The 2nd Battalion was to seize and hold the area north of Ste.-Mère-Église. On our right was the 2nd Battalion, 502nd Parachute Infantry [101st Airborne Division]. The 3rd Battalion [505th] was to seize Ste.-Mère-Église."[25]

After injecting morphine into his leg, Vandervoort loaded his Very pistol and "began to shoot up the green flares that were the visual assembly signal for my battalion. Troop-carrying aircraft continued to pass overhead. A bundle containing ammunition came down without its chute and exploded about fifty yards in front of where I sat."[26]

Descending almost on top of that bundle was Company D trooper, Sergeant Roy King. "I was fascinated by the sight of the tracers flying around everywhere, when I saw a huge explosion blossom directly below me."[27]

As he looked down at the explosion, King suddenly saw something else flash below him. It was "a plane between me and the ground. No, it was not in trouble; I was!

"I was above the stream of airplanes that had just dropped their troopers and equipment. My immediate concern was that I could be chopped to pieces by the propellers of the oncoming planes. [I was] trying furiously to turn and face the oncoming planes in order to be able to see how to safely maneuver through them. I dropped safely through them in spite of my near-hysterical struggles."[28]

Staff Sergeant Paul D. Nunan, jumping number eight in his D Company stick, was a veteran of the Sicily and Salerno jumps. "We weren't getting a lot of flak close to us, but we could see flak going up and bursting as we were flying in. We were closer to 1,200 feet and well over 110 miles an hour when we got the green light. I went out and the chute opened. The standard procedure was to check your canopy to see if you blew any panels in your parachute, which would make you come down a lot faster. So, I looked up and checked the canopy and about that time, I saw tracer fire from two weapons coming up from the ground by apparently two Germans down on top of a garage. They were trying to shoot at me because we were going fast enough and high enough so that there was nobody else I could see in the air. I couldn't see any aircraft, I couldn't see any individuals, I couldn't see any parachutes. These guys had Schmeisser machine pistols—it sounded like—and they were trying to hit me and they were shooting over my head or over the top of my chute. They realized that they needed to come down, so they brought their fire down and just about the time I felt the suspension lines jerking a little bit with bullets going through the canopy, here came a flight of three C-47s. They decided that those three airplanes were a better target than one man I guess, because they switched their fire up to the C-47s.

"I looked down and I was over an orchard and there were a couple of cows wandering around down there. I was oscillating and drifting toward where those two Germans were located who had been firing at me. I grabbed the risers, but I grabbed the wrong set of risers. What I wanted to do was grab the rear set of risers and slide back away from the area where these two Germans were; what I had done was grab the front risers and I was going right toward them. I wound up and saw this tree at the last minute. There was a tree about two feet in diameter or more that had grown up in the hedgerow over the years and I didn't land in the tree; I landed *on* the tree. I was oscillating in and drifting as well. By the time I spotted the tree, the only thing I could think of was, 'This is gonna' hurt.' And it did—I hit the trunk of that tree about six feet off the ground and collapsed into the ditch right by the hedgerow. I was convinced I had a broken leg. I didn't have time to get my feet up where my feet would hit the tree first. I also hurt my shoulder—I think I dislocated it."[29]

As Private First Class Charles H. Miller, with Company D, floated down he looked below and "was awed by the sight. You could just see everything. It was fantastic. It looked like a great big Fourth of July celebration. The whole sky was lit up like a big show. There was Ste.-Mère-Église down below on fire."[30]

As another D Company trooper, Private First Class Donald E. Ellis, descended, he saw cows in the field below. "I slipped trying to miss this cow, and I slid off her back, and I fractured one leg. So I was crawling around and hobbling around as best I could."[31]

Private First Class Robert M. Robinson, with Headquarters Company, 2nd Battalion, landed alone in a small field. "My M1 rifle was stowed in the Griswold case in three parts, so I was quite unarmed, except for my trench knife strapped to my jump boot. The first thing I saw were several creatures charging at me from the shadows. All I could see were white faces, and this unnerved me quite a bit. But when I realized that these creatures were cattle, I was really worried. Being a city dweller, I was afraid of being kicked or bitten, so I quickly cut myself free of my parachute and beat a hasty retreat from the field, with my 'adversaries' in hot pursuit."[32]

Private First Class Robert H. Dumke, with Headquarters Company, 2nd Battalion broke his ankle when he landed. "I had six rifle grenades strapped to my leg when I jumped, and they were pretty heavy"[33]

Sergeant Sampson found his Company E mortar squad on the drop zone and deployed it in a defensive position and took off to find Lieutenant Coyle, his plane's jumpmaster to report that he had his squad assembled. "I passed the 'T' light on my left and came across Colonel Vandervoort with his back against a wall and his legs outstretched. He was alone. He filled me in saying, 'Some of the planes have become lost. I have sent out to gather what men and equipment we have. We've got to get the situation in hand.' He paused for a spell and then said, 'I came down quite hard on this leg,' running his hand along his left one. 'I've done something to it; I have sent for a medic.'

"I could see he was in pain and favored the injured limb. There was nothing I could do for him and turned to go.

"'I'm proud to have you with us,' he said, as I walked away.

"'It is me who should be telling him that, with a busted leg and still in control of the situation. I feel confident with the reins in his hands; it was a nice compliment.' I made no reply."[34]

The 2nd Battalion surgeon, Captain Lyle B. Putnam, found Vandervoort about an hour after landing. "I located him near a small farmhouse. He was seated with a rain cape over him reading a map by flashlight. He recognized me and calling me close, quietly asked that I take a look at his ankle with as little demonstration as possible. His ankle was obviously broken; luckily a simple rather than a compound fracture. He insisted on replacing his jump boot [and] laced it tightly."[35]

AS SOME OF THE GERMANS pulled out of Ste.-Mère-Église, they took with them a number of prisoners, among them Company F trooper, Private John Steele, whose parachute had caught on the church steeple. Two Germans positioned in the steeple had pulled Steele in, cut him out of his harness, and taken him prisoner. "I was wounded in the foot and hobbling along on a stick under German guard with six or eight other GIs—being moved from a German battalion headquarters to their regimental headquarters. A small unit of German riflemen headed by a first lieutenant slipped out of the woods, stopping us. We were asked a lot of questions, which we didn't answer.

"The lieutenant cut my belt and flipped the buttons from the fly of my trousers with a hunting knife—tapping me on the chest with the point of the knife and said, 'So you won't run too fast,' in perfect English."[36]

AT THE 505TH DROP ZONE west of Ste.-Mère-Église, the 3rd Battalion, under the command of Lieutenant Colonel Ed "Cannonball" Krause moved out to capture the town. Lieutenant Colonel Vandervoort and the 2nd Battalion prepared to move northeast to block the N-13 highway north of the town. "I think it was about 0410 in the morning when I felt I completed the assembly sufficiently so that I could move out on our mission and take the town of Neuville-au-Plain. In the meantime, the regiment had told me to stand by. The news from Ste.-Mère-Église was so vague to the regimental commander that he had me stand by. General Ridgway happened to be in my CP during that period and he also directed me not to move without consulting him. It was not until daylight that I received orders to move. We actually started moving at 0600."[37]

Captain Lyle Putnam, the battalion surgeon, watched Vandervoort "pick up his rifle and, using it as a crutch, he took a step forward, looked at the men around him. 'Well,' he said, 'let's go!'"[38]

Landing north of Ste.-Mère-Église, the commanding officer of the 505th, Lieutenant Colonel Bill Ekman, came upon Major John "Jack" Norton, the regimental S-3, and together they moved south to find the regimental command post. On the way, they made contact with Vandervoort's 2nd Battalion moving north toward Neuville-au-Plain. Ekman used one of the battalion's radios to attempt to contact the 3rd Battalion, but was unsuccessful. Fearing that the 3rd Battalion had been misdropped or unable to capture Ste.-Mère-Église, Ekman ordered Vandervoort to move the 2nd Battalion south to assist the 3rd Battalion in capturing the town, or reinforce it if it was in control of the town.

Vandervoort made a decision that would prove critical to the success of the invasion. "I sent the 3rd Platoon of Company D to Neuville-au-Plain to outpost the area that originally was to have been held by our entire battalion."[39]

Arriving at Neuville-au-Plain, Lieutenant Turner B. Turnbull, the platoon leader of the 3rd Platoon of Company D, deployed most of his strength on the east side of the N-13 highway on a slight rise in elevation about forty yards north of the hamlet. His men were positioned along a hedgerow running slightly northeast to southwest, facing north with a good field of fire for six hundred yards. Turnbull positioned his bazooka team near a house next to the east side of the road, to give them some concealment.

Corporal Milton E. Schlesener was one of the assistant squad leaders. "We dug in along both sides of Route 13. Our mortar squad could not find their mortar, but they did find some machine guns and lots of ammo in supply bundles that were lying in the area. We had no idea to whom they belonged, but these were gathered and used. Lieutenant [Isaac] Michelman [assistant platoon leader] took charge of that squad since it was off to the left and part of it in an orchard."[40]

Lieutenant Michelman and the squad leader, Sergeant Robert J. "The Beast" Niland, organized some troopers, including Private First Class Horace H. Brown, Private John P. Slaverio, and Private Harold V. Dunnegan, to cover the field west of the highway with their .30-caliber light machine gun.

Corporal Schlesener noticed how peaceful everything seemed that morning. "It certainly did not seem like we were at war. Farmers were starting to gather their cows. People were walking along the road. There were no planes flying around. The fields were real lush with grass. Our boots made a sucking sound as we were walking through it. There were small drainage ditches along the edges of the fields, the dirt had been thrown into the hedgerows. Do this for a number of years [and] you get a deep bank to dig into."[41]

Private Gerald R. Weed was Lieutenant Turnbull's communications NCO. He had been a sergeant back in England, but had been busted. Weed was carrying a heavy SCR 300 radio, a roll of wire, and field telephone. "Lieutenant Turnbull said, 'Get a telephone.' So I strung a wire for a field telephone out there and I hooked it up."[42]

As Vandervoort and his men moved south on the N-13 highway toward Ste.-Mère-Église, he "noticed two 101st Airborne Division sergeants moving along with the 2nd Battalion column. They had dropped on the wrong DZ and lost their outfit. They were pulling a wheeled ammunition cart. Since I had a broken leg, I asked them if they would give me a lift into Ste.-Mère-Église. I was told, 'We didn't come to Normandy to pull a god damn colonel around.'"[43]

Vandervoort "persuaded them otherwise."[44]

As the column moved into the town, Sergeant Otis Sampson, with Company E, saw something that shocked and infuriated him. "There were [the bodies of] paratroopers still hanging from their chutes where they had been caught in the high trees before they could release themselves.

"Colonel Vandervoort's first command, 'Cut them down!'"[45]

Private Robert R. Hughart, with Company F, had also broken his left ankle on the jump, and had been trying "to stay with the company the best I could. But it was very painful."[46]

Upon arriving at Ste.-Mère-Église with the 2nd Battalion, Hughart also witnessed the terrible sight of the bodies of the dead troopers still in their parachutes hanging in the town square. "It makes one very sad to see dead Americans—torn apart—burnt, etcetera. It is really sickening to smell burned human flesh. Once you smell it—you will remember it forever and ever."[47]

When Vandervoort "got into Ste.-Mère-Église, an elderly French woman, noticing I was using a rifle to hobble about, went into her house and came out with an old fashioned pair of wooden crutches and gave them to me. With these I was able to get about much better."[48]

When the 2nd Battalion troopers entered Ste.-Mère-Église, they found it occupied by the 3rd Battalion. The 3rd Battalion commander, Lieutenant Colonel Krause and Vandervoort met and decided to divide the defense of the town—the 2nd Battalion taking responsibility for the northern and eastern portions, with the 3rd Battalion defending the western and southern approaches.

The 1st and 2nd Platoons of Company D were assigned to block the main highway and defend the area to the east of the roadblock. Company F was assigned to protect the eastern approaches to the town, where Germans retreating from the Utah Beach area were expected. The 2nd and 3rd Platoons of Company E had misdropped, so Captain Clyde Russell had only company headquarters and the 1st Platoon present. "Ben directed all 'strays'—some from the 101st and other 82nd units to join E Company. What an assortment to command!"[49]

Captain Russell formed the strays into a provisional unit, designated as the 2nd Platoon of Company E. "The company moved into a reserve position in the churchyard."[50]

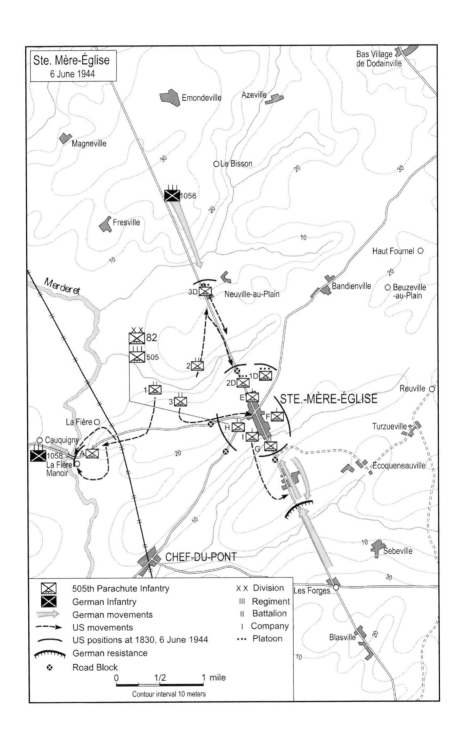

The 2nd Battalion surgeon, Captain Lyle Putnam, prepared for the inevitable flood of casualties who would soon need treatment. "We established an aid station in a large, two-story brick edifice on the [northern] edge of the town on the main road leading to Cherbourg, and began to collect our own casualties and some German [casualties]. We got all of the supplies we could find, beg, or steal."[51]

Private William A. "W. A." Jones and Company F were assigned to the eastern part of the Ste.-Mère-Église defensive perimeter. "My machine gun was set up in the cemetery. Now, the most horrible thing I saw during the war—to the right of where we were was a grove of trees. We looked over in the trees and Charlie Blankenship, [H. T.] Bryant, and somebody else were hanging in the trees dead."[52]

Captain George B. "Chappie" Wood was the regiment's protestant chaplain. "Colonel Vandervoort asked me to do something about the men hanging dead in the trees down in the village square. There were six of them. It was affecting the morale of the men to see their buddies' lifeless bodies hanging there. I had no burial detail, so I got a detail of six men with an officer from off the front line, which was just the other side of the wall of the cemetery where we were burying the men."[53]

The men Chaplain Wood found in the cemetery were from Company F. It had been their buddies who had overshot the drop zone and landed in the square the previous night. One of the Company F troopers chosen for the detail to cut the men down was W. A. Jones. "[Sergeant] Spencer Wurst, myself, and somebody else went over and cut them down. That was the hardest thing. Bryant was a good buddy of mine, even though he joined the regiment after we got to Quorn. He was from Fort Worth. Two of us would hold them while the third would cut them down. We cut them down, got their chutes down, and rolled them up in their chutes for Graves Registration. That has stuck with me more than anything else."[54]

Chaplain Wood and the men were finishing up when they began to receive an artillery barrage. "We got five men down and into the ground when all hell broke loose, and the men were ordered back to fighting. There was much anger among the men over the killing of their buddies hanging in trees, but I explained that this was what we could expect in our kind of an outfit."[55]

Lieutenant Charles E. "Pinky" Sammon commanded the Light Machine Gun Platoon, Headquarters Company, 2nd Battalion. "[Lieutenant] Colonel Vandervoort instructed me to set my platoon up in a defensive position one mile north and east of the town of Ste.-Mère-Église. There was no enemy activity in our area at this time, although I could hear some firing in the distance. We found the area assigned to us by the battalion commander, and I established three machine gun positions, which I felt would give us good protection. I then set up a platoon command post and together with my runner took turns wrapping up in a parachute in order to get a little sleep.

"Dawn of June 6th was just breaking as I started out to check the three positions to make sure everything was in order and find out if the men needed anything in the way of equipment or food. There was at the time sporadic firing in the distance, but we had not seen or heard anything of the Germans in our area up to that point.

"As I approached the first position, I called out to the corporal who was in charge—the answer came back in the form of a long burst from what was unmistakably a German machine gun and one or two machine pistols. The bullets hit the dirt at our feet, and the two of us hit the ditch beside the road.

"What had happened became very clear to me at this point. The Germans had infiltrated our positions during the night and had either killed or captured the men I had placed in this position. As I lay there in the ditch with bullets whizzing over my head, I was not only scared, I was thoroughly disgusted with myself for being outsmarted by the enemy. I was worried and concerned about my men, and at the moment felt helpless to do anything about the situation. We couldn't get up without exposing ourselves to their fire, but soon discovered that as long as we stayed flat on our stomachs in the ditch, we were protected from their fire. They were set up at the junction of two irrigation ditches and were unable to depress the muzzles of their guns any further and couldn't see us due to the relative height of their position.

"I then decided that we should turn around in the ditch and attempt to crawl back to our own positions. We had gone about half way with the bullets clipping the tall grass over our head, when my runner who was now ahead of me panicked and got up to run. I tackled him just as a long burst of German fire hit all round us. From then on, I kept one hand on his foot as we continued to crawl up the ditch. We were making fairly good progress when an American machine gun began firing at us from our own positions. Since we were approaching from the direction of the enemy and were unable to stand up to identify ourselves, I could see no way out of our predicament.

"This time however, the Germans came to our rescue. The first barrage of German artillery fire came into the position and forced the American machine gunner to abandon his position just long enough for us to jump up and make a run for it. We arrived at the machine gun just as the gunner did, who by the way, turned out to be one of my own men. Just for a moment I considered the irony of being killed by a machine gunner I had spent hours trying to train.

"All was confusion back in our own position. The Germans had infiltrated so well and struck so suddenly that no one knew what was going on. I managed to round up the remnants of my platoon and set up one machine gun to keep firing at the German position so they wouldn't attempt to advance further. I then had one of my men, who was armed with a carbine and rifle grenades, start firing grenades into their protected position.

"The best discovery of all, however, was a mortar man from one of the rifle companies with a complete mortar and a supply of ammunition. In parachute drops, this is a rare find, as often some vital part will be missing as a result of the drop. With the grenades and mortar shells falling into their position, the Germans had no choice but to move out. They couldn't go back up the same ditch they had used to get into the position, as we had set up a machine gun to cover their return. And besides, no doubt their orders were to go forward and wipe us out.

"One by one, they attempted to go over the top of their protective embankment and into the ditch I had used to retreat only an hour earlier. There were about twenty men in the position, and about half of them made it into the ditch, [while] the others were killed or wounded as they came out.

"Having become so familiar with that ditch earlier, I knew we couldn't reach them with our rifles and machine guns due to the difference in elevation of our positions. I decided the only way of reaching them was to go around on the flank and get above them and throw hand grenades into the ditch at the places I could observe the tall grass moving. We were so pinned down by artillery fire that I was unable to find anyone to go with me, and I hadn't seen hide nor hair of my runner since our narrow escape earlier. Equipment was scattered all over, and I found about ten ordinary fragmentation grenades and one Gammon grenade.

"From my position on the flank, I waited until I saw the grass move. I scrambled up the side of an embankment, ran across about fifty yards of open ground, which brought me to a position right over the ditch in which the Germans were working their way into our main defenses. I got rid of the Gammon grenade and headed back to the protection of my ditch. I disappeared over the side just as a German rose up out of the ditch and fired at me with a machine pistol. I waited for a loud explosion that never came—my Gammon grenade had misfired.

"Since they now knew where I was, I was hesitant about going back. About this time a lieutenant [Alexander F. Sweeney] from the airborne engineers came running up the road in a crouched position. He said he had three or four men with him and would like to help. We crawled up the embankment so I could show him what I was trying to do. As we cautiously poked our heads up over the top, a machine gun cut loose from the German ditch. We both slid back down the embankment. When the firing stopped I got up, but he didn't, so I rolled him over. He was shot right through the head.

"I decided to give it another try, as the Germans were getting in closer all the time, which I could tell by the movement of the tall grass in the ditch that they occupied. I pulled the pins on two grenades and started across the open area. This time they went off just as I got back to the protection of my own position.

"The firing from their position stopped, and I carefully looked over the top of the embankment. Believe it or not, a white flag was waving back and forth on the end of a tree limb. Soon a German soldier climbed up over the top carrying the white flag and started in our direction. Two or three of the dead lieutenant's men were with me, and they were all for shooting him. I pointed out that he didn't have any arms and that we had to honor any attempt to surrender. He turned out to be a German doctor about thirty-five [years old] who spoke fluent English. He explained that many of their men were dead and wounded and that they would like to give up. He looked all around and seemed surprised that there were only two or three men in the position.

"I told him that we would not stop firing unless he returned and got all of the Germans to throw down their arms and to come out with their hands over their heads. He agreed to do this and after he returned, we sat there waiting for something to happen. We did not have to wait long, however, as shortly after he disappeared into their position we were the recipients of the heaviest barrage of artillery and mortar fire I had experienced in the war up to that point. It was obvious that the doctor's surrender was all part of a very clever German plot. As a result, we had to abandon this position, and I returned to the area where the rest of my men were entrenched. The German firing was very light now, and with ten or fifteen men we started a counterattack toward the very positions my men had been driven from at dawn. We reached the position alongside the ditch where the Germans had been holed up, and I saw that my grenades had done the job. Those that were not killed by the grenades got up to run and were cut down by machine gun fire from our main positions. There were about fifteen dead and wounded Germans lying about the position."[56]

Lieutenant Sammon and his men had just repulsed the first German attempt to recapture Ste.-Mère-Église.

ABOUT A MILE SOUTH OF STE.-MÈRE-ÉGLISE, much of the German 3rd Battalion, 1058th Infantry Regiment, 91st Air Landing Division occupied Hill 20, astride the N-13 highway at Fauville, blocking the forces landing at Utah Beach from linking up with the 505th. Lieutenant Roper R. Peddicord and his 3rd Platoon, Company E, had landed near Les Forges, south of Fauville. One of his NCOs, Sergeant Cullen Clark helped set up a roadblock east of the village, where they stopped an armored reconnaissance unit of light tanks with the U.S. 4th Infantry Division moving west from Utah Beach. "Lieutenant Peddicord reported to the commander, and the commander asked us to join his outfit as scouts. Lieutenant Peddicord replied that we would join him and go as far as Ste.-Mère-Église, where we would join our own unit.

"Together, we all moved [west] down the road about two miles and turned right. About five hundred yards down the road we could see men moving all around and thought they were Americans. After we had gone about [another] two hundred yards, someone called us. We looked to our right and about fifty yards away was an American major. The major had broken his leg on the jump and had dug a hole to hide in. The major informed us that about three hundred yards in front of us were thousands of Germans, and that there were no American troops in that direction. The major said that he had been watching the Germans since dawn and that they were preparing for the seaborne troops.

"Lieutenant Peddicord asked the commander for three light tanks to make a reconnaissance. We put three men on the back of each tank and slowly proceeded down the road. Lieutenant Peddicord, a man named [Private First Class Fred J.] Hebein, and myself were on the first tank.

"Two German machine guns started firing at us, one from each side of the road. Lieutenant Peddicord and I pulled the pins from hand grenades, and were going to throw them at the machine guns as we went past. The gunner in the tank was also supposed to fire his machine gun at the Germans while we were attacking. He fired a few rounds, then ducked his head back into the tank and held his hands up trying to fire the machine gun. I took over his machine gun and fired about half of the rounds [of the belt] back at the German machine guns. The machine guns were firing at the tank and bullets were ricocheting in all directions. While we were approaching the machine guns, Lieutenant Peddicord had unscrewed the cap off a Gammon grenade and laid it on top of the tank.

"We were about fifty yards from the machine guns when the Germans fired an 88mm. The tank commander got all shook up and started to back up, right into the tank behind us, which was still coming forward. When the two tanks hit, the [Gammon] grenade was rolling all around and the safety was almost out—one more bump and it would have exploded. I scooped the Gammon grenade off [the tank], beside the road, as the other tank hit us again, and as it landed, it exploded.

"It blew me up against the tank and off of the tank, fracturing a couple of vertebrae, cracking my pelvis bone, and causing internal injuries. I fell in a ditch beside the road, but could not move from the waist down. I remember looking up and seeing one man named [George R.] McCarthy hanging upside down by his leg from one of the tanks. I learned later that he broke his leg. Temporarily paralyzed and with no weapon, I grabbed handfuls of grass and pulled myself to what I thought was the rear.

"While doing this, I heard a shout and looked up ahead. A German soldier had run up in front of me, and he fired a machine pistol at me and kept running across the road. I had my gas mask strapped to my leg, and he shot it completely off of my leg. Also, in my jump pocket of my trousers were some K-rations, which were all shot up.

"I got turned around and pulled myself to the rear. A German machine gun was firing at me, but the fire was a few inches above my head. Soon, I could hear American voices. I called out and an E Company man named [Jack S.] Flynn and another man, who I do not remember, picked me up and turned me over to the 4th Division medics. I learned later that Lieutenant Peddicord was killed the next day while on a patrol and never got to join E Company at Ste.-Mère-Église."[57]

SHORTLY BEFORE NOON, Private Gerald Weed, with the 3rd Platoon of Company D, finished laying a field telephone connection from the Company D command post on the north end of Ste.-Mère-Église to Neuville-au-Plain. "I was up on the road with Lieutenant Turnbull and I also had a radio, besides pulling that damned telephone wire. So I had to stay right with Turnbull. We looked down the road and here came a Frenchman riding up on a bicycle. We stopped him—he could speak just enough English that we could understand him. We [could] see some guys coming up the road. We asked him and he said, 'Paratroopers with some German prisoners.' They were so far away we couldn't tell. We thought this was great."[58]

At about that same time, Vandervoort arrived, bringing antitank support for Turnbull's blocking position. "About noon I went north to Neuville-au-Plain in a jeep with a 57mm antitank gun and gun crew. I told our 57mm antitank gun crew to go into position on the right of the road where a house offered some concealment. As we drove into Neuville-au-Plain, a French civilian passed us moving south on a bicycle. Lieutenant Turner Turnbull, the platoon leader, told me the Frenchman had just come from the north and had told them that a group of paratroopers had taken a large number of German prisoners and vehicles and were moving south on the highway and would arrive at Neuville-au-Plain shortly. As Turnbull and I walked over his position and talked, we kept watching the highway leading from the north. Shortly, a long column of foot troops appeared in the distance with vehicles scattered at intervals through their ranks. If these were prisoners, there was more than a battalion of them. We could make out the field gray of the German uniforms. On their flanks were individuals in paratrooper uniforms waving orange panels that were the recognition signal we were to have used to identify ourselves to friendly aircraft. Somehow, it looked just too good to be true. When the advancing column had closed to within about one thousand yards, I told Turnbull to have his light machine gun fire a burst into the field on the left flank of the column.

"That did it. The alleged German prisoners deployed instantly on both sides of the road and the leading vehicle, a self-propelled gun, instead of acting like the spoils of war the Frenchman said they were, opened fire on our position. Our 57mm antitank gun crew returned the fire and set fire to the leading SP [self-propelled] gun and one more that moved up behind it. A third German SP gun fired smoke shells into the road to its front to screen their position. The German infantry began to move forward on both sides of the road as their 80mm mortars started to range in on the 3rd Platoon position. I told Turnbull to delay the Germans as long as he could, then withdraw to Ste.-Mère-Église. With that, I returned to Ste.-Mère-Église to alert my troops as to what was on the way and to check our positions to meet it."[59]

Turnbull's men opened up as the Germans deployed into the fields on both sides of the road. With the slight high ground and six hundred yards of open ground east of the highway and a couple of two-story buildings on the west side, Turnbull had picked a great position from which to delay the Germans. However, the Germans sent troops from the rear of their column east and west, out of sight of Turnbull's platoon and out of range of its weapons, attempting to envelope the position. Casualties in Turnbull's platoon slowly mounted as enemy mortar and long-range machine gun fire took its toll.

By about 5:00 p.m., Vandervoort received a report by field telephone of the situation in Neuville-au-Plain. "The word came from Turnbull that the Germans were enveloping both flanks of his position and he couldn't hold on much longer. I sent one platoon of Company E, then in reserve, north on the left side of the highway to attack the enveloping German infantry by fire, then withdraw to their reserve position. We hoped it would help Turnbull to withdraw under the cover of this diversion."[60]

Lieutenant Theodore L. "Pete" Peterson led his 1st Platoon of Company E "quickly but cautiously north on the west side of the highway to Neuville-au-Plain. We saw groups of the enemy on the way, who apparently did not see us, so we did not engage them. Our primary objective was to assist Lieutenant Turnbull. As we approached his approximate position, my runner and [I] crossed the road, leaving our platoon in a concealed position in a hedgerow."[61]

Private Gerald Weed heard Turnbull shouting over the noise of the firing and explosions. "He hollered at me and said the phone wasn't working. I traced that wire—I just grabbed the wire and started running with it."[62]

As Weed ran south along the ditch bordering the east side of the N-13 highway toward Ste.-Mère-Église, he saw Germans to the west moving toward him to cut the highway behind Turnbull's platoon. "I saw these Germans, and I don't think they saw me. When I ran out of the wire, the other piece was lying on the ground; I just kept going, because I knew the Germans had cut it. The only thing I could do was run to battalion headquarters and report what was going on."[63]

While Lieutenant Peterson and his runner crossed the road to contact Lieutenant Turnbull, Sergeant Otis Sampson set up his 60mm mortar on the left flank of Peterson's platoon, concealing it in some high grass. "A dirt road ran across the front of us. There was little foliage to obstruct our firing across it. Our CP was set up under a tree to our right. A lane ran directly from the position I was in up over a crest of a hill less than a hundred yards away. Here, a paratrooper lay as he had fallen, crosswise in the lane's center."[64]

After crossing the highway with his runner, Lieutenant Peterson carefully approached Turnbull's position. "Lieutenant Turnbull had a guard posted at the position we entered, who seemed to be expecting us. This would confirm that [Lieutenant] Colonel Vandervoort had communications with Lieutenant Turnbull, and we were expected. Lieutenant Turnbull was very calm, and he had the situation well in hand, for the rough position he was in. He had about six men killed and eight or ten wounded, plus he was running low on ammunition. They were getting heavy large [caliber] mortar fire, plus machine gun and small-arms fire. One particular machine gun was causing him the most trouble, and he asked us to try to knock it out. This gun was to his left front behind a farmhouse. Also, he asked us to draw fire upon ourselves, which might relieve his platoon enough to withdraw with their wounded. He said as soon as he had withdrawn, he would send a runner to give us the word.

"We moved back to our platoon and set up a line of fire on Lieutenant Turnbull's immediate left, the farmhouse with the enemy gun to our immediate front. We formed a perimeter defense with our power to the front. We commenced firing on order, firing BARs, mortar, bazooka, and small arms fire, making quite a racket. This was to reveal our position to the enemy and to try to knock out the machine gun at the farmhouse. We ceased fire shortly, and waited. All was as quiet as a church. Two scouts and I crawled and ran to the farmhouse with our platoon covering us. There was no sign of the enemy, so we fired a few bursts from our Tommy guns into the barn and house and moved quickly back to our platoon position.

"After possibly five or ten minutes—all hell broke loose. The enemy, moving west down the road near the farmhouse and to our immediate front, walked right into our hidden left flank, who were stretched out along the hedgerow so that they were practically facing east. Corporal [Thomas J.] Burke, who had already won a Silver Star for bravery, with his Tommy gun; a [trooper with a] BAR; and three or four riflemen held their fire until the enemy was within a few feet of them. Then they opened fire. The surprised enemy took off in every direction, losing a good number of men. With that, the whole platoon opened fire with everything they had at the enemy. This included Sergeant Sampson, the greatest and most accurate mortar sergeant in the business. He fired at this close range and laid the shells down in a line right on their heads."[65]

As soon as Peterson's platoon opened fire, Turnbull ordered his platoon to withdraw. The medic, Corporal James I. Kelly, volunteered to stay behind with the wounded. Sergeant Bob "the Beast" Niland with his Thompson submachine gun, BAR gunner Private First Class Julius A. Sebastian, and Corporal Raymond D. Smithson volunteered to cover the withdrawal. Private First Class Stanley W. Kotlarz was in position behind a hedgerow on the west side of the highway. "The word got around that we should pull back because we were being surrounded. Shortly after that, we started pulling back. We lost a guy named [Private William H.] Neuberger; he got hit in the stomach. We walked him across the road; we had to move back, and we didn't have too much time, so we put him over to one side, and I took some branches that were lying there and covered him up. Kelly stayed back with Neuberger, but he [later] died.

"In the meantime, my squad leader, Bob Niland, was going across the road to set up a defense on the other side of the road. He was just stepping over a hedgerow and they nailed him. It was a machine gun...an MG-42...we heard the doggone thing. We could see the way he was hit...he was lifeless, he was bleeding, and wasn't moving. There wasn't any sense in trying to save him— because he'd had it."[66]

As Turnbull's platoon pulled out, the fire from Sergeant Sampson's lone 60mm mortar devastated the German infantry west of the highway. "I used the mortar with direct firing from an open, high grass area, with just [Private First Class Harry G.] Pickels [the gunner] up there with me to feed the tube. We changed positions often, using various objects as sighting stakes. Our firing, along with the rifles and machine gunners, finally started to tell on the Krauts and their firing began to slack off. Just over the hill, the Jerries were crossing the lane one man at a time on the run. I timed the interval, and when I thought another would cross over, the tube was fed a round. And as planned, when Jerry was in the center of the lane, the shell hit, right to the fraction of a second. On the easing off of the firing, I gave a couple of the squad men a chance to use the weapon as I did, to get the feeling of what it was like under fire. I kept a close watch with my Tommy [gun].

"We had come in a little to the left of town and had met a strong force, much greater than ours. They were going to cut off Lieutenant Turnbull's platoon. As soon as the Krauts quit firing, Lieutenant Peterson, with Lieutenant Coyle, took the rifle squads and went out to find Lieutenant Turnbull and his men. We knew the Jerries had suffered in our encounter with them, but had no way of telling how bad. So far, we had not lost a man. The fight had been short and heavy."[67]

As he and his men moved out to find Turnbull's platoon, Peterson saw a trooper approaching. "A runner from Lieutenant Turnbull reported to me that they had successfully withdrawn their platoon. We had firepower over the enemy, and having accomplished our mission, we made a tactical withdrawal, firing as we left, and continuing part way to our lines."[68]

With the help of Peterson's platoon, Turnbull's men had shot their way out of the German trap and then conducted a fighting withdrawal. Private First Class Kotlarz was one of just sixteen from Turnbull's platoon to make it out. "We were moving pretty fast. As we were going back, we'd stop and fire a few shots and then pull back."[69]

Private Gerald Weed arrived at Vandervoort's command post after running the mile or so from Neuville-au-Plain. "I told them what was going on. Vandervoort was propped up against a tree, and there was a naval officer who jumped in with us. They were talking and they gave me a couple of more men to go back. [Vandervoort said], 'Go back and tell the platoon that we're going to shoot up a white flare. When they see that white flare, withdraw. They've got five minutes to withdraw before the USS *Nevada* is to lay down a barrage.'"[70]

Weed immediately took off on a run back toward Neuville-au-Plain. "Me and these two others guys [headed] down the edge of this field because we didn't want to be right on the road. So we got close enough to where we could see where the platoon was. I could see where the platoon was supposed to be, and I saw a couple of German trucks driving through there, so I knew the 3rd Platoon wasn't there anymore. About that time I saw the white flare go up."[71]

Five minutes later, Weed heard a low roar, as a salvo of massive fourteen-inch shells, fired by the *Nevada* from twelve miles away, arced overhead and impacted along the road in front of him. "We wanted to watch what was happening, because we could see those German trucks out there. So we just lay there and watched the whole thing. I had never heard anything like that before. Every one of those things landed within a radius of a couple of hundred yards. They were right on target. It was real effective. The Germans took off; they got the hell out of there."[72]

Lieutenant Turner Turnbull and his fifteen troopers along with the Company E platoon walked back to Ste.-Mère-Église, arriving at dusk. Vandervoort was very proud of Turnbull and the 3rd Platoon of Company D for "having performed the magnificent task of delaying two heavily reinforced infantry battalions of the 91st German Infantry Division for more than four hours of intensive fighting. It was a small unit performance that has seldom been equaled."[73]

CHAPTER 4

"On One Leg and a Crutch"

D uring the night of June 6, the massive German Kampfgruppe moved south from Neuville-au-Plain to within a short distance of the northern edge of Ste.-Mère-Église. At dawn, the 1st Battalion, 1058th Regiment, attacked southward toward Ste.-Mère-Église east of the N-13 highway, the Seventh Army Sturm Battalion and seven self-propelled guns of the 709th Antitank Battalion attacked astride the highway, and the 2nd Battalion, 1058th, moved south toward the town in the fields west of the highway.

At his command post on the north side of town, Vandervoort received word that the German attack had commenced. "Shortly after first light 7 June, the 1st Battalion, 1058th Grenadier Regiment reinforced by elements of the Seventh Army Sturm Battalion, a specially trained counterattack unit, succeeded in driving the D Company platoon defending along the east side of the highway, back and away from the road on the north edge of the town. From the north, three battalions of German infantry supported by three artillery regiments and a number of 75mm and 7.62cm self-propelled guns marched south to clear a battalion and a half of American paratroopers off Highway N-13, the main road to the landing beaches. A fourth German infantry battalion south of Ste.-Mère-Église put the paratroopers in a vise. The German kampfgruppe operating with the usual German efficiency and ferocity powered methodically into the northern environs of Ste.-Mère-Église. A German breakthrough into the town appeared imminent."[1]

Defending the north side of the town east of the N-13 highway was the 1st Platoon of Company D, led by Lieutenant Thomas J. "Tom" McClean. The 2nd Platoon of Company D, commanded by Lieutenant Oliver B. "O. B." Carr, Jr., defended a roadblock on the highway.

The fighting was ferocious as the two platoons held off attacking hordes of German infantry supported by self-propelled guns, giving ground grudgingly. Private First Class Frank Bilich was a witness that morning to the heroism of the D Company executive officer, Lieutenant Waverly Wray. "In every attack that the Germans threw on us, he would go up and down the line, and as each guy was killed or evacuated, it was him running up and down the line, asking, 'Have you got enough ammunition?' changing positions, moving people. This guy was in the front of EVERYTHING."[2]

One enemy machine gun was inflicting a number of casualties among the Company D troopers. The company commander, Captain Taylor Smith observed that "at this point, Lieutenant Wray took ten hand grenades, crawled toward one enemy machine gun which had been firing into his platoon. The enemy directed continuous aimed fire at him, but he managed to reach the machine gun position located seventy yards in front of his lines. He demanded the surrender of the machine gun crew, but received instead their fire at close range. Lieutenant Wray then destroyed the position with grenades and killed the surviving members of the crew with rifle fire.

"Lieutenant Wray then occupied the position he had just cleared and remained in close contact with the enemy until he saw a German officer running toward another machine gun emplacement fifty yards away. He shot and killed the officer and then left cover and crawled toward the enemy emplacement, still under direct fire. He destroyed the crew with hand grenades and rifle fire and returned to his platoon. The elimination of the two German machine gun positions enabled him to reorganize his platoon and secure a resupply of ammunition."[3]

Lieutenant Wray's one-man counterattack had killed fifteen enemy soldiers.

However, the German forces astride the highway continued toward the northern edge of town. Lieutenant Charles "Pinky" Sammon, with Headquarters Company, 2nd Battalion was ordered to quickly withdraw his light machine gun platoon from its position northeast of the town to plug an enemy breakthrough. "Colonel Vandervoort told me that the Germans were now making their main effort to knock out our airhead at Ste.-Mère-Église by attacking with tanks and armored cars along the main road leading into the town. He instructed me to place my platoon in position about one block the other [north] side of the hospital on the east side of the main road. On arriving in the position we found the few American soldiers present in great disorder, with many dead and badly wounded soldiers lying about. There was a German armored car on the road at the time firing into the town with a small cannon. A lieutenant and a soldier were trying to fire a bazooka at it, but were unable to get it to function. I placed my men in position, but told them not to fire at tanks or armored cars as our light machine guns would do nothing but attract their fire. I told them to wait for the infantry, which most always accompany the armor and then to open up with the machine guns.

"I had just gotten into a hole myself when the German infantry came. They ran right into our position and I knew we would have to retreat if we were going to fight another day. I hollered at the men to fall back firing and took off myself, leaving my pack which contained all my worldly possessions at that moment. We lost three men getting out of there, but luckily most of the platoon arrived safely at the new positions around the hospital where we again set up the guns and started firing.

"While there, I took a couple of wounded men into the hospital, where I was greeted by a sight I shall never forget. Here were a couple of German doctors working alongside a couple of American doctors on what had once been a dining room table. They were sawing off arms, legs, etcetera, and throwing discarded limbs into a pile. The whole place was a mess of blood and bandages and I felt considerably better when I got back outside."[4]

Near the Company D command post, Staff Sergeant Floyd West, Jr., with Lieutenant Turner Turnbull's 3rd Platoon, moved out with the survivors of the previous day's fighting at Neuville-au-Plain. "We were laying in a ditch beside a road, and Turner started out in the lead, at right angles along a hedgerow. He was crawling. When he had gone about ten yards he stopped, turned around on one elbow and yelled, 'Sergeant, come here.' I left the ditch and when I was about six feet from him we heard the shell coming. We both flattened out, but we were in the open with no protection. Turner was killed by this shell. It hit in front and slightly to one side of him and he was hit by shrapnel."[5]

Private First Class Stanley W. Kotlarz "got hit in the wrist and in the arm, a guy by the name of Brown, got hit in the head, and Lieutenant Turnbull . . . it sheered the top of his head right off. When it hit, all of us seemed to go up in the air. When I got up, I saw Brown crawling away, staggering. Turnbull was lying there with his brains peeling out of his head."[6]

Just a day after he had led the gallant stand at Neuville-au-Plain, Turnbull's tragic death deeply affected everyone in the battalion who knew him. Sergeant Floyd West described Turnbull as "more than a damn good officer, he was my friend."[7] Vandervoort recommended Lieutenant Turnbull for the Distinguished Service Cross for his actions at Neuville-au-Plain. However, Lieutenant Turnbull was posthumously awarded the Silver Star.

The Sturm Battalion and the self-propelled assault guns pressed the attack to the very outskirts of Ste.-Mère-Église. A 57mm antitank gun, commanded by Lieutenant John C. Cliff, with Battery A, 80th Airborne Antiaircraft (Antitank) Battalion, engaged at long range a convoy of trucks transporting members of the Sturm Battalion, knocking out the lead truck and disrupting the convoy. A German armored car moved up and engaged the antitank gun, but Cliff's crew knocked it out. Then a German Sturmgeschütz self-propelled gun drove forward along the highway, projecting smoke canisters ahead to shroud its advance—then suddenly appeared out of the smoke, moving rapidly. Lieutenant Cliff maintained observation on the vehicle and gave verbal adjustments to the crew as they loaded and fired.

As Private First Class Turk Seelye and members of his Company E squad saw German infantry moving along the ditches of the highway, they "provided cover fire as the 57mm gun fired at the German [self-propelled] gun."[8]

The self-propelled gun got to within fifty yards of Vandervoort's command post before two rounds immobilized it. However, the vehicle's 75mm main gun continued to fire at Lieutenant Cliff's gun at almost pointblank range. The antitank gun crew fired two more rounds through the front of the vehicle, finishing off the enemy crew. They then moved the antitank gun forward to a point beside the knocked-out assault gun in order to have a clear field of fire. As they reloaded the antitank gun, another Sturmgeschütz in the distance up the highway fired, wounding the crew. Lieutenant Cliff was later awarded the Silver Star for his courageous leadership of his antitank gun crew.

With Lieutenant Cliff's antitank gun out of action, the self-propelled assault gun began moving toward the north end of town, projecting smoke canisters ahead to conceal its advance.

Private John E. Atchley, with Company H, courageously left his foxhole and single-handedly manned the antitank gun. Although Atchley had never fired an antitank gun, he loaded and fired, missing the oncoming self-propelled gun. He again single-handedly reloaded the gun and adjusted the aim as the assault gun drove toward him. At a range of about one hundred yards, he fired the second round, knocking out the vehicle. The other five German assault guns retreated, stopping the armored thrust at the very edge of Ste.-Mère-Église. Private Atchley was awarded the Distinguished Service Cross for heroic action.

However, Vandervoort didn't have much in reserve to counter the German infantry. "D Company's reserve platoon consisted of Lieutenant Turner Turnbull (half Choctaw Indian) and sixteen survivors from Neuville-au-Plain. His platoon, first to meet the juggernaut from the north, had delayed the Germans bravely, but at a terrible sixty-percent cost in casualties. Dug in behind D Company was Company E, the battalion reserve. They had only company headquarters and two platoons. One was Lieutenant Peterson's platoon of two lieutenants and about thirty-nine troopers. The other was an improvisation of glider pilots and 101st stragglers totaling about thirty-five men and officers armed only with individual shoulder weapons.

"The situation brought 1st Lieutenant Waverly W. Wray, executive officer of D Company, to the 2nd Battalion, 505 command post early in the morning to get help. Waverly was from Batesville, Mississippi. He had acquired all of the woodsman skills as a boy. In his hands, a rifle was a precision instrument. He claimed he had 'nevah missed a shot in mah life that ah didn't mean to.' In his early twenties, at the peak of physical fitness and mental quickness, he had the combat 'sixth sense' of the true warrior—an indefinable intuition, which warns of danger before it appears. A veteran of Sicily and Italy, he was as experienced and skilled as an infantry soldier can get and still be alive. Personally, he walked with the Lord. Some of the troopers called him 'The Deacon' because of his deep-South religious convictions—but never to his face. He didn't drink, smoke, curse, nor chase girls. When angered, he would resort to 'John Brown.' He was one of a few men in the regiment whom the chaplain could count on being present at services every Sunday. A God-fearing young man of uncompromising courage, character, and professional competence, combat leadership naturally gravitated to Waverly."[9]

Company D veteran, Private First Class Dave Bowman, described Wray as "fearless in his pursuit of killing Germans. Many accounts of his feats attest to that. He would go where no man would dare tread, unless he was leading them."[10]

Vandervoort listened intently as "Waverly explained the situation on the D Company front. The platoon, driven off the road, had suffered casualties, but was still intact and available for action. I told him to return to his company and counterattack the flank of the encroaching Germans. In his Mississippi drawl, he said, 'Yes, Suh,' saluted, about faced, and moved out like a parade ground sergeant major.

"Back in the company area he told his injured company commander, Captain T. G. [Taylor] Smith, what they had to do. He collected all of the grenades he could carry from the company headquarters personnel. Then, armed with his M1 rifle, an Army .45, and a silver-plated .38 revolver stuck in his jump boot, he went on a reconnaissance to better formulate his plan of attack.

"The terrain was mixed agricultural farm fields, orchards, and pasturage bound by man-high field stone and earthen embankments. These were the renowned hedgerows of Normandy, bordered by sunken cow lanes worn by centuries of traverse. Enemies could be a few feet apart and not be aware of each other. The fields were small—few running more than 150 by 300 yards. Infantry could cross only at great peril. The checkerboard layout of the land forced the combatants into close alignment at ideal ambush and small arms killing range. In that maze of natural fortifications, troopers and Germans exchanged fire and jockeyed for positions all along the northern environs of the town. It took real courage just to move about, much less voluntarily go alone to find the foe. Waverly knew the terrain because D Company had occupied the ground earlier.

"With utmost stealth and courage, he moved up the sunken lanes, across the orchards, through the hedgerows and ditches sprinkled with German units moving forward for their next drive to take the town. He went north about three hundred yards along the enemy left flank, then moved west a couple of hundred yards at right angles to the German axis of attack. That brought him a hedgerow or two away from the N-13. Then, moving like the deerstalker he was; he went south along a ditch until he heard guttural voices on the other side of the hedgerow. Stepping up and looking over the earthen embankment, he saw eight Germans in a sunken lane gathered around a radio. Covering them with his M1 rifle, he barked in his best command voice, 'Hande Hoch!' Most instinctively raised their hands, except one, who tried to pull a P-38 pistol from the holster on his belt. Wray shot the man instantly.

"At the same time, two Germans stood up in a slit trench about one hundred yards to his left rear. With burst from Schmeisser machine pistols, they tried to take his head off—clipping two 9mm pieces out of his right ear. Momentarily disregarding the hail of bullets from behind, Wray shot the other seven men in the lane dead.

"Whirling around, he jumped back down into the ditch, loaded another eight-round clip into his M1 and dropped the other two Germans across the field with a shot apiece. The eight dead Germans in the lane were the commanding officer and headquarters staff of the 1st Battalion, 1058th Grenadier Regiment."[11]

Lieutenant Tom McClean and his 1st Platoon arrived at the hedgerow across the field just in time to witness Wray's action. "My platoon was deployed along a hedgerow. I first saw Lieutenant Wray when he was approximately thirty to fifty yards to my left front. I saw him in a standing position firing down. I couldn't see who he was shooting at, as he was standing on a small rise from my position.

"I started to go to his assistance when I saw German troops approximately fifty yards to my right front. They were to Lieutenant Wray's left rear. Realizing that he did not see them as he was engaged in firing his rifle, I directed my platoon fire on the Germans."[12]

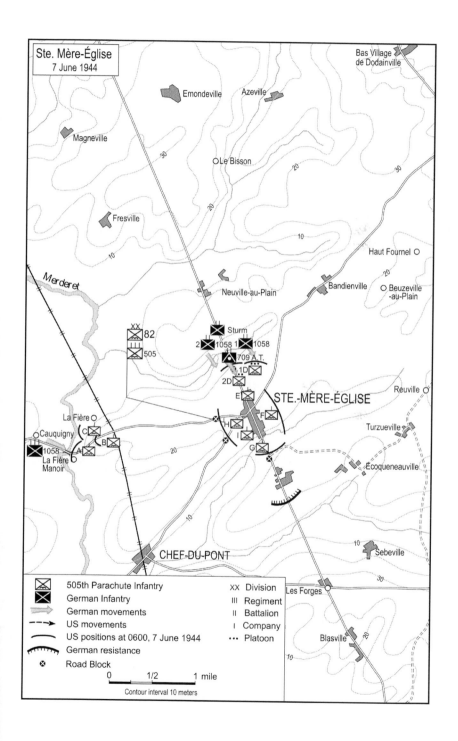

Ste. Mère-Église
7 June 1944

Bas Village de Dodainville

Emondeville   Azeville

Magneville

O Le Bisson

Fresville

Haut Fournel O

Merderet

Neuville-au-Plain   Bandienville   O Beuzeville-au-Plain

82   Sturm
505   2   1058 1   1058
       709 A.T.
       1D
       2D
       E   STE.-MÈRE-ÉGLISE   Reuville O
La Fière O   F
Cauquigny C   Turzueville
           B   H
1058   A   I
La Fière   G
Manoir   Ecoqueneauville

CHEF-DU-PONT   Sebeville

Les Forges O

	505th Parachute Infantry	XX	Division
	German Infantry	III	Regiment
	German movements	II	Battalion
	US movements	I	Company
	US positions at 0600, 7 June 1944	•••	Platoon
	German resistance		
⊗	Road Block		

Blasville

0   1/2   1 mile
Contour interval 10 meters

Private Frank V. "Barney" Silanskis watched Wray disappear from view as he continued his one-man reconnaissance. "The next time I saw Lieutenant Wray is when he came out of the hedgerow kicking two German prisoners. Lieutenant Wray had part of his ear and his helmet strap shot away. He was mad. He kept saying, 'John Brown Germans.'"[13]

Platoon Sergeant Paul Nunan was amazed that Wray was even alive. "The bullet had struck his steel helmet almost dead center at the front rim. A quarter of an inch lower and it would certainly have gone into his forehead. Instead, the bullet was deflected and struck the hinge of his chin strap and clipped a piece of Lieutenant Wray's ear, leaving his face, neck, shoulder, and part of his uniform covered with blood."[14]

Having completed his one-man reconnaissance, after finding the German battalion deployed in a sunken lane bordered by hedgerows, Wray found the end of the lane and positioned the platoon's 60mm mortar and a .30-caliber machine gun to fire down the lane into the enemy left flank. Lieutenant McClean's platoon spread out along a hedgerow perpendicular to the lane. Wray ordered the mortar to open fire at the far end of the lane, then observing the rounds exploding, gave adjustments to walk the shells up the lane toward his position. At the same time, the .30-caliber machine gun opened up, enfilading the German infantry packed into the lane.

The mortar rounds exploded as they struck overhanging tree limbs, raining shrapnel and large splinters of wood down on the Germans as machine gun bullets ripped into their flank. Germans spilled out of the hedgerows into the open fields, where McClean's platoon took them under small arms and machine gun fire. It was mass carnage.

Within minutes, Sergeant Nunan saw a German major carrying a white flag walked into the field in front of the platoon's positions. Nunan, Captain Taylor G. Smith, Lieutenant McClean, and an enlisted man, acting as a translator, moved into the field to speak with the German.

Nunan noticed the Red Cross brassard on the German major's sleeve, signifying he was a doctor. "He spoke English well, and at the request of our captain, T. G. Smith, we agreed to a one-hour truce so that the Germans be allowed to leave their medics and wounded with us, and that a wounded American glider pilot be turned over to us.

"Suddenly our men on the right flank opened fire. Captain Smith, the major, myself, and two others were still exposed in the open field. Only later did we learn the Germans on the right flank had started to withdraw as soon as the negotiations started, which caused our men on the right to open fire again. Captain Smith refused the German terms and shortly after, a green flare was fired by the Germans, and we began receiving fire from German 88's."[15]

Company D trooper, Private First Class Charles Miller, hit the ground as aerial bursts sprayed the field and hedgerow. "They told us, 'Get the hell out of here!'—and we did. But, on the way out there was a good friend of mine, Red . . . Big Red [Corporal Kenneth W. Auther]. I thought he was taking a leak. Instead of that, his blood was coming out of his stomach, just like urine, just pouring out of him. What had happened, a medic told me later, a shell or bullet had hit the artery, that main artery, and it just burst open and he was dead in three or four minutes.

"There was nothing we could do—we're not doctors. It was awful to stand there and watch him die, but there was nothing we could do, except hold his hand, and try to make it a little bit easier for him."[16]

Meanwhile, demoralized survivors of the German battalion fled north, exposing the left flank of the Sturm Battalion, causing it to withdraw, and effectively halting the German attack. Shortly afterward, Vandervoort learned that the German battalion east of the highway had been destroyed. "D Company moved back into their original defensive positions. Midmorning, Waverly returned to tell me the D Company area was secure. There he was—minus part of his ear. Blood had dried down his neck and the right shoulder of his jump jacket, fore and aft. I said, 'They've been getting kind of close to you haven't they, Waverly?'

"With just a grin, Waverly replied, 'Not as close as ah've been gettin' to them, Suh.' Waverly led Company D in throwing back the deepest penetration the Germans ever made into Ste.-Mère-Église, and in the process shattered the 1st/1058th."[17]

After Company D's devastating counterattack, German artillery and mortars shelled Ste.-Mère-Église for the remainder of the day and night.

Following restoration of the line by Company D, Technician Fifth Grade Alexander J. Matisick, with Headquarters Company, 2nd Battalion, moved into the area in front of the battalion's line in full view of the enemy to place colored panels to mark the area for aircraft strikes on the German positions. Despite intense fire from snipers, artillery, and small arms, Matisick laid the panels and started back when he spotted a wounded trooper. With snipers shooting at him, Matisick made it to the wounded comrade and was carrying him to safety when he was mortally wounded. Technician Fifth Grade Matisick was posthumously awarded the Silver Star for his self-sacrifice.

BY THE MORNING OF JUNE 7, seaborne forces landed at Utah Beach had not yet made contact with the division. General Ridgway had expected an armored task force, attached to the 82nd Airborne Division for the invasion and commanded by Colonel Edson Raff, to break through to Ste.-Mère-Église on D-Day. Raff's company of Sherman tanks would provide the 82nd Airborne Division with a heavier antitank defense.

About 10:00 a.m., Ridgway ordered Lieutenant James "J. J." Smith, the 2nd Battalion pathfinder team leader, to take a patrol to contact General Raymond O. Barton, commander of the 4th Infantry Division, to request tanks to support Ridgway's hard-pressed troopers. For the patrol, Lieutenant Smith chose pathfinders Corporal Lewis D. Allen, Headquarters Company, 1st Battalion; Corporal Howard W. Hicks, Jr., Company G; Corporal George H. Purcell, Company A; and Private Julius A. Wyngaert and Sergeant James Elmo Jones, both with Company B.

Sergeant Jones and the other pathfinders taking part in the patrol were told "we had to take all personal items such as billfolds, pictures, everything but our dog-tags off our uniforms. We could not take any prisoners because we needed to get to the beach, which was approximately four miles away, as quickly as possible.

"We started and it seemed everywhere we went we either had to evade or kill German soldiers that were either trying to fight or trying to get away. Many of them were in our way, and we simply could not take prisoners. We finally made it to the beach. When we got there, we saw the American tanks parked under trees with canopies from some American parachutes spread out for sunscreen. They were listening to the radios on the tanks as to how the invasion was coming. As we literally ran up, we bumped into a lieutenant colonel, and Lieutenant Smith said, 'Take me to your commanding officer.'

"The lieutenant colonel said, 'I'm the commanding officer.'

"Smith said, 'Hell, I don't mean you, I mean General Barton.'

"So, [the lieutenant colonel] put us in a jeep. He went along, and we took off to see General Barton, who was in his headquarters vehicle. We burst into his room, and he heard our story. We had not shaved, we were dirty, we probably looked terrible. But, he was very reluctant to send tanks that far away, because they had not penetrated in any way up toward the center of the peninsula. We didn't know it, but there were two or three men in the command vehicle.

One of them spoke up and said, 'I think you should do it. I think you should send the tanks up.' We turned around, and there was General Lawton Collins [the VII Corps commander], who happened to be there at the time. Within fifteen minutes, we had five tanks and we were riding on the back of them to show them the best way to get back. Five tanks on the way toward Ste.-Mère-Église."[18]

Early that afternoon, Lieutenant Colonel Krause, unaware of Smith's patrol, took some of his 3rd Battalion troopers to relieve Lieutenant Tom McClean's Company D platoon from the roadblock it manned northeast of town. Krause ordered McClean and his platoon to double-time to the command post of the 12th Infantry Regiment of the 4th Infantry Division, at St.-Martin-de-Varreville, over four miles away, to determine the location and status of the 8th Infantry Regiment, which should have already pushed into Ste.-Mère-Église from the south.

Lieutenant Colonel Vandervoort was unaware of Krause's order. "Tommy questioned the propriety of an order from a senior officer not part of his chain of command, but figured he'd better keep his mouth shut and do what he was told. He pulled his platoon out of the D Company position and went to the east edge of town. There, he told the platoon to wait and took five men on the patrol. He knew he could travel faster that way and if the Germans attacked again, the platoon would be there to help D Company, now down to about seventy men with McClean's people gone."[19]

As Lieutenant McClean and his men double-timed to St.-Martin-de-Varreville, they passed through an area occupied by the 1st Battalion, 8th Infantry, but somehow, the two units missed one another. When Lieutenant McClean and his patrol arrived at the CP of the 12th Infantry, he was informed that the 2nd Battalion, 8th Infantry, had been held up by the 795th Georgian Battalion defending Hill 20, then by artillery fire interdicting the approach from the south, along the N-13 highway. McClean and his platoon then left to double-time back the four miles to Ste.-Mère-Église with the information.

At about the same time, Company E assistant platoon leader, Lieutenant Jim Coyle was told to report to the company command post. "I received an order from our company commander, Captain Clyde Russell, to go to the beach by jeep with two men from D Company, and try to contact the 4th Infantry Division to get one of their artillery observers to Ste.-Mère-Église to give us fire support.

"I was able to reach the 4th Division as they were moving from the beach. But they had only one observer left alive and could not release him to aid us. I noticed a tank unit along the road and explained our needs to the lieutenant colonel in command. But he could not release any tanks to me without orders from his command. It was frustrating to see all those tanks not engaged while we were fighting so hard a few miles away. But there was nothing a lieutenant could do, so I returned to Ste.-Mère-Église with nothing but a bit of helpful information: The tank commander was in radio contact with tanks which were assigned to us. He told me they were on their way to Ste.-Mère-Église from a roundabout route through Chef-du-Pont.

"As soon as I reported to battalion headquarters upon my return, we were given an order to move into position north of Ste.-Mère-Église to prepare to attack the enemy who were closing in on the town."[20]

EARLY THAT AFTERNOON, Colonel Raff's armor arrived at Ridgway's command post by taking the road west from the N-13 to Chef-du-Pont, then the road from Chef-du-Pont northeast toward Ste.-Mère-Église, bypassing the Germans on Hill 20 at Fauville. Colonel James Van Fleet, commander of the 8th Infantry Regiment, 4th Division, arrived at Ridgway's command post a short time later. He told Ridgway that his regiment was fighting its way north up the N-13 highway and would reach Ste.-Mère-Église in about an hour. They decided to conduct a joint attack north from Ste.-Mère-Église at 5:15 p.m. The 2nd Battalion, 8th Infantry, would attack on the left flank of Vandervoort's 2nd Battalion, which would attack north along the N-13 highway.

Around 3:30 p.m., Lieutenant Eugene A. Doerfler, the 2nd Battalion S-2, arrived at Ridgway's CP and guided a platoon of four Sherman tanks from Raff's force to the battalion positions just north of Ste.-Mère-Église.

The situation north of Ste.-Mère-Église was still critical. Despite the near destruction of the 1st Battalion, 1058th Grenadier Regiment, five enemy self-propelled guns of the 709th Antitank Battalion and the Seventh Army Sturm Battalion remained just to the north astride the N-13 highway, and the 2nd Battalion, 1058th Grenadier Regiment was positioned west of the highway.

Lieutenant Frank P. Woosley had just become the acting commander of Company E, because Captain Clyde Russell had suffered a relapse of malaria on the morning of June 7. Woosley assigned Lieutenant Coyle to command the provisional platoon of about twenty to twenty-five misdropped troopers of the 101st Airborne Division and ten or so Company E headquarters troopers, designated as 2nd Platoon, Company E.

The plan of attack called for Lieutenant Coyle's platoon to attack north out of Ste.-Mère-Église, west of the N-13 highway, while the 1st Platoon, Company E, led by Lieutenant Ted "Pete" Peterson, would attack astride the highway. Lieutenant McClean's 2nd Platoon of Company D would attack north, east of the highway—if it arrived in time after double-timing back from the 12th Infantry Regiment's command post. The 2nd Battalion, 8th Infantry Regiment, 4th Division, would attack north on the left flank of Coyle's provisional 2nd Platoon. The attack would commence at 5:15 p.m.

Private First Class Earl Boling was a rifleman in Peterson's platoon. "As we were hearing rumors that the beach troops would be arriving soon, we were ordered to prepare to attack. Of course, this was good airborne strategy—when one is surrounded, tired, hungry, and low on ammunition, the best possible thing to do is attack."[21]

IN PREPARATION FOR THE PLANNED ATTACK that afternoon, Lieutenant Coyle moved the provisional 2nd Platoon of Company E into position just north of town. "We took up positions along a road which runs west from the main highway. It is the road which has the last house on the north edge of the town.

"Two tanks which had been attached to us arrived, and they would cover our open flank as we attacked. There was heavy machine gun fire coming across the field from our front. My original order was to take my platoon across this field, but in the interval before our jump off time, 17:15 hours, I got permission [from Lieutenant Woosley] to take them north up a dirt road on the left of the field, which provided better cover and concealment."[22]

It was a daring plan, which if successful would put Coyle's platoon on top of the Germans before they knew what hit them, if they weren't spotted coming up the road and cut to pieces with mortar, artillery, or machine gun fire.

Sergeant Sampson moved his 60mm mortar squad through town to a position where it could support the Company E attack. "I grabbed the mortar and with the rest of the squad, I followed the runner to the front where the forward squads had sought protection in a ditch on the near side of a sparsely planted tree hedgerow. Here, I was told by either [Staff] Sergeant [William] Smith or Lieutenant Peterson, 'Give us mortar fire in that next hedgerow. They are there in force.' The hedgerow ran west from the Montebourg road [N-13]."[23]

Shortly before 5:00 p.m., the 8th Infantry Regiment hadn't arrived and wouldn't be available for the attack. Company E would have to cover its left flank. Lieutenants Woosley, Doerfler, and Coyle met with the commanders of the two Sherman tanks supporting them and decided to use one tank and the provisional platoon strays to cover the left flank. Coyle, Woosley, Doerfler, and ten men from Company E headquarters would accompany the lead tank and cover the front and right when they reached the intersection with the hedgerow-lined lane, from which the German infantry was firing.

As the assault was about to commence, the 746th Tank Battalion taskforce that Lieutenant J. J. Smith had acquired earlier from the 4th Infantry Division approached Ste.-Mère-Église from the east. Smith's pathfinders were riding on top of the lead tanks. Company B pathfinder, Sergeant James Elmo Jones, had to jump off from the rear deck of the tank he was riding as it rolled through Ste.-Mère-Église. "The tanks never really stopped long enough to let us off, but kept attacking north [out] of Ste.-Mère-Église."[24]

The tankers, knowing nothing of the planned attack, just barreled right up the N-13 highway around 5:00 p.m., running head on into the remaining five German self-propelled assault guns and German infantry on the highway.

Lieutenant Houston Payne, commanding the lead tank, knocked out two self-propelled assault guns and a towed antitank gun before his tank was hit and he was wounded. He managed to get his tank pulled to the side of the road. Another Sherman moved past Payne's tank and continued the attack.

Just before the attack, Vandervoort received welcome help from a newly arrived forward artillery observer. "The 8th Infantry field artillery observer placed a 155mm barrage two hedgerows in back of the German front line position."[25]

The 2nd Battalion's 81mm mortar platoon, using an observer, fired indirect fire while Company E's 1st Platoon mortar squad, led by Sergeant Otis Sampson, fired from its exposed position on the German frontline positions with its single 60mm mortar. "We were in plain sight of the enemy and bullets were flying by. My men didn't hesitate—they tried to give us mortar gunners the protection we needed with their rifle fire. The teamwork paid off. My first rounds overshot the hedgerow. Once the range was found, we laid them in, one round landing in a machine gun nest, killing them all."[26]

Sampson's gunner, Private First Class Harry Pickels, fed the mortar while Sampson adjusted the aim, as rounds exploded above the entire length of the German-held lane. Simultaneously, Peterson's platoon unleashed a torrent of small-arms and .30-caliber machine gun fire into points in the hedgerow across the field where Germans were spotted or suspected to be positioned.

At 5:15 p.m., Lieutenant Ted Peterson's 1st Platoon of Company E attacked north, more or less in columns along both sides of the hedgerows bordering the ditch running beside the west side of the N-13 highway. Meanwhile, Lieutenant Coyle's provisional 2nd Platoon and the two Sherman tanks moved north up the lane, with Woosley, Doerfler, and Coyle and the Company E headquarters men walking on both sides of and just behind the lead tank. When the lead tank stopped, Lieutenant Woosley moved forward to investigate. "We came to a dead American soldier lying in the tank's path just short of the enemy's position. The tank commander didn't want to run over the body. I had what I consider a combat lapse and walked right in front of that tank. I lifted the body, even looked at his dog-tags, with sorrow for his family. I laid him in a ditch so the tank could move forward. I returned to the rear of the tank. Lieutenant Coyle told me he was amazed that I was not killed."[27]

The column continued forward cautiously, as Coyle watched for any signs the Germans had the lane covered by a machine gun or worse, a self-propelled or antitank gun. "When we reached the intersection of another dirt road running east to the highway, we found the enemy behind the hedgerow bordering this road. We had come up on his flank, and by pure chance he had left it unprotected."[28]

Woosley couldn't believe their luck, and immediately got the lead tank into action. "When we reached the lane that was the enemy's position, I had the tank make a ninety-degree turn and fire down the sunken lane."[29]

The tank fired its .50-caliber machine gun, the 75mm main gun, and .30-caliber coaxial machine gun, devastating the Germans packed into the narrow lane. Sampson's mortar rounds bursting overhead rained down on the helpless German infantry. Lieutenant Doerfler emptied his Thompson submachine gun into the surprised Germans positioned near the intersection of the lanes. Coyle deployed his ten Company E troopers into perfect enfilade positions. "We poured fire up the ditch from our positions. After about fifteen minutes of firing, a white flag appeared in the ditch. I called for a cease fire, and it was with some difficulty in all the noise of battle that I was able to get our firing stopped."[30]

Sergeant Sampson began to see some Germans emerge from the hedgerow to his front. "The rifle and machine gun fire along with the mortar shelling had many of the Jerries willing to come out with white flags. To stop those men from getting killed, I stood up and yelled, 'Cease fire! Cease fire!' But the tension was too high—the Germans ran back to the protection of the hedgerow."[31]

The Germans' intentions were not entirely clear to Private First Class Earl Boling. "The Germans started to surrender, then seemed to change their minds and started firing again. However, some had run into the open, and at this time Lieutenant McClean's D Company platoon opened up on their flank."[32]

The fire routed the Germans out of the lane, where Lieutenant Peterson's platoon decimated them. One of those troopers was Private John Keller, a rifle grenadier. "[Corporal Tom] Burke was to my right, and I noticed how close he was to the main road, which was also to our right. Next, I noticed he was standing up in the middle of the main road, blasting away with his Tommy gun. I ran up to him and saw a German running like hell down the road. I had a [high-explosive] grenade on my rifle and let the bastard have it. It landed in front of him by some yardage, but failed to explode. I don't know if I forgot to pull the pin, or if it just landed on the fin end and skidded. At that, he threw up his hands, turned and was walking back to us."[33]

The white flag convinced Coyle that the Germans had had enough. "Frank Woosley and I went up the road to accept the surrender. But before we got very far, two hand grenades came over the hedgerow. He went into the ditch on one side of the road and I on the other. We thought at the time that we had stepped into a trap.

"We returned to our position and resumed fire. This time we did not cease until the enemy ran out of the ditch into the large field next to it with their hands raised. When I saw that there were over one hundred of the enemy running into the field, I went through the hedgerow with the intention of stopping them and rounding them up. But as soon as I got through the hedgerow into the ditch on their side, I was hit by machine pistol fire coming down the ditch. The Germans had not quit yet. One of my men followed me through the hedgerow and fired an unmanned German machine gun up the ditch, ending any further fire from the enemy."[34]

Sampson suddenly saw some Germans attempting to escape up the ditch bordering the highway. "I was set up on the extreme right flank of the field and when some tried to escape in the mouth of a ditch to the right front of me, I quickly brought my mortar into play there. It paid off.

"Mortar ammunition gone, I used my Tommy gun on the escaping Jerries. The ditch was their death trap. . .

"I saw the backs of four still going. As long as the enemy had a gun in his hands, even though he was running the other way, to me it was open season on them. . .

"It was Lieutenant Packard's Tommy gun I was using. It had more than paid for his death that occurred back there on the Volturno railroad yard in Italy. It was so easy, I felt ashamed of myself and quit firing. That was the one time I felt I had bagged my quota."[35]

The Germans, realizing there was little chance of escape, emerged into the field in front of their hedgerow. The number of Germans coming out of the lane worried Lieutenant Woosley. "The enemy seemed to come from everywhere with raised hands until it looked like an army. I had difficulty locating enough soldiers for the guard detail. I wondered what would have happened if they knew how small a unit I had left at this point.

"Corporal Sam [J.] Appleby, in helping to round up the prisoners, came across one officer who refused to move for him. With Appleby's own words, 'I took a bayonet and shoved it into his ass and then he moved.'

"You should have seen the happy smiles and giggles that escaped the faces of the prisoners to see their lord and master made to obey, especially from an enlisted man."[36]

Sampson, for the first time, became aware of the appalling scene he had been too busy to notice during the fighting. "I remember very vividly looking over the dead and wounded in the ditch and the surrounding area. One mortar shell had landed on top of the bank near the deep ditch and partly covered some of the dead and wounded with a heavy layer of dirt. Every time a wounded man breathed, the soil would rise and lower. I could partly see the eyes of one man who was lying on his back. An awful scared look was in his eyes as I looked down on him. Fearing, I guessed, that I would put a bayonet into him. I made no attempt at helping them.

"I looked up. No more than fifty feet from me in the open field next to the hedgerow were about fifty to sixty Germans with their hands up, standing in a group. I saw the tall form of Lieutenant McClean from D Company. He was on the other side of the road with some of his men, where more of the enemy had surrendered. . .

"I started from the Montebourg road and walked west on the north of the hedgerow with my men trailing. It was a double hedgerow with a sunken lane in between. Here was where Jerry had made his stand.

"One wounded German looked at my canteen and asked what sounded to me like, 'coffee.' I gave him my canteen and moved on, forgetting the incident. .

"At the end of the field, I ran into Lieutenant Coyle. He had a large group of prisoners guarded by our company headquarters men.

"He told me part of the story of his attack. 'We caught them unaware. It took twice to make them surrender and then I got hit in the rear,' he said, laying his hand on his rear cheeks.

"'Let me take a look and see how bad it is,' I said as he lay on the ground. A bullet had almost completed its journey through both cheeks. I applied a bandage, saying, 'Lieutenant, just remember, I put your first granny rag on. 'Completing the job, I said, 'Just lie here and I'll see someone picks you up.'"[37]

Coyle replied that he'd been all right before Sampson came along. "I was given first aid after the prisoners were collected, and rode back on a tank to the battalion aid station in the old school in Ste.-Mère-Église. The next day I left Ste.-Mère-Église in an ambulance to return to England and the hospital."[38]

After leaving Coyle, Sampson returned to the highway. "I was hailed by the wounded Jerry I had given my canteen to. I had forgotten all about him. He passed it back empty, but the look he gave me was one of thanks. . .

"I met [Private First Class] Jack Hill, roaming around the area on my return to the Montebourg road. He showed me a beautiful watch, saying, 'A German officer lost his arm and I bandaged it up for him. He could speak English well. He offered me the watch and I refused it. I didn't want him to think he had to pay me. The officer said, 'You might as well have it, for it will be taken from me later.' He seemed to be a very pleasant man and showed little sign of the pain he must have been in. . .

"Our partial company, still minus two platoons, returned to our area in Ste.-Mère-Église without getting a man killed. The price the Germans paid for that short encounter in dead and wounded was terrific, not counting the men captured. We hit fast and hard, each man doing his part. The sight that met our eyes after that encounter was a gruesome one."[39]

As Private Keller was escorting prisoners to the POW area, he noticed a high-ranking German officer, "A colonel, I believe—a man slightly grey at the temples, with a serious leg wound, who was being carried by two of his men. We hadn't gone too far when he asked me for a drink of water. I hesitated to give him one, as I didn't trust him—but I did and I couldn't help but notice, in spite of his defeat and pain, a look of relief or gratitude in his eyes.

"I relieved him of his Iron Cross, and we proceeded on our way. We came to a cluster of buildings, where I had his men place him on a door. Here, I searched him and took a Mauser pistol he had in his hip pocket, and then rejoined my outfit at the front."[40]

The battle was an overwhelming victory. Before he was evacuated, Coyle received a preliminary prisoner count. "In this battle E Company, with two platoons, captured 168 prisoners. I do not know the number of dead left in the ditches. Lieutenant Peterson's platoon on my right flank captured the German commander. Corporal Sam Appleby shot one German captain as he tried to escape the trap. A platoon of D Company, commanded by Lieutenant Thomas J. McClean, captured a great number who tried to escape across the main highway [N-13] and ran into his position."[41]

While the paratroopers destroyed the German infantry, Lieutenant Colonel C. G. Hupfer, commanding the 746th Tank Battalion and his executive officer, Major George Yeatts, reconnoitered a route around the German flank by taking the road northeast toward Bandienville, then turning north. They skirted the open flank created by the destruction of the 1st Battalion, 1058th, that morning, via a secondary road to Neuville-au-Plain, in time to destroy two more German self-propelled assault guns, while losing two of their own tanks. They took about sixty German prisoners and liberated nineteen American prisoners, most of them members of the 3rd Platoon, Company D, captured the previous afternoon.

Lieutenant Colonel Vandervoort was justifiably proud of his battalion's overwhelming victories that day. "We had annihilated the 2nd Battalion, 1058th German Infantry Regiment. The 1st Battalion, same unit was completely routed. Four hundred eight prisoners were captured and counted. Thirty-six enemy vehicles and guns destroyed. Four hundred fourteen enemy dead were counted within and in front of our positions."[42]

Lieutenant Eugene Dorefler was awarded the Distinguished Service Cross for his heroism in single-handedly bringing the tanks through enemy fire to the battalion and for his part in leading the attack that afternoon.

Commenting on the attack by Company E, Vandervoort would learn that "later in the war, Major General Lawton Collins, VII Corps commander, said the 505 had conducted 'one of the most perfectly coordinated combined attacks laid on in Europe.'"[43]

The following morning, Vandervoort asked Lieutenant Waverly Wray to show him the area where he had killed the German battalion staff. "We went to a sunken cow-path bordered by six foot high hedgerows north of the town. His very presence there, all alone at the risk of his life in the midst of the attacking Germans, was unbelievable and beyond the call of duty. There were the bodies of three or four German officers and four or five enlisted men—each killed by a single shot. Two were communicators who had been operating a radio. The ranking officer was a lieutenant colonel. They were the commanding officer and staff of the 1st Battalion, 1058th Grenadier Regiment. This left the battalion without leadership when Wray launched his attack half an hour or so later. Two other dead Germans were across a narrow field, each shot in the head. Unforgettably, all bodies were sprinkled with pink and white apple blossoms from an adjacent orchard.

"Questioned closely, Wray described how he had shot them on his reconnaissance inside enemy lines. I had served with Waverly for the past two years and knew what he said was the gospel truth. He was a devout, God-fearing young man who was sending half his pay home to help build a Methodist church. He would not exaggerate or lie about his incredible adventure. Although his right ear was almost shot off, he continued deep into the enemy deployment to fix their positions prior to launching his attack with his understrength parachute company.

"Highly impressed by the unprecedented solitary performance and accomplishment, I confirmed the story. I checked with his injured company commander, Captain T.G. Smith, his first sergeant, John Rabig, and other D Company troopers. His reconnaissance was really a one-man combat patrol of great grit. Encountering isolated Germans in the hedgerows, he destroyed those he could not avoid with hand grenades and rifle fire. D Company eyewitness glimpses of the lieutenant's crusade sustained the truth of his deeds in depth.[44]

"John Rabig, Waverly's first sergeant, summed up Wray's performance the next day with the comment, 'Colonel, aren't you glad Waverly's on our side?'"[45]

Vandervoort recommended Lieutenant Wray for the Congressional Medal of Honor, but Wray was subsequently awarded the Distinguished Service Cross.

The next day, when General Gavin viewed the fields just north of Ste.-Mère-Église littered with German dead from the pervious day's fighting, he commented to Vandervoort, "Van, don't kill them all. Save a few for interrogation."[46]

Lieutenant Colonel Vandervoort was awarded the Distinguished Service Cross for his inspirational leadership and heroism during the first day of the Normandy campaign:

Lieutenant Colonel Benjamin H. Vandervoort, 0-22715, 505th Parachute Infantry, United States Army, for extraordinary heroism in action against the enemy on 6 June 1944, in France. Though he sustained a broken foot in his jump, Lieutenant Colonel Vandervoort refused to be evacuated. He immediately, despite his painful injury, assembled and organized all the available troops from his battalion and personally led it through enemy held territory to the initial objective. With only first aid treatment for his broken foot, he remained with his unit and directed the defense of its newly won position against a vastly superior enemy. With complete disregard for his own safety, he continually moved about the foremost elements, subjecting himself to intense enemy rifle, machine gun, and artillery fire. Inspired by his presence, his men successfully withstood repeated enemy counterattacks. The personal bravery, devotion to duty, and outstanding leadership displayed by Lieutenant Colonel Vandervoort reflects great credit on himself and is in keeping with the highest traditions of the armed forces. Entered military service from Ohio.

In his recommendation, the 505's commanding officer, Lieutenant Colonel Bill Ekman stated in part, "Throughout the continuing engagements with the enemy and under hostile enemy machine gun, rifle, and artillery fire, he moved among his troops directing and encouraging them. He personally inspected the positions of all elements of his command to insure that they were the best available on the terrain. In spite of the pain from his injured foot he was tireless in his effort to maintain his battalion in an offensive defense against enemy repeated counterattacks. Inspired by his ever present encouragement, his men inflicted heavy casualties on the enemy infantry and panzer forces. He maintained a successful defense of the town of Ste.-Mère-Église until the seaborne forces were able to contact his outpost on the 7th of June. Ste.-Mère-Église was a key town in the enemy defensive system because it was the center of the many roads used by the Germans for troop movement and supply of their many defensive positions. Control of the town removed dangerous pressure by hostile forces in the area between Ste.-Mère-Église and the Utah Beachhead, being established by the United States Army invasion force from the sea to the east."[47]

DURING THE EVENING AND NIGHT OF JUNE 7, large-caliber German artillery pounded the 2nd Battalion. Sergeant Eldon M. Clark, with Company D, hugged the bottom of his slit trench as explosions rocked the ground. "They had zeroed in on us. I was literally bouncing up and down.

"[Private First Class Allen B.] Davis was dug in about thirty feet behind me. Davis was in a slit trench and he got a direct hit—blew him to pieces. I got up to check on the guys [in my mortar squad]. The guys wouldn't let me look at him. They knew we were good friends."[48]

At the aid station in the schoolhouse in Ste.-Mère-Église, Captain George Wood, the regimental chaplain, witnessed the heroic efforts of the medical personnel. "Captain Putnam, [2nd Battalion] medical officer, performed major surgery, even to amputations, all night long with the few instruments he jumped in with on his person, in a blacked-out room of the schoolhouse, to the music of a rain of shells which never ceased."[49]

COLONEL EKMAN exploited the destruction of two battalions of the 1058th Regiment, ordering an attack north toward Montebourg Station, commencing shortly after midnight, the morning of June 8. Lieutenant O. B. Carr's 2nd Platoon, Company D conducted a combat patrol at 9:00 p.m. astride the N-13 highway to reconnoiter the area north of the 2nd Battalion's front line. Private Leonard M. Skolek "was assigned as the get-away man, on the right rear of the platoon, to protect the platoon's right rear flank. My combat days in Sicily and Italy made me very cautious. On the way to Neuville-au-Plain we stopped and laid in the ditches next to the hedgerows and listened for danger. After the third stop, everyone got up and moved forward It was a quiet night and I had a strange feeling we were being followed, so I did not get up. I laid flat on the ground and faced the rear skyline. After our platoon moved about 200 feet, I saw someone coming behind us. I quickly ran to the rear of our platoon and told everyone to get in the ditches.

"Sergeant [Paul] Nunan then came behind me. We both called, 'halt.' Instead, they opened fire on us. I killed every one with my M1 rifle. No one else fired for fear of hitting me. The Germans were about twenty feet in front of us."[50] Skolek later received the Bronze Star for his actions in killing five enemy soldiers and preventing an ambush of his platoon.

As the 2nd Battalion moved up to the line of departure, Staff Sergeant Russ Brown, with Company F, saw a gruesome sight along the road. "A tank had gone down a ditch with its track and ran over some Germans in the ditch. I heard some Germans call, 'Hilfe! Hilfe! (help).'"[51]

By 4:30 a.m., the 2nd Battalion reached Neuville-au-Plain, where nineteen wounded troopers, including some from Lieutenant Turnbull's Company D platoon, were found holding the town. Hupfer's tanks had liberated them the previous evening.[52] As they came into the hamlet, Private First Class Frank Bilich, with Company D, noticed "there was a guy lying on his back with his head facing down the hill. It was [First Sergeant] John Rabig's buddy, Bob Niland. As we pulled up there, John Rabig took one look at him and started walking away. He had tears in his eyes."[53]

The 505th was ordered by VII Corps Headquarters to wait at Neuville-au-Plain for the 4th Infantry Division to close up on its right flank. The 2nd Battalion sent out strong combat patrols and then continued the advance that evening toward Fresville.

Like almost all of his troopers, Vandervoort was exhausted from almost three days of fighting. "It was just before sunset and my CP was being shelled by a German 88. I issued orders for the CP to move and fell asleep in my foxhole. The next thing I knew I was waked by beautiful music. I looked up and saw beautiful blossoms above me. I knew I had been killed and was in heaven and thought, 'What a lovely place it is.' When they had moved the CP they had been unable to wake me and poured me into a jeep and then a foxhole under one of the Normandy apple trees which was then in full blossom. The music was BBC broadcasting over a small portable radio one of the troopers had carried in with him. It was early morning and no firing was going on at that time."[54]

At 5:30 a.m. on June 9, the 505th pressed the attack toward Montebourg Station, with the attached 2nd Battalion, 325th Glider Infantry Regiment (GIR), the division's organic glider infantry regiment, attacking on the right flank of the 2nd Battalion. The 1st Battalion, 505th followed behind in reserve, while the 3rd Battalion protected the left flank and guarded crossings over the Merderet River.

The Norman hedgerow country was tailor-made for defenders. The Germans were masters of defensive warfare; taking advantage of the hedgerows, terrain features, and stone buildings at tactically advantageous points. In a hedgerow-lined field, they typically would dig in machine guns in the corners of the hedgerows to provide crossfire of the field and direct fire along the hedgerows parallel to the axis of an enemy advance. These machine gun positions were usually made by digging a tunnel through the base of the hedgerow instead of on top to provide better cover and concealment for the gunners. German infantry would typically occupy dug in positions to fire over the top of the hedgerow between the two machine gun positions. Secondary positions were usually prepared in advance and in depth, with planned routes of withdrawal to them.

The Germans established field telephone or radio contact with artillery and mortars already zeroed in on the fields in front of the dug in infantry. The Germans laid antitank mines along roads and lanes as well as covering them with machine guns and antitank weapons such as Panzerfausts, Panzerschrects, antitank guns, and tank destroyers to block armored vehicle routes of advance. If available, local commanders employed a mobile counterattack force of armor and infantry to stop an enemy breakthrough.

Captain Hubert Bass, commanding Company F, realized that "hedgerow fighting was to be something new and we quickly adjusted our tactics to close range fighting with limited observation of the terrain and enemy."[55]

It was during the advance that day that one of the Company F platoon leaders and elements of his platoon became trapped by a numerically superior German force. Technician Fifth Grade Hubert G. Pack, the platoon's radio operator, voluntarily made his way through enemy machine gun fire and found a covered escape route. Pack led his platoon leader and most of the men out of the trap, but discovered that four troopers were missing. Pack made the dangerous trek back to locate and bring out two of the troopers. Returning a third time under heavy enemy fire, Pack crawled to within ten feet of a German mortar position to verify that the two remaining troopers were dead. Technician Fifth Grade Pack was awarded the Silver Star medal for his gallantry.

OVER THE NEXT FEW DAYS, the combat-wise 505th Parachute Infantry intuitively developed a method of attacking through this hedgerow country, while incurring minimum casualties. Sergeant Spencer Wurst was squad leader of the 1st Squad, 3rd Platoon, Company F. "Whether we were attacking as part of a larger unit or on patrol, we sent scouts out ahead to the next hedgerow. They crossed the open field or moved along the hedgerow in the direction of the attack. The remaining squad members would deploy along the hedgerow we occupied, ready to give them fire support. Sometimes this worked, and sometimes it didn't. If the scouts made it to the other side of the field without drawing fire, they looked around as best they could, then the rest moved across. If they got fired on, we knew we had a fight on our hands, and we deployed and fired, or tried to maneuver to the next hedgerow."[56]

When the Germans were found to be defending a hedgerow, the paratroopers employed shock and speed to overwhelm the enemy and once they had them on the run, kept pursuing them so they couldn't get reorganized and set up at a secondary position. Fortunately, the battalion had limited tank support for the drive. Sergeant Otis Sampson, with Company E, found the tactic effective, but tough on his heavily laden 60mm mortar squad. "The tanks would rake the forward hedgerows with their heavy machine guns and fire against a target or so with their 75s and then we would be given the command to 'charge'.

"We did just that, yelling like a bunch of Indians on the warpath; we kept pushing the enemy back. With the load we had to carry, I was glad that kind of advance wasn't kept up."[57]

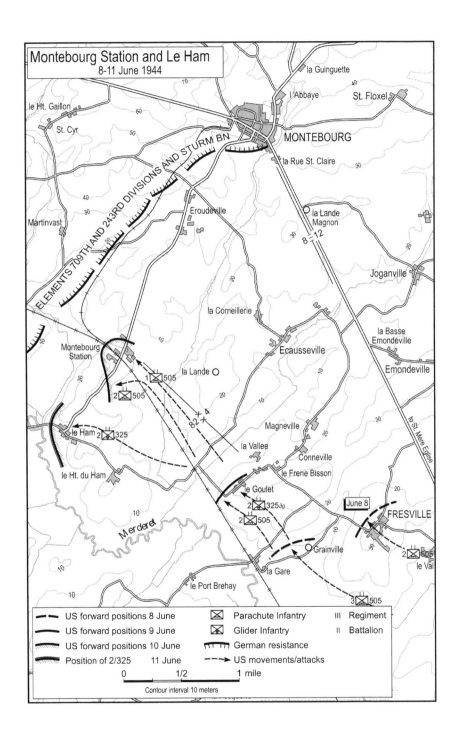

Montebourg Station and Le Ham
8-11 June 1944

la Guinguette

l'Abbaye   St. Floxel

le Ht. Gaillon

St. Cyr   MONTEBOURG

STURM BN

la Rue St. Claire

ELEMENTS 709TH AND 243RD DIVISIONS AND

Eroudeville   la Lande Magnon

Martinvast   8 ÷ 12

Joganville

la Corneillerie

la Basse Emondeville

Montebourg Station   Ecausseville   Emondeville

1 ⊠ 505   la Lande

2 ⊠ 505

le Ham 2 ⊠ 325   82 × 4

     Magneville

la Vallee

le Ht. du Ham   Conneville

le Frene Bisson

le Goulet

Merderet   2 ⊠ 325   June 8   FRESVILLE

2 ⊠ 505

Grainville   2 ⊠ 505   le Val

la Gare

le Port Brehay

3 ⊠ 505

to St. Mere Eglise

– – – US forward positions 8 June	⊠ Parachute Infantry	III Regiment
—— US forward positions 9 June	⊠ Glider Infantry	II Battalion
—— US forward positions 10 June	⊓⊓⊓ German resistance	
⫫⫫ Position of 2/325 11 June	– – → US movements/attacks	

0   1/2   1 mile

Contour interval 10 meters

The 2nd Battalion, 505th attack reached a point just south of Montebourg Station. That evening, the old commanding officer of the 2nd Battalion, Lieutenant Colonel Mark Alexander, who was the regimental executive officer and now acting commander of the 1st Battalion, reported to the regimental command post to discuss plans for the attack the next morning. "Lieutenant Colonel Bill Ekman had requested that I give the attack order. My order was for the 1st Battalion to lead, followed closely by the 2nd Battalion. After the 1st Battalion had taken Montebourg Station, the 2nd Battalion was to take the lead, turning to the left forty-five degrees and take Le Ham."[58]

That night, Lieutenant Frank Woosley, acting commander of Company E, reported to the 2nd Battalion command post to receive the attack order. "We were to move northwest towards Le Ham, with E Company on the left, D Company on the right, and F Company in reserve. A railroad track was our line of departure."[59]

The 1st Battalion broke through the German front line and drove forward to capture Montebourg Station. The 2nd Battalion passed through the town and jumped off on its attack toward Le Ham. Private First Class Turk Seelye was advancing across open ground just outside of Montebourg Station with Company E when "our skirmish line was spotted by the enemy as we crossed a railroad grade. Artillery airbursts were directed toward us. We passed through a lightly forested area. Corporal Ralph H. McGrew, Jr. was killed by a sniper. At about 1700 hours, Germans were spotted up ahead. Shortly thereafter, a mortar shell exploded at my side. I was blinded, [had] broken bones, and [was] bleeding. I spent the next twelve months in an Army hospital."[60]

Lieutenant Woosley tried to get Company E moving again. "I was suddenly appalled at the confusion. I had temporarily lost contact with battalion headquarters and with D and F Companies. I didn't know what was in front of me, or on either flank. I followed my original orders and moved into the attack until my company was pinned down by enemy small arms fire and by artillery shelling that grew more intense through the evening and night. Three men were killed that night—they were all 101[st Airborne] men who were in their fourth day of combat."[61]

The 2nd Battalion, kept attacking until Company F reached the edge of Le Ham that night, but Ekman ordered a withdrawal about 11:00 p.m. The 2nd Battalion stopped several German platoon-sized counterattacks during the night.

On the morning of June 11, following a fifteen minute barrage by the 456th Parachute Field Artillery Battalion, the 2nd Battalion made a limited attack on Le Ham. As Lieutenant Woosley led Company E forward, "enemy fire and shelling continued, and we were temporarily pinned down. An artillery shell hit close by—a dud. A messenger came, and hit the ground beside me. He told me that a flank of E Company was not holding. As I started to the area to assess the situation, a shell hit close by me—the blast caught me mostly in the face—one eye was blinded, and I received a small wound in my back. I was taken to an aid station, and then by truck to the coast."[62] Captain Clyde Russell, even though still affected by malaria, took command of Company E, being the only company grade officer remaining.

The 2nd Battalion laid down a base of fire on Le Ham, as the 2nd Battalion, 325th GIR assaulted the town. A storm of enemy machine gun and rifle fire stopped the glider troopers, who withdrew to reorganize. At 6:00 p.m., they renewed the assault, behind a ten minute artillery concentration on the town, fired by the artillery of the 456th. By about 8:00 p.m. on June 11, the 2nd Battalion, 325th had secured Le Ham. The 505th remained along the eastern side of the Merderet River, patrolling across the river until relieved by the 90th Infantry Division on the evening of June 12–13.

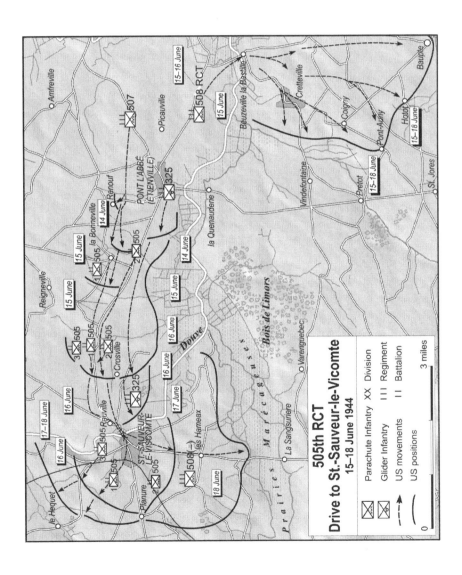

THE 505TH MOVED BY TRUCK to an area west of the Merderet River, near the confluence with the Douve River on June 13. The next day, the division attacked from west of Étienville westward toward St.-Sauveur-le-Vicomte. The severely depleted 507th PIR ran into strong enemy resistance, but captured La Bonneville that night, and repulsed several enemy counterattacks. The understrength 325th GIR attacking west along the highway on the left flank of the 507th, engaged in savage fighting with exceptionally strong enemy opposition, but that night pulled up even with the 507th.

At 5:00 a.m. next morning, the 507th advanced about six hundred yards against light opposition before an enemy counterattack, supported by tanks and intense artillery and mortar barrages, struck its open right flank, halting the advance. The 505th, following in reserve behind the 507th, took over the attack.

Advancing astride the highway toward St.-Sauveur-le-Vicomte, Company D approached a group of farm buildings at Les Rosiers, where a German platoon supported by two 75mm antitank guns and two 37mm antiaircraft guns employed in a direct-fire, antipersonnel role opened fire. Private First Class David Bowman, a machine gunner with Company D, advanced through the extremely heavy enemy fire during this "combined infantry-tank attack, which developed into the most heated battle in which I participated in Normandy. We were moving forward under constant artillery and small arms fire. The resistance was so heavy that we could move forward only in spurts. We'd hit the ground, open fire, get up, rush forward a short distance, and hit the ground again. A few men were hit during these movements. Some just lay there; others limped to the rear. Tanks were on our left flank, and I heard the rumble of some to our right.

"After moving forward some distance, our unit was halted and [William R. "Rebel"] Haynes and I were instructed to direct fire so it would complement that from the machine gunners to our right, Private [John D.] Donald MacPhee and Private First Class Thomas [B.] Byrd.

"The enemy fire from small arms, tanks, and artillery was heavy. After an indeterminable passage of time, I heard Byrd shouting, 'MacPhee! ''MacPhee!' (I later learned that both had been killed around that time.) Shortly after this unfortunate incident, Haynes was hit and went to the rear.

"We continued our advance . . . but for some distance we endured the sight of burning tanks and their hapless crews. One would see tankers, mostly German, I believe, but also many Americans, draped over the turrets, burning atop their burning tanks. Evidently, no quarter was given by either side, as would be expected under these conditions. When the tanks were disabled and the surviving crew attempted to abandon them, the enemy would mercilessly cut the men down."[63]

Fire from the German high-velocity guns was terrible. Corporal Wilton H. Johnson with Headquarters Company, 2nd Battalion, was working his way up the highway looking for a place to set up his machine gun, when he was wounded in the back by shrapnel from an aerial burst. "Private Elmer Pack, who was in my squad, pushed a rag in my back to stop the bleeding and probably saved my life."[64]

Vandervoort personally led the 1st Platoon of Company D and two tanks from Company A, 746th Tank Battalion around to the right flank of the German position as the 2nd Battalion's 81mm mortars suppressed the German fire. As the 1st Platoon advanced north in a skirmish line across an open field toward a hedgerow running east and west, Sergeant Roy King was deployed on the extreme left flank of his squad. "I was hit by a very small piece of shrapnel in the calf of my right leg. It felt like when you get popped with a towel in the shower room. I did not even know that I was hit until later.

"We reached the next hedgerow when Lieutenant McClean called for squad leaders to meet in his location, which was a gun pit for a large gun, about five feet by ten feet by eight inches [deep]. We had been assembled for a short time when the enemy fired a burst from an antiaircraft gun, hitting the hedgerow and bursting into flak—a piece of which hit me in the neck at the level of my Adam's apple and about an inch and a half to the right. My mouth and throat filled with fluid.

"I thought, 'Blood.' *I knew fear.*

"Because I did not recover from hitting the dirt, the lieutenant asked, 'King, are you hit?' I did not answer, fearing that I'd pour blood forth. The lieutenant asked, 'King, are you all right?'

"My answer was, 'Hell no, where's the medic?'

"He said, 'Right up the hedgerow to the east.' I leaped from the pit to the border and over the hedge, and ran to the medic. When I arrived, he was holding one of us [troopers] in his lap, with blood pumping from his back. I immediately sat down and recovered normality. When he looked up at me, he turned pale, and I was frightened again. After a sulfa powder application, he bandaged my neck. Then he put me on a stretcher and said, 'Lie still until they come for you.'"[65]

A short time later, as Lieutenant McClean's platoon hit the German flank, Company E and a couple of tanks moved up behind them to carry the attack through the enemy positions.

Private Earl Boling, an assistant BAR gunner with E Company, was carrying a heavy load of ammunition for the BAR as well as his own M1 rifle. "It was in this area that Private First Class Julius Eisner was wounded in the calf of the leg by a 37mm projectile, and as an aid man attended to him, we passed through D Company and took up positions along a hedgerow to gain a field of fire, since we had by this time many casualties.

"As we placed the BAR in firing position, an enemy machine gun fired. John [W. Burdge], Private [William H.] Nealy, and I were about a foot apart, John being in the center. A burst of machine gun fire started—neither Private Nealy nor I were touched, but Burdge was struck in the left thigh—the bullet going through the left leg and entering, but not exiting the right leg."[66]

Boling quickly got a medic for Burdge. "As the aid man was treating the wound, Private Nealy and I found a position to return the enemy fire, and as the company started to advance and broke the enemy line, we were advancing up a long grassy field.

"We had gotten a couple of tanks in support for a change—as we neared the crest of the hill, one of the tanks seemed to slow a bit, and Nealy and I saw a beautiful sight. There was Colonel Vandervoort with the cast still on the leg [of the ankle] he had broken on the jump—hopping on one crutch and pounding the back of the tank with the other one. I don't remember his exact words, but they were something to the effect that if the driver couldn't drive the tank up the hill, that he would put one of his men in to drive.

"Needless to say, the tank moved and Private Nealy, who was on his first campaign and had been a little nervous to that point, smiled and said, 'If that so and so can make it on one leg and a crutch, I can make it on two good legs.'"[67]

At around 7:00 p.m., the 2nd Battalion halted and dug in for the night.

The following morning, the 505th continued the attack westward toward St.-Sauveur-le-Vicomte, with the 1st Battalion attacking on the right, north of the highway and the 2nd Battalion on the left. By midday, the 2nd Battalion reached the high ground on the Douve River overlooking St.-Sauveur-le-Vicomte. Vandervoort entered a chateau on the bluff overlooking the town to conduct a preliminary reconnaissance. When he looked through his binoculars from a window on the top floor, Vandervoort saw thousands of German troops and horse-drawn heavy equipment moving south on the main north-south highway running through St.-Sauveur-le-Vicomte, attempting to escape to the south before the Cotentin Peninsula was cut. Vandervoort immediately radioed Major Jack Norton, the regimental S-3, describing the situation, but terminating the conversation before providing the coordinates. Norton deduced the location and quickly got word to Lieutenant Colonel Ekman, who in turn contacted General Ridgway, to request artillery fire on the enemy. General Omar N. Bradley happened to be visiting Ridgway at the division command post. Bradley arranged for all available VII Corps artillery to fire on the target. Ridgway and Bradley then left the command post and drove to the chateau where Vandervoort was located to witness the fireworks.

Using a forward observer, every available artillery piece in the VII Corps within range, not engaged in support of another unit, fired a massive TOT (time-on-target) barrage. Artillery batteries fired at slightly different times depending upon the distance to the target and velocity of the shells fired so that all of the rounds fired would arrive on the target simultaneously.

At St.-Sauveur-le-Vicomte, German soldiers moving down the main road heard the unmistakable sound of more than a hundred incoming 75mm, 105mm, and 155mm artillery shells filling the air just seconds before exploding on the town and the Germans along the highway. After a slight adjustment to the fire, a second TOT barrage destroyed those German troops, vehicles, and horses not hit in the first barrage.

Private First Class James V. Rodier, an ammo bearer with the 81mm Mortar Platoon of Headquarters Company, 2nd Battalion, positioned on the high ground above the town "could see a self-propelled gun being knocked out in the town. There was other artillery coming from the same direction our mortars were firing. I do not know what kind of guns the enemy was using, but they were getting the worst of the deal."[68]

As the second barrage lifted, Vandervoort ordered Company F to cross the bomb damaged bridge over the Douve River, circle the town to the north, and block the road running west from the town. Company D would follow, skirt the town to the south and cut the north-south highway, then Company E would move through the town and clean it out.

Sergeant Spencer Wurst and his squad led Company F down a ditch along the main road leading into town, waiting for the inevitable German fire to hit them. "The Germans had taken position on the other side of the river to our left and right front, on slightly higher ground. They let us get almost fully deployed along that open road before they opened up. We hit the dirt as the shells skimmed the top of the roadbed, passing over our heads by two or three feet."[69]

Wurst knew they had to keep moving to avoid casualties. "The best we could do was to get the hell out of there as fast as possible. We had to jump up and run across the bridge. The instant before we made our dash, [John P.] Corti, a BAR man in my squad, was severely wounded. He had been in a prone position close to a cement power pole, which was hit by one of the shells. As we made our rush, we couldn't stop, but the medic did."[70]

The German fire increased as Wurst and his men sprinted toward the bridge. "We were taking considerable small arms fire, which was particularly deadly in our situation. The Germans had us in sight and were firing rifles and machine guns directly on us.

"About a hundred fifty yards from the bridge, we were also taken under very heavy direct artillery fire. This was a minimum of 75mm, and probably larger, most likely from self-propelled guns. These were HE—high explosive shells, not antitank."[71]

Watching from the chateau overlooking the town as Company F dashed across the bridge under withering enemy fire, General Bradley turned to Ridgway and said, "My God, Matt, can't anything stop these men?"[72]

Ridgway replied, "I would rather have a platoon of those men than a battalion of regular infantry."[73]

As Company F turned right and began working around the north side of the town, Sergeant Paul Nunan, with Company D, got his men across the river, where they turned left and began moving around to the south side of the town. "They sent my platoon around to the left and we were going back into hedgerows. I had a man out in front of the platoon and he was down in the roadway. All of a sudden, he jumped back into the corner of this hedgerow and he said, 'There's a German out there, and he jumped into the hedgerow.'

"I told the people right up front against the hedgerow, 'OK everybody stay down until I give the word, then everybody stand up and open up against that hedgerow that's along the road.' I had a guy named [Private First Class] Norman [M.] Pritchard, who either didn't hear what I said or didn't care, so he stood up all by himself. A shot rang out and he had been drilled right through the heart. I told our guys to fire into the other hedgerow that was parallel to the road. Pritchard keeled over and after we had doused the area with small arms fire, I went up to him and saw he had taken one bullet. I thought of shooting him with the morphine syrette. I put it in his arm, and it stayed in a lump. And I realized he was dead. I've reviewed that in my mind I don't know how many times."[74]

As Company E moved along the road down the slope toward the bridge, Sergeant Victor M. Schmidt, with the 2nd Platoon, watched in disbelief as "Colonel Vandervoort and his aide came through us in a jeep, drove right down the road, and crossed the bridge into the town. They drove around part of the city, then came back about a half block from the other side of the bridge and parked their jeep on the side of the street. Colonel Vandervoort got out and he waved his crutch at us to come over the bridge—that all was clear.

"Our 1st Platoon was first to start over the bridge. This bridge had no guardrails on it, only a curb and a sidewalk on either side of it. When we got to the center of it, the Germans opened fire on us with a couple of 88s and machine guns, etcetera. We all hit the dirt immediately. The shells hit the cement and ricocheted over us, spinning about a foot over our bodies. We lay there about thirty seconds. It was either do or die. We all got up and ran headlong into that hail of gunfire coming down the street. We were in two columns about eighteen feet apart. When we got over the bridge, we split to each side of the street for cover. I still can't believe to this day why we weren't all killed."[75]

Shortly after Company E crossed the bridge, Staff Sergeant Russ Brown, a 60mm mortar squad leader with Company F, positioned on the high ground east of the Douve, and firing in support of the crossing, heard the sound of planes and looked up. "Some P-47s tried to skip bomb the bridge while our men were still crossing. They missed, turned around, and tried again, but missed again."[76]

The 505th PIR had moved past the bomb line that ran along the Douve River for that day. None of the planners believed the regiment would be able to cross the Douve until the following day. Therefore, Allied aircraft sighting any troops west of the river considered them as enemy and attacked them accordingly.

West side of the river, Sergeant Wurst looked back, "I could see Colonel Vandervoort, who had crossed shortly after we did, standing out in an opening with a huge orange blanket or panel. He was waving it like mad, standing there with orange smoke everywhere, trying to deter the planes. The bombs missed the bridge, but the planes also made some strafing runs."[77]

Private Earl Boling was acting as a scout for the 1st Platoon as Company E moved through the streets into the heart of St.-Sauveur-le-Vicomte. "As I turned the corner and moved a few feet down the street, a machine gun opened fire. I jumped over a nearby stone wall, about three feet high, and raised my head to try and ascertain where the fire was coming from.

"The German immediately tried to write his name on the wall with the weapon."[78]

Boling moved back along the wall to find his platoon. "At this time, [Battery C, 80th Airborne Antiaircraft (Antitank) Battalion] brought forward a 57mm antitank gun and attempted to fire on the enemy guns, but immediately received a round of enemy fire, which killed one and wounded two of the crew.

"Some of the platoon members decided to use the gun for our protection and as I recall, Private Clyde [M.] Rickerd went to a second story window with binoculars to direct and correct fire.

"As he was looking at the enemy position, he received a sniper shot which hit him in the second joint of the small finger of the right hand, and he had to vacate the window view. As Clyde later explained, 'I was looking at their positions and suddenly spotted this German looking back through a sniper scope, and before I could duck, I was shot in the hand. It was like looking through a keyhole and seeing an eye looking back.'"[79]

As Company E pushed through town, Private Donald D. Lassen and another trooper were called up front to act as scouts for the 3rd Platoon. "As the assistant BAR man in my platoon, I was sent to lead an exploratory advance up a road in St.-Sauveur-le-Vicomte along with the BAR man, [Private First Class James E.] Jimmy Keenan. We got about 50 yards up the road and hit the dirt with the objective of bringing some BAR fire on the Krauts who were just up ahead of us. Keenan fired one round and the BAR jammed. We were out in plain sight, fair game for the Krauts, no way to get back without totally exposing ourselves.

"[Private First Class] Fred Hebein saw our plight, and he ran out into the middle of the roadway we were in and started firing at the Kraut positions that were preparing to deliver withering fire upon Jimmy Keenan and me and shouted, 'Come on back, I got you covered!' We jumped up and got the hell out of there before the Krauts could find a way to get us. And they didn't get Fred Hebein either.

"It seems that Fred Hebein had gotten a 'Dear John' letter from his girl back home just before the Normandy invasion, and he seemed to have developed a death-wish. He was always volunteering to go on patrols and wanted to be the first scout in an attack. Fred Hebein was one helluva tough soldier. Fred came from Wisconsin, and incidentally, he married that girl that sent him the 'Dear John' letter."[80]

The Company F troopers kept out of the built-up areas as they skirted the north side of town, with Sergeant Wurst and his squad still leading. Scouting ahead, Wurst and Corporal William E. "Bill" Hodge observed to their front three Germans walking along a hedgerow in a column, unaware of their presence. Wurst aimed and fired, hitting one of the Germans, then took aim on another. "Just as I was about to shoot, Bill opened up with his .45-caliber Tommy gun. One instant the German was in my sights and the next he was flat on the ground. He must have been hit by a number of the .45 slugs, because he went down very fast. The other German threw his hands up in surrender, and we approached him after an intense visual search of the surrounding area. Bill and I moved up to where the bodies were lying, and Lieutenant [Jack P.] Carroll came up with a few others from the platoon. One of the Germans was dead, and three or four of our men gathered around to watch the other one die.

"This is one of the few times I actually saw at close range the result of my own fire, or that of my squad. I thought the German was suffering terribly, and without thinking, I asked the lieutenant whether I should finish him off. Much to his credit, he absolutely refused. The sight of that man lying there slowly dying lingers in my mind to this day. He has been the subject of many nightmares over the years. I hesitate to think what kind of dreams I'd have now, if I'd put the man out of his misery."[81]

Private First Class Dale C. Hudson was acting as scout when his Company F squad came under fire from a high velocity gun. Hudson voluntarily drew the attention of the crew by making himself a target. This allowed his squad to deploy and bring effective fire on the crew, causing them to surrender and the gun to be captured. Later that day, when his squad came under heavy fire from several automatic weapons, Hudson again moved into the open to draw fire. Machine gun fire was concentrated on Hudson, allowing the squad to get close enough to kill all of the gunners of the machine gun positions, but sadly Hudson was killed before the enemy machine gun nests were knocked out. Private First Class Hudson was posthumously awarded the Silver Star for his gallantry.

Company F fought its way to the main north-south highway, where it ambushed German traffic moving south, scattering it, then pushed on until reaching the road that ran west from town. There, it set up a roadblock, preventing the Germans from using it as an avenue of retreat. Company D cut the road leading south from St.-Sauveur-le-Vicomte.

The 505th consolidated and expanded the bridgehead west and north, while the 508th PIR arrived and did the same, to the south and southwest of the town. The next day, the 9th Infantry Division passed through the bridgehead and attacked west to the coast, cutting the peninsula.

Over the next couple of days, the troopers' barracks bags arrived and they were able to bathe, shave, and change clothes. They now had bedrolls and blankets, and the much better five-in-one and ten-in-one rations.

ONE OF THE WORST STORMS in fifty years struck the English Channel, lasting from June 19 to 21, damaging and sinking many Allied small ships and destroying the Mulberry harbor at Omaha Beach that brought much of the ammunition, rations, equipment, vehicles, guns, and men to Normandy. The supply tonnage at the onset of the storm, only seventy-three percent of plan, dropped to only fifty-seven percent. This forced Allied commanders to accelerate the capture of the Cherbourg port to replace the destroyed Mulberry harbor. The VII Corps was given priority for supplies.

On June 20, the 2nd Battalion moved south of the Douve River into the Bois de Limors, digging in behind the 3rd Battalion in the forest. It carried out aggressive patrolling while preparing for the next attack. Two weeks of almost continuous combat had severely depleted the battalion, and like the rest of the division, it had received no replacements during the Normandy campaign.

From June 19 through July 2, overcast skies and rain kept the troopers wet and cold, even though they covered their waterlogged foxholes with wood and mud. A shortage of rations caused the troopers to be continually hungry. Both Allied and enemy aircraft strafed them while in the Bois de Limors. In short, life was miserable.

The battalion conducted many patrols into the German positions to the west to gain knowledge of the strength and disposition of the enemy in the coming attack. Corporal John Durst led one such patrol of Company F troopers into German lines on June 23, when they were trapped by a numerically superior force. Durst led them to the temporary shelter of a large monument, where they took up defensive positions. However, Durst knew that if they stayed they would eventually be killed or captured. Without regard for his safety Durst deliberately crossed the road in plain sight of the enemy drawing their attention and fire, allowing his patrol to make an escape. Corporal Durst was killed as he did so and was later posthumously awarded the Silver Star for his self-sacrifice.

Sergeant Eldon Clark's Company D mortar squad, now just four men, shared a single hole, which they had covered with branches and earth piled about two feet high. On the night of June 24, Clark received an order to fire a flare shell from his squad's 60mm mortar, because of enemy activity in front of the company's line. "We knew that firing that flare would mark right where we were. Right after we fired it, those 88s were coming in. We crawled in the tunnel of our hole—during the night the ground was just shaking. We had about two feet of soil above us and we were kind of worried that it might cave in on us.

"When the morning came, everything was quiet and we crawled out of there. [Private John O.] Haggard told me, 'You know Clark, I didn't go to church, but I did learn the Lord's Prayer in school. I just said the Lord's Prayer over and over all night long.'

"I said, 'That's what the Lord said, "When you pray, pray our Father Who art in heaven."

"We were all standing out of the hole and we had this lemon concentrate that you put water in to make this lemon drink. All of the sudden—[an explosion]—and all of us just jumped back in the hole, except Haggard. He just bent down to be behind that ledge [of earth piled on top of the hole]. Then another explosion and he hit the ground. There was a hole above his right eye about the size of a silver dollar—you could see his brain. It had just killed him right then and there."[82]

The Germans took advantage of the respite caused by the bad weather to reorganize and dig fortifications, plant minefields and booby traps in front of the line held by the 82nd Airborne Division, and registered their artillery and mortars on likely routes of approach.

On July 2, the division issued orders for an attack commencing at 6:30 a.m. the following day, with the objective of capturing the high ground northeast of the town of La Haye-du-Puits. On the division's right flank, the 505th PIR would attack with the 2nd Battalion leading, followed by the 1st and 3rd Battalions in a column of battalions. The regiment would move out of the Bois de Limors at 3:00 a.m. to the line of departure, a crossing over a creek that ran south through the village of Varenquebec. At that point, the 1st Battalion would move up and attack on the right of the 2nd Battalion, with the 3rd Battalion mopping up. The regimental objectives were to seize the northern slope and crest of Hill 131 and cut the St.-Sauveur-le-Vicomte to La Haye-du-Puits highway. The 79th Infantry Division would be on the right flank of the 505th.

AT 3:00 A.M. ON JULY 3, the 2nd Battalion moved out in the darkness in a column of companies. Sergeant Spencer Wurst was one of only about fifty-five officers and men remaining with Company F. "As we moved up to the line of departure, we saw that Colonel Vandervoort had preceded us. There he was, in a raincoat with his crutch, his leg either still in a cast or heavily bandaged. It was pretty tough going for me and my squad, let alone for someone with a crutch and only one good leg."[83]

Upon reaching the line of departure, the battalion went into attack formation. Captain Hubert Bass, now the 2nd Battalion executive officer, watched the battalion's troopers drive forward. "A heavy English fog had settled over the countryside. Enemy heavy artillery pounded our positions. Their infantry continued to withdraw in great haste."[84]

The 2nd Battalion's primary opposition was mines, booby traps, and mortar and artillery fire. Shortly before 10:00 a.m., it reached Phase Line "B," where it wheeled to the left and attacked the northern slope and crest of Hill 131, while the 1st Battalion pushed west to cut the St.-Sauveur-le-Vicomte to La Haye-du-Puits highway. Private First Class Frank Bilich was carrying D Company's heavy SCR 300 radio. "E Company was on the left, D Company up the middle, and F Company on the right. There was a little winding road that went back and forth up to that hill, and went around and disappeared. Our job was to come up from the front. At that time, we thought that was a real strong position."[85]

Sporadic artillery shells landed in the area as Private First Class Bilich moved up the hill with company headquarters. "There was a little stone wall about two feet tall that separated the fields. There was a piece torn out of it, like a shell had hit it. We were crawling along that wall as we were going up the hill. We got about three-quarters of the way up and an artillery barrage came from a different direction. [Private First Class George J.] Rajner was up about two guys. There was Captain [Taylor G.] Smith, Sergeant [John] Rabig, a couple of other guys, and me. All of the sudden an SP [self-propelled gun] or something fired a direct round right through that opening, right where Rajner was—shrapnel just hit him all over. He moaned for a couple of minutes and told John Rabig, 'I'm in bad shape.' Orders were to keep moving—you can't do anything. They threw a couple more rounds in, but nobody got wounded.

"We made it to the top of the hill, and there was a dug in communications center, and the phones were still ringing."[86]

A brief firefight broke out with surprised Germans at the observation post. Private First Class Robert Robinson, with Headquarters Company, 2nd Battalion, was shot by a German officer with a pistol at a range of about four feet. "The shot knocked me to my knees—it felt like a heavy blow. I disarmed the officer and took the pistol. It wasn't until several minutes later that I realized that there was a hole in the front and back of the shoulder of my raincoat. It was then I realized that I had been shot clean through the shoulder."[87]

Vandervoort's troopers quickly overran the observation post, capturing eighteen Germans, and securing Hill 131. This effectively ended the battalion's fighting in Normandy.

On July 8, the battalion as part of the 505th went into corps reserve and moved to the rear to clean up. Three days later, the 82nd Airborne Division loaded on to LSTs at Utah Beach for the return to England the following day.

For its actions in the defense of Ste.-Mère-Église, of which Vandervoort and the 2nd Battalion played a major role, the 505th received a Presidential Unit Citation. Additionally, Lieutenant Colonel Vandervoort, Lieutenant Wray, and Lieutenant Doerfler were awarded the Distinguished Service Cross for heroism and leadership during the defense of Ste.-Mère-Église.

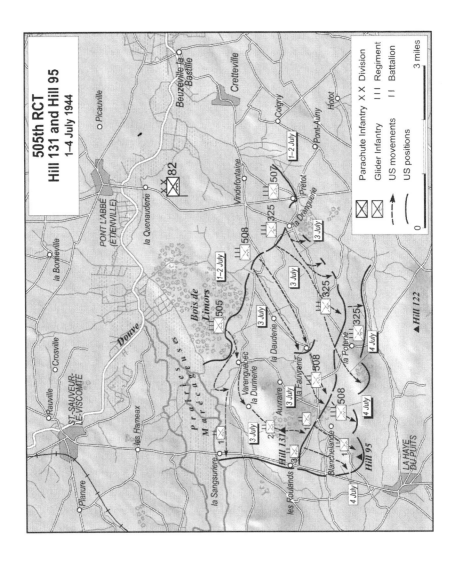

PHOTO GALLERY

Major Ben Vandervoort (right) and Colonel Jim Gavin (center) inspect the 505th Parachute Infantry at Oujda, French Morocco. *U.S. Army photograph, National Archives*

Paratroopers recover equipment bundles and set up an 81mm mortar in the back ground, during a practice jump near Oujda, French Morocco, in June 1943. *U.S. Army photograph, National Archives*

AN IRRESISTIBLE FORCE

Medics administer aid to a paratrooper injured during a practice jump near Oujda, French Morocco, in June 1943. *U.S. Army photograph, National Archives*

Equipment bundles are loaded on racks under a C-47 in preparation for an upcoming jump. *U.S. Army photograph, National Archives*

PHOTO GALLERY

Paratroopers prepare
for the Sicily jump,
July 9, 1943.
*Photograph courtesy
of Jan Bos*

This pillbox is typical of those encountered and destroyed by the 2nd Battalion,
505th Parachute Infantry Regiment upon landing in Sicily, July 10, 1943. *U.S.
Army photograph, 82nd Airborne Division War Memorial Museum*

AN IRRESISTIBLE FORCE

The awful price of combat—dead paratroopers await burial near Vittoria, Sicily, July 1943. *U.S. Army photograph, National Archives*

Heavily laden paratroopers with Headquarters Company, 2nd Battalion enter Naples, October 2, 1943. *U.S. Army photograph, National Archives*

PHOTO GALLERY

An aerial photograph of the town of Arnone, Italy was the final objective of the 2nd Battalion. It was located in a bend of the Volturno River at the upper right. The railroad yard, the scene of heavy fighting by Company E is at the left center. *U.S. Air Corps photograph courtesy of Mark Sparry*

AN IRRESISTIBLE FORCE

The 505th Parachute Infantry Regiment encampment located the grounds of the Quorn House on Wood Lane in Quorndon, England. *Photograph courtesy of the 82nd Airborne Division War Memorial Museum*

Company D officers: Lieutenant Oliver B. "O. B." Carr, Jr. at top left and kneeling left to right, Lieutenants Wavery W. Wray, Charles W. Qualls, and Thomas J. McClean. *Photograph courtesy of the 82nd Airborne Division War Memorial Museum*

PHOTO GALLERY

The 2nd Platoon Mortar Squad, Company F. From left to right: Sergeant John P. Ray, Private First Class Philip M. Lynch, Private John M. Steele, and Private Vernon L. Fransisco ready for an inspection. *Photograph courtesy of the 82nd Airborne Division War Memorial Museum*

The three 505th pathfinder teams, including the 2nd Battalion team (above) were largely responsible for the successful drop by the 505th Parachute Infantry Regiment in Normandy. *U.S. Army photograph courtesy of Julius Eisner*

AN IRRESISTIBLE FORCE

The primary D-Day objective of the 505th Parachute Infantry Regiment, the key crossroads town of Ste.-Mère-Église, the capture and retention of which was vital for the protection of Utah Beach against German armored counterattacks. *U.S. Army photograph, National Archives*

A Company F light machine gun team dug in east of Ste.-Mère-Église on the morning of June 6, 1944. *Photograph courtesy of Michel De Trez*

PHOTO GALLERY

Lieutenant Colonel Vandervoort at his command post on the northern edge of Ste.-Mère-Église on June 6, 1944. Vandervoort's left ankle is wrapped in a gasmask bag. The crutch he would use for the entire Normandy campaign, given to him that morning by a lady citizen of Ste.-Mère-Église, lies at his side. Note the portable radio at the lower left of the photo. *Photograph courtesy of Michel De Trez*

AN IRRESISTIBLE FORCE

A German Sturmgeschütz knocked out at the northern edge of Ste.-Mère-Église by a 57mm antitank gun manned by troopers with Battery A, 80th Airborne Antiaircraft (Antitank) Battalion. *Photograph courtesy of Robert M. Piper*

The 57mm antitank gun sits beside the destroyed self-propelled gun shown in the preceding photograph shortly after the action by Private John Atchley, with Company H, to destroy the second self-propelled gun shrouded in smoke in the distance. *Photograph courtesy of the 82nd Airborne Division War Memorial Museum*

PHOTO GALLERY

The German self-propelled gun, single-handedly destroyed by Private John E. Atchley, just north Ste.-Mére-Église. *U.S. Army photograph, 82nd Airborne Division War Memorial Museum*

Looking south, the same German self-propelled gun as seen above. The self-propelled gun on the opposite page can be seen in the background. *U.S. Army photograph, 82nd Airborne Division War Memorial Museum*

AN IRRESISTIBLE FORCE

An 81mm mortar is fired by a crew with Headquarters Company, 2nd Battalion in defense of Ste.-Mère-Église, June 7, 1944. *Photographic still of U.S. Army combat camera film, courtesy of Tyler Alberts and www.combatreels.com*

Troopers with the 505th Parachute Infantry move along a hedgerow lined road in Normandy. Note the Browning Automatic Rifle (BAR) carried by the trooper looking back at the camera. *Photographic still of U.S. Army combat camera film, courtesy of Tyler Alberts and www.combatreels.com*

PHOTO GALLERY

Lieutenant Eugene A. Doerfler, the 2nd Battalion S-2 at the left and Lieutenant Colonel Vandervoort at the center of the photograph were awarded the Distinguished Service Cross for extraordinary heroism during the Normandy campaign. Captain James T. Maness, the 2nd Battalion adjutant is at the right. *Photograph courtesy of Michel De Trez*

One of the two German 75mm antitank guns that opposed Company D at Rosiers, east of St.-Sauveur-le-Vicomte on June 15, 1944. *Photograph by Dr. Daniel B. McIlvoy, courtesy of Mrs. Ann McIlvoy Zaya*

Wounded German prisoners await treatment, while their dead comrades lie in the ditch on the right side of the photo. *U.S. Army photograph, 82nd Airborne Division War Memorial Museum*

Aerial photograph of St.-Sauveur-le-Vicomte. The Douve River along the lower portion and the bridge at the lower right of the photograph. *U.S. Army photograph, National Archives*

The 2nd Battalion moves through the rubble strewn streets of St.-Sauveur-le-Vicomte on June 16, 1944. Lieutenant Colonel Vandervoort is at the left center with his left leg in a cast and using a crutch. *U.S. Army photograph, National Archives*

AN IRRESISTIBLE FORCE

The 2nd Battalion moves through St.-Sauveur-le-Vicomte, shortly after an American artillery barrage destroyed German forces in and around the town, June 16, 1944. *U.S. Army photograph, National Archives*

General Omar Bradley, commander of the First Army during the Normandy campaign decorates Lieutenant Colonel Vandervoort with the Distinguished Service Cross for his extraordinary heroism during the defense of Ste.-Mère-Église. *U.S. Army photograph, 82nd Airborne Division War Memorial Museum*

CHAPTER 5

"The Best Damned Soldiers In The War"

Lieutenant Colonel Vandervoort's courage and combat leadership during the fierce fighting in Normandy had inspired loyalty and respect from the officers and men of the 2nd Battalion. Vandervoort was now *their* colonel and commanding officer. Private First Class Frank Bilich observed that "after Normandy you didn't hear one guy say a bad word about him. Everybody said the same thing: 'That son of a bitch has got balls.'"[1]

Captain Lyle Putnam, the battalion surgeon felt that Vandervoort had "convinced every man of his battalion of his merits and qualities."[2]

Lieutenant Claiborne Cooperider, the executive officer of Headquarters Company, 2nd Battalion, felt that Vandervoort had "gained the respect of every enlisted man and officer in the battalion as a combat leader 'second to none.'"[3]

From his perspective, Vandervoort observed that the bonds among the troopers had strengthened as well. "The esprit-de-corps of the regiment grew with combat experience. Their motivation was 'mutual faith.' Every soldier knew that every other man would do his job in combat or die trying. They would not let each other down. Within the mutual faith, all competed to make the play to win the game. That faith and competitive spirit welded the regiment into a rough, tough, winning combat team."[4]

Back at Quorndon, England, empty cots in their tents reminded every officer and enlisted man of the price paid in blood for spearheading the assault on Hitler's fortress Europe; none more so than Vandervoort. "From an initial strength of 629, the 2nd Battalion, 505 had 298 casualties during its twenty-eight combat days in Normandy."[5]

Sergeant Spencer Wurst had been one of the men who had cut down the dead bodies of other Company F troopers hanging in the trees and on telephone poles in the town square at Ste.-Mère-Église. He had also witnessed men in his squad killed during the terrible fighting in Normandy. "The memory of these men was sharp in my mind as I trained their replacements in my squad at Quorn."[6]

The battalion received a large number of replacements for those killed in action, captured, missing in action, or wounded too severely to return to the unit. Even though Sergeant Wurst was a veteran of the fighting in Italy, he had not been a squad leader, as he had in Normandy. He had learned a great deal about being an infantryman and as a squad leader after two campaigns. Wurst was determined to teach those lessons to his new replacements. "After I had been shot at a few times, many things became second nature. Whenever we were moving, whether in an attack or approaching the front lines, whether in artillery, mortar, or small arms range, I kept my eyes open, continuously looking for signs of the enemy. This became automatic, as 'natural' as looking both ways before crossing a street. With every step, I asked myself, 'If I'm shot at now, where will I go? Where am I going to find cover?' To react quickly, you must prepare where you're going to go, minute by minute, second by second.

"I knew a soldier cannot afford to become tired. Get a little wavy, and things catch up with you. Mental alertness and quick reaction time were two essentials that enable soldiers to come back alive. I had seen its opposite, the thousand-yard stare in the eyes of solders—almost a trance. A soldier like this has been too long in combat. He will become one of the next casualties.

"I learned the tricks of the trade. When to dig. How deep to dig. Whenever I was placing my BAR and machine guns, I asked myself, 'What can the guns cover here that they can't cover over there?' In a defensive position, I always thought, 'How the hell am I going to get out of here if I have to? What's the safest and quickest way if I need to withdraw?' I always picked an alternate position from which to cover the same field of fire. I always thought about where I was going to move if I was attacked from the left, the left rear, the front, etc. Much of this is standard procedure, but being shot at really drums it into you. Only after you've been under fire do you *really* understand the importance of your training."[7]

Virtually every 2nd Battalion trooper who was a veteran of Normandy now understood why Lieutenant Colonel Vandervoort had emphasized tough and realistic training before Normandy. They now had to teach those tricks of the trade to the replacements before the next operation.

Lieutenant James J. Meyers, a replacement officer, arrived at Camp Quorn on July 18, 1944, and was assigned to Company D. "Upon entering the pyramidal tent that served as the D Company orderly room, the XO, 1st Lieutenant Waverly Wray, greeted me. Wray introduced me to the first sergeant, John Rabig, and he informed me the company commander would return shortly. In the meantime, he assembled the other company officers.

"I stood a quarter inch short of six feet, which made me the runt of the litter of platoon leaders. They were: 1st Platoon, 2nd Lieutenant Thomas J. McClean, three combat jumps, a big Irishman and a former New York City policeman; 2nd Platoon, 1st Lieutenant Oliver B. Carr, three combat jumps, a son of the old South from Palm Beach, Florida; 3rd Platoon, 2nd Lieutenant Charles K. Qualls, two combat jumps, a giant of a man.

"Assistant platoon leaders were Lieutenant [Isaac] Michelman, hospitalized and recovering from wounds; and 2nd Lieutenant Russell E. Parker, a former first sergeant, three combat jump veteran, and the recipient of a recent battlefield commission. I was a replacement for 1st Lieutenant Turner B. Turnbull, killed in action in Normandy.

"Following the introductions, McClean asked me, 'What do we call you?'

"I replied, 'Jim.'

"He paused, looked at me and said, 'We have too many Jims in this outfit. From now on your name is Joe.' I thought he was joking. He was not and to this day my airborne colleagues know me as 'Joe.'

"When the CO, Captain Taylor G. Smith, returned, he met 'Joe' Meyers. He assigned me as Tom McClean's assistant. I had much to learn and Tom had extensive combat experience. He could teach me the ropes."[8]

Lieutenant Meyers was briefed on the unofficial table of organization and equipment that had been adopted before Normandy, adding a squad to each platoon in a parachute infantry company. "Company headquarters had a CO, XO, first sergeant, operations sergeant, company clerk, supply sergeant, supply clerk, and armorer. Each of the three rifle platoons had three twelve-man rifle squads, a 60mm mortar section, a rocket launcher (bazooka) team, and a platoon headquarters with a platoon leader, assistant platoon leader, platoon sergeant, and a radio/telephone operator (RTO). Each rifle squad had a light machine gun (LMG) and a Browning automatic rifle (BAR). One squad member was the assistant LMG gunner and the rest of the squad's riflemen had the additional duty of carrying added ammunition for the LMG. In our company, the only true rifleman was the squad leader. As long as the ammunition held out, the airborne platoon had roughly two to three times the firepower of a straight infantry rifle platoon.

"I soon met the men of the 1st Platoon and I noted this unit was different. Although I was only twenty-one, I was slightly older than most of the men and about the same age as the NCOs. Although I was one of the youngest officers in the regiment, the age spread was smaller. The captains were in their mid-twenties; the battalion commanders in their early thirties; Bill Ekman, the regimental commander was about thirty-four; and General Gavin was thirty-six or thirty-seven. Ridgway was the old man at fifty-one. Age wasn't a problem, but the men took note of my lack of combat experience. In various ways, they let me know I was the new kid on the block. D Company officers were close knit. They made it crystal clear: 'Make your friends within the company.'

"Enlisted replacements also joined the company, some from the packet I brought overseas. D Company set about integrating us into the organization.

"Our diet in England consisted of endless meals of Brussels sprouts and Spam. The troops could do nothing about the Spam, but during training, they never missed an opportunity to step on Brussels sprouts growing in the fields.

"Wartime England was a heavily populated country and space was at a premium. Tactical training took place on pastureland or uncultivated fields. This presented a problem to our troops. The English farmers used human feces for fertilizer. Although the feces was usually hard and dry, crawling through turds was not a popular pastime.

"Corporal Edward J. 'Ozzie' Olszewski shared some of his knowledge with me. While undergoing training in daylight scouting and patrolling, Ozzie and I sat on a high hill overlooking the training area. Ozzie quizzed me on the location of the patrols as they moved along fence lines and hedgerows below. My efforts to detect the movement of members of the patrols failed. But, Ozzie knew the exact location of the patrols and the direction of their movement.

"He let me in on the tricks of the trade. As a patrol moved along a hedgerow, nesting birds took flight. Although I was familiar with livestock, I had not noted or taken advantage of the curiosity of cows and horses. They almost always turn and stare at nearby humans. In combat, this type of information is life insurance."[9]

During the remainder of July and the month of August, some of those wounded or jump injured during the Normandy campaign returned to the 2nd Battalion.

IN EARLY AUGUST, General Eisenhower promoted Major General Ridgway to command the newly formed XVIII Airborne Corps, consisting of the 82nd, 101st, and 17th Airborne Divisions as part of the newly constituted First Allied Airborne Army. Ridgway recommended Brigadier General Gavin for promotion to major general and command of the 82nd Airborne Division, which General Eisenhower approved. At thirty-seven year old, Gavin was the youngest major general since George Armstrong Custer. On August 16, 1944, Gavin assumed formal command of the division.

The 2nd Battalion made a number of changes in command and staff positions as the regiment reorganized and trained for new operations. Captain Taylor Smith remained as the commander of Company D. Captain Clyde Russell, still suffering from repeated bouts of malaria was returned to the United States. The 2nd Battalion pathfinder team leader, Lieutenant James J. Smith, took command of Company E. A West Point graduate fresh from the United States, Captain Robert H. Rosen, was assigned to command Company F. Hubert Bass was promoted to major and remained as executive officer of the battalion.

LED BY GENERAL GEORGE S. PATTON'S THIRD ARMY breakout near St. Lo, France in mid-August, the Allied armies encircled and destroyed most of the German forces west of the Seine River. Those Germans who escaped what became known as the Falaise pocket were pursued toward the German border by the highly mobile Allied ground forces. The major obstacle to the complete destruction of Germany was one of logistics and fatigue of the soldiers. The Allies were still bringing supplies in over the beaches at Normandy. The most acute shortage was gasoline. General Bradley turned to the IX Troop Carrier Command to ferry gasoline across to the continent to keep the tanks, trucks, half-tracks, jeeps, and countless other vehicles rolling eastward.

The commanders at the Supreme Headquarters Allied Expeditionary Force (SHEAF) wanted badly to get the newly formed airborne army's elite troops sitting at its bases in England, into the fight. Several missions were devised to accomplish that desire. The first, a three division operation to capture the bridges over the Escaut River, north of Tournai, Belgium, planned for September 3, was briefed to the commanders of the 82nd, 101st, and British 1st Airborne Divisions at British General Frederick Browning's British I Airborne Corps headquarters on August 29. Fortunately, the 82nd Airborne Division maintained a high degree of readiness and was largely prepared for the operation when the orders for the operation came down. The division was sealed in at the airfields when the operation was cancelled because of rain and Allied armor overrunning the area of the planned operation.

General Browning then developed an airborne plan to jump near Liège, Belgium to block the retreat of the German Army through that area.

On September 10, Gavin attended another briefing at Browning's headquarters. "It was conducted generally by Browning and had to do with a new plan envisioning a drop for the 82nd to seize bridges at Grave and Nijmegen and the high ground between Nijmegen and Groesbeek. That the plan would go through was all agreed to; Browning was to command it and had it all set up. The troop carrier lift was not set, however."[10]

The plan was part of British Field Marshal Bernard L. Montgomery's Operation Market Garden. General Lewis H. Brereton, commanding the First Allied Airborne Army, wanted the operation to commence on September 14, but availability of troop carrier aircraft forced the delay of the operation until Sunday, September 17, less than seven days away.

The operation entailed dropping three airborne divisions behind German lines in southern Holland to seize and secure bridges over canals and rivers for a drive by the British Second Army north from the Dutch-Belgian border to the Rhine River, where it would turn east into the Ruhr valley and overrun the heart of Germany's industrial war production.

The 101st Airborne Division would jump north of the city of Eindhoven, seize bridges over the Aa River and Zuid Willems Vaart Canal at Vechel, over the Dommel River at St. Oedenrode, and the Wilhelmina Canal at Zon, then drive south through Eindhoven to link up with the British XXX Corps, spearheading the British ground force.

The British 1st Airborne Division and the attached Polish 1st Independent Parachute Brigade would drop north of the 82nd to capture and hold a single bridge over the Rhine River at Arnhem, sixty-four miles deep in enemy territory.

The 82nd Airborne Division would jump fifty-three miles behind German lines to seize two bridges over the Maas River at Grave and Mook, two across the Waal River at Nijmegen, and five bridges across the Maas-Waal Canal. The division would also have to seize and hold high ground east and southeast of Nijmegen that dominated the route of the British Second Army and landing zones southeast and northeast of Groesbeek for glider-borne units to follow. The division's perimeter would be enormous and the objectives ambitious—only an elite veteran unit could accomplish the mission.

The intelligence reports of the likely enemy opposition in the area were ominous. The Order of Battle Summary report dated September 11, stated: "It is definitely established that many of the SS training units which were near Amsterdam are now quartered in the excellent barracks in Nijmegen. It is estimated there are four thousand of these SS troops; moreover, troops are also reported in St. Canisius College and the Marienboom Girls' School. There is little doubt that our operational area will contain a fair quota of Germans, and an estimate of a divisional strength in this area may not be far wide of the mark."[11]

Upon landing, the division had to engage and destroy German forces in the immediate area, including the SS troops reportedly around Nijmegen, and be prepared to defend against armored attacks from the Reichswald to the east and the Arnhem area to the north.

The 82nd Airborne Division's three parachute infantry regiments would jump south and southeast of Nijmegen. The 50th and 52nd Wings of the IX Troop Carrier Command would transport 7,250 paratroopers of the division to Holland in the first lift of 480 planes in eleven serials plus one fifty plane glider serial, September 17. Five-second intervals would separate each nine-plane V-of-V in each parachute serial.

Concerned about the possibility of German armor hidden in the Reichswald, General Gavin decided not to use pathfinders to mark the drop zones for the 505th and 508th prior to the jump. The 504th PIR pathfinders would lead the 82nd into Holland and jump at 12:30 p.m. to mark DZ "O" north of the Maas River.

The 505th would jump at DZ "N" southeast of Groesbeek, capture the town and the high ground to the west, and establish blocking positions south and east of Groesbeek to protect against attacks from the Reichswald and the Nijmegen-Gennep highway. The 2nd Battalion was scheduled to arrive at 1:00 p.m., the 3rd Battalion at 1:04 p.m., and the 1st Battalion serial at 1:08 p.m. Elements of regimental headquarters would accompany the 2nd and 3rd Battalion serials, while division headquarters personnel would jump with the 1st Battalion.

The veteran 504th Parachute Infantry Regiment, which had rejoined the division after the Anzio campaign in Italy, would jump southwest of Nijmegen at DZ "O" near Over Asselt between 1:10 and 1:18 p.m., and capture the bridge over the Maas River at Grave and bridges over the Maas-Waal Canal.

The 307th Airborne Engineer Battalion, less Headquarters and Headquarters Company and Company A, would jump on DZ "N" at 1:24 p.m. Company C would support the 504th, with Companies B and D providing security for the division command post.

The 508th would jump at DZ "T" northeast of Groesbeek, between 1:28 and 1:35 p.m., seize the high ground and establish roadblocks south and east of Nijmegen, and upon the completion of these objectives, move to capture the bridges across the Waal River in Nijmegen.

The veteran 376th Parachute Field Artillery Battalion would jump at DZ "N" at 1:40 p.m. and support the 504th and 505th as required.

The twelfth and last serial of fifty C-47s towing gliders transporting Battery A, 80th Airborne Antiaircraft (Antitank) Battalion and elements of division headquarters, division artillery headquarters, the 82nd Airborne Signal Company, the 82nd Airborne Reconnaissance Platoon, a forward air controller team, and a British SAS Phantom detachment would land on LZ "N" at 1:50 p.m.. Battery A, 80th Airborne Antiaircraft (Antitank) Battalion's eight 57mm guns would provide the division's initial antitank defense.

The planed parachute and glider operation would take just one hour and twenty minutes from beginning to end, with only fifty minutes from the arrival of the first battalion-sized element.

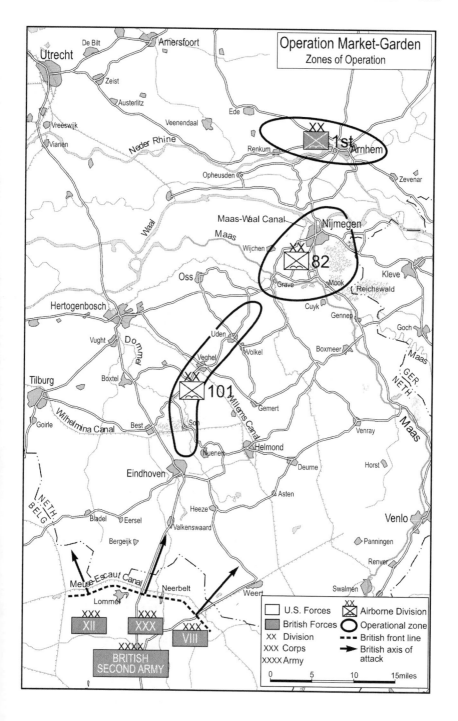

Operation Market-Garden
Zones of Operation

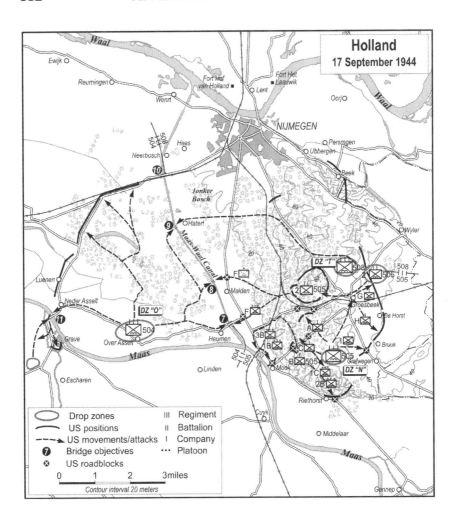

The remainder of the division's artillery (including the 456th Parachute Field Artillery Battalion), the rest of the 80th Airborne Antiaircraft (Antitank) Battalion and Company A, 307th Airborne Engineer Battalion, would arrive by glider on D+1.

The 325th GIR would land on D+2 and assemble in the division reserve area. The remaining elements of the division would move by sea, then over land to join the division.

The 505th commanding officer, Colonel Bill Ekman, issued orders for the 1st Battalion to "establish roadblock at Point 'A' [Mook], seize and hold railroad bridge at point 'B' [Maas River railroad bridge] and be prepared on regimental order to occupy high ground to southeast."[12]

Ekman ordered the 2nd Battalion to seize the high ground east of the Maas-Waal Canal and "establish and maintain contact with 504th Parachute Infantry at canal crossings at points 'J' and 'K' [Bridges 7 and 8] and if necessary in order to gain contact, assist in the seizure of these crossings."[13] The 2nd Battalion would act as the division reserve after capturing the high ground.

The 3rd Battalion was ordered "to seize and hold Groesbeek. Send reconnaissance patrol at once to ridgeline to southwest of Groesbeek, clear and secure LZ 'N' for glider and resupply lifts, and secure roadblocks [east and southeast of Groesbeek] as indicated after seizing Groesbeek."[14]

IN THE PREDAWN HOURS OF SUNDAY, September 17, people all over southern England awoke to the sound of 1,094 U.S. and British heavy and medium bombers taking off from airbases that dotted the countryside, to bomb German flak positions, airfields, and barracks in Holland in preparation for the airborne landings. The U.S. Eighth Air Force dispatched 872 B-17 Flying Fortress bombers, escorted by 147 P-51 Mustang fighters to strike 117 German targets along the troop carrier routes. The British dispatched 85 Lancaster, 65 Mosquito, 48 B-25, and 24 A-20 bombers accompanied by 53 Spitfire fighters to attack German defenses on the coast of Holland and troop barracks at Nijmegen, Arnhem, and Ede.

Later that morning, as paratroopers boarded their C-47s, they saw the sky beginning to fill with the more than 4,700 planes that would take part in the largest airborne operation in history. More than 1,500 fighter escort planes and fighter-bombers would provide protection. It was a comforting sight for the troopers.

At 10:19 a.m., C-47s from six airfields began lifting off the runways at five-second intervals, climbing to altitude, and vectoring to form up into formation. The 505th PIR flew in three serials. The 3rd Battalion serial, with elements of regimental Headquarters and Headquarters Company, and the 2nd Battalion serial, with elements of regimental Headquarters and Headquarters Company, took off from Folkingham airfield, while the 1st Battalion serial took off from Cottesmore airfield.

Lieutenant Bill Meddaugh, the Company E executive officer, was a veteran of three night combat jumps. "One of our company officers, Lieutenant Ted Peterson, had been wounded in the leg in Normandy, evacuated at that time, and returned to the company prior to our move to the airfields. He was limping badly, and it was obvious that his days in the airborne were numbered. His duties were limited to supply and administration, and he was very helpful during the few weeks prior to our departure.

"It became official, however, when we settled at the airfield that Pete was through as a paratrooper. It was a very poignant and painful time for all of us company officers who had served with Pete for the past eighteen months and had made three combat jumps with him. It was obvious that he wanted to go with us. I'm sure he felt like he was letting us down as he stayed behind. And we would have liked to have "old Pete" with us. He was dependable and we knew his capabilities. It was not in the cards, however, and as I strapped on my parachute and the rest of my gear, Pete was there to give me a hand. The word came down to board our aircraft, so I shook Pete's hand and he wished me good luck. He limped away to say goodbye to the rest of his good buddies as I climbed aboard my plane.

"In a few minutes our engines came to life and we were ready to roll. Planes began to move out of their parking positions and form a long line moving towards the active runway. I was standing in the open door in my customary place looking across the tarmac at what might be my last look at the English countryside.

"Suddenly, there was Pete, running alongside of my plane waving wildly in a frantic effort to get my attention. I waved back through the open door and Pete yelled at me. His words were drowned out by the roar of hundreds of engines, as more and more planes rolled out on the taxiways and began to take off. We picked up speed as we taxied and Pete was soon left behind. I had mixed emotions, which were impossible to sort out during this moment of intense excitement and anxious butterflies.

"But, I must have been thinking, 'You lucky son of a bitch, I wish it was me staying behind.' But, I knew I would have felt just like Pete—staying behind would have been unthinkable if there was any choice in the matter. As anxious and nervous as I was, I knew I couldn't be anywhere else at that moment. I had burned my bridges behind me when I volunteered for parachute duty so many months ago. This was where I wanted to be, even if some part of me rebelled somewhat. The die was cast!

"Our takeoff and movement into formation was routine but as always—exciting. We were to fly in a battalion serial, which consisted of three rifle companies and headquarters company—approximately forty aircraft. Each company was carried in nine or ten aircraft, depending on total number of personnel on the roster at that time. Each company flew in a V-of-Vs and the four companies flew in trail.

"After circling a few times to tighten up the formation, we headed towards the English Channel. What I saw in the next two hours prior to the jump was the most breathtaking and awesome experience I had ever been a part of. Aircraft formations, such as ours, were all over the sky. Three airborne divisions were involved in this operation—all of which were either airborne or close to it at this very moment.

"Takeoff points were scattered all over England from the Midlands to southern England—all converging on the drop areas which were about a sixty mile stretch from Eindhoven, through Nijmegen to Arnhem. In addition to all the troop carriers, squadron upon squadron of fighter aircraft were flying above us to provide protection from German fighters and to suppress flak installations. As we flew along our prescribed route and altitude, other formations, some carrying paratroopers, others towing gliders, would pass overhead or underneath on a different heading, giving the appearance of mass confusion.

"Standing up in the door of my plane I had a much better view of what was going on around us than the rest of my stick, who were reduced to watching through the small windows of the aircraft. I hooked up my static line in case I fell out, and stuck my head out of the open door as far as I could to enjoy the magnificent scene. It took my mind off the jump and upcoming fight."[15]

As jumpmaster, Lieutenant Meddaugh had a perfect view of the one-hundred-mile-long sky train of troop carrier planes and gliders, moving in three columns, ten miles wide. Above and on both flanks of the sky train Meddaugh saw fighter planes of all types—P-51 Mustangs, P-47 Thunderbolts, P-38 Lightnings, British Spitfires, Hurricanes, and Typhoons. "The sun continued to shine brightly, and as we passed over the channel it reflected off the water into a blaze of fire. It was a Sunday afternoon—in other times we all would have been off to the local swimming hole for a picnic. But today would be no picnic."[16]

Private First Class Dennis O'Loughlin, with Company E, "could see some of the damn fools sitting in the open doors of the planes with their feet hanging out. There was some nose thumbing going on back and forth while flying along in formation—a few antitank grenades being tossed out. We didn't like the ack-ack setting those things off in the planes. They always sent us more grenades anyhow."[17]

As the 2nd Battalion serial crossed the flooded coastal areas of Holland, Lieutenant Meddaugh "watched the tempo of the mission start to pick up speed. Sporadic small-arms fire rose to meet us, but in our immediate formation it was ineffective. I would estimate we were flying about 1,500 feet above the ground. And as I looked out the door I could see Dutch civilians running from their homes and waving to us. I was low enough to see their faces. I waved back. I could imagine their excitement, as it was obvious they recognized us as Allied forces—and their liberators! It was a rare form of flattery.

"I was brought back to reality rather abruptly when flak began to burst intermittently around the formation—ugly black puffs of smoke. I began to see fighters diving toward unseen antiaircraft batteries, which added to the overall scene of pandemonium. I clearly remember at one point an air burst exploding straight out from the door of my plane, and I flinched—an involuntary but normal reaction I guess. No damage anywhere that I could see and the formation drove on. It wasn't long before the crew chief came to my position at the door to warn me we were ten minutes from the DZ. I alerted my guys, and everyone made their individual last-minute preparations for the jump. At four minutes out, the red light over the door flashed bright and the show got underway."[18]

Lieutenant Meddaugh, upon seeing the flash of the red light by the door, began getting his stick ready. "'Stand up and hook up!'

"I shouted the command over the noise of the engines and eighteen men struggled with the weight of the equipment they were carrying and got to their feet. Their static line was hooked to the anchor line cable running the length of the C-47 in the same motion.

"Sergeant Roy Joster, who was jumping number two right behind me, was carrying a large radio used for communications with battalion in addition to all his other equipment. He needed help to rise up and get steady on his feet. I had him jump right behind me, as I knew he could crowd the door and step out more easily when I exited.

"'Check your equipment!'

"My next command was hardly necessary, as these men were all pros with enough jumps under their belts to be counted on to be properly rigged up. Their safety was their own responsibility in these circumstances—hardly a school jump.

"'Stand in the door!'

"There was a visible rush as everyone crowded forward and closed up tight behind me and Sergeant Joster. Each man's reserve chute on his chest, pressed tightly against the backpack of the man in front of him. The slightest gap or interval between each man as he went out the door was multiplied many fold in the spacing between men as they landed on the ground below. Not as important in a daylight jump as it is at night, but good habits are not tossed aside easily."[19]

Lieutenant William R. "Rusty" Hays, Jr., an assistant platoon leader with Company F, was a replacement making his first combat jump. "About five minutes out, we started running into flak. Since our altitude was only five hundred feet and we were slowing to one hundred miles per hour, preparing for the jump, we were pretty easy targets. As jumpmaster, I was standing in the door where I could get a clear view of all the black flak bursts. I could see every burst, I could hear the fragments as they zinged through the skin of the plane, and I sure wanted that green light to come on telling me it was time to jump."[20]

As the 505th neared the drop zone southeast of Groesbeek, there was a sudden problem—the 3rd Battalion serial and the 2nd Battalion serial were approaching DZ "N" at the same time almost side by side. With quick thinking on the part of Lieutenant Colonel Vandervoort, Colonel Ekman, and the pilot of the lead plane of the serial, the 2nd Battalion changed the drop zone to the open ground northeast of Groesbeek, near Kamp, on the edge of DZ "T," where the 508th would jump shortly.

Lieutenant James J. "Joe" Meyers, an assistant platoon leader with Company D, was also making his first combat jump. "We passed over the Maas-Waal Canal, one of our checkpoints. I watched the lead aircraft in the formation for the silk of Vandervoort's parachute—our signal to jump. We had descended to drop altitude, six hundred feet above the ground. The green light went on, and I saw Vandervoort's silk appear beneath his plane. I hit the toggle switches that released the parapack bundles, gave the door bundle a shove, and followed it out the open door. My parachute opened, and I oscillated once or twice before I landed in a large, open field along with dozens of other jumpers."[21]

Germans positioned around DZ "T" unleashed machine gun and 20mm antiaircraft fire on the C-47s and paratroopers as they descended.

Private Michael A. Brilla, with Company F, was a veteran of the Sicily and Salerno combat jumps. "The lad next to me in the plane was making his first combat jump, and flak came through our plane and cut his leg. I asked him if he wanted to jump or go back in the plane, but he said he would rather jump. So he did, and we patched him up when we hit the ground."[22]

Lieutenant Meddaugh watched for the sight of his company commander jumping as his signal to go. "I waited for the green light to flash, the signal from the pilot to jump. But, I watched the other planes in our company formation intently as well, because, green light or not, if I saw J. J. Smith jump from the lead plane, I would go immediately, to insure the company landed in as tight a formation as possible to facilitate our assembly on the DZ. This was standard operating procedure throughout the battalion.

"As I stuck my head farther out the door, I could see hundreds of parachutes in the air and on the ground out in front of the formation—Company D and Company F had led the battalion into the DZ and had already jumped. Adrenaline was flowing—I couldn't wait to get out of that airplane—my usual instinct seconds before a combat jump.

"Suddenly, I saw our six equipment bundles flash by underneath us. 'Shit, the pilot released the bundles too soon.' I knew this would make it more difficult to recover heavy equipment on the ground during the assembly phase. No time to worry—things are moving too fast. Let's get the hell out of here—flak bursts still in the vicinity of our formation. I see bodies coming out of the lead plane to my left front. J. J. has taken off!

"'Let's go!' I turned my head in the direction of the men behind me as I shouted the command and exploded from the door of the C-47. 'One thousand'—I'm floating, head tucked down on my chest. 'Two thousand'—my feet start to rise up and the weight of the chute rotates my body backwards as if I am sitting in a reclining chair. The roar of the engines begins to recede and the relative quiet is deafening. 'Three thousand.' I can see the silk deploying in front of me; 'come on baby, do your thing.'

"The chute pops open with a bang. God, we must have been flying too fast. It feels like I hit a stone wall. The parachute harness bites in my flesh and my body jerks violently as the brakes go on. The forward momentum slows dramatically, and the shock is absorbed in my leg and chest straps. I look up at the canopy and breathe a sigh of relief as I confirm a normal opening and no blown panels. Looks like number fifteen is going to be O.K. A quick look behind me and I can see that all the guys in my plane are out O.K. The sky is full of silk—what a sight. I turn my attention to the descent—we had jumped higher than planned—probably about 1,500 feet. There is a slight breeze, and the DZ is a huge open field with no trees or obstacles that I can see—a piece of cake. Five hundred feet—ah, ah! Do my eyes deceive me?

"A group of four German soldiers are running full speed across the DZ heading towards the spot where I expect to make contact with the ground. Are they after me personally? I frantically try to reach the .45-caliber pistol in the holster hooked to my pistol belt. My Thompson submachine gun is inaccessible, stowed underneath my reserve chute on my chest. The opening shock pulled my harness so tight across my entire body that I can't stretch my arm low enough to reach the pistol. I know I was the most vulnerable when I hit the ground and was still in my harness, and watch apprehensively as the group below me continues running like gangbusters.

"One hundred feet—to my relief I can see that my presumed executioners are not the least bit interested in me as an individual as they pass underneath me and continue to run towards the Motherland. One of them is unfastening his cartridge belt as he runs so he can increase his speed. I concentrate on my landing now and gather myself together for the impact. I land hard, as usual, but without further incident. I get out of my harness in record speed, throw my pack back over my shoulders, and ram a magazine of thirty rounds of .45-caliber ball into my Thompson. The adrenaline is still flowing, but all the butterflies are gone. Our parachutes and C-47s have done their job—transportation to the objective. Simply put, that is their function. We now revert to our primary role of combat infantry. Elite infantry in our own minds—but infantry, bottom line!"[23]

As he floated down, Captain Robert "Doc" Franco, the assistant regimental surgeon, could see tracers rising up and looked over just as "a man near me, descending at the same speed, was hit. He screamed obscenities at his unknown assailant and promised to get him as soon as he reached the ground—he probably did."[24]

As Private Edwin L. Raub, with Headquarters Company, 2nd Battalion, descended he was targeted by a 20mm antiaircraft gun. Knowing that the antiaircraft gun could do significant damage to the C-47s and paratroopers in their chutes, Private Raub slipped his chute toward the enemy position, instead of away from it, as 20mm shells ripped through his canopy. Landing on the edge of the emplacement, Raub pulled a pistol, and still in his parachute harness, hurdled into the position, where he killed one of the crew and captured the remainder. He disabled the gun before marching his prisoners to the assembly point. Private Raub was later awarded the Silver Star for his heroism.

Private First Class Frank Bilich, a radio operator with Company D, landed and quickly got out of his chute. "[Private First Class George] Fotovich and I landed near Lieutenant [Tom] McClean. The DZ was drawing fire from German soldiers in a home across the road. Men were gathering up equipment bundles, and next to me was one with a bazooka and rounds.

"Lieutenant McClean said, 'Put a round into that house.' Fotovich loaded it—I took aim and fired. The shot went right through the window, but nothing happened. Lieutenant McClean said, 'Hit it again.' Again, we followed the same procedure and nothing happened.

"Lieutenant McClean's platoon moved out and we joined company headquarters. His platoon went to clean out the Germans from the farmhouse. Most of the Germans faded into the woods or left in vehicles. When he went inside, he saw a large group of women crouched and praying. Both bazooka rounds had hit the interior wall and didn't explode. In our haste to fire, I suppose we forgot to pull the arming pin [on the bazooka rounds]."[25]

Bilich later found out from Lieutenant McClean that "in the front room of the house where the window was, was nothing but school children and a woman sitting there praying."[26]

A number of wooden flak towers mounting 20mm antiaircraft guns where the 2nd Battalion landed were put out of action in less than twenty minutes. Troopers climbed the towers and shot or grenaded anyone who didn't surrender.

After landing, Lieutenant Meddaugh helped get Company E organized and ready to move out to the objective, the high ground overlooking Groesbeek. "The task of assembly, recovering heavy equipment from the equipment bundles, and moving towards our objective got underway with the usual confusion which always followed a mass drop. The SNAFUs were greatly reduced however, since it was broad daylight. We soon discovered we were not dropped exactly as planned, but the battalion was organized, oriented on the ground and moving off the drop zone in rapid order. The jump phase of Operation Market Garden was over—and very successfully for E Company: no casualties and only a few minor jump injuries. What lay ahead of us for the next six weeks was to be much more painful and bloody."[27]

Upon landing northeast of Groesbeek, Lieutenant Colonel Vandervoort radioed his company commanders, telling them the 2nd Battalion assembly point would be an observation tower to the west at Molenberg, on the northern edge of Groesbeek. After gathering weapons and supplies from equipment bundles, the battalion moved to the assembly point. The battalion executive officer, Major Hubert Bass, and a group of troopers in the lead came under 20mm antiaircraft, machine gun, and small arms fire from the observatory, which was being used as a flak tower. The 20mm gun on top of the tower was able to be depressed enough to fire at the battalion. Major Bass and the small group of troopers with him immediately rushed the tower, drawing intense fire, killing three troopers and wounding several others. Bass and his group knocked out the 20mm antiaircraft gun with small arms and bazooka fire, and cleared the observatory, killing or capturing all of the Germans occupying it. Major Bass' quick reaction and decisive leadership saved further casualties and he was later awarded the Silver Star for his valor.

Major Daniel B. "Doc" McIlvoy, the regimental surgeon, found a German ambulance abandoned near where he landed. McIlvoy directed his men to load his unit's medical equipment in it and they joined the 2nd Battalion column. "On nearing the edge of the town, we saw a Volkswagen coming down the road, and after [it passed] several of us, we realized a Volkswagen wasn't GI issue. So finally, one of us decided to stop it. It turned out to be a German officer, who was driving down from Nijmegen and almost drove past a company or more of Americans without anyone knowing that this was anything unusual."[28]

After assembly, the 2nd Battalion moved west through the northern part of Groesbeek. Staff Sergeant Paul Nunan was a platoon sergeant with Company D. "As we moved through Groesbeek against very light resistance, the Hollanders began appearing from their hiding places. They seemed overjoyed at our arrival and eager to help. A group of them approached me, dragging and pushing a man wearing civilian riding boots, breeches, shirt, and brown jacket. After several minutes of scrambled conversation and sign language, it developed that the man was a local official appointed by the Nazis. As my men led him away, he received several sound kicks in the rear end from the townspeople."[29]

The battalion cleared the northern part of Groesbeek against almost no resistance. Doc McIlvoy moved in and set up an aid station. "We set up our regimental aid station in a German PX, which was abundantly supplied with the usual delicacies of a PX, plus an unlimited supply of Bendectin, [an anti-nausea drug,] which we stored among our medical supplies to use at a later date, at such time when we had a little bit more to celebrate."[30]

The 2nd Battalion then moved out toward its assigned objective, Hill 81.8 and the high ground west of the town. As platoon leader Lieutenant Jim Coyle, with the 1st Platoon, Company E, moved through the heavily wooded area, he had the fate of Staff Sergeant Otis Sampson's squad weighing on his mind. "I was afraid that he and the 1st Platoon 60mm mortar squad might have been shot down.

"As we approached the high ridgeline that we were to attack, I realized that it could be a difficult assault. There was some low brush, but no cover from enemy fire, which might come down the hill. We moved up the hill rapidly, although it was a hard climb with all the equipment we carried. We reached the crest without being fired upon. At the top, we found many small barracks, all empty, although there were fires going and warm food on the stoves. I saw no weapons or combat equipment anywhere. It appeared to me that the troops who had occupied the barracks were from a Todt Battalion, a work group, which had simply fled as we came up the hill. I could not believe the Germans did not have machine guns or artillery on the ridge. It was the only high ground in the area and they did not defend it.

"We set up a company perimeter on the hill. In a little over an hour, Sergeant Sampson came climbing up the hill with the mortar squad and the men who had jumped in his plane. They had had engine trouble on his C-47 and had to turn back to England. He had transferred the bundles and his planeload of men to another plane, when they reached the airfield and had taken off immediately for Holland again. I was very relieved to see him and the mortar squad and was quite surprised that he was able to rejoin the company after only a delay of an hour or two."[31]

Company F was assigned to contact the 504th Parachute Infantry Regiment at Bridge Numbers 7 and 8 across the Maas-Waal Canal and if needed, assist in securing them. Lieutenant Jack P. Carroll was the platoon leader of the 3rd Platoon of Company F. "The 1st Platoon of our company was sent to take the bridge west of the hill [Bridge Number 8 near Blankenberg]. The bridge had been blown, but the platoon went there anyway. The 2nd Platoon was sent to the bridge and lock southwest of the hill [Bridge Number 7 at Heumen]. This platoon was to take the east side of that bridge and a unit from the 504th Parachute Infantry was to take the west side and the lock. My platoon took over the company sector."[32]

After finding Bridge Number 8 blown, the 1st Platoon moved east and established a roadblock on the highway leading south from Nijmegen to Mook. Private First Class Robert R. Hughart was one of the troopers at the roadblock. "We were standing in and out of foxholes on both sides of the street. There were large two-storied homes and very large trees on both sides of the street. At dusk, two Germans came down the middle of the street on bikes. We waited until they got into the middle of us, then jumped out from behind trees and out of the holes, and tried to get them to surrender. One went for his pistol and was shot dead for his stupidity. The other got off his bike and we cut him down as he tried to run down the street."[33]

A short time later, Sergeant Russ Brown heard the sound of an approaching vehicle from the south, behind the roadblock. "A weapons carrier tried to run our roadblock, but the machine gun and everyone shot at it. The carrier hit a house and caught on fire. All night long the people in the house poured water on the fire from an upstairs window."[34]

Sergeant Spencer Wurst and his squad of the 3rd Platoon, Company F were dug in on ground overlooking a railroad track. "Our area ran northeast to southwest and was parallel to a railroad track, whose bed was 150 or 200 yards down the slope. Although the battalion was in reserve, not much over half of Company F was in the reserve defensive position. We dug in and passed the rest of the day uneventfully, awaiting orders. We sent some small patrols out to our front, and some contact patrols with the 1st Platoon roadblock out on one of the hardtop roads."[35]

Around dusk, Vandervoort's troopers heard a train approaching from the direction of Nijmegen. Everyone just stood dumbfounded as the train passed. Moving through Groesbeek, the train chugged past startled 3rd Battalion troopers on its way to Germany. Afterward an order was issued to stop all trains attempting to pass through the area. Sergeant Wurst, who had attended demolition school, took his squad down to the tracks. All of the antitank mines had been allocated to the 1st and 3rd Battalions for roadblocks, so Wurst and his men very carefully molded the Composition C from Gammon grenades to the sides and tops of the rails. They did this in darkness, where one wrong move would result in the whole group being killed or wounded. The improvised mines were then armed, and Wurst and his men returned to their positions.

THAT NIGHT, the 1st Battalion of the 508th Parachute Infantry Regiment attempted to capture the highway bridge over the Waal River in Nijmegen. The arrival of reinforcements from the 10th SS Panzer Division, which had been refitting in the Arnhem area, and confusion resulting from night urban combat stopped the Red Devils short of the objective.

JUST BEFORE DAWN ON SEPTEMBER 18, Lieutenant Rusty Hays, a replacement with Company F, heard the sound of a second train approaching from the direction of Nijmegen. "First the machine guns opened up; then it hit the Gammon grenades, which derailed the train. The engine came to a stop with steam hissing from the holes made by the machine guns. My guys went charging down the hill to shoot up the Germans on the train. I remember them bringing a German officer back who spoke English and was offended that even though he was wounded, they made him hold his hands up. He didn't get much sympathy; in fact, he was told that if he put his hands down, he would be shot."[36]

Later that morning, at the Company F roadblock south of Nijmegen, Private First Class Hughart inspected the vehicle that the platoon had ambushed and set on fire during the night. "With daylight, we found two dead Germans in the cab all burned to a crisp, and found out the truck was carrying meat, bread, and jam.

But this cargo was one big black mess. If only we had known at first, we might have been able to save something to eat."[37]

IN NIJMEGEN, the 1st Battalion, 508th was preparing to resume the assault to capture the Nijmegen highway bridge, when word was received that the Germans had overrun the landing zones for the reinforcements due to arrive later that day. The battalion was ordered to withdraw from Nijmegen to make an attack to recapture the landing zone northeast of Groesbeek.

ON THE MORNING OF SEPTEMBER 19, elements of the British Guards Armoured Division affected a linkup with the 82nd Airborne Division. There was no radio contact between the British 1st Airborne Division and the British Second Army. However, Vandervoort was aware of the desperate situation of the British airborne, thanks to the Dutch Underground's use of the country's modern telephone system. "Sometime on September 18, 1944, the telephone rang in a little railroad substation in the Groesbeek woods. The caller was a British paratrooper at Arnhem. He said the British Airborne had experienced stiff German resistance and needed the British armored column to link up and provide help as soon as possible. That information was passed to our regimental command post. Several follow up calls in the same vein were received before we were ordered out of the area."[38]

BY THE EARLY AFTERNOON OF SEPTEMBER 19, German forces defending the two massive Waal River bridges in Nijmegen were formidable. Kampfgruppe Euling, commanded by SS Captain Karl-Heinz Euling, defended the highway bridge. The force consisted of elements of the attached 9th SS Reconnaissance Battalion, one company of 10th SS engineers, and Euling's understrength battalion of panzer grenadiers, transferred from the 9th SS to the 10th SS the previous week. It was dug in in Hunner Park on the southern approach to the highway bridge. Other units, also under Euling's command, defending the highway bridge were the 4th Company, 572nd Heavy Flak Battalion (with four 88mm dual-purpose guns and eight 20mm antiaircraft guns), and a company of paratroopers of the Hermann Göring Training Regiment, defending the Villa Belvoir east of Hunner Park. A battalion of 10th SS tank crews without their tanks were dug in around Lent near the north end of the highway bridge. Defending Nijmegen south of the river between the two bridges were a group of reserve police companies and an assortment of other rear area units known as Kampfgruppe Melitz. Kampfgruppe Runge, consisting of an understrength NCO training school company of the Hermann Göring Training Regiment, three companies of a reserve battalion of the 406th Division, and some combat engineers, totaling some 500 to 750 men, defended the railroad bridge and the rail yard. In all, approximately two thousand Germans defended the two massive bridges.

Antitank guns covered all streets approaching the bridges, with strongpoints in key buildings leading to the open areas around the bridges. The SS grenadiers and engineers had dug deep trenches and gun pits in Hunner Park, the railroad embankment, fortified the ruins of the ancient Valkhof, and positioned 20mm antiaircraft guns in an antipersonnel role at the approaches of the two bridges. The company of paratroopers defending the Villa Belvoir placed machine guns in windows on the upper floors, dug trenches around the building, and encircled it with barbed wire entanglements. Two Mark IV Panzerjäger self-propelled guns concealed in Hunner Park and two more at the railroad bridge provided a mobile antitank defense.

An SS artillery training regiment north of the river near Oosterhout and an artillery battalion of the 10th SS near the Pannerden ferry crossing provided indirect fire support. On the north side of the river, SS Major Leo Reinhold directed the overall defense.

It was imperative that the Nijmegen bridges be captured as soon as possible to allow the British ground forces to drive to Arnhem and relieve the hard pressed British 1st Airborne Division. General Gavin chose the 2nd Battalion, 505th to make the assault to capture the bridges. Vandervoort was confident that his combat tested battalion was up to the challenge. "They were the fortunate survivors of three hard parachute night combat assaults—Sicily, Italy, and Normandy. Excepting a few handpicked replacements, yet to be bloodied in combat, they were aggressive, skilled warriors. Their marksmanship, battle reflexes, and survival instincts were finely tuned by being shot at—close and often. There were fraternal bonds between the battalion officers and men, especially the lieutenants. They were outstanding. They were raised to be last in the chow line and first out the door in the jump line. Their creed was, 'take care of the men and they'll take care of you.' Based on mutual faith, it worked well. What the troopers had was esprit de corps. They thought of themselves as AMERICAN PARATROOPERS—the best damned soldiers in the war."[39]

CHAPTER 6

"You Fired Fast And Straight"

Vandervoort received orders on the morning of September 17, attaching his battalion to the famed British Guards Armoured Division. "We were honored to be a momentary part of their distinguished company. Our job was to help the armor attack through the city of Nijmegen to seize the southern ends of the highway and railroad bridges over the broad Waal River. The British were to then continue north without us. General Allan Adair, commander of the elite Guards Armoured Division was to command the operation."[1]

British infantry of No. 2 Company, 1st Grenadier Guards Battalion and four troops of Sherman tanks of No. 3 Squadron, 2nd Grenadier Guards Battalion were selected for the joint British and American operation. Some of the Guards' Sherman tanks were the Firefly version, with a 17-pounder main gun, which had enough velocity and penetrating power to take on any German tank.

This force was divided into two task forces. The Western Force consisting of Company D, 505th; one troop of tanks from No. 3 Squadron, 2nd Grenadier Guards; and a platoon of infantry from No. 2 Company, 1st Grenadier Guards, were assigned the capture of the railroad bridge as its objective. The Eastern Force, composed of Companies E and F, and Headquarters Company, 2nd Battalion, 505th; three troops of tanks of the No. 3 Squadron, 2nd Grenadier Guards Battalion; and three platoons of No. 2 Company, 1st Grenadier Guards Battalion, were assigned the objective of capturing the highway bridge.

The paratroopers and Grenadier Guards rendezvoused at the Sionshof Hotel just north of Groesbeek. The combined forces moved out at 1:45 p.m., northeasterly along the tree-lined Groesbeeksweg for four miles into Nijmegen.

Twelve Dutch guides familiar with the Nijmegen streets rode on the lead tanks. Lieutenant J. J." Smith, the E Company commander, was glad to have them. "Dutch underground assistance was very valuable at this time, as they had intimate knowledge of the German disposition and their latest movements. We had been informed by the underground representative we had with us, that there would be no resistance until we reached a point some six hundred yards south of the bridge. Their information stated that the Germans had extremely strong positions all around the bridge and that [they] had a number of antitank guns all around the position."[2]

The order of the column was Company E, Company F, and Company D, followed by No. 2 Company, 1st Grenadier Guards Battalion, riding in Bren gun carriers. Some of the paratroopers hitched ride on the Guards' Shermans, while others piled their musette bags and heavy weapons on the back decks of the tanks and marched ahead and alongside.

Private First Class Don Lassen and the 3rd Platoon were following behind the 1st and 2nd Platoons in the Company E column. "We walked into the south edge of the town in a squad column. When we first approached the town, there was no resistance. I remember that before we got into Nijmegen proper we took a ten minute break along the road and the people were coming out from their houses with apples and pears and water, giving us anything they could. They started hoisting their Dutch flags on their flag poles and were genuinely happy.

"About that time, an artillery shell came from nowhere and the picture changed immediately. They pulled down their flags and rushed back into their houses and locked the doors, fearful for what may lie ahead for them."[3]

As the column moved into Nijmegen, First Sergeant John Rabig, riding on one of the tanks with other D Company troopers, made a similar observation. "The nearer we got to Nijmegen, the fewer people there were. Soon the people just disappeared, and we were smart enough to know that the shooting would soon start—and it did."[4]

When the column reached Wezenlaan, the Western Force took that street west around the outskirts of the city via Groenestraat. Lieutenant Colonel Vandervoort remained with the Eastern Force. Lieutenant J. J. Smith was up front with the lead elements of Company E when at approximately 3:15 p.m., the enemy opened fire upon them. "The Sherman tanks that were leading the attack ran into enemy resistance and were receiving extremely heavy fire from 88s and other high-velocity antitank weapons. The enemy immediately placed [small arms and mortar] fire on the lead elements of the infantry, which was the 1st Platoon of Company E. All the mortar fire and artillery fire at this time came from this side of the bridge, and it seemed to be observed fire. We later determined this to be true, as we discovered snipers and enemy observers had radios and seemed to be in communication with the guns firing. The tanks, having been fired on, proceeded to place fire in the adjacent buildings and covered the area to our front with fire."[5]

Private First Class Lassen and the other E Company troopers had difficulty locating the well hidden German positions. "They were firing at us out of the windows of the third and fourth story apartment buildings. We couldn't see them nor tell where the firing was coming from."[6]

The Germans had positioned several strongpoints, consisting primarily of well hidden antitank guns covering key intersections, as well as snipers and machine gun positions in key houses, between the Eastern Force and the primary defensive area around the bridge. Lieutenant Colonel Vandervoort deployed his paratroopers into the buildings on both sides of the avenue of advance. "Two rifle companies, E and F—abreast— began to clear a corridor two city blocks wide. There was no preoccupation with the security of our flanks. If anything jumped us, we would have a tank or two jump back. The two companies worked forward in the center of the blocks to avoid casualties inherent to city street fighting. We were in a residential neighborhood of tall, two-story, brick and stone row houses. Some were topped with attics and flat roofs. The troopers fought over the rooftops, in the attics, up alleys, out of bedroom windows, through a maze of backyards and buildings. Nijmegen wasn't all that neat and tidy. In the labyrinth of houses and brick walled gardens, the fighting deteriorated into confusing, face-to-face, kill-or-be-killed showdowns between small, momentarily isolated groups and individuals. Friend and foe mixed in deadly proximity. Germans would appear where you least expected them. You fired fast and straight or you were dead. A lot of gallantry took place unnoticed and unrewarded. The spontaneous nature of the combat required cool heads, courage, skill, and tremendous self-discipline.

"At times, the two rifle companies fought three platoons in line, which gave lateral width to the corridor. Eighty-eight–millimeter antitank guns were the main focal point of resistance. Some were well placed to stop armor, but not situated well to greet paratroopers coming over the rooftops. Among the heavy-caliber antitank guns, one had been disassembled and carried into a corner house to fire at street level from a cellar window. Where the troopers came at them from the middle of a block under cover of the houses, they were manageable.

"By far the most dangerous part of driving the Germans back fell to our rifle squads. They were thirteen-man squads organized and trained to split into three four-man assault teams. One team had a light machine gun; two had Browning Automatic Rifles. The squad leaders moved the assault teams around to support each other. Lieutenant platoon leaders controlled the show. With the self-assured instincts of veteran combat leaders, they kept all units moving forward more or less together. Eight to a company, they provided officer participation in all crucial actions."[7]

Vandervoort's troopers assaulted a city block by deploying squads from the same platoon into row houses in the middle of the block across the street with light machine gun teams on the top floors and each squad's second assault team on the rooftop to provide covering fire. Any Germans firing from windows or doorways in buildings across the street were exposed to fire from the paratroopers above. British Guards' tanks added suppressive fire with their .30- and .50-caliber machine guns. Under the cover of this fire, the third team from each squad would charge across the street, throwing grenades through windows, then kicking in the doors, and fighting room-to-room to clear each house in the building. As soon as the assaulting force entered the building across the street, the covering force moved up behind it to assist. Then the teams would do it again, but instead of crossing a street to the next row of houses, they would have to cross a brick-walled backyard, the alley, and then the brick-walled yard of the houses being assaulted. These squad-level teams worked side by side as a platoon to clear three or four connected houses in the middle of a city block, then blasted holes in the common walls with Gammon grenades and bazookas to assault adjacent houses, working outward from the middle to the houses on the corners. Platoons sometimes worked forward behind one assaulting platoon and sometimes fought together in a line to clear a wide enough corridor, depending upon the nature of the opposition.

Private First Class Jimmy Keenan, with Company E, had not experienced street fighting, but he and the other paratroopers quickly adapted. "In fighting during the first day's assault on the city of Nijmegen, we were under heavy artillery and antitank fire in the street. Instead of advancing outside, we went from building to building by blowing holes in the walls and thus clearing street by street in this ingenious fashion."[8]

Vandervoort was impressed by how well his paratroopers and the British Guardsmen worked with the other. "For soldiers of different allied armies, it was amazing how beautifully the tankers and troopers teamed together. It was testimony to their combat acumen as seasoned veterans—both Yanks and Tommies. It required an intuitive sense of balance not to exploit the tanks as protection for the infantry, nor to preoccupy the infantry with screening the tanks. That depended on a lot of individual initiative. [Lieutenant] Colonel [Edward H.] Goulburn, a perceptive commander, more or less turned individual tanks loose and let them go up the alleys and through the yards with the infantry. The spearhead of the British column, which included the paratroopers, blasted its way up the avenue and into the side streets as required by the enemy dispositions."[9]

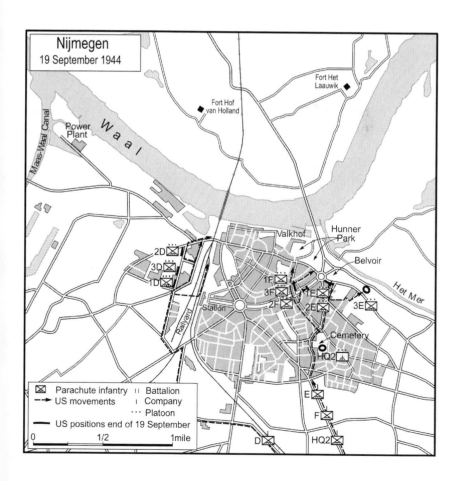

AS THE EASTERN FORCE fought toward the highway bridge, the Western Force approached the railroad yard about 4:15 p.m. Company D was supported by a section of Headquarters Company, 2nd Battalion's light machine gun platoon, five Sherman tanks, five Bren gun carriers, two weapons carriers, and a platoon of British Grenadier Guards. Lieutenant Joe Meyers, an assistant platoon leader with the 1st Platoon of Company D, was riding on a tank at the rear of the column as it turned from Nieuwe Nonnendaalseweg on to Koninginnelaan, just west of the railroad tracks, south of the train station. "As we approached the rail yard, the lead elements of our column came under both tank [from a self-propelled gun] and automatic weapons fire. All D Company troopers immediately dismounted from the exposed tank decks and took cover."[10]

First Sergeant John Rabig could see tracers hitting the tank in front of him. "I kept behind one of the tanks, which was shielding me. I felt safe enough. I began to see crazy Dutch boys, young kids about sixteen or seventeen, with an orange band on their arms, with guns, risking their lives. I tried to get them to go back, but they took no notice. All hell broke loose on the approach to the bridge. I learned later that six hundred Dutchmen had volunteered their services to General Gavin, using the weapons from our dead and wounded."[11]

Staff Sergeant Paul Nunan, with the 2nd Platoon, was riding on one of the tanks in the middle of the column. "We climbed off the tanks not far from a railroad yard and moved along the tracks leading to it. One platoon of the company was ahead of us. As we approached an underpass, we began receiving sporadic sniper fire. With a thousand places to hide, it was hard to tell where the fire was coming from."[12]

With the 3rd Platoon in the lead, Company D and the five British tanks advanced up a street parallel and adjacent to the railroad tracks to the east, north to the railroad station and then north up Oude Heselaan. A section of light machine guns with Headquarters Company, 2nd Battalion, moved up onto the railroad embankment to cover the advance, but heavy enemy fire forced it to withdraw to the west. One machine gun squad rejoined the main force on Oude Heselaan, and the other, reinforced by a D Company bazooka team, moved to the next street west, Krayenhofflaan, and advanced north to cover the left flank.

Captain Taylor G. Smith then ordered Lieutenant Waverly Wray, the executive officer, to take some men, a bazooka team, and a machine gun team to fire north up the tracks to keep the enemy on the east side of the tracks. Wray approached the company communications NCO, Sergeant Gerald Weed. "Wray said to me, 'Get a bazooka team, we're going up on the railroad tracks.'"[13]

Lieutenant Meyers and the 1st Platoon were at the rear of the column, behind the 2nd Platoon. "As we advanced, we came to a building I took to be a railway station, or a freight depot. [Lieutenant] Wray came rushing to the rear of the column. He pointed to Lieutenant Michelman, who had returned from the hospital a few days before the operation, and to me and beckoned us to join him. He had a rocket launcher team and a few men with him, and he instructed Michelman and me to take one rifle squad and come with him. We followed Wray around the station or depot and stopped briefly just short of the rail yard.

Wray said a German tank was holding up the advance of the company. He would take his group and the rocket launcher and work his way down the west side of the rail yard and try to get in a position to take a clear shot at the German tank. Michelman and I were to take the squad and move through the rail yard to his right. Wray did not state precisely what he wanted us to do, nor did he indicate why his plan required a total of three officers. He was XO and an experienced combat veteran, while I was inexperienced. It is safe to assume he wanted us to cover his right flank and rear, and that's what we did. Wray moved to the left with his group, and he was quickly out of sight."[14]

Staff Sergeant Roy King, with the 1st Platoon, was ordered to detach the machine gun team from one of his squads to support Lieutenant Wray, who would lead the advance along the railroad tracks toward the railroad bridge. "My machine gun crew went to the west of the railroad station, [but] I still had my BAR team. My remaining squad was assigned to guard the left flank of one of the tanks as we approached the bridge from our southwesterly position."[15]

The team's machine gunner, Private First Class Dave Bowman, and his assistant moved out, attacking north up the railroad tracks. "[Private First Class William R. "Rebel"] Haynes was again with me on the machine gun, to the right flank of the advance. A number of riflemen, including a BAR team, led by Corporal Julius Eisner, to the left, were supporting Lieutenant Wray and Corporal [Richard J.] Lord as they advanced up the tracks toward the bridge.

"We, on the machine guns, would fire a few bursts, then move forward with the bazooka team. Heavy fire—mortar, small arms, and maybe artillery—was coming from different directions at ground level."[16]

Suddenly, Bowman's machine gun jammed and he worked furiously to clear it. "I glanced to my left and was shocked to note that Haynes was nowhere in sight, so I assumed he had been hit and left for the rear. (I later learned what had happened. When I next saw him in France following the campaign, he chided me for ignoring him when he punched and yelled at me as he lay 'bleeding to death.' He was great for hyperboles. I guess because of the noise and distraction at the time, I was just oblivious to his efforts.) I worked with the gun for a while, trying to get it operating again."[17]

In the meantime, Lieutenant Joe Meyers and the squad on the right moved up the tracks toward the bridge. "After advancing about fifty yards, we met a hail of automatic weapons fire coming straight down the tracks from the direction of the bridge. We hit the ground. But, there was almost no cover or concealment. Michelman crawled under a boxcar, and I was a few inches away to his left. A steel rail separated us.

"We couldn't locate the source of the automatic weapons fire, and we were discussing what to do. Michelman's body rose a few inches into the air, then settled back to earth. He was hit, and he commenced to check out his wound. The bullet entered his left breast, traversed his chest and abdomen, and exited at the waistline forward of his right hip. I glanced to my rear to check on the squad and saw Private Jacob T. Herman, Jr., kneeling directly behind me. I shouted an order for him to get down, but he did not move. I took a second look and saw a bullet hole in his forehead. He was dead."[18]

As Lieutenant Wray and his group moved north along the railroad embankment, the 3rd Platoon moved into the houses facing the railroad embankment on the left side of Oude Heselaan, while the 2nd Platoon and the lead tanks moved along the street. Private First Class Donald E. Ellis, with company headquarters, was moving with the 3rd Platoon. "We got in the houses, and come to find out they [Germans] were in there, too. So, we were looking for a way to get up on top and shoot down."[19]

Ellis and other troopers moved upstairs to the top floor; found a door to the attic; and from there a door up to the roof. Ellis and his group moved across the roof to the next house north and found the door that opened to the attic of that house. "When we got ready to go down, we lifted the door to make sure it was clear."[20]

Ellis and the group found Germans in the lower floors of some of the houses. "A couple of times, we were shooting at them going down the stairs. They would shoot at us and take off and go into the other houses [on Krayenhofflaan, west of Oude Heselaan] and we would get a shot at them."[21]

On the embankment, pathfinder Corporal Julius "Ike" Eisner, armed with a BAR, worked forward up the tracks with Wray's group. Suddenly, a burst of machine gun fire ripped Eisner's jumpsuit pants, tore into his thigh, and knocked him to the ground. Eisner was hit by four or five bullets. "They split my leg wide open, from the knee to almost the crotch. Went right through, didn't hit the bone or nothing. I was lucky."[22]

One or more of the bullets struck a Gammon grenade in the right leg pocket of his jumpsuit. "It took the whole top off the grenade, detonator and all. It was in two pieces."[23] Eisner was extremely fortunate the grenade did not detonate.

Private First Class Bowman, unable to clear his jammed machine gun, picked up a carbine lying nearby and moved forward. "At this time, I was some distance behind and hastened to catch up. A couple of men who had been hit passed me, going in the opposite direction—one of whom I remember was Eisner, who had a large chunk of flesh torn from his right leg, just above the knee."[24]

Eisner, struggling, made his way back some distance, until he could go no further on the severely wounded leg. He was alone and bleeding profusely from multiple wounds. "There was nobody around there. And who comes along, but a Dutch guy with a bicycle stretcher. I was bleeding and he put a patch on me from the first aid kit I was carrying. He looked after me. Just patched me up, gave me the penicillin I was carrying, and put some sulfa powder on it. He put me on the bicycle stretcher and took me to a German hospital."[25]

Bowman continued to work his way forward up the tracks. "At one point in the advance, while lying on my stomach firing at the tower, movement of Germans slightly to my right caught my attention. They were running on a low, concrete platform, apparently heading to reinforce their comrades to our front. By the time I repositioned myself and began firing at them, only the characteristic German boots were visible between the platform and the bottom of a freight car, through which I was sighting. I emptied the carbine at them— but because of the small targets, the fact that I had, of course, never zeroed in the weapon, and the rapid pace at which they were moving, I am uncertain if I had hit a single one of them."[26]

Private Frank Aguerrebere, carrying an M1 with a grenade launcher attached, followed Lieutenant Wray north on the railroad embankment. "We were under heavy fire and we were looking for cover. There were a few sheds and boxcars in the area with troopers already using them. I lay on the ground by the railroad tracks next to a trooper with a boxcar above us. The bazooka man [Private First Class Frank V. 'Barney' Silanskis] was standing alongside the boxcar and below him on the ground was his [assistant] gunner [Private First Class Joseph J. Rajca]. As we were under heavy fire, a bullet ricocheted up and hit [Silanskis] in the face. He yelled and went to the rear. Another bullet, this time hit the [assistant] gunner on his buttocks, and he was carried back by four troopers. Other troopers were also hit and went back."[27]

While hugging the ground, Private Aguerrebere heard Lieutenant Wray, who was well out in front of the rest of the troopers, shout for the bazooka team to move up. "I yelled to him that the bazooka man and some of his men had been hit and [had] gone back. I told him that I had a grenade launcher and some grenades. He said for me to come forward. I went and laid next to him, noticing that he was alone, risking his life, and appeared to be without fear.

"He pointed to a tower, way up in front, and said, 'See if you can hit it. I think someone is up there.' I got up on one knee, aimed, and fired. The grenade went short. He said, 'Let me try it,' grabbed my rifle, aimed and fired. Again it was short. The tower seemed to be very far [away].

"Suddenly, a trooper came up with a bazooka and ammunition for us to use."[28]

Bowman could see "to my left front, just a short distance away, were Corporal Lord and Lieutenant Wray still doing their thing: loading, firing, and advancing, loading firing. Enemy fire continued to increase. Then, either as Wray was preparing to fire another round from his bazooka, or immediately after he had just finished firing one, I glimpsed the sight of his helmet flying off and he hit the ground on his back."[29]

Aguerrebere wasn't sure if Wray was still alive, and decided to check on him. "We crawled to him, shook him, and asked if he was all right. He did not respond, so we figured that he was dead."[30]

From where he was lying, Bowman watched Corporal Lord and Aguerrebere check on Wray. "The corporal then stood up, faced the rear, waved his arm, and shouted, 'Let's go!'

"We hastened to the rear with Corporal Lord in the lead. As I rushed on, I heard bullets zing by that spurred me on, while gravel to our front continued to be kicked up by shells and small-arms fire. After we reached the rear, a quick debriefing took place, primarily between Corporal Lord and the officers."[31]

On the east side of the rail yard, Lieutenant Meyers saw a trooper moving back toward him through heavy automatic weapons fire. "Corporal Gerald R. Weed, a member of Wray's group, hit the ground at my side and reported that Wray had been killed attempting to destroy a German tank with a bazooka and that the remainder of the group had withdrawn. There was no point in remaining in our exposed position and taking more casualties, so I decided to pull back. Michelman said he couldn't make it and to leave without him. I told him to remain, to play dead, and I would return for him in a few hours when it was dark.

"I issued the squad orders to withdraw in a single rush to the nearest cover, an earth berm used as a stop at the end of a rail siding. As we jumped to our feet and moved to the rear, streams of blue tracers enveloped us. Fortunately, no one else was hit."[32]

An attached machine gun squad from Headquarters Company, 2nd Battalion, and led by Private First Class Robert Robinson and a bazooka team which moved north on Krayenhofflaan to the west of the main advance, received automatic weapons fire from a small park—Krayenhof Park, to the north. Robinson moved down the middle of the street firing his machine gun from the hip, knocked out two German positions, killing five and wounding another four. From a building on the left side of the street, Robinson and the ammo bearers laid down a base of machine gun and rifle fire, while the bazooka team advanced and knocked out the automatic weapon firing from the park. The squad moved up to join the bazooka team, and they took the park after a brief but intense firefight. Realizing they were too far out in front, the machine gun squad and bazooka team withdrew south to buildings on Krayenhofflaan that overlooked the park. Private First Class Robinson was awarded the Silver Star for his gallantry.

With the 3rd Platoon moving through the houses and the 2nd Platoon moving behind the lead tanks on Oude Heselaan below, the force turned left and moved to Krayenhofflaan and then north to Voorstadslaan, which ran east underneath the railroad overpass. As the first two British tanks turned onto Voorstadslaan and attempted to charge the overpass, an antitank gun firing down the street from the other side of the trestle knocked out both tanks. Company D trooper, Private First Class Frank Bilich, saw one of the tanks catch fire, trapping its crew inside. "[Private First Class] Charlie Miller ran out under intense fire and pulled some of them out, then dragged them around the corner to a Dutch house. (We were later told that he was written up for a medal.)"[33]

As the two tanks charged the overpass, Lieutenants O. B. Carr and Russ Parker, Staff Sergeant Paul Nunan, and a squad of 2nd Platoon troopers ran across Voorstadslaan to Krayenhof Park. As he entered the park, Nunan scanned the area surrounding it looking for enemy. "Buildings faced the park on all three sides, and in one corner was a small air raid shelter. As we moved into the park, a sniper fired at us. I took cover in the entrance of the shelter behind a baffle, which protected the entrance. I had been carrying a white phosphorous grenade and a Gammon grenade in the pockets of my jumpsuit. After I took cover in the entrance of the air raid shelter, I took the grenade from my pocket and laid it on a parapet behind the baffle.

"On my left side was [Staff Sergeant] Herbert J. Buffalo Boy, a Sioux Indian from Fort Yates, North Dakota. We were also receiving sporadic machine gunfire from our right flank. The fire seemed to be coming from a railroad overpass, and the gun seemed to be well located.

"Lieutenant Carr, the platoon leader, moved to the rear in an attempt to contact the company headquarters and ask that a tank be sent forward to assist.

"Lieutenant Russ Parker, his ever-present cigar clenched in his teeth, moved out into the open and sprayed the roofs across the street in order to discourage the sniper. There was a lull in the action for a few minutes as we stayed under cover, trying to locate the enemy positions.

"Buffalo Boy nudged me and pointed across the street to our left front. There, walking along the sidewalk, was a German soldier, obviously unaware of our presence. He was wearing an overcoat and had his rifle slung over his shoulder, and seemed intent on continuing down the street, which ran across our front. I told Buffalo Boy to shoot, and as he fired his M1, I opened up with my Thompson. I still don't know if we hit him, because at that instant, all hell broke loose.

"The entire park seemed filled with tracer slugs. There seemed to be three colors of tracer—red, orange, and light greenish color. The fire was coming from a fast-firing automatic weapon, just at the corner to our left and across the street. My first reaction was that a German tank had moved in on us. I remember thinking that if they had infantry with them it was going to be a very tough day."[34]

The "fast-firing automatic weapon" was in fact two 20mm antiaircraft guns, which were pouring grazing fire into and across the small park. Private Frank S. Slugai and a couple of other troopers moved to knock out the 20mm antiaircraft gun at the corner across the street to the left, but were quickly pinned down. Private Slugai, using only natural concealment provided by the bushes and trees in the park, worked his way to the flank of the enemy gun while exposed to heavy small arms and 20mm fire. He opened fire and pinned down the enemy crew. The other troopers then managed to get closer and knock out the gun and the crew with Gammon grenades. Private Slugai was awarded the Silver Star for his gallantry.

While the squad continued to engage Germans to the front, another group of German infantry infiltrated the park on the flank and charged Lieutenant Parker and his troopers, who destroyed the enemy at close range with Gammon and white phosphorous grenades. Parker then led an attack on the remaining Germans to the front, killing another ten and wounding several more. For his courageous leadership, Lieutenant Parker was awarded the Silver Star.

After the attack, Staff Sergeant Nunan noticed that "the firing stopped as suddenly as it started. The Germans had either pulled back or were preparing for another attack. We had entered the park in the late afternoon and it was now getting dark. The word came up that we were to pull back about a block and consolidate our position for the night.

"As we began to pull back across the street to our rear, I was nearing the intersection when it started all over again. Another gun of the same caliber opened up. I was in the open and I could see that the gun was on wheels and was about a 20mm antiaircraft type. I saw the outline of a German lying behind a utility pole and cut loose with a burst from my Thompson. Three yards to my left, also caught in the open, a machine gunner from 2nd Battalion Headquarters

Company [Private First Class Robert Robinson] fired his .30-caliber machine gun from the hip, Audie Murphy style.

"I felt a weight against my right thigh and realized it was my white phosphorous grenade. Grabbing it, I pulled the pin and threw it in the general direction of the enemy. It landed to the right rear of the position of the enemy gun and their fire ceased temporarily. Diagonally, across the street from me on the opposite corner, were some men from the platoon with a bazooka. I yelled at them to fire on the gun.

"As I recall, there was difficulty before they could get the first round to fire, but two rounds were finally fired. I couldn't tell if the enemy gun had been hit, but it quit firing. We crossed the street and began to retrace the route we had come. Only then did I realize that I had left the Gammon grenade in the entrance to the air raid shelter. I told someone I was going back for the grenade to try to finish the gun before we pulled back. As a couple of men covered me, I hastily went back to the park and retrieved the grenade.

"As the rest of the platoon moved back, I moved as close to the gun as I dared. It seemed to be abandoned in the middle of the street, but I was certain some of the enemy were still nearby. I took cover behind a pole or a tree, unscrewed the fuse cap of the grenade, and pitched it. It exploded on the gun with a roar. I turned to rejoin my platoon and felt a blow at the back of my left knee, as though I had been struck with a club. I went down on the sidewalk and quickly got up. Although my leg wouldn't function properly, I hobbled back to the men covering me and they helped me back to the rest of the platoon. I was later awarded a Silver Star for this action.

"The platoon quickly set up defensive positions for the night and I joined the platoon headquarters in a yard near a wall of a house as German heavy artillery began to smash into the city. Our platoon medic, [Private Leland C.] Lee Heller, cut open my pants leg and began patching my wound. I began to shake violently. A combination of shock, reaction from the fight, and the chill of the night air, I suppose.

"Lieutenant Carr ordered me back to the company command post, and Heller and another man helped me hobble a block or so to the house where our CP was located. The missile that struck me nicked a tendon just behind my knee, but by keeping my knee locked, I could navigate after a fashion. If I attempted to bend my leg, it would not support me.

"I entered the house where the CP was and found a spot on the living room floor and lay down. The house was spotless, and although there was an empty davenport in the room, I couldn't bring myself to climb on it in my dirty, bloody uniform."[35]

Throughout the ten hour assault that day, Captain Taylor Smith, the commanding officer of Company D, had been at the forefront of the action, personally directing his troopers in spite of heavy enemy fire and snipers specifically targeting leadership personnel. Captain Smith was later awarded the Silver Star for his valiant and inspirational leadership.

Lieutenant Wray, always up front with the NCOs and enlisted men, wherever the action was the hottest, was posthumously awarded the Silver Star for his heroism and leadership in the assault on the rail yard and the southern end of the railroad bridge. When Sergeant Nunan learned of Wray's death, he was shocked. "That really hurt. First Lieutenant Wray was one of the finest small-unit combat leaders I have ever known."[36]

As word spread, it stunned the entire 505th and the division. It had been Wray who had single-handedly killed the commander and entire staff of the 1st Battalion, 1058th Grenadier Regiment, in Normandy only three months earlier. Lieutenant Colonel Vandervoort described Wray as "one of our finest officers. Wray was a Congressional Medal of Honor nominee."[37]

In the growing darkness, Company D and the three remaining British tanks pulled back and occupied buildings on Krayenhofflaan. But, Private First Class Bilich and a couple of D Company headquarters troopers holding a house on Oude Wertz, across the street from the railroad embankment, weren't told to withdraw. "Captain Taylor Smith told us to stay there, nobody was pulling out. 'We are going to hold this position' were his last words. All of a sudden, the Germans were all over the nearby railroad track and we were cut off. What we didn't know was, the company had pulled back, leaving us to our fate."[38]

In the house with Bilich were only two men, "[Private William T.] Bill McMandon, and another guy. With us were three members of a Dutch family; the mother, who spoke English, and her two young daughters. Around my neck I had my dog-tags and a rosary my mother had given me. The Dutch lady asked if I was Catholic.

"The Germans were getting very close, so we went down into the basement from the kitchen. Those houses were built so there was another door and stairs from the basement that came up under the back porch, into a fenced backyard. All three of us were hiding under the stairs as a German officer brought his platoon into the building. Twice he came halfway down the stairs from the kitchen to give orders to the Dutch lady to fix coffee or something. By then the shooting had died down and it was all quiet. Every time he came down we thought about shooting him, but the rest would have got us. Her daughters were against a wall—she had only one small light on, and we had not been spotted in the darkness."[39]

Bilich and the other two men were trapped and could do nothing except hide and wait.

MEANWHILE, THE PARATROOPERS AND TANKERS of the Eastern Force fought their way through the city in over three hours of continual house-to-house street fighting. As always, Lieutenant Colonel Vandervoort was right up with his troopers, observing the action. "The Jerries fought hard and courageously, but the relentlessly closing tanks and troopers forced them to scramble to alternate positions and to fall back to continue the fight. To do so, they had to abandon some of their heavy weapons and bulky ammunition. The Guards Armoured Division gave us all the tank support we needed. Some Shermans and their crews were lost as we went along. Usually, it happened because the tank was employed too aggressively. There were street intersections a man could run across, but a tank would be hit by a high-velocity gun. In order not to lose tanks, the armor had to wait until the troopers moved ahead and solved the problem from the flanks. The formula was learned quickly, but unfortunately, the hard way. With the overwhelming preponderance of armored firepower, the foot soldiers and tanks moved methodically the last few blocks toward our objective."[40]

The 1st Platoon of Company E, at the point of the advance, came to a wide intersection with Mariaplein Boulevard, which ran to the Keiser Lodwijkplein traffic circle, just south of the highway bridge. Lieutenant Colonel Vandervoort, Lieutenant J. J. Smith, Lieutenant Jim Coyle, and the 1st and 2nd Squads sprinted across the wide boulevard, accompanied by four British Sherman tanks before the surprised Germans opened up with machine gun, antiaircraft, and antitank fire, raking the boulevard. The platoon sergeant of the 1st Platoon, Otis Sampson, waited at the corner of a building on the left side of the street to send the rest of the platoon across the intersection. "A shell fired from our left down the avenue caught the corner of the building and exploded. Lucky no one was hit. It had been close. Lieutenant Colonel Vandervoort crossed over from the other side and informed me to send a machine gun forward; then he took off back [across the street]. Clyde Rickerd volunteered, and with his machine gun across his shoulder, he hurried across the open area. The rest of the platoon followed: one at a time. I brought up the rear, and as I was about in the middle of the thoroughfare I sent a burst from my Tommy gun down its wide area as I continued to run to the safety of the buildings on the other side. The gun that fired the shell must have been moved so as not to give its position away or they would have used it against us."[41]

Heavy fire from the traffic circle covering the intersection with the Berg en Dalshe at the Mariaplein cut off the remainder of the column from the 1st Platoon of Company E. Lieutenant J. J. Smith wanted to get the remainder of Company E forward to join the 1st Platoon. "The 2nd and 3rd Platoons were following up the 1st Platoon and had been stopped by enemy fire which covered the road intersection immediately in the rear of the 1st Platoon position. They were unable to move, and the situation at the time was looking rotten. Under cover of smoke from hand grenades which the British gave us, Lieutenant Meddaugh succeeded in bringing up the two remaining platoons."[42]

The point elements of the column moved along Dr. Claes Noorduynstraat, reaching the last houses before the traffic circle and the highway bridge. It was here that Lieutenant Coyle "cleared the last house and could see the bridge. I got quite a shock. I didn't expect it to be so large."[43]

Company E trooper, Private First Class Earl Boling, was advancing along the sidewalk as the lead platoon of four tanks slowly passed him. "As they passed, one of the drivers said the phrase used by kids all over England, 'Any gum, chum?' I gave him a pack of gum and he said, 'Thanks mate,' closed the hatch of the tank, and turned the corner to his left."[44]

As the tanks neared the open area around the Keiser Lodwijkplein traffic circle, Lieutenant Coyle watched the lead tank open fire with its main gun. "The roar was deafening, and I am sure they were not firing at any particular target, but to pin down the enemy."[45]

YOU FIRED FAST AND STRAIGHT

137

As the first Sherman moved into the intersection with the cross street, Graadt van Roggenstraat, an 88mm dual-purpose gun positioned on the west side of the traffic circle opened fire. The first round hit the tank, which immediately caught fire. Private First Class Boling saw it happen. "He immediately tried to back around the corner. As we ran to the tank to try to help, it was engulfed in flames as the fuel burned and the ammunition exploded. We stood helplessly as the tank went up in flames, a second tank tried to locate the hidden gun and knock it out. It too was disabled, but the crew did manage to escape from this one and retreat back around the corner."[46]

Lieutenant Coyle was moving up the street approaching the traffic circle with the third tank, when it suddenly "went into reverse and backed up about fifty feet to the houses we had just left. I went storming back to the third tank shouting at the commander to get back with us. He said he was hit. I told him he was not hit. (I could not see a mark on the tank.)

"A British sergeant jumped out of the tank and said, 'What's that then, mate?' pointing to a large hole on the other side of the turret which I had not seen.

"I felt about two feet tall. I didn't know how that tank took that hit without suffering any wounded or catching fire. I could see that the tanks were not going to make a move at that point and was trying to figure a way to get to a point where I could observe the position in front of me without being spotted.

"Just then, an elderly man and woman came out the back door of one of the houses facing the park and ran as fast as they could back the way we had come. I realized that if I could get the men on the second floor rooms in the front of the row of attached houses, we would be able to see and fire on the enemy in the park. I moved the platoon quickly into two of the buildings, cautioning them not to open fire before I gave the command. I knew that as soon as we opened fire we would receive heavy fire in return. I hoped that we would be able to spot the antitank guns and knock them out so the tanks and the rest of the battalion could advance on the bridge."[47]

Meanwhile, Private First Class Boling and the 1st and 2nd Squads of the 1st Platoon cleared the row houses on Graadt van Roggenstraat. "We entered the back yards, which each had a block of brick wall about four feet in height around them. We crossed and checked the yards and houses—the First Platoon moving forward through and past about four or five houses for the other platoons to use, then going into the next house to try to set up a field of fire over the park area from the second-floor windows.

"We could see the Germans milling around the park, bringing up more weapons and supplies. [Private] Carl Beck and [Private First Class] Earl Hable set up a .30-caliber machine gun at a window on the left side of the room and I had the BAR at a window on the right side."[48]

Lieutenant Coyle's 1st Platoon now occupied the row houses on Graadt van Roggenstraat, facing the Villa Belvoir and the bridge to the north, with the traffic circle to the left and Hunner Park to the left front.

Meanwhile, the 3rd Platoon moved across the Mariaplein and into the houses on the east side of Dr. Claes Noorduynstraat. The platoon leader,

Lieutenant John D. Phillips, Jr., and his troopers "proceeded to fight from one building to another, at times in hand to hand combat. Fighting lasted for about an hour in this area before the entire block was secured. The 2nd Platoon was ordered to take over this area as the 3rd Platoon was withdrawn to the cover of a large church in the block."[49]

Meanwhile, in the houses on Graadt van Roggenstraat, Lieutenant Coyle "kept the men back from the windows so they could not be seen by the enemy and set up our machine guns on tables near the front windows of two of the adjacent buildings. I could see German soldiers streaming across the bridge from the other side on foot and on bicycles. It was difficult to keep men from opening fire on them, but I wanted to get as many men in firing position as possible before we gave our position away.

"The Germans had no idea we were there. I knew this for certain when a crew manhandled a [50mm] antitank gun out of the park, and proceeded to set it up not thirty feet in front of us, pointing up the street to our right where the tanks had been knocked out.

"Suddenly, [Lieutenant] Colonel Vandervoort, the battalion commanding officer, and Captain Bill Harris, the S-3, came into the room where I was setting up our position."[50]

From the second floor, Vandervoort, standing back from the windows, observed the German positions below. "Hunner Park was congested with Germans. Some were established in a small cluster of buildings, bricked walled gardens and walks leading to an ancient stone ruin on the river bluff—the castle of Charlemagne on the northwest corner of the park.

"Other enemy elements were concealed in air raid shelters and sandbagged small group trenches in the open park. The Germans had hastily converted an antiaircraft position [of three 88mm dual-purpose guns] at the south end of the bridge to ground defense. Some self-propelled guns were visible, and one or two high velocity antitank guns fired from the left.

"We had to cross the park to reach the highway bridge. The Germans, in sizable numbers, had to be dislodged to give the tanks unmolested access to the bridge. From the second floor windows we looked down their throats. Time was running out for them unless they got help. Whatever their number, we had them outmaneuvered, outgunned and, in our bones outclassed. Why not? We had driven them back for blocks."[51]

Coyle told Vandervoort what he planned to do. "I knew we could knock out the gun as soon as we opened fire. I told the colonel I would hold our fire for five minutes. He told me he would try to move the British tanks forward when we opened fire. Then he left to see the British commander."[52]

Staff Sergeant Otis Sampson walked into the room about that time. "I saw a German soldier running across the street to the other side. I raised my Tommy gun to shoot him, but Coyle pushed it down. 'Not yet!' he whispered, 'It will give our position away.'

"It was such a perfect shot I hated to miss it. I had figured the Germans knew we were there. Coyle had quietly moved into this building with his men before I came up. He was right; if they didn't know we were there, the burst from the Tommy gun would have told them.

"I went into the cellar where some of our platoon men were waiting quietly in the dark, watching through the street windows. I had just left the building by the back door when . . . ."[53]

Someone opened fire from the house next door to Coyle, who "immediately had the men in the house where I was open fire with the machine gun and BAR, and Private First Class John Keller knocked out the [50mm] antitank gun with a rifle grenade."[54]

The sudden concentrated automatic weapons and rifle fire caught some of the surprised Germans out of their holes, cutting them down. Others in the trenches and gun pits methodically blasted each house on the block with small-arms and machine gun fire, while trying to locate the paratroopers' individual positions. Private First Class Boling shoved in clip after clip of ammunition as he fired his BAR on full automatic, when he felt something sting him. "I received flying brick chips to the right side of my neck. I reached up and got a handful of brick dust and traces of blood. In the dim light I thought I was wounded, but a check by others confirmed it was only a nick."[55]

When the firing began prematurely, Lieutenant Smith signaled the Grenadier Guards to move their tanks up to the intersection on the right side of the 1st Platoon as planned. "Some high-velocity 75s opened up that had not done any firing as yet and made the positions of the tanks untenable. Two Shermans were knocked out in this bit of action, and the tanks retired to a cover position to wait for a new thrust."[56]

Without warning, as Lieutenant Coyle and the men in the room were firing at the Germans below, "there was a terrific explosion in the room and it filled with plaster dust blinding everyone. When it cleared, I could see that an antitank gun shell had come through the wall from the room in the house next door on our left and continued through the wall to the house on our right. By some miracle, the only man wounded was Private Carl Beck. But, he was seriously wounded in the left side of his head and face. We pulled him into the back of the house, and some men got him out to the back yard where the medics could pick him up."[57]

Sergeant Sampson watched Beck and [Earl H.] Hable being carried out the back door of the building. "Beck was badly wounded. As Hable passed, I heard him tell his buddies, 'I'll be back as soon as I can.' It was a sincere statement."[58]

Private First Class Hable would later be awarded the Silver Star for his courage in continuing to fire his light machine gun in spite of heavy enemy automatic weapons fire until the antitank round wounded him and Private Beck.

Beck's wound was life threatening. "A piece of shrapnel went into my mouth and came out the left side of my head, taking everything with it. I now know that it was my lieutenant, James Coyle, who saved my life by his prompt first aid."[59]

As soon as Lieutenant Coyle had taken care of Beck, he returned to the front room. "Private First Class Clyde Rickerd and I then manned the machine gun and reopened fire, but we could not see exactly where the antitank gun firing to our left was located. Just as I realized that tracer rounds included in the ammunition were pinpointing our position for the enemy, another shell burst into the room from the left, hit the wall on our right, and fell to the floor in the room. We could not continue firing, and we moved back out of the front room.

"I went to the front room next door where the other squad of my men was, to check them out. No E Company men were hit, but a British [artillery] observer with a radio, who had moved into our position without my knowledge, had been killed by the concussion when the shell went through the room. He did not have a mark on him."[60]

When Coyle asked his men who had opened fire without orders, they told him that a British artillery observer "had walked into the room where our men were waiting, and seeing the Germans in the street in front of us, opened fire on his own."[61]

After reorganizing the 3rd Platoon, Lieutenant Phillips received the order "to move [north] across the street opposite the buildings we had previously secured and take up positions in the buildings along the east side of the park [on Reinaldstraat, facing the Villa Belvoir and the traffic circle to the west and the highway bridge to the northwest]. When all men were in position to open fire on the enemy with LMGs and BARs, the remainder of the platoon was to move into the park and close with the enemy. The 2nd Platoon would assist in the assault from its present positions and would jump off when the 3rd Platoon opened fire.

"The platoon moved a block to the east and crossed the [Barbarossastraat] street into the buildings, being covered from enemy machine gun fire by two knocked out tanks burning in the street and cutting off the fields of fire. These buildings had been large three story apartment houses of brick construction, but the Germans had set them on fire on D plus 1 to prevent troops from taking positions in them should they progress that far. The majority of the walls were still standing, but all of the wooden parts had burned and fallen through to the ground level, the rubble still smoldering and very hot.

"Shortly after entering the buildings, enemy artillery began to fall on the area, but the men continued to work their way forward to take up their pre-designated positions. As the platoon was going into position a runner from the company arrived and stated that the company commander wanted the platoon brought out before it was eliminated by the artillery.

"Three men were hit and had to be carried back to the location of the company command post."[62]

While Easy Company was infiltrating the area south and east of the highway bridge, Vandervoort ordered Company F to move around the left flank and approach the bridge area from the southwest. Lieutenant William "Rusty" Hays was a new assistant platoon leader with Company F. "As we crossed streets perpendicular to our line of march, we would pause, gather into small groups, and run across to reduce exposure to enemy fire. The Germans were expected to be on our right, so as the tanks would cross a wide street, they would swing their big guns to the right, so if they received fire from down the street they'd be ready to return it.

"We came to a wide boulevard [Canisiustraat]. We'd been told there was a German 88 antitank gun at a traffic circle two blocks down the boulevard to the right. My platoon ran across without drawing fire, and the tanks followed us, swinging their guns to the right as they crossed."[63]

As one of tanks crossed, its gun hit a small tree, causing the turret to spin around, accidentally firing a round from the 17-pounder main gun, hitting a group of troopers from Hays' platoon who were resting with their backs against the wall of a building. One of those in the group was Sergeant Spencer Wurst. "When the gun went off, the detonation was close enough to stun me. I was momentarily knocked out or lost my senses. I couldn't hear much for the next few hours, but I recall coming to and immediately remembering what had occurred. As for the tank, it just kept rolling down the street. Luckily, the round was armor piercing. If it had been high explosives, it could have been catastrophic, but it was already very bad.

"The second man to my right [Private Alfonso R. Aguirre] was killed instantly. The man next to me [Corporal George S. Ziemski] was seriously wounded but survived. As soon as I came to I grabbed my first-aid packet and started to bandage him as best I could. We had been taught to use the first-aid packet of the wounded man rather than our own, to insure we still had bandages if we were wounded ourselves. In the confusion, I wasn't thinking all that clearly, although my training did click in well enough for me to start working on him."[64]

As the rifle companies moved toward the bridge, the 81mm Mortar Platoon, Headquarters Company, 2nd Battalion moved into position to support the assault.

The 2nd Battalion S-4, Lieutenant Claiborne Cooperider and his supply section had the critical responsibility of bringing up ammunition to support the operation. He had at his disposal a captured German truck and two jeeps with trailers. Cooperider had left some of his men back at the supply dump to load the captured German truck while he and his other troopers followed the battalion into Nijmegen in the two jeeps and trailers, heavily loaded with ammunition. "We arrived at Nijmegen about dusk with two vehicles, carrying as much mortar platoon equipment as possible. We unloaded in a Nijmegen graveyard where the mortar platoon was to set up its guns. Both vehicles were unloaded and contents set up at this point."[65]

Because of the density of multistory buildings, the 81mm mortar platoon had found only one place with the vertical clearance from which to operate the weapons. When he checked on the dispositions of the mortar platoon that evening, Vandervoort observed that the "mortars were dug into deep gun pits between the headstones and monuments of an ancient cemetery a few blocks back. When firing, the troopers' torsos bobbed above and below ground. There was a ghoulish appearance to the scene—not for the superstitious or squeamish. It wasn't irreverence but necessity that placed them there. The old graveyard was the only open space in the neighborhood giving sufficient vertical clearance from the tall buildings to permit wide, full-range horizontal arcs of fire.

"The Tommies thought the layout was hilarious. Good natured banter about fornicating Yank grave robbers was run into the ground. It was well the Dutch residents had evacuated the area.

"Our 81mm mortar platoon was walking high-explosive shells up and down the roadbed of the massive stone-piered and steel-arched bridge. They hoped to get lucky and cut any exposed wires leading to demolition charges. Someone asked, 'What if they hit a charge causing the bridge to blow sky high?'

"'Then we'd know the bloody thing was booby trapped' was the reply. The 81mm shelling also sealed off access between enemy elements on the opposite sides of the Waal.

"One German tried to run north across the bridge. Our mortar observer fired one round that knocked him flat. He got up and began running away without his rifle. Then he stopped, turned around, came back, picked up his piece, and started away again at a full jog—weapon in hand. The mortar platoon leader ordered 'cease fire' and watched the good soldier run away."[66]

After unloading the ammunition at the cemetery, Lieutenant Cooperider left for the regimental supply dump. "I took one vehicle and trailer and headed back to the location of the German vehicle, dropping a man at that point to take the vehicle up to the graveyard, and then headed for the regiment CP at Groesbeek and loaded on all the 60mm mortar ammunition that I could carry. I returned immediately to the graveyard, finding the mortars in the process of considerable firing.

"Figuring they might draw considerable counter fire, I set out looking for another point to establish the battalion supply dump. I located a former garage slightly to the east of the graveyard about 400 yards. It had an entrance way of about twenty-five yards and then a plaza. Within the garage and on the plaza were six or seven abandoned German trucks and several German motorcycles. As this plaza was protected by surrounding buildings and being the first to discover this place along with these vehicles, I determined to set up a supply dump there, and in turn did so. By this time the ammunition had been divided into two piles; 81mm along with 60mm mortar ammunition being left in the graveyard as it was more easily accessible there, and the remainder, from small arms ammunition and all inclusive, was put in this garage."[67]

Meanwhile, Lieutenant Cooperider's men shuttled the 60mm mortar ammunition to the squads in the rifle companies.

Company F mortar squad leader, Sergeant Russ Brown, and his troopers set up their 60mm mortar along Canisiustraat, the wide boulevard that ran southwest from the traffic circle, providing the overhead clearance needed for Brown's mortar. "Lieutenant Dodd stopped and called me aside. He got out his map and showed me the targets he wanted me to fire on. We set up the mortar and set up aiming stakes that I plotted from the map. Lieutenant Dodd had a truck drop off a load of mortar shells. We had never had so much ammo to fire.

"[Private First Class] Douglas [J.] Trieber and [Private Harold E.] Harry Peterman fired the mortar, switching from stake to stake—sometimes firing for effect. We must have been effective, because we were hit by a large gun, much bigger than an 88. They had us zeroed in, and Harry Peterman was killed."[68]

After checking on his men, Lieutenant Hays and the rest of the 2nd Platoon of Company F moved north along both sides of a street. "About a block further on, just as it was getting dark, I was told that my platoon would be attached to the British tank company we were with. Our objective would be a wooded park area [Hunner Park] down the street about two blocks. Whenever the tanks stopped, the platoon's job was to 'nip up into the houses on both sides of the street and be sure there were no Germans with Panzerfausts in the houses.'"[69]

Sergeant Wurst and his squad were moving behind the tanks. "The British tanks were abreast of one another. We followed them as closely as we could, seeking maximum protection as we peered ahead into doors and windows. I don't know if I fired or saw any enemy soldiers, but they were there. As soon as we turned the corner, the tanks fired rapidly with their two .30-caliber MGs and 75mm cannon. The din was deafening.

"We got a lot of return fire from the head of the street, heavy small arms fire. In addition to machine guns, rifles, and machine pistols, the Germans had dug in some 20mm antiaircraft weapons. I don't know if they were twins or quads, but when they're shooting at you, it hardly matters. They fired tracer rounds with a ratio of about one to four. It was late enough for the tracers to show up well in the dark.

"The fire became so heavy that the tanks momentarily stopped. They weren't damaged by the small arms and the 20mm fire, but it was a dangerous situation for the rifle squads. I got flatter than flat on the street, trying to get below a six-inch curb in a desperate search for cover. The fire immediately over my head cracked the air a foot or two above my body. I lay prone, hugging that curb for dear life, and I wasn't the only one. I don't think it gave us much protection except from our right front. If it hadn't been for the pavement, I'd have started digging."[70]

The tanks began moving again, and Lieutenant Hays and his men advanced behind them. "The tanks moved slowly down the street towards the wooded park, and we followed. Just before we reached the park, the tanks encountered a roadblock, some trees that had been felled across the road. Fearing that there may be some antitank mines hidden in the trees, they stopped and my platoon tried to 'nip up into the houses on each side of the street.' On my side of the street, this wasn't possible; the house had been set on fire by artillery shells. Not only was this house on fire, silhouetting us against the flames, but there were houses on fire up the block behind us, also silhouetting us, including the tanks, against the flame. This was particularly scary to the tankers, since they knew somewhere in front of us the Germans had a big 88.

"By that time it was pitch dark. The troops of my platoon on my side of the street, unable to move into the house because of the fire, were milling around outside in front of the house, not knowing what to do."[71]

Meanwhile, Sergeant Wurst's squad moved around the tanks on the opposite side of the street. "I was reluctant because of the tank episode earlier in the day. At night, a buttoned up tank is practically blind. To advance around and move in front of those tanks would expose us to friendly fire as well as heavy fire from the enemy. We had almost gone forward enough for the traffic circle to come in view to our right front. It was a large area, and the Germans had dug in with at least one 88, as well as other heavy weapons. There were also most definitely mobile 20mm guns.

"We nevertheless moved around to the left of the tank to clear away the debris. At that very instant, a German antitank gun let loose. The German gunner was anxious and missed. The fire came from our right front and went across in front of the tanks. The gunner probably couldn't see them, but he had anticipated their movement into his field of fire.

"When an 88 fires on you at a distance of a hundred yards or less, you don't get much time to react. The tanks reversed, moving to the rear as quickly as their engines could get them there. One thing, and one thing only, saved us from being crushed—my squad had already started around to the left of the tanks."[72]

Hays and his men were now exposed on the street without the protection of the tanks. "Just after the tanks left, someone called out, 'counterattack!' and a German hand grenade exploded in the front yard of the house where we were. One of the British soldiers was hit bad.

"Because of the fire behind us, we were reluctant to move from where we were. We didn't know how many Germans were in front of us and expected them to counterattack any minute. Then, suddenly, here came the tanks roaring back and [they] stopped in front of us. We carried the wounded man out and put him on the back of a tank, and keeping the tanks between us and the Germans we moved two blocks down the street to a school, where the rest of the company was and where we were to spend the night."[73]

As the British tanks backed up, the platoon leader, Lieutenant Jack Carroll, along with Sergeant Wurst's squad took refuge in an outside cellar entrance off the street. After an exchange of hand grenades in the darkness with enemy troops, Lieutenant Carroll decided to break into a house down the street, get into the backyard, and then move through the backyards to join the remainder of the platoon. A couple of Carroll's men found an unlocked house a short distance down the street and the remainder followed them through it into the backyard. One of Carroll's troopers had pulled the pin on a grenade, but had not released the lever, during the earlier exchange and was still holding it. Carroll "told him to throw it over the wall, and when he did this, it hit a wire and came back in the courtyard and went off not over ten feet away. We didn't even get a scratch. We had a real tough time getting back to our own lines that night, as we could hear them talking all around us."[74]

Lieutenant Colonel Vandervoort had his men in position for an assault on the southern approaches of the highway bridge. "Companies E and F deployed in houses on the southern edge of the park waiting to be unleashed to finish the job. Our ammunition was plentiful with the exception of 60mm mortar rounds. All battalion communications—radio and telephone—were tied in 'five by five' [loud and clear]—better than 'Ma Bell.' A dozen or more Sherman tanks, motors idling, were ready to roll when ordered. Company D was downstream, fighting and dying for the railroad bridge. Except for Company D, our casualties, tanks and troopers, were negligible. In short, the battalion and the tanks were on the line of departure ready for a joint infantry/tank assault to put the armor over the river. There was time to establish a bridgehead north of the Waal before dark if the bridge wasn't demolished.

"So—I reported to the generals that 2nd Battalion was ready to take Hunner Park and put their tanks on the bridge. After consideration, they decided to consolidate our positions for the night and have their infantry, the Coldstream Guards, mop up the area to our left the next morning. The decision to pause was disappointing. The momentum was ours all afternoon. We wanted to continue while we had the upper hand.

"From dead and wounded enemy, our intelligence officer identified the reconnaissance battalion of the 9th SS Panzer Division. Were they the forerunners of the whole damn panzer division? That was what recon battalions usually did. The SS recon battalion T/O [table of organization] strength was six hundred, coincidentally about the same as 2nd Battalion's strength. The SS identification explained why few prisoners had been taken. The deaths-head skull and cross bones were the SS insignia. . . . In combat they were deceptive, prisoner-shooting bastards. Despite our mean opinion of them, they were tough S.O.B.s and could not be taken lightly."[75]

AS DARKNESS FELL, exhausted paratroopers, Guardsmen, and German troops tried to get some sleep, knowing the next day would undoubtedly bring more combat. But sleep was risky, as both sides used the night to conceal their movements. The Germans set fire to the buildings around their perimeter in order to prevent infiltration, and dispatched night patrols to infiltrate the American positions.

Lieutenant Jim Coyle and the 1st Platoon of Company E maintained their positions in several of the row houses overlooking the German positions south of the Nijmegen highway bridge. "We received the word that the attack was being held up for the night and that we were to hold our position. Enemy fire had stopped, and I placed men in the three houses on the ground floor to prevent enemy infiltrators from getting into position.

"I was in the upper front room shortly after dark observing the enemy area in front of us as best I could. Suddenly, a British tank opened fire across my front from the right, and a German tank replied from my left. I don't know how they could see each other in the dark, but a terrific crossfire of heavy-caliber tracers continued for almost five minutes. (The next day I saw the German tank, an old French model, knocked out near the traffic circle to the left of our position.) When the firing ceased, I saw that the tracer fire had set a public building on fire, and I could now observe the area to my front by its light.

"The company runner then gave me a message that I was to report to the E Company CP—about two blocks behind the 1st Platoon position. When I got there, the CO told me to plot my platoon's position in on the company's overlay. I had just completed the map when my platoon runner came in with the information that a patrol was moving in front of our area. The men thought the patrol was British and had not fired on it. But, some thought it was an enemy patrol.

"I had returned to the platoon and went to the front of the house where Sergeant Ben Popilsky was observing from the doorway. He told me two men walked past on the sidewalk earlier, but he thought they were British tankers. Just then, the two returned and I could see in the light of the burning building that they wore the helmets and smocks of German paratroopers.

"Popilsky and I opened fire with our Thompson submachine guns. One of the Germans went down, but the other ran to our left and got behind a tree. He yelled at us in German, and Ben who understood it said he was asking to come back and help his comrade. I told Ben to tell him that we would take care of his comrade, who was groaning on the sidewalk. When Popilsky yelled back, I realized that Ben was speaking Yiddish to the German. The German then called us, 'Verdamdt Americanische Schweinhunds' and we called him a 'Kraut bastard.'

"I wanted the wounded German soldier as a prisoner, and I was not about to let the other man come back and pick us off in the doorway, now that he knew exactly where we were. He finally ran away, but when we crawled out to get the wounded German, we discovered that he had died."[76]

The paratroopers also used the darkness to get close enough to assault the German strongpoints around the approaches to the bridges. Between 6:00 and 6:30 p.m., the 2nd Platoon, Company E moved into two houses occupied by the 3rd Platoon on the southeastern corner of Graadt Van Roggenstraat and Barbarossastraat on the right flank of the 1st Platoon.

After receiving an order to penetrate the German bridge defenses from the east, Lieutenant John Phillips led his 3rd Platoon "two or three blocks to the east and then north to a parkway in an effort to flank the enemy or get in behind his park positions. The platoon, with one section of light machine guns attached, moved six blocks northeast to the eastern end of the parkway. Here, the platoon was halted and left under cover of the buildings."[77]

Lieutenant Phillips decided to make a reconnaissance of the area and selected the platoon sergeant, Staff Sergeant John C. Porter; Private First Class Edward T. Pryzborowski; and Private Joe Elizondo for the patrol. It was dark at around 8:00 p.m. when Phillips and his patrol moved out. "The section of town being fought over was well illuminated from the fires that were burning. Using the cover of a sunken lawn to conceal our movement to the opposite side, we moved in behind a bank on the north side of the parkway, and discovered that it extended along the rear of the enemy positions for about two blocks, dropping off steeply to a street some twenty or thirty feet below. This was the break the platoon had been looking for; so the patrol moved along behind the enemy positions using Tommy guns, hand grenades and knives to eliminate the enemy in this area in less than an hour's time. The bank was perfect cover for movement of the patrol from the rear of one position to the rear of another; and with fires burning in front of the enemy, their heads protruding above the foxholes made perfect targets. In some instances an enemy's head was no more than two feet from the muzzle of a gun when the trigger was pulled.

"Artillery was still falling and the enemy along the parkway was so busy pouring fire into the buildings across the street that the activities of the patrol went unnoticed until it reached the point where the parkway converged with the park. Here it was discovered and fired on by a machine gun. The fire was returned by the patrol, but none of the men could get into a position to assault the enemy gun."[78]

Lieutenant Phillips and two of his troopers maintained their positions, while he sent one of the men "back with an order to the assistant platoon leader to bring the platoon forward and occupy the recent enemy positions. Two LMGs were to be brought forward to [my position] and set up to cover the enemy machine gun. By 2200 the platoon was in position and the enemy gun that fired on the patrol had been forced to take cover.

"All automatic weapons were left in position and the remainder of the platoon was organized into four man patrols to enter the north section of the park in an effort to destroy the enemy antitank guns and all of the enemy that could be found. This section of the park was on a lower level than the south section and offered a defiladed area in which the patrols could operate in and not be endangered by small arms fire from our own troops on the south.

"Patrol activities continued throughout the night with the net result of one 50mm antitank gun and crew being destroyed, several enemy killed and a few taken prisoner. The patrols were withdrawn to their own lines prior to daylight and resupplied with ammunition."[79]

For his intrepid leadership that night and the next day, Lieutenant Phillips would be awarded the Silver Star.

During the night, the 3rd Platoon occupied the foxholes taken by the reconnaissance patrol, with the four machine guns of the attached 2nd Section, Light Machine Gun Platoon, Headquarters Company, 2nd Battalion, led by Lieutenant Vernon L. Autrand, defending the northernmost positions.

Private First Class Don Lassen was one of the 3rd Platoon troopers occupying the captured German foxholes. "[Private First Class] Fred Hebein and I were talking and we heard some noise about halfway down the hill.

"Fred said to me, 'Let's go down and see what the hell that is.'

"I said, 'Just a minute, Fred, I gotta go back to my foxhole and tell [William A.] Muller'—he was my foxhole buddy—'where I'm going,'—because we always kept each other informed of what we were going to do. It took a couple of minutes to get back to my foxhole, and then I started back to join Fred in an exploration. Just as I got back to Fred, all hell broke loose from that area halfway down the hill. There was a whole squad of Krauts in there, and if I hadn't taken those couple of minutes delay, we'd have walked right straight into that squad of Krauts."[80]

While Lassen felt very fortunate not to have walked into the German squad, "it didn't bother Fred, hell he was always game for a good firefight."[81]

NEAR THE RAILROAD BRIDGE, Lieutenant Joe Meyers took a few D Company troopers under cover of darkness back to the rail yard to find and evacuate Lieutenant Michelman, who had been wounded during the earlier fighting. "I found [Private Jacob] Herman's body, but Michelman, who was only a few feet away, was gone. Apparently, he crawled out on his own. Later, we received word from the aid station of his evacuation.

"Fires from the burning buildings illuminated the streets, and the fighting continued as we advanced from one building to another. During lulls in our fighting we could hear sounds of heavy fighting coming from the direction of the highway bridge."[82]

THAT NIGHT, the 1st Platoon runner found Staff Sergeant Otis Sampson, known as the "mortar artist" to the men in E Company, to report to Lieutenant Smith's command post. "Our company command post was in the cellar of a house [in] back of the one Lieutenant Coyle was holding. [Lieutenant] Smith told me to take two mortar squads and go to the east of where we were and shell the area across the street from Lieutenant Coyle. He showed me the position I was to set up in. I asked for a ruler to lay out my field of fire [on a map]. The spacious cellar room was dimly lit. I had entered the room during an interrogation of a large-built German soldier. The prisoner was using both hands to hold his pants up, for his belt had been removed and the buttons or zipper ripped open. I was given a table and a light to see by, and with the aid of a compass and a ruler, I oriented the map and measured the distance as 550 yards.

"Wesley [A.] Forsythe, our platoon runner, guided me to the chosen area by back alleys. I believe it was to the very end of the front street going east. A platoon of E Company men was already dug in across this front street in the open area that ran to the river.

"I set the two mortars up in the back yard of the corner house and distributed men in defensive positions. A telephone line from the company CP had been laid for the platoon across the street, but it seemed to be continuously out of order. The lieutenant of the platoon told me to hold my fire. I knew he was right, but that wasn't the reason I did it. The firing had quieted down. All I would have done is bring artillery down on us and the platoon in the open field. I could send one round over at a time, [but] between each round fired I would have to use a light to reset the delicate M4 sightings on the mortar. I wouldn't trust the weapon to hold its setting. I would be taking a chance of hitting my own platoon across the street. Taking one man with me, we went across the east side street in some shelled-out houses and picked up some couch covers and draperies for the mortarmen to keep warm. It was quite chilly. During the night, I heard cries for help, but not in our area. I had wondered if the cries were for real or someone trying to lure a victim in. Many parts of the city were burning. I didn't sleep that night, but kept guard."[83]

DURING THE NIGHT at the Champion CP south of Nijmegen, General Gavin struggled with how to capture the two Nijmegen bridges intact. The fate of the British paratroopers at Arnhem weighed heavily on his mind. "General [Brian G.] Horrocks, commanding British XXX Corps, General Browning, commanding the airborne corps, and General Allan Adair, commanding the

Guards Armored Division, and I had a meeting near the sidewalk in front of the Malden schoolhouse late in the afternoon of September 19.

"Earlier Browning had warned me, 'The Nijmegen bridge must be taken today. At the latest, tomorrow.' The capture of the Nijmegen bridge was squarely on my shoulders. This I knew. But most important to me were the lives of General [Robert F.] Urquhart and the British First Airborne."[84]

Gavin knew that Vandervoort's battalion and the British Guards Armoured Division could seize the southern approaches to the bridges, but that the Germans would simply blow them up as they retreated. "I decided therefore, that I somehow had to get across the river with our infantry and attack the northern end of the bridge and cut off the Germans at the southern end. The question was how. There were no boats around Nijmegen. They had long ago been removed by the Germans."[85]

Gavin discussed his plan with General Horrocks and told him if he could get boats brought up quickly, that the 504th PIR would make an assault crossing of the Waal River as soon as possible. Horrocks agreed to the plan and instructed his staff to immediately have the boats brought forward. Gavin wanted to make the crossing in the predawn darkness, but Horrocks couldn't assure him if the boats would arrive by that time.

Later that evening, there was a large meeting at the Champion CP. Assembled were Gavin, British Generals Browning and Horrocks, officers of the Guards regiments and divisional staff, the 82nd divisional staff, and Colonel Reuben Tucker and his 504th regimental staff.

An observer at this meeting, Colonel George Chatterton, commander of the British Glider Pilot Regiment, noted that the British officers were wearing "corduroy trousers, chukka boots, and old school scarves. They seemed relaxed, as though they were discussing an exercise, and I couldn't help contrast them to the Americans present, especially Colonel Tucker, who was wearing a helmet that almost covered his face. His pistol was in a holster under his left arm, and he had a knife strapped to his thigh. Tucker occasionally removed his cigar long enough to spit and every time he did, faint looks of surprise flickered over the faces of the Guards' officers."[86]

Gavin laid out a very bold plan. "Speed was essential. There was no time even for a reconnaissance. As I continued to talk, Tucker seemed to be the only man in the room who seemed unfazed. He had made the landing at Anzio and knew what to expect."[87]

Browning was "by now filled with admiration at the daring of the idea."[88] He immediately granted permission to Gavin to proceed with the assault crossing. Gavin planned to launch the boats in the Maas-Waal Canal close to where it empties into the Waal River, providing a covered position to load the boats and time for the men to become familiar with the boats before leaving the canal to cross the river. Gavin wanted to use every artillery piece the division and the British could employ to shell the opposite side of the river, together with direct fire from the British tanks and Tucker's 81mm mortars and machine guns as the 504th troopers crossed. Finally, Gavin wanted a heavy smoke screen laid on the far shore to conceal the crossing.

BACK IN NIJMEGEN, Vandervoort and most of the battalion spent the night with little or no sleep. "There were small patrol clashes. Outposts listened for vehicles on the bridge. A prisoner or two was taken. Illuminating flares burst over the front. Minor shellings were exchanged. Someone wounded cried in the park—or was it the SS baiting a trap? The Germans wanted a truce to take out wounded in the E Company sector. The troopers magnanimously stood by— weapons ready—while the evacuation took place. German patrols (some probable would-be looters) tried to enter houses we occupied. They were gunned down through the lace curtained front doors and windows. In the Nijmegen fighting the .45 caliber Thompson submachine gun didn't penetrate doors and walls as well as our .30-caliber weapons. Some innovative troopers switched to German Schmeisser machine pistols. To obtain more 9mm ammunition clips, they would shoot another Jerry. It was a self-sufficient if somewhat chancy supply system."[89]

During the night, Private First Class Earl Boling stood watch with two other E Company troopers in one of the houses overlooking the traffic circle. "A patrol with hobnailed boots was heard approaching. Since both the British and the Germans wore hobnailed boots, we were waiting to get a look at them to ascertain if it was friend or foe. As they passed from the back of a large tree and arrived almost in front of our positions, we could see their German uniforms and helmets in the light of the burning house, and it looked to be a five- or six-man patrol. At this time [Private First Class] John Keller, who was armed with a rifle grenade launcher, pulled the pin and threw a rifle grenade into their midst.

"I believe at least one was killed and one wounded in the blast. Another two or three ran toward the building where Private George [M.] Wood and I were at the first floor window. I opened fire with the BAR and one dropped near the sidewalk. I thought two more were outside the window ledge, so I tipped the BAR up and fired the last two shots of the clip over the window ledge; then tried to change a clip, when I saw the enemy soldier less than two feet away, holding to the window ledge with one hand and raising a Luger automatic with the other.

"I was so nervous that I dropped the clip and started to reach for my trench knife on my right boot when Private George Wood said, 'I'll get him,' and fired four times at point-blank range into the face of the German. With each shot I could see his head bounce, but he didn't fall until the fourth shot.

"Private Wood had used a Beretta automatic that he had been carrying into combat since his days in the Sicily invasion. I was certainly glad he had it along. I told George that I was sure that another German soldier was outside the room below the window level or behind some nearby bushes in the shadows.

"We 'sweat it out' until daylight was approaching. Meanwhile, one of the wounded near the curb of the street was moaning throughout the rest of the night. As dawn was breaking we could make out the figure of a German underneath the edge of some bushes with a grenade in his hand.

"Sergeant Popilsky, who had been raised in Chicago and spoke some of several languages, called out to the German to put down the grenade and come in the window, which he did. Sergeant Popilsky interrogated him and learned that he was a Polish soldier, conscripted into the German unit, and was not of the diehard SS troops that we were fighting."[90]

That night, Corporal Ronald F. Adams, Sr., with Headquarters Company, 2nd Battalion's light machine gun platoon moved up with his squad in the dark to get into position to support the attack the following day. However, Adams and his squad ended up in the middle of a group of Germans already in the area. They were soon discovered and fired at from a dugout at close range. Too close to deploy his machine gun, Adams quickly fixed the bayonet on his rifle and single-handedly assaulted the position, killing one and capturing four others. As he took the prisoners back to the platoon CP, a sniper seriously wounded him. But despite this, he delivered the prisoners to the command post before he was evacuated. Corporal Adams was awarded the Silver Star for his bravery.

MEANWHILE, NEAR THE RAILROAD BRIDGE, Private First Class Frank Bilich, along with the two other D Company troopers trapped under the stairway in the basement of a house occupied by German soldiers, faced a dilemma. "By 2:30 in the morning all was quiet. We knew there was a guard on the back porch. If we stayed until daylight they would soon find us. The three of us had a whispered council of war. It was decided that we would make a run for it just before dawn. We talked about who was going first, second, and last. The way out would be up the stairs and out under the porch.

"Again, the officer came halfway down the stairs from the kitchen and asked for coffee. After he went back, we decided that this was our chance. We came up to the backyard and saw a wooden fence with a gate blocking our path.

"McMandon took off, hit the gate with such force that it burst open, and [he] went through. I followed. There was a call to halt in German and somebody fired some shots. We were all through the gate and running down the backs of those houses, running until our lungs were ready to explode. We ran across a road and right over an E Company machine gun position and fell into a ditch. All the E Company boys could say was, 'Where the hell have you come from?' We didn't care. We had made it."[91]

CHAPTER 7

"No Quarter Combat"

As dawn broke on September 20, embers still glowed in the ruins of burned out buildings as smoke rose into a dreary gray sky over Nijmegen. A light rain fell. Most troopers like Lieutenant Joe Meyers, an assistant platoon leader with Company D, had not received more than a couple hours of restless sleep in the eerie surroundings while taking turns on watch. "D+3 found us facing a determined enemy in well prepared defensive positions guarding the approaches to the railroad bridge. The rail yards to the east, our right, were elevated about twenty feet above the street level. To reach them, you had to negotiate a steep embankment. Our attack followed a main street to an underpass of the main line. A German minefield, protected by fire, was sited in this underpass. In the distance, we were not far from our goal, the railroad bridge, but in time it was another matter. It was a temporary stalemate.

"Tom [McClean] and I set up platoon headquarters in the remains of the basement of a two- or three-story brick building. Except for some rubble, the entire building was gone. Sound-power phone lines connected us to the nearby rifle and mortar squads, and a telephone line linked us to company headquarters.

"Shortly after dawn on the morning of D+3, a jeep sped down the main street, through our lines, and into no man's land. The Germans greeted the vehicle and its occupants with bursts of automatic weapons fire. The sound of a German machine gun or machine pistol was very distinctive, since each had a higher cyclic rate of fire than similar U.S. weapons. The jeep carried an artillery forward observer (FO) and his team, who had come to join us. Instead of approaching with caution, the FO team raced straight through our position. The FO, a lieutenant, and his NCO died. The driver escaped and returned to our lines, where he joined Tom and me in the basement ruins. We gave him a cup of coffee and a cigarette to calm his nerves, before sending him to the rear."[1]

Lieutenant J. J. Smith, commanding Company E, who had not slept the previous night, worked under the dim light of his command post in the cellar of a house just behind the frontline held by his company. "At dawn heavy artillery began dropping in on us and did not cease all day long. During the night, snipers had succeeded in gaining positions within our company sectors, and sniping was carried out all day long. Details were formed to ferret out these men, but they were so well hidden that it was almost an impossible task."[2]

Lieutenant John Phillips, the platoon leader of the 3rd Platoon of Company E, was sitting in one of the enemy foxholes captured during the prior night's fighting. "At 05:30, 20 September, the battalion ordered a direct assault into the park from the three sides held by our troops.

"The platoon was to move back into the north end of the park where they had been patrolling, assault the enemy gun positions from the rear, then proceed on to the bridge.

"The Germans had brought reinforcements across the bridge during the early morning, and when the platoon moved into the assault it was met by a terrific volume of automatic weapons fire and forced back into its previous positions.

"Two bazooka teams were brought forward and put into action against the gun positions in the park and an old Dutch fort (the Valkhof) that was located near the bridge. They were successful in eliminating the gun positions to their front in the park, but their weapons had no effect on the fort.

"Enemy snipers that had infiltrated into the buildings behind the platoon were beginning to make their presence felt and it was necessary to put a four man patrol into these buildings in an effort to eliminate them. By 1200 they had killed six Germans and the harassing fire in the rear of the platoon had subsided. The Germans however, had succeeded in killing three men and wounding four others so seriously that they had to be evacuated.

"Artillery had started to fall on the platoon positions about 0700 and continued throughout most of the day. The enemy batteries were located behind a dike on the opposite side of the river and each time they fired, the report gave sufficient warning for everyone to get down in their foxholes. Their efforts were not totally unrewarded, as the platoon was receiving numerous casualties."[3]

The 2nd Battalion attack was held up that morning while the British Grenadier Guards cleaned out the built up area of Nijmegen between the railroad and highway bridges. Vandervoort knew that his men were very hungry, having exhausted the rations they had brought with them on the jump. "Every back porch seemed to have a cage of Belgium hares and every house a garden. There was time to cook, so GI rabbit stew came on the menu. I don't recall that it qualified as gourmet."[4]

That morning, Private Wayne W. Galvin, with Company F, decided to look for food. "[Private Kenneth V.] Mickey Hungerford and I were shaking down some two-story brick flats. Close to the Nijmegen bridge, we had entered a house and were upstairs when seven or eight Germans ran in on the first floor. As we were a block from any help, we decided to get out. I looked out a back window onto what looked like a porch roof. I stepped out and crashed through to the back porch. What I thought was a roof was glass painted black. Hungerford jumped through a second behind me and we ran out through the backyard. All the noise of the crashing glass must have frightened the Germans and kept them inside as we got away easily.

"Hungerford said, 'Boy, you sure are one helluva guy to follow!'"[5]

While waiting for the order to attack, Company E platoon leader Lieutenant Jim Coyle decided to try to knock out the 88mm dual-purpose gun which had fired the previous afternoon through the row houses that his platoon occupied. "I took five men through the backyards of the buildings on our left and worked our way to the end of the block, where I hoped to be able to spot the antitank gun which had fired. When we got into the attic of the corner building, I could see the gun with its crew in the street at the corner [across from the traffic circle]. We opened fire with M1s from the attic window. The crew could not spot our firing position. When one of their men was hit, they abandoned the gun and withdrew to a nearby trench where there were other enemy troops. We were firing down on them and hit some. The rest retreated into the park."[6]

Lieutenant Coyle later received the Silver Star for his courageous leadership during the previous day's action and for knocking out the 88mm gun.

In one of the row houses in the middle of the block that the 1st Platoon had occupied since the previous afternoon, Corporal Thomas Burke and Private First Class Earl Boling decided to check the house next door for food. As Boling stepped out of the back door and into the yard, "we both heard a bullet snap over our heads, and as we ducked for protection near the wall of the house, I saw the body of Sergeant Popilsky. I checked him and he appeared to have been shot in the head as he had come over the garden wall, apparently to join us. I checked his pulse and found that he was dead."[7]

Meanwhile, Coyle maintained his watch on the 88mm antiaircraft gun. "While waiting to see if they would re-man the gun, I sent Private [John L.] Gill back to the company CP to tell the CO where I was and what we were doing. When he didn't return as I had instructed, I sent another man. This man returned immediately and told me that Gill was lying wounded in the back yard next door. Gill told me that as he started back he had been shot from the back door of the adjacent house. We pulled him to cover. We threw grenades in the windows of the house, but the Germans kept firing out of the door. Corporal Burke tried to rush the door, but was hit with machine pistol fire and killed immediately."[8]

He fell backward into Boling's arms. "As I tried to drag his body out, a grenade was thrown at me and I felt a numbing pain in my left leg near the knee. I fired a burst of BAR fire up the stairs where the Germans had run. Some men attempted to throw grenades into the second floor windows at the Germans, but they were also throwing concussion grenades as well as potato masher grenades with a fragmentation sleeve on them."[9]

While his men fired into the house, Coyle saw his medic signal him from over the wall at the next house. "He had heard us firing and had come by himself from the platoon CP to see if anyone was wounded. He shouted to me that Sergeant Popilsky was lying dead on the other side of the wall. Popilsky had apparently heard our fire from the attack [on the 88mm gun crew], and had left the platoon on his own and had been killed as he started over the wall by the Germans in the house, who later wounded Gill.

"A grenade flew out of a window in the house and badly wounded Corporal [Richard] Crouse. I realized that we had to get out of the yard as we had no cover. And despite all our fire, the Germans were in a position in the house where we couldn't hit them, but they could hit us. I pulled the men out of the yard and blew the back of the house with a bazooka round. I then took the men back to our original position down the block. We had knocked out the antitank gun. The Germans abandoned it and did no more firing. But, we lost three men killed and one wounded."[10]

Despite the back of the house being blown by a bazooka round, two Germans remained well hidden inside. When Lieutenant Coyle and the others moved back to their positions in the other houses, the Germans slipped out of the back of the house and into any alley to make their way back to German held positions. About that time, Lieutenant Bill Meddaugh, the Company E executive officer, left the company CP with Lieutenant Smith to inspect the dispositions in the front line buildings. "Smith had a .45 caliber automatic [pistol] stuck in his hip pocket. I was carrying my Tommy gun. As we came out of the cellar and started to move across our backyard towards the alley—suddenly the two Germans in their camouflage outfits appeared from around the corner of the wall moving directly towards us. We were in single file—J. J. in the lead. My reaction when I saw them was that they were *prisoners* and I expected to see one or more of our men following close behind. But it suddenly dawned on me that they were both armed with machine pistols. This thought process probably took a couple of seconds while we stared at each other. Then they broke and ran to the rear around the corner of the wall—J. J. and I in hot pursuit. He was able to get a couple of fast shots away with his pistol and I got off a burst with my Thompson. The Kraut to the rear was killed, but the front runner managed to get around another corner and out of view. We chased after him and heard shouting—the German had run head on into three or four of our men and he surrendered promptly. How these two managed to survive for two days in our midst, I'll never know—but this ended the affair."[11]

Lieutenant James J. Smith received the Silver Star for unhesitatingly and aggressively attacking the two heavily armed Germans and for his heroic conduct during the operation in Nijmegen.

Corporal Thomas Burke was posthumously awarded an oak leaf cluster to his previous award of the Silver Star for his courage in rushing the house to clear it of the hidden enemy.

The interminable wait for the order to attack weighed heavily on the minds of every trooper as German artillery and mortar fire rained down on their positions and snipers harassed them. Corporal Clifford W. Putman and two other 2nd Platoon, Company E troopers were buried alive when their position was hit by enemy artillery fire. Putman, although wounded, extracted himself and the other two men, carried them to safety, and refused evacuation. Corporal Putman knew that every available trooper would be needed for the coming assault.

German troops had succeeded in infiltrating into the area held by Lieutenant John Phillips' 3rd Platoon of Company E, southeast of the highway bridge during the night. "At 10:00 the three 60mm mortar squads in the company were grouped and attached to the platoon. These squads were put into position and given several targets to fire on. They had fired on the first target for effect when the enemy artillery located the position and knocked it out. Five men were injured and two mortars damaged so badly they could not be used.

"It was learned later that the enemy had observers to the rear of the platoon, thus accounting for their accurate fire on every move being made by the men.

"The battalion medics were unable to evacuate all the casualties, so the platoon aid man moved the injured men into the basement of a building where he could care for them and await help to effect their evacuation."[12]

Two of the wounded troopers with the mortar squads were Staff Sergeant Otis Sampson and Private First Class Dennis O'Loughlin. Despite being wounded, O'Loughlin left the area unarmed, except for his .45 caliber pistol to find help. He located an unoccupied jeep during a German barrage and made an incredibly daring drive through the city while being shot at and as artillery shells fell all around him. He was finally able to find the position and evacuate the wounded mortarmen to the battalion aid station.

One of the 3rd Platoon troopers, Private First Class Fred Hebein, did a great deal to eliminate the threat of the infiltrating enemy soldiers. He shot a German in an adjacent field about to open fire on Lieutenant Phillips. Hebein then spotted two more Germans, who had infiltrated into a nearby foxhole. He charged the position and killed both. When he observed enemy fire from the window of a building on Batavierenweg, he crossed an open yard and tossed a Gammon grenade into the window, wounding several and forcing the surrender of all of the Germans inside the house.

BEHIND THE DIKE on the southern side of the Waal River, just west of the railroad bridge area, troopers of the 504th Parachute Infantry Regiment waited for boats to arrive in order to make an assault crossing of the river. Tucker's tough veterans would make the assault crossing and capture the northern ends of the two Nijmegen bridges, while Vandervoort's troopers and the British Grenadier Guards would assault the southern ends of the highway and railroad bridges.

THE 2ND BATTALION ASSAULT PLAN on the highway bridge called for the 1st Platoon of Company F, supported by two British tanks, to attack Hunner Park from Walstraat on the left flank; the 3rd Platoon of Company F to attack Hunner Park from Gerard Noodstraat in the center; and the 2nd Platoon of Company F on the right would attack the traffic circle from Canisiustraat.

The 2nd Platoon of Company E, led by Lieutenant Nicholas J. Psaki, and two British Sherman tanks, would attack from Graadt Van Roggenstraat due north toward the bridge approach. The 1st Platoon of Company E and a section of the light machine gun platoon of Headquarters Company, 2nd Battalion, would provide overhead cover fire from the houses on Graadt Van Roggenstraat. The 3rd Platoon of Company E would provide suppressive fire on enemy positions, interdict Germans attempting to reinforce the position, and assault the enemy positions from the rear.

However, Captain Robert Rosen, the commander of Company F, who had no combat experience prior to Holland, ordered a premature assault on Hunner Park without first informing or receiving permission from Lieutenant Colonel

Vandervoort. Company F would make the attack without coordination with, nor help from, Company E and British armor.

Company F moved toward Hunner Park and the traffic circle with the 1st Platoon on Walstraat on the left, the 3rd Platoon on Gerard Noodtstraat in the center, and the 2nd Platoon on Canisiustraat on the right. As the 3rd Platoon moved through a portion of the street containing shops with large plate glass windows, incoming heavy-caliber artillery could be heard. The troopers took cover in doorways of the shops as a shell exploded in the middle of the street. Deadly shrapnel and flying glass from shattered windows filled the air. The 3rd Platoon leader, Lieutenant Jack Carroll, "was wounded in the leg and taken out through the apartments by jeep and just escaped being captured."[13]

As Company F continued its advance, heavy automatic 20mm antiaircraft fire filled the street, ricocheting off the wrought iron fences and hitting the brick fronts of the houses. It was just before 2:30 p.m., and Lieutenant Rusty Hays, assistant platoon leader of the 2nd Platoon, was about to get his baptism of fire. "Soon we had the whole company in the front and back yards of the houses just across the street from the park, the company objective.

"About that time, the company commander comes up, swings his Tommy gun around his head, and shouts, 'Follow me!' and runs across the side street into the park. About twenty men—those that were nearby, and who heard him—followed him.

"As I started to follow him, I looked to my left and saw two Germans, carrying a machine gun, come out of the door from the stone wall about two hundred yards to my left. They put it down on the street and began to get in position to fire it. I stopped in the middle of the street and fired at them with my Tommy gun. Since a Tommy gun fires pistol ammunition, the Germans were a little too far away for accuracy, but they heard the slugs hitting around them and ducked back inside the stone door, leaving the machine gun sitting in the street.

"Since the machine gun was still a threat, I stopped in the middle of the street and looked around for a bazooka man who was nearby. I told him to fire into the door where the Germans had come from. When the bazooka round exploded in the door, I knew we had seen the last of those two Germans, even if we hadn't hit them. They wouldn't dare come out again."[14]

As this took place, Sergeant Spencer Wurst led his squad forward as the company poured out of the houses. "We got to the street and started into the park under direct small-arms, grenade, and machine gun fire at ranges of fifteen to seventy-five yards. We formed a crude line on the run and assaulted across the street. The enemy was well dug in, fighting from foxholes and trenches located between the sidewalk on back to a hundred yards into the park.

"Just as we got into the skirmish line, a crucial thing happened. A very big, scared German soldier—I only saw him flash in my mind—leaped up from a foxhole just inside the park. He lifted his hands up over his head as he ran across the sidewalk toward us. There was absolutely no doubt about his intentions. He had his hands up high over his head, very evidently wanting to surrender. But as he leaped up, many men fired on him. In combat you must react instinctively and quickly. This is what we did, and the man was practically a sieve before he hit the ground."[15]

This happened in plain sight of the SS grenadiers defending Hunner Park, who now believed the paratroopers were not going to take prisoners. Wurst and some of the troopers made it into the edge of the park. "I don't know how many men from either platoon made it across the street on the first assault, but we took many casualties. I got across and into the park. Just before I took cover, I saw Captain Rosen run back down the middle of the street. He passed me going full speed to the rear, holding both his hands over his mouth. He had evidently been shot through the face."[16]

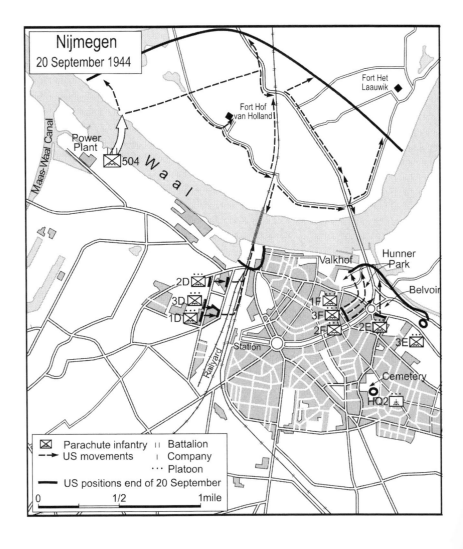

Nijmegen
20 September 1944

Fort Het
Laauwik

Fort Hof
van Holland

Maas-Waal Canal

Power
Plant

504

W a a l

Valkhof

Hunner
Park

Belvoir

2D

3D

1D

1F

3F

2F   2E

3E

Station

Cemetery

HQ2

Parachute infantry   ‖ Battalion
US movements   ‖ Company
                               ⋯ Platoon
US positions end of 20 September

0   1/2   1mile

With that, the attack fell apart—before Lieutenant Hays could follow them into the park. "The men who had gone into the park came running back, many of them wounded. The company commander was hit in the face and died just as he got back to my side of the street. A couple of more wounded came back, and then the man who asked me to get him out of the stockade so he could make the jump with us, ran up to me and pointed to a wound in his chest and said, 'Quick, put a tourniquet on it.' Just as I grabbed him, he died.

"As we looked into the park, we could see one of our men on the ground, with a medic bandaging him. Finally, the medic came trotting back and said the man was still alive but would soon die from loss of blood if we didn't get him soon. Another officer and I dropped weapons and ran over to get him. I'm sure the Germans saw us, but didn't fire because we were there to pick up our wounded. The other officer grabbed his shoulders and I grabbed his feet. As I did, he opened his eyes. We carried him out of the park. I presumed he lived; I never heard from him again."[17]

In addition to Captain Rosen, Corporal Max D. McCleary and Private William L. Hall, with the 3rd Platoon, and Privates Jack C. Williams and John J. Baynes with the 2nd Platoon were killed and two others seriously wounded. Lieutenant Joseph W. "Little Joe" Holcomb, the executive officer and a veteran highly respected among the men, assumed command of Company F. The troopers cleaned and reloaded their weapons, brought up more ammunition, and prepared for the next attack they knew would come very soon.

As the 3rd Battalion, 504th made its daring and epic crossing of the Waal River, Lieutenant Colonel Vandervoort received the orders for which he and his battalion had been waiting. "Finally, it was decided to 'go for the bridge.' General Adair ordered a coordinated paratrooper/tank attack to put his armor over the Waal. Our company commanders and key officers gathered at the battalion observation post. Toward the north, from windows twenty feet above street level, we looked down into Hunner Park crowded with enemy emplacements. The park was the place the great bridge would be won or lost. We held the high ground, the good ground, from which to launch our attack. The smooth sloping area was, as I remember, a little less than one quarter of a mile deep and a little more than that wide. A 'bare-assed' prospect, somebody observed. There was no concealment, and firepower would be the only cover when we moved. E Company on the right and F Company on the left would assault the park. They would hit the park simultaneously with Goulburn's tanks, all moving together and try to finish it fast."[18]

After receiving the attack order, Lieutenant Holcomb waited with his troopers for the assault to commence. Time seemed to stand still as Sergeant Wurst waited for the attack. "As we got ready to go for the second attempt, Lieutenant Holcomb calmly walked out on the street and gave the order to assault."[19]

At 4:20 p.m., from the roofs and upper story windows of houses fronting the park and the traffic circle, Company E's 1st Platoon and a section of the light machine gun platoon of Headquarters Company, 2nd Battalion, and from the ridge to the southeast, the other section of the light machine gun platoon of

Headquarters Company, 2nd Battalion and machine guns of the 3rd Platoon of Company E unleashed a torrent of automatic weapons fire into the trenches, gun pits, and buildings occupied by the enemy.

Private First Class Charles R. Varvakis, with the 3rd Platoon of Company E, trained his .30 caliber light machine gun on the Germans defending the north end of Hunner Park and the bridge approach, pinning them in their holes, denying them observation and movement to mount a counterattack.

Additional firepower from a captured French heavy machine gun that Private First Class Fred Hebein had brought up, added its weight to the fire covering the assault.

Vandervoort's paratroopers moved out to assault Hunner Park, the traffic circle, and southern end of the bridge. Veteran Company F trooper, Corporal W. A. Jones, Wurst's assistant squad leader, did not want a repeat of the earlier attack that had failed. "Everybody went in with the idea that we were not going to pull back. If they take us back, they're going to have to carry us back."[20]

As the paratroopers poured out of houses, Wurst watched them deploy "into a rough skirmish line, formed on the run. I glanced to my right and left, and what a sight I saw! A nearly perfect, coordinated attack by two infantry companies on line."[21]

The Germans held their fire until everyone was exposed in the street, then the whole area exploded as almost six hundred trained infantrymen opened up with every available automatic weapon and rifle. The paratroopers fired from the hip as they ran forward. Tracers—waist high, chest high, head high, and a foot or so off the ground crisscrossed the park and traffic circle. The firing was at almost point-blank range—25 to 150 yards. Plunging fire from enemy paratroopers firing machine guns from the upper-floor windows of the Villa Belvoir and SS gunners from the Valkhof filled the air. Wounded and dead paratroopers littered the street in front of the park.

Corporal Jones had never experienced anything like the volume of fire in the park that day. "It was tremendously heavy . . . machine guns, 20mms, 88s, everything. On the wall along the left, they had taken out bricks and put machine guns in the portholes."[22]

German snipers targeted anyone displaying signs of leadership. Lieutenant Hays fired his Thompson submachine gun as he ran forward into the park. "Everywhere I looked men were falling. . . . I saw the new company commander [Lieutenant Holcomb] fall; a bullet had gone into the front of his helmet and had come out the back. 'He has to be dead,' I thought."[23]

Lieutenant William H. Savell, commanding F Company's 2nd Platoon, was shot through both arms as he crossed the street into the park. Private Arthur L. Gregory saw this and moved through the intense fire to get to Savell. Gregory picked him up and carried the stricken lieutenant toward safety, when a sniper's bullet struck Gregory, mortally wounding him. Private Gregory was later posthumously awarded the Silver Star for his self-sacrifice. The 3rd Platoon leader, Lieutenant Jack Carroll, had already been wounded seriously by artillery fire that morning. Company F had now lost four of its eight officers.

Vandervoort "was with Lieutenant [John H.] Dodd's platoon in the park at Nijmegen. Lieutenant Dodd was hit in the stomach by a small bore exploding antitank shell. It shattered every one of his vital organs."[24]

Vandervoort knew "it was a mortal wound that should have killed him instantly, but he was a hard dying young man.

"His platoon aid man, with tears in his eyes, gave his dying young lieutenant an overdose of morphine to ease his pain. His platoon attacked the Kraut gun crew that killed their lieutenant. Furious, they gave no quarter, and the gun crew stood its ground."[25]

Private Wayne Galvin and other 1st Platoon troopers attacked and wiped out the crew of the 20mm antiaircraft gun that had killed Lieutenant Dodd. "Sergeant [Vernon L.] Francisco, being so upset about Lieutenant Dodd, stood right out in the open, throwing grenades at the Germans."[26]

For Vandervoort, the loss of Lieutenant Dodd "made me mad and very sad, but at that time I had seen so many of my men die. I felt he was the most beloved officer by his platoon of anyone in the battalion. For that alone he was a great loss to us all."[27]

Company F trooper, Private First Class Bob Hughart, was pinned down by enemy machine gun and 20mm fire upon entering the park. "We lost our platoon medic [Private First Class Vernon D. Carnes]. He was lying on the ground beside me—a white tracer hit him in the left side of his chest."[28]

Sergeant James T. Steed, the Company F communications NCO, tried to help one of the badly wounded troopers, a "European kid who had served in the armies of four countries and spoke seven languages. He was very religious and so proud to be an American. He prayed and I yelled for a medic, but none came—there were too many wounded. He died with his head in my lap."[29]

A short time later, Steed narrowly escaped death when he was shot down as he advanced. "I was wounded by machine gun fire. It hit my 536 radio. The shrapnel from the radio hit my face and shoulder."[30]

Lieutenant J. J. Smith, commanding Company E, watched the 2nd Platoon, supported by two tanks, move out of the buildings toward the highway bridge approach. "Covered by automatic weapons fire from the 1st Platoon, the attacking echelon moved out with fixed bayonets. A hand-to-hand battle followed in which the 2nd Platoon men had to literally drive the Germans from their holes with grenades and cold steel."[31]

Lieutenant Nicholas Psaki led the 2nd Platoon assault, blowing a gap in a barbed wire obstacle with a Gammon grenade and leading them through it to engage a dug in platoon of SS infantry at close range. The fight soon turned to hand to hand combat, as Psaki and his men bayoneted, clubbed, and grenaded the SS troops in their holes. For his courageous leadership during the assault Lieutenant Nicholas Psaki was awarded the Silver Star.

That afternoon, incredible bravery was commonplace. Private Camille E. Gagne, a rifle grenadier with Company E, in position on the roof of a building overlooking the highway bridge approach, fired grenade after grenade at the German mortar positions, preventing them from having direct observation of the attacking elements of the two companies. From his position on the same building, Private Robert E. Nurse fired his BAR to interdict any traffic on the bridge approach. Their fire was so devastating that an enemy Mark IV self-propelled gun fired at them from only four hundred yards away. Despite the high velocity fire from the 75mm gun, Gagne and Nurse courageously kept firing.

Private First Class Clyde F. Knox, a Company E medic, watched German artillery zero in on the building that Gagne and three others occupied. "A German 88 gun crew spotted them—after the first round landed close by, they moved off the top of the building into a small shack. Corporal [Clifford] Putman, who was the squad leader, said, 'The only way they will hit us now is by a direct hit.' A direct hit came in demolishing the building, killing Private Nurse and Private Gagne, and wounding Private Paul C. Trotman and Corporal Putman."[32]

Privates Gagne and Nurse were posthumously awarded the Silver Star for their heroism.

Private Kenneth Hungerford, with Company F, deliberately exposed himself to draw fire in order to locate some very well camouflaged positions which were being used by the SS grenadiers to pin down his squad. He then led them forward to assault the enemy manning those positions.

German artillery, direct fire from high-velocity antiaircraft and antitank guns across the river, and long-range machine gun fire hit the Company E troopers of 3rd Platoon occupying the ridge on open ground southeast of the bridge, severely wounding Private First Class Jimmy Keenan. "I was hit in five places, including a nerve separation wound in my right ankle by a 240mm airburst. [Private First Class Edward W.] Ed Arndt, at the risk of his life, came down the ravine into which I was blown, and carried me bodily up the steep incline into cover."[33]

Private First Class Charles Varvakis, with the 3rd Platoon of Company E, kept firing his machine gun despite being almost blown from his position by airbursts from German 88mm antiaircraft guns across the river.

Enemy snipers in buildings and in the woods fired at the 3rd Platoon and Headquarters Company, 2nd Battalion machine gunners to suppress the heavy fire they were placing on the Germans defending Hunner Park and the bridge. Private First Class Edward Przyborowski, the 3rd Platoon's runner single-handedly manned an abandoned German MG-42 to protect the platoon's flank. He also carried ammunition to the other machine guns under extremely heavy artillery fire.

Private Robert H. Cooper, with the 3rd Platoon of Company E, dashed across open ground under sniper and artillery fire to bring up a bazooka team and pointed out sniper positions in buildings to the bazooka gunner. Together, they killed three snipers in well concealed positions. One of the machine gunners told him about snipers firing at them from woods to their left. Cooper directed his rifle fire at the hidden enemy snipers, drawing their fire away from the machine guns and eventually silencing them. A short time later, a sniper who had infiltrated into a building behind his foxhole, shot and killed Cooper.

Private First Class Fred Hebein, Charles Varvakis, and Edward Przyborowski and Private Robert Cooper, all with the 3rd Platoon of Company

E, would each later be awarded the Silver Star for their valor in support of the assault. Sadly, Przyborowski would be killed in action on September 26. With genuine modesty typical of these veterans, another 3rd Platoon trooper, Private First Class Don Lassen stated that those four "are the guys that are responsible for me being alive today. They were the bravest and the toughest guys I have ever known."[34]

Vandervoort was very thankful to have the British Grenadier Guards tanks supporting his troopers. "With those Shermans bearing down on them, the Germans aimed most of their fire at the tanks. Otherwise, more of the troopers would have been wiped out. Bullets bounced off Shermans like hailstones. Some were chipped, but none were holed. The Germans, stiffened by elements of the 9th SS Recon Battalion, kept firing full bore until overrun. Moving with the troopers, the tanks rolled over trenches and fired point blank into air raid shelters. It was 'walking fire' with tanks—the effect was devastating. The air in Hunner Park turned blue with hand grenade, cannon, rifle, and gun smoke generated by hundreds of combatants."[35]

In Hunner Park, Company F troopers were getting enfilade fire from the Valkhof ruins on their left flank as they moved forward. Lieutenant Hays, one of the few officers left in Company F by this time, "realized something had to be done or all our men would be killed. To our left was a fifteen-foot stone wall; somehow it had to be coming from there. I looked behind me, and there in the street was a British tank. I ran back, banged on the tank with my Tommy gun, and climbed upon the tank. The tank commander stuck his head out. I told him my men were being slaughtered and we needed help. He was reluctant to leave his position. I begged him to come help, and finally he agreed.

"Before I jumped down from the tank, he handed me a bottle of brandy and said, 'Here, you need some of this.' I must have looked as shook up as I felt. I don't remember if I took his brandy or not, but I did direct him into the park.

"When he got there he said, 'What do I shoot at?'

"I said, 'I don't know. That wall must have something to do with this; shoot at that wall.' I thought at the time, it sounded pretty silly; but I didn't know what else to say.

"He may have fired his machine guns; I know he didn't fire his cannon; but suddenly the firing stopped. Later, I learned that the stone wall was a retaining wall for the ground in the old fort and the ground was flush with the top of the wall. The Germans had dug a trench along the top and were firing at us from point-blank range. The reason the firing stopped was that the British infantry had captured the fort."[36]

The fire coming straight at the paratroopers in the park did not subside, however. If anything, it increased as SS grenadiers, now pinned in their foxholes and trenches, fought with the fury of cornered animals. The firing was so heavy that Sergeant Spencer Wurst took cover behind a tree. "From behind my tree, I observed [Howard R.] Krueger as he crawled fifteen or twenty feet to my right front. He actually reached down into a foxhole, grabbed a German, and pulled him out. He motioned the prisoner to the rear, and both of them crawled back to our skirmish line. The German didn't stop; he crawled another twenty feet and stopped to help our medic bandage one of our wounded. Very shortly thereafter, he was killed by German fire.

"I glanced to my right rear and saw Colonel Vandervoort, our battalion commander, approaching my position. Our dead and wounded were lying all around us, hit only moments earlier. We pleaded with the CO not to expose himself to the heavy fire, but he continued until he reached my position. He looked at me and calmly said, 'Sergeant, I think you better go see if you can get that tank moving.'"[37]

The same tank that Lieutenant Hays had used to suppress the fire from the Valkhof was still at the edge of the park, the commander justifiably concerned about the 88mm dual purpose guns and Panzerfausts.

Corporal W. A. Jones witnessed 88s even firing at individuals. "There was one 88 in the park and one down by the bridge. If you stuck your head up they would fire that thing at you."[38]

Sergeant Wurst asked Vandervoot to take cover, then jumped up and ran through a blizzard of fire to the tank. Wurst beat on the turret with his helmet and the tank commander once again raised the hatch. "I hollered to the tank commander, relating the colonel's order to move forward and continue firing. We talked a minute or two, and I pointed out targets. While I was showing him where he should shoot, I had to remain standing. Finally the tank lumbered forward, and I gave arm and hand signals to what was left of my squad to get up and start moving."[39]

Corporal Jones jumped to his feet and started forward beside the tank, raking the holes and trenches with his Thompson as he advanced. "We just kept going. Some of the Germans stayed in their holes, and some of them saw we weren't going to stop and left their guns and tried to run."[40] Jones and the others mercilessly shot them as they attempted to run.

Sergeant Wurst and his men came to a barbed wire entanglement that ran through the middle of the park. "We wanted the tank to move through to make a path. Instead, it advanced a little to our left front. We went to the right and had a real time getting through the wire. [Larry] Niepling, with a shortened belt of ammo, was actually firing his light .30 caliber machine gun from the standing position as he moved through the wire. Then there was a little Greek from the 1st Platoon, George [A.] Pagalotis, a bazooka man whose bazooka was almost as long as he was tall. He ran right up to a fortification dug into a bank by the Valkhof and fired a round directly into the opening. I think someone from the 1st Platoon got the tank's attention and moved it over to the bank, where it fired rounds into the fortification from five to six feet away. Talk about direct, point blank fire!

"My squad was the first to break through to the east side of the park. When we got on the east side of the barbed wire, we dropped into a well constructed, World War I–type trench the Germans had dug. From here we had a good view that overlooked the approach road, the entrance to the bridge, and the bridge itself. I heard some shouted commands from my distant left rear that I later learned was British infantry moving up by the numbers."[41]

Vandervoort's paratroopers shot, bayoneted, or grenaded the Germans in their holes as they advanced through the park. "'No quarter' combat became the order of the day throughout that quarter-mile-square area. The fighting was so close, individual Germans were either too brave or too scared to surrender— probably both. The Germans seemed indifferent to death. The paratroopers retaliated with ice-cold ruthlessness. That gladiatorial test of wills gave a shocking crescendo to the battle. The British Shermans gave the troopers the cumulative edge. Position by position, the trooper/tank collaboration closed down Hunner Park. The enemy finally broke and ran east and west. Others were driven into the Waal."[42]

Sergeant Wurst and his men caught the Germans attempting to escape. "As we dropped down into the trench, groups of Germans started to withdraw across the bridge, taking cover behind the girders. This was a bad move. We had seized the high ground overlooking the bridge and had a perfect view. As soon as they dashed to the next girder, we had them."[43]

Sergeant Wurst's squad and the machine guns on the ridge southeast of the bridge opened up on the fleeing Germans, cutting them down. From his position in the trench Sergeant Wurst could see that "there were thirty or so to start, but I don't believe a single one got across.

"Right after, another group of Germans came from our left. This group was pretty smart. They rushed up the left side of the bank all together, went over the top, across the road, and down on the right side of the road that led to the bridge. There was a large drop-off on the east side of the road, so they gained the cover of the roadbed. They took us by surprise and got away with it."[44]

This group of about sixty Germans led by SS Captain Euling was the only one to escape. A few individuals were able to make it across the highway bridge. Of the six hundred or so, mostly SS grenadiers and German paratroopers, who defended the south side of the highway bridge, only about sixty were taken prisoner, and about sixty in Captain Euling's group escaped in the darkness east along the south bank of the Waal. Vandervoort's veteran troopers and the Grenadier Guards killed or mortally wounded the remainder.

A British officer with the Royal Engineers came up and asked for volunteers to remove demolition charges from the bridge. Private Kenneth Hungerford, with Company F, volunteered to accompany him. Hungerford was the first 505 trooper to reach the highway bridge. Private First Class Bob Hughart observed him "on the ground under the bridge when he got shot. He was our company barber. I had loaned him four pounds back in England before we left."[45]

For his gallantry in the assault by his platoon, Private Hungerford was later posthumously awarded the Silver Star.

As the fighting around the southern approach of the highway bridge wound down, Vandervoort's troopers and British Guards infantry mopped up small pockets of Germans. Private First Class Ken Russell and three Company F buddies were "standing, watching our last medic [Technician Fifth Grade Lloyd G. Ellingson] doctoring one of our guys, when an SS trooper near the rubble of the castle (that we thought a rabbit couldn't live in) dashed by us and shot the medic and killed him. It was such a surprise that we all opened up on him as he ran over the hill and killed him."[46] Private Michael A. Brilla was one of the F Company troopers who shot the fleeing German. "I have never seen so many tracers from our machine guns go through one man before he hit the ground."[47]

One of the SS prisoners taken at Hunner Park was a paymaster who Private First Class Bob Hughart found to have "had about twenty thousand dollars in German Marks in a briefcase. We could not use the money of course—but made it do for toilet paper."[48]

During the assault, a mortar shell had wounded Company F trooper, Private Wayne Galvin. "My left wrist was shattered—I was also hit in the left thigh. I stayed for several more hours, then was helping to escort some prisoners back when my leg gave out."[49]

The scene in Hunner Park and the traffic circle was appalling. German corpses and mortally wounded were lying half in their trenches and foxholes where they had been bayoneted or shot. Wounded and dead troopers littered the street and the park. Weapons and the debris of war were strewn everywhere.

MEANWHILE, NORTH OF THE RIVER, the 504th PIR, with incredible courage, had captured the north ends of both bridges, despite suffering heavy casualties during the river crossing. Its troopers were reorganizing and consolidating positions to establish a perimeter to protect the bridgehead.

DESPITE GERMAN ARTILLERY FIRE falling just south of the bridge, the Grenadier Guards commander, Lieutenant Colonel Edward Goulburn, ordered a troop of four Sherman tanks led by Sergeant Peter Robinson to cross the great highway bridge. Everyone fully expected the bridge to be blown any moment. From his observation post in one of the houses held by Company E, Vandervoort had a front row seat to watch Robinson's four tanks cross the bridge. "As Sergeant Robinson's lead Sherman approached the midpoint of the bridge, from dead ahead, an 88mm antitank gun opened fire. It should have been a mismatch. One or more tanks, knocked out, could block the bridge. Our tanks stopped and returned fire. The lead Sherman fired its cannon as fast as it could load and sprayed the road ahead with its .30-caliber machine gun. The 88 fired half a dozen—more or less—near misses, ripping and screaming with an unforgettable sound—past the turret of the tank. In the gathering dusk they looked like great Roman candle balls of fire. Brightly glowing, 17-pounder cannon shots rocketed back along with flashing machine gun tracers. Suddenly, the 88 went silent. One of the tanks' .30-caliber armor-piercing rounds had penetrated the soft metallic end cap of the 88's recoil mechanism, causing the gun to jam. That improbable, long-odds happenstance of good marksmanship and good luck ended the shoot-out on the bridge."[50]

As Robinson's Sherman tanks continued across, German General Heinz Harmel, commander of the 10th SS Panzer Division, looked through his binoculars from a concrete pillbox northeast of the bridge near Lent. Lieutenant

General Wilhelm Bittrich, commanding the II SS Panzer Corps, had been ordered by Field Marshal Walter Model not to blow the bridge. Harmel was determined not to allow the bridge to fall into Allied hands. He didn't want to be brought to Berlin to be executed for allowing the British to cross the Waal River. When he saw Robinson's tank reach the center of the bridge, Harmel gave the order to the engineer waiting nearby to push the plunger on the detonator. "Get ready . . . Let it blow!"[51]

Nothing happened. "'Again!' I was waiting to see the bridge collapse and the tanks plunge into the river. Instead, they moved relentlessly, getting bigger and bigger, closer and closer."[52]

Harmel turned to his staff and said, "My God, they'll be here in two minutes. Stolley, tell Bittrich. They're over the Waal."[53]

Upon reaching the north side of the bridge, Robinson's tanks linked up with 3rd Battalion, 504th PIR troopers, who held the northern end of the bridges. At around 7:15 p.m., the highway bridge was firmly in Allied hands. German artillery pummeled the southern approaches to the highway bridge while snipers fired from across the river to interdict British infantry attempting to cross the bridge to reinforce the bridgehead.

The attack to capture the two bridges had been costly for the 2nd Battalion. Company F lost seventeen killed and twenty-three wounded in the two days of the attack on the bridges. Company E suffered nine killed and twenty-five wounded.

Company F trooper, Private Donald W. McKeage, one of the extremely fortunate individuals not killed or wounded in the assault on Hunner Park looked over the area in the aftermath of the assault. "The park was covered with dead and wounded Germans; the road was covered with our dead and wounded."[54]

McKeage noticed that the citizens of Nijmegen began to appear from their cellars, even as German artillery fell just north at the bridge approach. "They had blankets and flowers for our dead troopers. They didn't show the same respect for the dead Krauts; they kicked the hell out of some of them."[55]

That evening, Corporal Clifford Putman, wounded earlier that day, volunteered to lead a patrol of Easy Company troopers to mop up the area. The patrol captured nine prisoners before Putman was again wounded by shrapnel and had to be evacuated. Corporal Putman was later awarded the Silver Star for his courageous actions throughout the morning, afternoon, and evening of September 20.

THE RAILROAD BRIDGE was also in Allied hands, as the Germans defending the southern approaches to it, had stampeded across the bridge after the 3rd Battalion, 504th PIR had successfully crossed the Waal River and threatened to cut off the path of retreat. As they fled across the railroad bridge, nineteen troopers with the 3rd Battalion, 504th, opened up on them. The next morning, 267 dead Germans were counted on the bridge.

On the evening of September 20, Company D moved into a factory building near the railroad bridge. Lieutenant Charles Qualls took over as executive officer, replacing Lieutenant Wray, and Lieutenant Joe Meyers was given command of the 3rd Platoon. The responsibility of guarding the railroad bridge that night was assigned to Lieutenant Meyers and his platoon. "[Sergeant Edward F.] Murphy, my platoon sergeant, and I deployed one rifle squad under Sergeant Donald H. Olds to secure the south approach, [and] Sergeant [Milton E.] Schlesener's squad to guard the north approach. In addition, we placed a guard in a sentry box located in the center of the bridge. The balance of the platoon remained at the factory, prepared to relieve the deployed squads if we remained in position for any length of time. Murphy and I took turns inspecting the positions at night."[56]

THE 2ND BATTALION was awarded a Presidential Unit Citation for its actions in the capture of the two Nijmegen bridges:

The 2nd Battalion, 505th Parachute Infantry Regiment, 82nd Airborne Division, is cited for outstanding performance of duty and extraordinary heroism in action against the enemy on 19 and 20 September 1944 at Nijmegen, Holland. This battalion was given the mission of capturing the city of Nijmegen and the southern approaches of the vital Waal River bridges in that city. The enemy had strong defensive position in the park area and had resisted all efforts during three days to eliminate their forces. With British tanks in support, the 2nd Battalion moved to the attack at 1445 hours, on 19 September, along the main road to the city in the face of artillery and small arms fire. In the city the companies fanned out to their separate missions. The principal effort was aimed against the approaches to the highway bridge. The lead tank was knocked out by direct fire. The troops fought their way through the town and flanked the bridge plaza, while Company E commenced a frontal assault. By 1900 hours all elements were in close contact with the enemy. Patrols from both sides were very active and snipers commanded all streets. Paratroopers rushed the foxholes and trenches and knifed or bayoneted the occupants. Fighting continued through the night. Burning buildings surrounding the bridge-park area revealed every attempt to penetrate enemy defenses. By dawn the situation was a stalemate with the enemy still determined to fight. At 1530 hours on 20 September, the battalion commenced a direct assault from all sides. Fighting with every available weapon, the troopers closed with the enemy. Many Germans chose to die in their foxholes rather than surrender and continued fighting even when their situation seemed hopeless. The battle was not won until 1800 hours, and all organized resistance was eliminated south of the bridge by 1915 hours. British tanks were enabled to cross to the north shore. In this engagement, the battalion suffered 82 casualties, but killed 155 of the enemy, captured 91, and wounded hundreds. The superb achievement of the 2nd Battalion 505th Parachute Infantry Regiment, 82nd Airborne Division in the battle of Nijmegen was characterized by high courage, dogged determination, and superior tenacity, and reflects the highest traditions of the U.S. Armed Forces.

For his heroism and leadership, Lieutenant Colonel Vandervoort was awarded an oak leaf cluster (second award) to the Distinguished Service Cross:

> *Benjamin H. Vandervoort (O-22715), Lieutenant Colonel, U.S. Army, for extraordinary heroism in connection with military operations against an armed enemy in Holland from 17 to 23 September 1944. On September 17, the Second Battalion, 505th Parachute Infantry, Lieutenant Colonel Vandervoort commanding, landed near Groesbeek, Holland. Lieutenant Colonel Vandervoort hastened the reorganization and advanced with his leading element to capture the initial battalion objective in three and one half hours. On the afternoon of the 19th of September 1944, the Second Battalion moved into Nijmegen to attack prepared defensive positions including dug in anti-tank and machine gun nests and camouflaged snipers posts. Lieutenant Colonel Vandervoort supervised and directed the assault while continually under direct fire from these snipers. A coordinated attack was launched on the afternoon of 20 September 1944. Lieutenant Colonel Vandervoort established himself at a forward and exposed position to personally supervise and coordinate the progress of the infantry and attached armored elements. Throughout the entire engagement, his total disregard for his own safety made possible the continued coordination which led to the final seizure of the bridge. Lieutenant Colonel Vandervoort's coolness, outstanding courage and initiative, and his resolute leadership contributed to the success of the mission of seizing intact the railway and highway bridges.*

The actions of the 2nd Battalion contributed to the already legendary mystique of the 82nd Airborne Division's fighting prowess, causing General Sir Miles Dempsey commander of the British Second Army to say to General Gavin on September 23, "I'm proud to meet the commanding general of the finest division in the world today."[57]

EARLY ON THE MORNING OF SEPTEMBER 21, Lieutenant Joe Meyers checked on his Company D platoon, which was responsible for security of the railroad bridge. "I took a stroll across the bridge, stopped to talk to the men on duty, and ended up at [Sergeant Donald] Olds' position on the south end. Olds had occupied the German flak crew's quarters in the stone bridge keep. He invited me to join the off-duty members of his squad for coffee and some abandoned German rations. After our meal, Olds and I walked outside the keep and stopped briefly to talk.

"Someone sounded the alarm when three German fighters suddenly appeared downstream, flying in our direction about fifteen or twenty feet above the water. As they neared the railroad bridge, the planes pulled up, dropped their bombs, and cleared the bridge by a few feet. Not one bomb hit the bridge. However, the upward force of the explosions blew away forty or fifty feet of train rail and decking from the bridge's center span. Although twisted and bent, the I-beams that supported the missing rails and decking remained intact.

"Olds and I ran to the edge of the decking and looked down about fifty or sixty feet to the water below. Although jumping out of an airplane did not bother men, walking on a twisted steel girder, sixty feet in the air, was a frightening experience. Olds and I negotiated the twisted beams and safely reached the far side. The sentry box was intact, but there was no sign of the guard. We ran to the box and found the sentry seated inside unharmed, but stunned by the explosions. Although badly shaken and hard of hearing, he was able to walk around after a few minutes.

"The German attempt to destroy the bridges indicated the importance they attached to the structures. I deployed the balance of my platoon to defend it."[58]

The following day, the 2nd Battalion moved out of Nijmegen and went into division reserve near Groesbeek. Lieutenant Harold E. "Casey" Case also took command of Company F.

On September 23, the battalion marched two miles and relieved the 1st Battalion, 505th at positions running from the north of the Kiekberg Woods in an arc along the Gennap-Nijmegen highway to the town of Mook.

THE BRITISH SECOND ARMY was unable to force a crossing over the Rhine River by September 24 and had to evacuate the remnants of the British 1st Airborne Division from the north side of the river. Of more than 10,000 officers and men who had jumped and landed by glider north of the Rhine, only about 2,400 came back across the river. Operation Market Garden had failed, but not because of the the three airborne divisions and the Polish brigade.

ON THE MORNING OF SEPTEMBER 24, the newly arrived 325th Glider Infantry relieved the 2nd Battalion from its defensive positions and the entire 505th moved to Nijmegen to guard the two bridges across the Waal River. During the five days and nights in which the regiment guarded the two bridges, the Germans shelled the highway bridge sporadically to interdict traffic.

The first mail arrived on September 26, and the letters from home raised the morale of the troopers considerably. The following day the battalion's barracks bags arrived with the seaborne elements of the division and the men got cleaned up for the first time since jumping.

At 8:00 p.m. on September 28, elements of the British Army relieved the regiment of responsibility for the bridges and the 505th moved back into the frontline east and southeast of Groesbeek area the following day. At 5:00 a.m. the following morning, September 29, German frogmen floated down the Waal River and detonated explosive charges at both bridges, dropping the center span of the railroad bridge into the Waal River and blowing a hole in part of the road surface of the highway bridge, but it remained usable and was subsequently repaired.

The 1st and 3rd Battalion of the 505th manned the frontline defending Groesbeek, with the 2nd Battalion in division reserve. However, on the afternoon of September 30, British intelligence advised the division that a heavy

German attack was expected that night. The 2nd Battalion was brought up and put into the line, relieving elements of the 325th Glider Infantry Regiment, defending Mook and the area around the Kiekberg Woods, on the right flank of the regimental sector. The battalions were all issued double combat loads of ammunition. The expected attack didn't occur that evening.

At midnight of October 1-2, the Germans fired heavy artillery and Nebelwerfer concentrations for an hour and a half prior to launching the anticipated large scale tank and infantry attack to overwhelm the perimeter of the 82nd Airborne Division and recapture the bridges at Nijmegen and over the Maas-Waal Canal. The attack was thrown back with heavy German losses.

The situation in Holland now settled into defensive static warfare, with the next month and a half marked by night patrol actions, sharp local attacks by both sides, and the inevitable attrition resulting from such actions.

On October 3, Private First Class Dave Bowman and his new assistant gunner, Private Frank Aguerrebere, were manning a .30-caliber machine gun outpost on the Company D sector of the line near the edge of the Kiekberg Woods south of Groesbeek. Around noon, Bowman saw two troopers approaching their position. "Lieutenant McClean and Private Ulysses [S.] Emerick came by carrying binoculars, clipboards, etcetera, and informed us they would be forward of our position. In other words, hold fire until they returned. Several minutes passed with no shelling, then a mortar shell exploded to the front, closer than usual. Less than a minute passed after that when Lieutenant McClean appeared, blood-splattered and visibly shaken, exclaiming that Emerick had been killed."[59] Lieutenant Tom McClean, a veteran of the regiment's four combat jumps, had suffered severe wounds to his chest and arms, and was evacuated to the United States.

That afternoon, Staff Sergeant Irving N. Syrene, the S-2 section sergeant with Headquarters Company, 2nd Battalion, led a patrol to reconnoiter a route for a combat patrol to be conducted that night. During the reconnaissance, Syrene observed concertina wire strung directly across the planned route of the combat patrol. Syrene reported the obstacle, volunteering to personally remove it.

That night, friendly artillery fired a preparatory barrage on the combat patrol's objective. Just five minutes before the combat patrol moved out, Staff Sergeant Syrene rushed forward into the barrage and grabbed the concertina wire with his bare hands and removed it from the path of the patrol. Four different times, artillery shells fell so close by that Syrene was blown off of his feet and his clothing was perforated with shrapnel. Miraculously, Syrene was not wounded. He joined the patrol when it moved through the wire, then personally captured a German soldier during the patrol. For his bravery, Staff Sergeant Syrene was awarded the Silver Star.

The British infantry relieved the 2nd Battalion that night and the battalion moved into the woods near Groesbeek, where it spent the next day resting and cleaning its weapons. On the night of October 4, the battalion moved out at 10:00 p.m. to relieve the 3rd Battalion, 505th which was defending a sector east of Groesbeek. Over the next six days the battalion was heavily shelled by artillery, mortars, and Nebelwerfers—the famed Screaming Meemies. The flat ground and close proximity to the enemy resulted in several firefights. The terrain presented great observation for the battalion's mortars which hammered the German positions.

Private First Class Earl Boling was manning a Company E outpost near the railroad tracks east of Groesbeek on the morning of October 9. "Since our outpost position was very vulnerable, a mortar observer from the headquarters company mortar platoon was sent up. I recall his name being [Sergeant Roy M.] Tuttle. He was in the position or foxhole next to mine, and we started to receive sniper fire.

"The sniper was using tracer ammunition—I told the men to keep low.

"Tuttle said, 'I will spot him and get a fire mission.' He raised his binoculars up for a look and was immediately shot. At this time, I ordered all men to fire at the enemy positions to our front, and under this covering fire, I crawled from the next hole to check on Sergeant Tuttle.

"When I slipped into the foxhole, I found that he had been shot in the left temple and was still alive, but unconscious, and was having difficulty breathing. As I picked up his phone to the mortar platoon, they were trying to contact him. I explained the circumstances, and the officer [Lieutenant John L. Cooper] on the line called one of our battalion doctors to the phone.

"[Captain Lyle Putnam] asked me to describe the appearance of the wound and the exact location. I then asked if there was anything I could do to help Tuttle. He answered, 'No—from the description of the wound and point of entry of the bullet, I don't believe you can do anything except try to make him comfortable, and if you know any prayers, say them.'

"About this time, there was a gasp from Tuttle and his breathing stopped. I could not get a pulse—I let the doctor know this, and he said, 'You have done all that you can,' and turned the phone over to the officer of the mortar platoon.

"The headquarters mortar platoon officer said, 'We are sorry to hear about Tuttle, but since he has been at your position (two days), he has plotted several targets, and we have the map coordinates. We are going to fire a saturation barrage. You stay on the phone to correct our fire if needed.'

"With that, the barrage started, and the German positions were smothered in mortar fire from the heavy mortar section. Within one hour or less, the Germans were waving a Red Cross flag, asking for a ceasefire. I notified the mortar section and the barrage stopped. The Germans came out under Red Cross flags to pick up dead and wounded, while one of their officers watched our position with binoculars.

"That night, as we were to go for rations, etcetera, we removed Tuttle's body. With three other men, I carried Tuttle on a litter, and without an audible word, the four of us removed our helmets and knelt for a moment's silent prayer. I was to think later that there were three different religious groups represented in this action of a prayer for a fallen comrade."[60]

Sergeant Tuttle had directed accurate 81mm mortar fire on the enemy positions that day, despite constant fire by enemy troops to silence him. For his heroic actions that day, Sergeant Tuttle was posthumously awarded the Silver Star.

The British 130th Brigade relieved the 505th from its front line position east and south of Groesbeek on the night of October 10-11. The 505th moved to defensive positions along the flatlands south of the Waal River, where it relieved the 504th PIR. The 1st and 3rd Battalions held the frontline, while the 2nd Battalion was held in reserve.

Lieutenant J. J. Smith was sent to the hospital with a recurrence of malaria on October 16, and Lieutenant Bill Meddaugh temporarily replaced him as E Company commander.

On the night of October 17, the 2nd Battalion relieved the 3rd, occupying positions that ran south from the river to where it tied in with the 1st Battalion on its right. Company D occupied a brickyard adjacent to the southern bank of the Waal River. Lieutenant Joe Meyers was the platoon leader of D Company's 3rd Platoon. "First Lieutenant [Lawrence M.] Price joined the company and took over McClean's 1st Platoon. The yard consisted of three massive brick kilns, with smoke stacks that towered 150 feet skyward. These kilns were located atop a thirty-foot, east-west levee that paralleled the river. Behind the levee was a large, open area with a multitude of open-sided sheds, used to store bricks. The surrounding area was level farmland, cut up into small plots by a series of drainage ditches and dikes.

"Captain [Taylor] Smith deployed the 1st and 3rd Platoons on line, and he held [Lt. O. B.] Carr's 2nd Platoon in reserve. Price's 1st Platoon extended from the river across the levee, south to the edge of the brickyard, where he tied in with me. I defended a three hundred–yard sector extending south and tied into another company from our battalion."[61]

At 6:40 p.m. on the night of October 20, the battalion launched a mock attack by firing its machine guns and mortars at prearranged targets, while British tanks drove around to give the Germans the impression an attack was imminent. This was to cover a Dog Company combat patrol led by Lieutenant O. B. Carr to engage and kill the enemy, reach two objectives for the purpose of determining the enemy strength and disposition, and capture prisoners for interrogation. The patrol was almost 100 yards from the first objective when suddenly the familiar "pop" of flares bursting above was heard and the area was soon illuminated. Carr and his troopers instinctively hit the ground. Just seconds later, heavy concentrations of 50mm and 80mm mortar shells exploded all around and among them. Tracers from machine guns crisscrossed just overhead as the patrol crawled toward the German frontline. The troopers wanted to get close to the German positions so the enemy would lift the mortar concentrations for fear of hitting their own troops. The troopers got to within twenty-five yards of the positions and the mortar fire lifted. However, the German platoon defending the sector tossed hand grenades at them while grazing fire from their automatic weapons increased. The troopers fought back with small arms fire and hand grenades. During the firefight, the squad leader, assistant squad leader, and two of the men were hit, causing confusion and loss of direction and contact.

Private Harry Garlick took charge of the squad and got it reorganized, all while under heavy fire and illumination from enemy flares.

Private First Class Dominic J. "Little Joe" Dippolito, on the point, became separated from the patrol during the firefight, but infiltrated through the German positions, crawling across open ground, devoid of cover or concealment, until he reached the first objective, which he discovered was a German company command post. Dippolito crept up to the entrance, then burst in firing his Thompson submachine gun, killing three and wounding four others. Meanwhile, Lieutenant Carr took the point of the patrol and led the remaining eight men to the objective. Dippolito started for the second objective, but found a second German platoon dug in along a ditch between the command post and the second objective. Dippolito returned and reported this to Lieutenant Carr, who decided the patrol would take with them two of the walking wounded at the enemy command post and ex-filtrate back to friendly lines. After the patrol returned safely, Private Garlick volunteered to accompany Lieutenant Carr to evacuate the four wounded troopers lying just yards from the German positions. Much information was gained from the prisoners the patrol brought back with them. Lieutenant O. B. Carr, Private First Class Dominic Dippolito, and Private Harry Garlick were each awarded the Silver Star for their actions during the patrol.

The 3rd Battalion relieved Vandervoort's troopers on the night of October 24-25 and the battalion moved into reserve. Everyone had an opportunity to get cleaned up the next day at field showers set up at Nijmegen. The Company D commander, Captain Taylor G. Smith was promoted to 2nd Battalion executive officer. Captain George D. Carlson replaced Smith as commanding officer of Company D.

One of the big problems during the stay in Holland was food. Meyers found that "the Dutch civilians were willing to share their meager rations with us, but they had so little food to spare, we were reluctant to accept their offerings."[62]

Occasionally, Meyers and others picked fruit from trees, where it was available, but this did little to supplement their rations. "For the entire period of our stay in Holland, we were on cold rations: Ks and Ds initially, and later we switched to C-rations. Although no gourmet delight, C-rations were an improvement over Ks and Ds. Issued in a cardboard box, one ration consisted of three canned bread units (large round crackers and a can of jam), three canned food units, and an accessory package. As I recall, the food units were ham and eggs for breakfast, pork and beans for dinner, and meat and vegetable hash for supper. The accessory pack contained cigarettes, matches, toilet paper, a miniature can opener, and candy. The ration is fine for a few days. When you eat it seven days a week for two straight months, you are willing to face enemy fire to get a decent meal."[63]

Company F platoon leader, Lieutenant Rusty Hays, witnessed a humorous incident, had it not been so serious to the parties involved. "The last two to three weeks in Holland were pretty calm. We got word that C-47s with coffee were being flown in. Up to this time, we had been on English rations, which meant tea instead of coffee. The only way to get coffee to us was by plane. Our guys were ready to revolt if they couldn't get coffee. It got bad enough that they loaded a C-47 with coffee and flew it in to us.

"Not being a coffee drinker, it made little difference to me, but the rest of the fellows could hardly wait. The 1st squad had found a cow that had gone dry because it hadn't been milked regularly. In anticipation of getting coffee, they worked with it until it started giving milk again.

"Finally, the coffee arrived. The next morning the 1st squad brewed up a big pot of coffee and went over to milk the cow. It was dry, and they were mightily disappointed.

"The next morning they found out what happened to their milk. They happened to go out to the cow a little earlier than the morning before, and found the 2nd Squad milking their cow. It looked for a while that a firefight would develop."[64]

The last week of October and the first week of November were mostly quiet for Vandervoort's troopers, with mostly night patrols and light enemy shelling. On November 10, Canadian forces relieved the 82nd Airborne Division. The men were happy to be leaving Holland, even though most had made friends with the Dutch citizenry. The fighting had once again been costly.

PHOTO GALLERY

Paratroopers gather around a map for a briefing of the unit orders and assigned objectives. *Photograph courtesy of Jerome V. Huth*

Paratroopers enjoy a combination fried chicken dinner and breakfast, before dawn on September 17, 1944. *U.S. Army photograph, courtesy of the Cornelius Ryan Collection, Alden Library, Ohio University*

PHOTO GALLERY

Blocks of C2 plastic explosive, detonator caps, and cloth covers used to make Gammon grenades are issued, September 17, 1944. *U.S. Army photograph, 82nd Airborne Division War Memorial Museum*

AN IRRESISTIBLE FORCE

Scale maps of Groesbeek (1:25,000) and Hertogenbosch (1:100,000)
are issued, September 17, 1944. *U.S. Army photograph, courtesy of the
Cornelius Ryan Collection, Alden Library, Ohio University*

PHOTO GALLERY

A stick of 505th paratroopers finish putting on their parachutes, weapons, and equipment and wait to board their plane, September 17, 1944. *Photograph by Daniel B. McIlvoy, courtesy of Ann McIlvoy Zaya*

The 505th paratroopers pose for a photo before boarding their aircraft, September 17, 1944. Note the trooper on the left has a BAR enclosed in a padded case and strapped to his right leg. The two other troopers have M1 rifles in Griswold cases under their reserve parachutes. *Photograph courtesy of Weldon Grissom*

Opposite bottom: An officer refers to a map while giving his men a last-minute briefing on the morning of September 17, 1944. *U.S. Army photograph, 82nd Airborne Division War Memorial Museum*

AN IRRESISTIBLE FORCE

A stick of paratroopers await takeoff for Holland, September 17, 1944. *U.S. Army photograph, 82nd Airborne Division War Memorial Museum*

C-47s of the IX Troop Carrier Command carrying paratroopers of the 82nd Airborne Division over Holland, September 17, 1944. *U.S. Army Air Corps photograph, 82nd Airborne Division War Memorial Museum*

PHOTO GALLERY

The parachutes of the 2nd Battalion, 505th Parachute Infantry Regiment fill the sky northeast of Groesbeek, Holland on September 17, 1944. *Photograph by William Jenks*

Second Battalion paratroopers have stopped these two cars and are searching a German soldier with his hands over his head in the center of the photo, near the observatory on the northern edge of Groesbeek, Holland, September 17, 1944. *Photograph by William Jenks*

AN IRRESISTIBLE FORCE

Lieutenant Colonel Vandervoort (fourth from the right) and Colonel Ekman, commander of the 505th PIR (second from right), confer with Lieutenant Colonel Edward H. Goulburn, commander of the 1st Grenadier Guards and overall commander of the combined force, in his scout car on Groesbeekseweg as the force moves into Nijmegen, September 19, 1944. *U.S. Army photograph, courtesy of the Cornelius Ryan Collection, Alden Library, Ohio University*

The main body of the Eastern Force column is stopped by fire coming from the traffic circle through the open area of the Mariaplein plaza, effectively separating it from the lead elements, September 19, 1944. *U.S. Army photograph, courtesy of the Cornelius Ryan Collection, Alden Library, Ohio University*

PHOTO GALLERY

Company E paratroopers with the 2nd or 3rd Platoon dash across the Mariaplein plaza as automatic weapons fire from the traffic circle area rakes the street. The 1st Platoon occupies houses on Graadt van Roggenstraat and British armored vehicles are parked on the short street just south of Graadt van Roggenstraat and the open area south of Villa Belvoir and east of the traffic circle. *U.S. Army photograph, 82nd Airborne Division War Memorial Museum*

The lead Grenadier Guards Sherman tank, moments after being hit by antitank fire, as it moved into the open area near the traffic circle, killing the troop leader and catching fire. Two other tanks moved into the intersection just after this photo was taken and were damaged by antitank fire. *U.S. Army photograph, courtesy of the Cornelius Ryan Collection, Alden Library, Ohio University*

AN IRRESISTIBLE FORCE

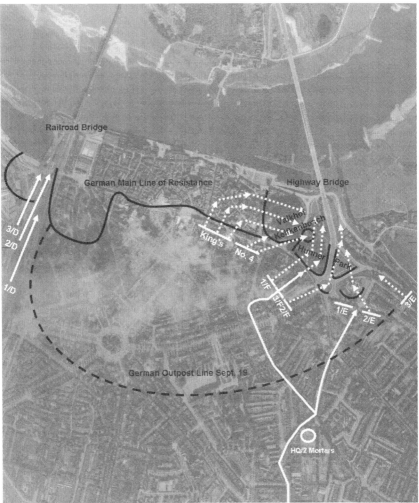

An aerial photo of the Nijmegen bridge areas taken by British RAF Number 541 Squadron on September 19, 1944. The view is oriented to the north, with the railroad bridge on the left and the highway bridge on the right. The 2nd Battalion fought to capture these bridges and the southern approaches on September 19-20. The solid white arrows depict the routes of advance by the 2nd Battalion on September 19. The positions of the platoons of the three rifle companies are shown as of the morning of September 20. The dashed white arrows depict the attacks by the 2nd Battalion and the British Grenadier Guards on September 20. *Photograph courtesy of Frits Janssen*

PHOTO GALLERY

Headquarters Company's 81mm Mortar Platoon was set up in the Nijmegen cemetery, one of the few areas with the overhead clearance required for effective use of mortars in the city. *U.S. Army photograph, courtesy of the Cornelius Ryan Collection, Alden Library, Ohio University*

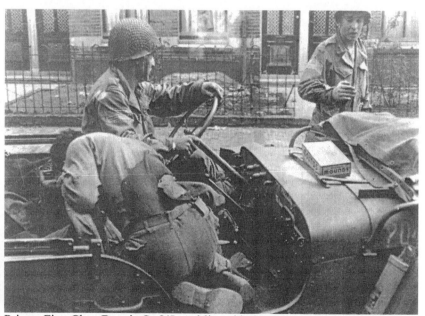

Private First Class Dennis G. O'Loughlin, with Company E, in a commandeered jeep, drives wounded Company D trooper, Technical Sergeant Buffalo Boy Canoe, to a Nijmegen hospital used by the division for treating its casualties, September 20, 1944. *U.S. Army photograph, courtesy of the Cornelius Ryan Collection, Alden Library, Ohio University*

AN IRRESISTIBLE FORCE

This 88mm antiaircraft gun, located on west side of the Keizer Lodewijkplein traffic circle in Nijmegen, did much damage to British armor. This gun was put out of action by Lieutenant Coyle and his Company E troopers on the morning of September 20, 1944. *Photograph courtesy of the Cornelius Ryan Collection, Alden Library, Ohio University*

A rare photograph of Hunner Park after its capture by Company F during savage fighting against an SS kampfgruppe, September 20, 1944. *Photograph courtesy of the Cornelius Ryan Collection, Alden Library, Ohio University*

PHOTO GALLERY

One of the Company D squads early in the Ardennes campaign. Kneeling on the left with a BAR is Private Melvin P. Brown, Private First Class David V. Bowman is standing on the far right, and to his immediate left is Private First Class Stanley W. Kotlarz. *Photograph courtesy of David V. Bowman*

Paratroopers with the 505th advance behind a tank destroyer of the 636th Tank Destroyer Battalion, January 4, 1945. The Sherman tank on the left side of the photograph was out of action with a missing right tread. *U.S. Army photograph, 82nd Airborne Division War Memorial Museum*

AN IRRESISTIBLE FORCE

Well built and concealed bunkers such as these, manned by soldiers of the 62nd Volksgrendier Division, had to be cleared during the costly attacks of January 3, 1945. *U.S. Army photograph, 82nd Airborne Division War Memorial Museum*

An enemy prisoner (center) smiles as he marches with his hands up into captivity. He knew that the Americans treated POWs well. He could expect a warm place to stay and hot food, unlike the troopers who had to continue the attack. *Photograph by Daniel B. McIlvoy, courtesy of Mrs. Ann McIlvoy Zaya*

PHOTO GALLERY

Paratroopers with the 505th inspect a German Mark VI Tiger II tank knocked out near Goronne, Belgium, January 7, 1945, killing the entire crew. This is likely the tank that Lieutenant Joe Meyers describes during the attack on the high ground overlooking the town. Belgian girls (left) smile and look admiringly at the troopers as they pass. *U.S. Army photograph, National Archives*

Members of the division reconnaissance platoon test German Panzerfausts and a U.S. bazooka on the frontal armor of a Mark VI Tiger II tank at La Gleize, Belgium. The Panzerfausts made the deepest penetration, only four inches of the seven inches of the frontal armor. *U.S. Army photograph, National Archives*

AN IRRESISTIBLE FORCE

This wreckage of American vehicles along the road through the Kall River valley in the Hürtgen Forest had been there since the previous fall. *Photograph by Robert M. Piper, courtesy of Robert M. Piper*

Bodies of members of the 112th Infantry Regiment, 28th Infantry Division, killed the previous fall during fighting in the Hürtgen Forest. *Photograph by Robert M. Piper, courtesy of Robert M. Piper*

PHOTO GALLERY

Troopers of the 2nd Battalion, 505th Parachute Infantry Regiment board boxcars at Düren Germany, April 26, 1945. *U.S. Army photograph, National Archives*

Troopers with the 505th rest against the dike on the east side of the Elbe River as others dig in, April 30, 1945. *U.S. Army photograph, National Archive*

CHAPTER 8

"We Had Never Retreated"

After being relieved in Holland, the 82nd Airborne Division was trucked to France for rest, refitting, and reorganization. After arriving at Suippes, France, the 505th Parachute Infantry Regiment was billeted in stone French army barracks buildings. The men were given time to rest and relax, passes were generous, and many officers were on furlough. No one in the regiment could know that a catastrophe in Belgium would soon plunge them into the most costly campaign of the war.

The regiment soon began receiving replacements. One of those assigned to Company D was Private William E. Slawson, a veteran of the 1st Special Service Force, which had fought spectacularly in Italy and southern France. It had been disbanded December 5, because it had sustained very high casualties. "I got assigned as an assistant machine gunner with a guy by the name of Julius Eisner. Eisner was a great man—he was a pathfinder in the Normandy drop. He would share anything he had—smokes, socks, etcetera."[1]

On December 16, 1944, the German Army launched an massive offensive in the Belgian Ardennes. Thirteen infantry and five panzer divisions in the initial attacking force overwhelmed four American infantry divisions defending the sector. Most in the 82nd Airborne Division took notice of the event, but didn't believe it would affect them.

The following night, Lieutenant Rusty Hays, with Company F, had turned in early and was asleep at the officer quarters in Suippes. "About 1:00 in the morning, there was pounding on the door. 'Officer's meeting in the battalion commander's room.' There, we were told that the Germans had broken through our lines in some place called the Ardennes in Belgium. We would leave for combat at 8:00 in the morning. 'Alert your men, then get yourself ready for winter combat and report back to your company in an hour. Dismissed!'

"With that, I broke and ran as fast as I could to the company area. There was one extra BAR in the company, and I wanted it for my platoon. After I got my platoon alerted and prepared for winter combat, I went back to my quarters to get myself prepared.

"Here's what I wore: regular cotton underwear, long underwear, wool pants, wool shirt, a field jacket (short, medium weight), combat pants, combat jacket, [and] wool overcoat. With the cotton underwear, I had four layers of clothes, and since we had buttons on our pants instead of zippers, I found it more convenient not to button any of the pants. Because jump boots fit snug and were

176

not warm, I wore combat boots instead of jump boots. The only gloves we had were woolen with leather palms—not much help in the cold weather we would face. To keep our heads warm, we had a wool knit cap that we wore under our helmets.

"For a bedroll I had: a cocoon-type blanket sleeping bag, which is not very warm, but I could at least zip it up around my head. Two woolen blankets [and] a shelter half, which is a half-tent—not warm, but fairly waterproof and usually used as a ground sheet, and to roll my bedroll in to keep it dry. I was lucky. There were some men who, for one reason or another, did not have many of these items and had to leave for combat without them.

"All in all, our clothes and bedding would be far from adequate for the below-zero weather we would be in. The army had completely neglected to provide cold-weather gear for their troops.

"But there was another, even more critical shortage. We did not have a combat load of ammunition for our weapons and no magazines for our BARs, and BARs couldn't be fired without magazines to hold the cartridges."[2]

Private John R. Jackson was a new replacement assigned to Headquarters Company, 2nd Battalion, as a battalion message center runner. "I went to the supply room for equipment, and there were no packs to carrying supplies. I wound up with a gas mask [and container, from] which I removed the mask and used the canvas bag as a pack for some socks and underwear. There were no overshoes available, so I went out with regular jump boots."[3]

Private First Class James Rodier was the acting supply sergeant for the 2nd Battalion when the word came that the regiment was moving out. "I had weapons in the supply room to send to ordnance for repair and maintenance. Captain [William] Schmees said to give the weapons to the people, and they would have to use them."[4]

COLONEL EKMAN was in England on the evening of December 17, and heard radio news broadcasts regarding the German offensive. He received a call at 11:00 p.m. from Colonel Robert H. Wienecke, the division chief of staff, who told him the division was moving out and that he was to report to the airport at 9:00 the next morning. Ekman knew the problems were immense in getting his regiment prepared for the move. "The equipment situation was critical. Many of the weapons were in Ordnance, [and] there were shortages in field rations and ammunition. All requests for such items had not been completely filled. Clothing was in the laundry, equipment was stored, [and] winter clothing had not been issued to the regiment. The personnel shortages were most serious in the case of specialists—particularly for crew-served weapons.

"The training program was not completely underway when the alert came; there had only been a week of very serious training during the month, and even this had been somewhat haphazard because the mortars had to be borrowed from the 508th Parachute Infantry. These mortars were returned at the time of the move and as a result, the 505th went into battle with only three 81mm mortars and seven or eight 60mm mortars for the entire regiment.

"To complicate the personnel issue, at 0300 on 18 December, after the alert for movement had been received, but before the regiment left Suippes, two hundred replacements arrived. This left no time to get them oriented, classified, or properly distributed, and they were just thrown into the move."[5]

The next morning when the trucks arrived at Suippes to transport the 505th to Belgium, Private First Class Malcolm Neel, with Battery A, 80th Airborne Antiaircraft (Antitank) Battalion, was one of the last to board his truck. "I was in a 2 1/2-ton, 6x6 truck sitting near the tailgate when I heard one of our guys, looking out at a group of cold, wet paratroopers standing packed into an open semi-trailer, say, 'Boy, I feel sorry for the first Germans those guys get a hold of.'"[6] The original destination for the truck convoy carrying the 82nd Airborne Division was Bastogne, Belgium. However, this was changed while en route.

GENERAL GAVIN, who had left France the previous evening and driven blacked-out on treacherous roads all night, arrived in Spa, Belgium. "I reported to General [Courtney] Hodges [commanding general of the U. S. First Army] in person at about 09:00 hours 18 December. At that time the situation appeared rather vague. The first reports of enemy contact at Stavelot were just coming in. It was reported that an enemy force at Stavelot had driven our troops across the river and had succeeding in capturing and destroying a large map supply. They apparently blew the bridge upon driving out our forces. The situation south and west of Stavelot was unknown except that the enemy had evidently overrun our front positions. There appeared to be a large force of U.S. troops centered on St.-Vith. There also appeared to be a large pocket of the 106th Division surrounded in the Eifel.

"After some staff discussion, the commanding general, First U.S. Army decided to attach the 82nd Airborne Division to V Corps. It was to close in an area in the vicinity of Werbomont. The 101st Airborne Division was to be attached to VIII Corps and would assemble in the vicinity of Bastogne. I placed a request with the First U.S. Army for tanks, TDs [tank destroyers], 4.2s [4.2-inch mortars], and medium artillery, and left the CP for Werbomont. At this time there was considerable movement west of service and command installations in and around Spa. It was apparently being evacuated."[7]

AS THE CONVOY transporting the 505th neared Werbomont, Private John Jackson, a new replacement assigned to Headquarters Company, 2nd Battalion, heard the sound of artillery in the distance. "I was nervous when I heard some loud reports. The older men said not to worry, because that was outgoing. I asked how they knew that, and was told that when you hear incoming, you will know."[8]

COLONEL EKMAN arrived in Werbomont at approximately midnight on December 18, after landing at an airfield near Suippes at 3:00 p.m., driving for two hours to his now abandoned CP, and then through the night to catch up with the regiment.

BECAUSE OF THE FLUID SITUATION, the locations of the enemy armored spearheads were unknown. On the morning of December 19, the 505th was ordered to push east to the village of Basse-Bodeux. At about noon, during the march, trucks belonging to the division arrived. As Lieutenant Rusty Hays, with Company F, moved along the road, he saw them parked up ahead on the shoulder of the road. "Along the right side of the road was a line of trucks, their tailgates facing the road. As our men reached the trucks, someone would ask each one, 'What do you need?' As we passed the trucks, we were fully supplied with all that we needed."[9]

Hays would later learn the story of how those trucks got there from a captain with the transportation corps. "The officer in charge of the depot was told that when the trucks from the 82nd arrived, they could have anything in the depot without signing for it—something unheard of before in the army. This captain was put in charge of the convoy, and told to take it to wherever the 82nd was in Belgium.

"To get there in time, they had to drive all night with their lights on, rather than using the blackout lights. With their lights on, they would attract any German tank column in the area.

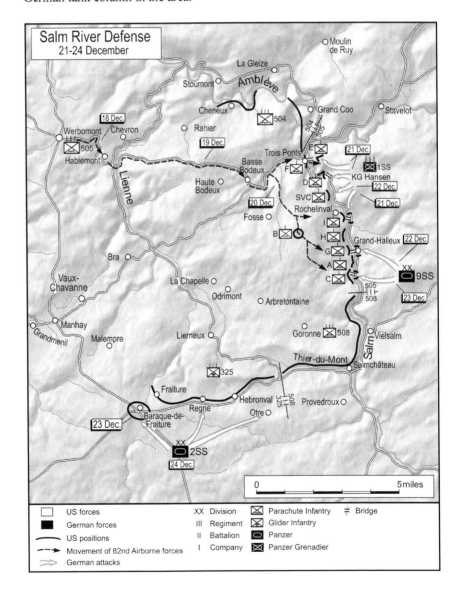

"These were 82nd trucks and 82nd drivers. From time to time, MPs would stop them and tell them they may be running into a German roadblock, and they better turn off their lights and stop there for the night.

"In every case, the drivers would say, 'No sir, we're 82nd Airborne and our men need this stuff up there in the morning.' And on they drove.

"We did need this stuff, and we got it just in time."[10]

Around noon the next day, December 20, the 505th moved out of Basse-Bodeux toward the Salm River. The 1st Battalion marched southeast to hold the sector between Rencheux on the right, where it tied in with the 508th PIR to just south of Grand-Halleux. The 3rd Battalion moved southeast to defend a sector from Grand-Halleux on the right, north to La Tour. The 2nd Battalion moved eastward to defend the town of Trois Ponts, where key bridges across the Salm and Amblève Rivers were located, extending south to La Tour.

Lieutenant Bill Meddaugh and his Company E troopers led the 2nd Battalion column as it moved out. "We pulled out of a bivouac area and began an approach march along a narrow mountain road leading to Trois Ponts. No maps were available and I wasn't sure where we were headed. I was asked to send one platoon forward by truck as an advance force to occupy the town and reconnoiter the immediate area around the town. I selected the 2nd Platoon, under Lieutenant John Walas, who boarded the trucks and headed for Trois Ponts. The rest of the company (and battalion) continued the march."[11]

Lieutenant Colonel Vandervoort didn't know much more than his men about what to expect. "There was no information about either enemy or any friendly forces in the area."[12]

Vandervoort and his command group drove toward Trois Ponts in jeeps, at the head of the truck column carrying Lieutenant Walas' platoon. They didn't know whether they would run head-on into a German armored column or if they might be ambushed en route. But, they needed to reach Trois Ponts if possible before the Germans.

The column entered the town without incident. Vandervoort made a reconnaissance in order to be able to deploy his battalion immediately upon arrival. "Trois Ponts was a small, rural village of two-story stone houses and shops. The town was in a narrow valley, overpowered by mountains, at the confluence of the Salm and Amblève Rivers. At Trois Ponts, the steep-banked Salm was a definitive barrier for vehicles. But its shallow headwaters were easily fordable by infantry willing to chance frostbitten feet. A few women and children were the only civilian occupants when we walked into the town. A handful of combat engineers (Company C, 51st Engineer Combat Battalion) were setting up a defensive position at the Salm River bridge in an attempt to prevent anyone's crossing. Those engineers were glad to see that parachute battalion.

"Holding Trois Ponts was the keystone of General Courtney Hodges' plan for the First U.S. Army to stop, drive back, and then destroy the German winter offensive. [Colonel] Ira P. Swift, assistant division commander of the 82nd Airborne Division, newly assigned to paratroops, took a personal interest in Trois Ponts. He ordered the 2nd Battalion to establish a bridgehead with just one company on the high ground to the east side of the Salm River. The remainder of the battalion was deployed on the west bank of the river in order to prevent the enemy from crossing.

"At the foot of the town the highway crossed the Salm River going east over a heavy timber bridge. Immediately across the bridge, the highway ended at the base of a bluff. It then split; turning north and south. The northern road led to two bridges crossing the nearby Amblève River. Hence the name 'Three Bridges.' The southern road climbed gently a few hundred yards, then turned left one hundred eighty degrees to the north over railroad tracks paralleling the river. The narrow two-lane road climbed steeply along the side of the one-hundred-foot-high bluff, cleft with a long, sheer highway and railroad cut. At a point opposite the bridge, now well below, the highway turned ninety degrees to the east then sloped gradually up to level ground. No vehicles could come into Trois Ponts from the east along this road without exposing themselves broadside to 2.36-inch bazooka fire from short range as they negotiated a hairpin turn for two-tenths of a mile."[13]

Companies E and F would defend Trois Ponts on the left flank of the regiment, while Company D would hold the section of the river across from La Tour.

Late in the afternoon of December 20, as the 2nd Battalion column approached Trois Ponts, the acting E Company commander, Lieutenant Bill Meddaugh took a jeep the short distance ahead into town. "I went forward to meet with Lieutenant Colonel Ben Vandervoort, 2nd Battalion commander. Lieutenant Walas had set up the platoon as a base of fire along the Salm River, on both sides of the damaged bridge, to cover the area across the river directly opposite the town. The terrain rose sharply across the river, giving the appearance of a cliff or bluff. A narrow road wound up the side of the cliff and disappeared in the woods to the left of the top of the mountain.

"A three-man patrol, under the command of Corporal Clifford Putman, was working its way up the side of the mountain (not using the road) to determine the presence of any enemy troops in the woods over the crest of the bluff. The patrol disappeared over the crest and returned shortly, waving that all was clear."[14]

Vandervoort deployed his battalion to defend against a potential river crossing. "On the west side of the Salm River, F Company and the battalion headquarters company—particularly the light machine gun platoon and bazookas—set up a main line of resistance (MLR) among and in the houses on the river bank. Machine guns were sighted to provide flanking fires onto both sides of the bridge.

"A few more U.S. Army engineers drifted down from the hills into town. We were glad to take in those orphan engineers. They were scattered throughout the MLR so they could use their .50-caliber machine guns to provide an overlapping final protective line of fire.

"D Company was sent south on the riverbank road to defend the next nearest bridge, still intact, across the Salm. They were to destroy the bridge if attacked in force. Second Battalion habitually teamed with a platoon of

Company B, 307th Airborne Engineers. They were sent with D Company to perform the demolition task. D Company and F Company maintained twenty-four hour contact with foot patrols on the west bank of the Salm.

"Our 81mm mortar platoon found a lovely observation post (OP) on the side of the mountain sloping to the north above Trois Ponts. From there they could see the road net to the east, the bottoms of both rivers, and the open field east of the E Company position."[15]

Lieutenant Meddaugh was ordered to take E Company across the Salm River, "to the high ground and to establish a defensive position denying enemy troops and vehicles the use of the road. I sent for the rest of the company and immediately ordered Lieutenant Walas to move the 2nd Platoon across quickly and set up a defensive position straddling the road, inside the woods, just over the crest of the mountain. When the balance of the company arrived, we moved across the bridge and up the winding road to get into position. I ordered Lieutenant Jack [N.] Bailey's 1st Platoon to move into the woods and dig in on the right flank of the 2nd Platoon. Lieutenant Howard [E.] Jensen's 3rd Platoon was kept in reserve and located in the immediate vicinity of the Company CP, which I established in a small home located on the road about one hundred yards from the 2nd Platoon positions."[16]

After crossing the river, Sergeant Julius D. Axman took two of his E Company troopers on a reconnaissance patrol. "We went into the woods along the road about twenty-five yards and stopped. It was dark by now—I was the rear man and didn't hear the other two men move out. About then, I heard a lot of troops moving up [from the southeast], so I headed in that direction. They were Krauts—they were setting up their radios and bringing up a lot of equipment. Well, I made the sign of the cross about a dozen times and said goodbye to my mom, when our [81mm] mortars started up across the river with three rounds. They didn't hit anything, but they fired again and hit the road the Krauts were on. All hell broke out—[the mortar fire] hit some trucks and started a fire. I could see shadows of Krauts running all over the place. I thought the whole German Army was after me. I put my hand on my helmet, my BAR under my arm and ran for the sound of the mortar blast. I got challenged by my squad—still not yet dug in. They sent me down to the CP. I told Lieutenant Meddaugh everything I saw, and then rejoined my platoon."[17]

Later that evening, Vandervoort crossed the river to check on the Company E positions. "The men dug in with their left flank slightly astride the road. Facing east, the bulk of the company selected positions in the edge of a dense wood at the top of the bluff. The wood ran off to the right, gradually expanding into a forest. To their front, the left side of the road was solid woods. The right side of the road was a wide-open field with little vegetation other than pasture-like stubble. From their positions inside the tree line, the paratroopers had ideal fields of fire on the road and across the open area.

"Antitank mines were sprinkled across their front. The E Company command post was located a short distance to the right of the road with the front line platoons. A 57mm antitank gun was dug into the right road shoulder, twenty or thirty yards behind the riflemen. First Lieutenant Meddaugh, the company commander, put a battery of six bazooka teams just ahead of the position in the woods on the left of the road. Behind the bazooka ambush, they placed antitank mines across the road. Before dark they settled down to wait in the bitter cold—no fires—no lights—no smoking.

"It was an excellent position for an ambush, but inherently a weak one to defend against armor accompanied by infantry. But up on the bluff, it was the best position available. The heavy woods left of the road provided the natural infantry approach, and the open area to the right of the road was good tank terrain. The Salm River separated the company from the rest of the battalion and prevented mutual support."[18]

ON THE NIGHT OF DECEMBER 20–21, the 1st SS Panzer Division's Kampfgruppe Peiper, the armored spearhead for the entire Sixth SS Panzer Army, was trapped near La Gleize. Tucker's 504th paratroopers were attacking Obersturmbahnführer Joachim Peiper's bridgehead at Cheneux, and the 30th Infantry Division was squeezing the noose tighter. Peiper's men badly needed food, medical supplies, ammunition, and most of all gasoline. The 1st SS Panzer Division's Kampfgruppe Hansen, consisting of the 1st SS Panzer Grenadier Regiment, a heavy tank destroyer battalion (Panzerjäger Abteilung 1), and a battalion of self-propelled 105mm artillery (Abteilung 1, Panzer Artillery Regiment 1), located at the town of Wanne, was ordered to break through to Peiper and open the way again to Antwerp, Belgium.

The closest road bridge spanning the Salm River in the vicinity capable of carrying heavy armored vehicles and tanks was at Trois Ponts. If Kampfgruppe Hansen could seize this bridge along the Salm intact, it could then drive north and attack toward the bridge at Cheneux and link up with Peiper's trapped men and armor.

Along the west side of the Salm River, a half mile south of Trois Ponts at La Tour, Company D defended a railroad bridge, a footbridge, and the bridge where a road following the Salm River crossed to the west side. Just after dark on December 20, the company's demolition man asked Lieutenant Virgil D. Gould to cover him while he set up booby traps on the footbridge. "Sergeant Jerry Weed chose me because I was armed with a Thompson submachine gun, and the other trooper that went with him was an Indian from North Dakota, Sergeant Herbert J. Buffalo Boy, who carried a BAR.

"We went with Jerry down to this swinging hand bridge and out on the bridge, and he set up booby traps in a series of three white phosphorous grenades connected to the rings to pull wires, with trip wires. We went up the hill and got behind this stone wall. Pretty soon there was a flash, when the first one blew up, then the second one blew up. By this time, there were two splashes in the water, because I suppose some people were burned pretty badly by this white phosphorous. We could hear a set of boots coming across that bridge and part way up the hill. Buffalo Boy and I poured fire on this bridge."[19]

Gould, Weed, and Buffalo Boy destroyed the German patrol.

A Sherman tank, positioned in the woods behind the company, covered the road and the railroad bridges. Just after dark, Company D platoon leader, Lieutenant Joe Meyers heard the tank start its engine and move out. "I tried to stop him, but he was gone before I reached his position.

"Our bedrolls were in Werbomont. We had nothing to keep us warm during the coming night. The temperature dropped below freezing and it snowed. There were two small farmhouses nearby, and we raided them for anything that would help us to survive the night. [Sergeant Edward F.] Murphy and I ended up with a mattress over the top of the prone shelter we had dug. It did not help much."[20]

At about 3:00 a.m. on December 21 at his position on the east side of the Salm River, Lieutenant Bill Meddaugh, the acting commander of Company E, heard the sound of tracked vehicles approaching. "Two armored half-tracks slowly approached the 2nd Platoon positions. The Germans were noisy, shouting back and forth and seemingly unaware of our presence. The first vehicle struck a mine and was disabled. Almost immediately, the second half-track was hit by bazooka fire and was destroyed. A brief firefight developed, and several enemy soldiers were killed. We had no casualties. The rest withdrew, and there was no further activity that night. We still had no firm information on enemy strength, but it was obvious that we were facing some sort of mechanized unit.

"At dawn or shortly thereafter, the Germans attacked straight down the road into the 2nd Platoon's positions—infantry was accompanied by armored vehicles. The enemy infantry must have worked their way in close to our positions before they opened fire, because Lieutenant Walas' call to me in the company CP was that 'the Krauts are all around us.'

"I was able to get immediate 81mm mortar support from battalion in front of the 2nd Platoon area, which was the most critical point. Lieutenant [John] Cooper of the 81mm Mortar Platoon came over to our position immediately and moved into the 2nd Platoon area, so he could direct mortar fire more effectively. Cooper did a tremendous job and was probably mainly responsible for slowing down the attack.

"I went forward to see what the 2nd Platoon's situation was at that time. They had suffered some casualties, but seemed to be organized and holding their own with the 81mm support. I then made a hasty visit to the 1st Platoon area. The attack was on a wider front than I thought, and the 1st Platoon was receiving a lot of pressure also, but not as concentrated as the 2nd [Platoon]. I returned to the company CP and committed the 3rd Platoon. I instructed Lieutenant [Howard E.] Jensen to move forward and reinforce the 1st Platoon and attempt to extend the right flank in a way which would allow enfilade fire to be brought down on the advancing enemy troops."[21]

Jensen's platoon moved up to a stone wall at the edge of the woods facing the road. This position gave perfect enfilade fire into the left flank and rear of the attacking German infantry. Sergeant Julius Axman and his men spread out behind the wall just moments before they were hit. "A Kraut half-track sent four rounds of [77mm] heavy artillery at us."[22]

Private First Class Samuel D. Durbin moved forward over the stone wall and engaged the half-track with his bazooka, scoring a direct hit and knocking it out, just as he was mortally wounded. For his courageous self-sacrifice, Private First Class Durbin was posthumously awarded the Silver Star.

Sergeant Axman saw another half-track open fire on the platoon. "Lieutenant [John J.] Fields was wounded. John Burdge, Jules Lankford, and I were sent up to the extreme right flank and started to shoot up a lot of Krauts. The half-track also came after us and was shooting his machine gun at us—I can't believe how lucky we were. I'll never know why that half-track didn't come over that rock wall."[23]

A 57mm antitank gun dug in near the bend in the road, just behind the 2nd Platoon, had a field of fire on the road and the open ground in front of the 1st Platoon. A second antitank gun positioned along the road farther down the hill could deliver a flank shot on any vehicle attempting to negotiate the bend in the road. The Battery A, 80th Airborne Antiaircraft (Antitank) Battalion gun section was commanded by Lieutenant Jake L. Wertich.

The two half-tracks, destroyed earlier, blocked the road, and thick woods prevented armor from using the north side of the road. Any armored vehicle would have to use the field south of the road to go around the knocked-out half-tracks. That ground was soggy, making movement by the twenty-eight ton Jägdpanzer tank destroyers difficult. As enemy half-tracks moved through the field, Wertich's gun knocked out an SdKfz 250/8, mounting a 75mm gun, with a flank shot. Together with Durbin's destruction of another half-track, it discouraged German armor from moving across the open field toward the edge of the woods to blast the Company E troopers at point blank range.

At his command post at Trois Ponts, Vandervoort received news that his battalion was facing elements of the most powerful division in the German Army. "First Lieutenant [Eugene] Doerfler, the battalion intelligence officer, confirmed the identification of the Germans killed during the night and early morning. The battalion reported to the division that E Company was engaged with elements of the 1st SS Panzer Division.

"In mid-morning a full-scale infantry attack, supported by four or five [tank destroyers], was launched against the company. The attack ended with German soldiers lying dead among the E Company foxholes and with other Germans taken as prisoners. The resistance probably surprised the German commander. The terrain dictated a tentatively held blocking position. The crazy American paratroopers didn't seem to know how to read a map and persisted in staying at the edge of the woods and covering the road with fire.

"From the mortar OP we could watch the panzer formations maneuvering and massing for another attack. The road was clogged with panzer grenadiers (in vehicles and afoot), self-propelled artillery, and mobile flak towers. It was an exceptionally well-equipped panzer kampfgruppe of great size—and an ominous sight for a unit that had one small 57mm antitank gun. The young German 'blackshirts' killed in the E Company foxholes were determined to power their way to the west. Some of the panzer artillery, mortars, and 20mm flak wagons began firing into the E Company area."[24]

Because the 3rd Platoon had moved into position after the fighting commenced, they had not had an opportunity to dig in. Private First Class Ed Arndt was a machine gunner with the 3rd Platoon. "We were fighting Germans at close range all morning. I thought we were all ready to meet our Maker. [Private First Class] Charlie Varvarkis, a Greek trooper, 3rd Platoon, never got up from his prone position—mortars and 88's exploding in the treetops and waist high machine gun and rifle fire—ground fire—all you could do was lie down and take it.

"Fred Hebein knocked out a half-track full of Germans that a.m. with a bazooka. I got a squad of Germans with my machine gun—I always carried it with a belt of 285 .30-caliber bullets, ready to fire."[25]

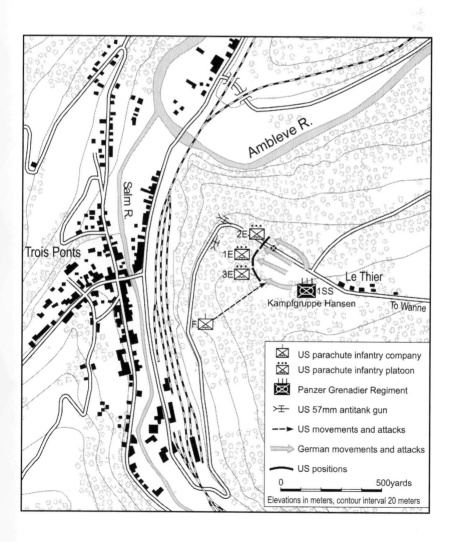

Private First Class Earl Hable, with the 1st Platoon, mowed down the SS grenadiers with his machine gun as they charged toward the platoon's foxholes, dug in about twenty yards inside the tree line, despite being under fire from a self-propelled gun less than 150 yards in front of him.

Arndt, Varvakis, Hable and others left heaps of enemy dead in front of their positions.

Lieutenant William W. Reed, Jr., a forward observer with Battery C, 456th Parachute Field Artillery Battalion, directed the fire of all of the battalion's 75mm howitzers, while the 2nd Battalion 81mm mortars and E Company 60mm mortars pounded enemy troops and vehicles.

However, the fanatical attacks by German infantry, supported by fire from armored vehicles, continued and Lieutenant Meddaugh had no reserve to counter a breakthrough. "As the morning wore on, the situation became more tenuous. 2nd Platoon was suffering heavy casualties, and it appeared they were not going to be able to hold on much longer. The 1st and 3rd Platoons were also being pressured badly, and casualties were mounting. The 2nd Platoon's situation particularly was getting desperate. The Germans had overrun part of the platoon area and were occupying some of the foxholes dug by our own men. They had captured two or three men in the process. They were last seen being moved to the rear of the enemy lines.

"Captain T. G. Smith, 2nd Battalion executive officer, joined me to get a firsthand assessment of my ability to hold on. It was my opinion that we should withdraw. I felt like we had our back to the wall and, although we had never retreated in our combat history, I was very concerned for the safety of my men, and I began to feel that I was losing control of the fight."[26]

Lieutenant Colonel Vandervoort requested permission from the assistant division commander, Colonel Ira Swift to withdraw Company E. "With this vastly superior force bearing down on them, and with their backs to the river, the bluff position was rapidly becoming a trap. Prudence dictated that we pull the company back to the more favorable defensive position on the west side of the river. The terrain would help us separate tanks from infantry and put the clambake on more equal footing. The assistant division commander did not concur.

"There was no better combat company commander than [Lieutenant] Bill Meddaugh. He and his company—about 140 men and officers—were proud, tough, battle-seasoned soldiers. His orders were to stay and try to hold the Germans east of Trois Ponts. Unless ordered off of the position—[and] confronted with being surrounded and captured, they probably would have gone down fighting under the treads of the tanks.

"Disaster seemed imminent. Facing the better part of a panzer division, not one man of E Company left his fighting position. They were superb.

"Determined not to lose E Company, I sent Company F across the river to the south to try to hit the next German tank attack in the flank. This would facilitate breaking off the engagement if we could get permission (or when I decided, to hell with permission) to pull E Company back."[27]

Vandervoort ordered Company F to move up the hill through the wooded area to the east of Lieutenant Meddaugh's position. When they emerged from the woods, they would be on the right flank of Company E and would be able to deliver devastating fire into the German infantry attacking across the open field toward Company E.

Lieutenant Rusty Hays' Company F platoon, on the right flank, moved just inside the eastern edge of the woods. Unknown to Hays, SS panzer grenadiers were moving to strike the right flank of Company E. "With our scouts out in front, we started through the woods. On our right was a foggy, open field, with a ditch running along the edge of the woods in the direction of our advance. The scout [Private First Class Paul V. Zahurance] with the BAR was walking down the ditch. Suddenly, he threw his BAR up and emptied his twenty-round magazine straight down the ditch, knocking out an entire German squad trotting along the ditch toward us. That BAR saved some lives of my platoon. He couldn't have knocked out the entire squad if he had been armed with a rifle.

"Right then, I knew we were facing a well trained enemy. Almost immediately, the rest of the Germans began moving through the fog to get around our right flank. With the fog, we couldn't see them. But, we could hear them shouting commands as they ran. They may have been well trained, but our men could think for themselves. Without a word from me, the machine gunner ran a few steps into the open field, knelt, and put his machine gun across his knee, and ripped off a six-foot belt of grazing fire in the direction of the voices. We could actually hear the bullets hit home. His assistant gunner came up with a tripod and a box of ammo, and they hosed down the field pretty thoroughly. That stopped the attack, dead."[28]

Corporal Don McKeage and the rest of Company F emerged at the edge of the woods "just in time to save E Company's ass, as the Germans really hit them head on. We ended up on E Company's right flank, as the German column plowed on. We shot the hell out of them."[29]

Meanwhile, the 505th commander, Colonel Ekman, alerted to the situation while coordinating the tie-in of the regiment's right flank with the 508th, drove to Trois Ponts. He received a briefing, and after conferring with Colonel Swift, they decided to order a withdrawal. Swift told Vandervoort, "Bring them back." Vandervoort immediately told his S-3, Lieutenant Pinky Sammon, to radio that order to Lieutenant Meddaugh and Lieutenant Harold Case, the Company F commander.

Vandervoort then jumped into his jeep and was driven to the E Company command post. "As we passed the 57mm gun, the crew was getting ready to move back into the town. We arrived at the Company CP at the same time that a combined infantry and tank assault was culminating its attack on the company's foxholes. Four or more [self-propelled guns], with infantry, were closing across the open area to the right front and spraying the edge of the woods with machine gun and cannon fire.

"The first wave of the German infantry assault was momentarily piled up on the left side of the highway by a deadly fusillade across the open road. I ran to Meddaugh and told him to get his men back into town to constitute the battalion reserve, and to DO IT NOW! Bill passed the word to his company to withdraw. They began moving back through the woods accompanied by a hailstorm of bullets pruning bark and leaves from the trees. A panzer grenadier company pushed across the road—some shouting in English, 'Halt, Americans! You are surrounded.'

"Meanwhile, Corporal Jerome [B.] Russell, my driver/radio operator, had whipped the jeep around. Taking T. G. [Smith] with me, I jumped back in and we started down to Trois Ponts—urged on by swarms of 9mm slugs from Schmeisser machine pistols. Halfway down the road we passed the 57mm AT gun jackknifed into a ditch and abandoned by its crew.

"The left flank of E Company, hit by the full weight of the panzer infantry's flanking assault, maintained their composure and kept their weapons. But with the Germans flowing behind them on the other side of the road, they could only move into the concealment of the thick woods and towards the bluff. Farther to the right, tanks and their accompanying infantry were slower to close. The E Company troopers were making the panzer grenadiers with their [tank destroyers] pay a high price for progress across open ground. Ordered to withdraw, the troopers, with their previously learned lessons in close-quarter fighting at Nijmegen, Holland, intuitively improvised 'walking fire' in reverse. Moving backward and using the trees for cover, they simply out-shot any pursuer who crowded them too closely."[30]

Lieutenant John Walas covered the withdrawal of the survivors of his partially overrun 2nd Platoon until he was cut down by the horde of oncoming SS troopers. Walas was posthumously awarded the Silver Star for his heroism and inspirational leadership in repulsing five enemy attacks by an overwhelming number of enemy. His steady leadership had helped the platoon hold its positions despite a very desperate situation.

Private First Class Ed Arndt, with a .30-caliber machine gun to carry, waited for the right moment to make his move. "Us old timers were yelling at the new replacements to lie down until a break in the fire came—but they got up and ran and got cut down."[31]

Lieutenant Jake Wertich and the crew of the 57mm gun near the sharp curve on the edge of the bluff assisted the withdrawal by maintaining fire on enemy infantry and vehicles. However, SS grenadiers had penetrated through the woods immediately north of the road, overrunning part of the 2nd Platoon and the six bazooka teams. The Germans suddenly opened fire on Wertich and the gun crew from the woods at close range, killing and wounding some of them. Corporal Stokes M. Taylor grabbed a BAR, ordering those who could, to withdraw, while he covered them. Taylor fired clip after clip, pinning down the Germans in the woods, allowing the others to withdraw. Wertich remained with the gun, manning it by himself, keeping German armor from gaining the road, until both he and Taylor were shot and killed. Lieutenant Jake L. Wertich and Corporal Stokes M. Taylor were both later posthumously awarded the Distinguished Service Cross.

Around the bend in the road, Corporal Gordon Walberg hitched up the other 57mm gun to the jeep, but before they could pull away, Germans coming through the woods shot down the crew, killing and wounding almost everyone. Walberg and a couple of others managed to make it down the hill.

Private First Class Charlie Varvakis was killed as he covered the withdrawal with his machine gun. Private First Class Earl Hable was shot down by a sniper as he threw his machine gun over his shoulder and began moving out. For his key role in stopping the earlier assaults, Hable was posthumously awarded an oak leaf cluster to the Silver Star he was awarded for heroism in Holland.

Another machine gunner, Private First Class Arndt, withdrew through the woods. But as he started down the hill, he emerged into open ground. Fortunately, fog partially hid Arndt from view. "All of a sudden, I was on the ground—it was like an electric shock to my leg. I couldn't believe it—my foot and boot were facing another direction and blood running like hell.

"[Private Gordon M.] 'Stinky' Stiner got it at the same time through the head.

"How I kept my cool, I don't know. I took off my belt as a tourniquet above my left knee, took my aid packet off my belt, injected myself with morphine in my left arm, took sulfa tablets with a gulp of water from my canteen, and I started doing pushups and crawling as fast as I could down the hill.

"Had I found my combat knife, I would have cut off my left foot—it was grotesque and hurting like hell. I cinched up my belt tighter and yelled for George McCarthy and [Richard L. 'Mickey'] Johnson to come back and help me. They too, were crawling for cover and heading for the road above the railroad yard. They waited for me to catch up and helped me to the edge of a forty-foot precipice above the rail yard.

"How to get me down to the aid men with stretchers down below—funny how your mind works so clearly when in distress. I spotted a huge stack of [2 x 12] lumber planks [thirty-feet long], where the medics were below, and yelled to them, as did George and Johnson, to lay the planks against the cliff wall as a slide, which they did. Johnson—that beautiful, big nosed bastard—grabbed me by the collar and lowered me as far as he could, while bullets and shrapnel were flying everywhere. He let me go on the planks—I slid down to the waiting medics, who put me on a stretcher and carried me across what seemed like two hundred yards of bullets and railroad tracks to a Red Cross truck with stacked litters."[32]

Private First Class Dennis O'Loughlin was carrying his 60mm mortar down the hill. "We were rolling and tumbling down that steep hill, all trying to stay below the bullets. I soon left the mortar again, and picked up speed. I remember looking back up at the Germans on top of the hill and thought of movies I'd seen of Indians coming out on the hills and firing down. It was a hell of a time to be thinking about movies.

"We were pushed right down to the top of the bluff over the railroad at the foot of the hill, and some guys went tumbling right over the edge. Some were hit and some weren't. I had a slight draw spotted before I got there and went down it in a hurry, so I wouldn't have quite so far to fall. I ended up rolling, trying to break my fall and lay on the speed, too.

"At the bottom of the bluff on the railroad tracks, some of us got up and ran across the highway and over the river bank to cover, and some didn't. Some were shot up, so they weren't able to, I think."[33]

Lieutenant Meddaugh had not had time to direct an orderly withdrawal back to Trois Ponts. "The withdrawal was disorganized, and men formed small groups in the attempt to get out. I had the company headquarters group and a few men from 3rd Platoon who had become separated and drifted back. As we started to move down the road, we came under automatic weapons fire. The Germans had been able to break through at some point and put fire on the road.

"We considered dropping down the side of the cliff to the ground below, but it was about a twenty-foot drop. I rejected that move, and by moving in single file and staying close to the bank on the side of the road, we managed to work our way down the road to the bridge.

"This was not the bridge at the edge of town; this bridge went over railroad tracks. Due to the small-arms fire being directed at the bridge, we were forced to dash, one by one, across it. We crossed the river on a small foot bridge and moved through town to an assembly point. The rest of the company made their way back by similar means and drifted in over the next hour or two."[34]

Lieutenant Colonel Vandervoort barely made it back in the jeep. Now, he watched his troopers appear at the top of the bluff created by the railroad cut. "When they reached the edge of the bluff, they jumped down the sheer cliff, picked themselves up, and ran the one hundred yard gauntlet across the two roads, railroad bed, and river, under the cover of friendly protective fire delivered by our troops on the other side of the river. The latter had been told to engage any Germans appearing on the bluff.

"A number of troopers injured their backs and limbs—sprains and breaks—leaping down the cliffs, but no one was left behind. Other members of the company would grab the injured and drag them along.

"It was an opportune time for the Germans to start pushing into the town of Trois Ponts. E Company was in momentary disarray. F Company was still on the other side of the Salm. D Company was downstream holding off another attempted German crossing. Battalion headquarters, the headquarters company, and those 'damned engineers' were all that stood in the way of a major breakthrough. Troopers and engineers, dug in along the riverbank and in the Trois Ponts houses, fought back with their .30-caliber and .50-caliber machine guns. We blew the highway bridge over the Salm as soon as the last E Company trooper cleared the area. More German infantry opened fire along the bluff. The Germans and Americans engaged in rapid-fire machine gun and rifle fire at ranges from 150 to 300 yards. The Germans began hosing the streets of Trois Ponts with their automatic weapons. But the exposed rim of the cliff was no place to duel with dug-in defenders. The paratroopers settled down to some old fashioned sharpshooting and spilled a lot of blood on the bluff."[35]

Corporal Don McKeage and some of the Company F troopers assisted the troopers who had been injured jumping from the sheer cliff near the railroad depot. "Private First Class [Richard R.] Baldwin of E Company was coming down the road. He was an ammo bearer for a machine gunner by the name of

[Private] George [R.] Sonnenburg. He told me that George was hit bad, and wouldn't make it. George was from California, We went through basic training in Texas in 1943 and jump training at Fort Benning, Georgia. I and a few others stayed by the depot until we had all troopers back across the river."[36]

Lieutenant Colonel Vandervoort watched with pride as his troopers made their way across the bridge and into Trois Ponts. "The E Company survivors were a tired, ragged, rugged looking bunch when they reassembled in the town after dropping off their injured at the battalion aid station. What I saw was beautiful. About one hundred troopers, with weapons and ammunition, still ready to fight. E Company had taken about thirty percent casualties, mostly during the ill-timed withdrawal. That was nothing compared to the damage they inflicted on the enemy. They were remarkable."[37]

Lieutenant Meddaugh reorganized the Company E survivors behind a hill to the west of Trois Ponts. "The casualty figures—killed, wounded and/or captured—were high compared to previous combat situations. It was a particularly traumatic experience in that the company was for the most part overrun, or at least penetrated in some areas. Our relatively disorganized withdrawal added to the shock. As we regrouped, most of the men were in a high state of excitement. I remember one 2nd Platoon man specifically losing control of himself, and he had to be restrained and ultimately evacuated. We never saw him again.

"In spite of this, we were able to quickly reorganize and prepare to move back into Trois Ponts. That order came through shortly, and we moved into defensive positions in houses on the edge of the river, where we stayed for the next day or two."[38]

The Germans now shifted their effort to cross the Salm River south of Trois Ponts, in the Company D sector across from La Tour, where both railroad tracks and a highway crossed the river. At about 8:30 p.m., 1st SS grenadiers charged across an open area near the east bank of the river as automatic weapons fire from the wooded hill on the other side covered them. Lieutenant Joe Meyers, caught out of his foxhole, took cover behind the railroad embankment. "As the Germans advanced, we opened fire and slowed their progress. Suddenly, friendly artillery fire began to fall on the attacking force and they withdrew into the dense woods."[39]

Later that night, Meyers was lying in his hole, trying to sleep for the first time in four days. "We heard screams for help in English coming from the German-held hill. The Germans had captured several wounded E Company troopers. We assumed the 1st SS Panzer was torturing our comrades. I was one of many troopers who made a mental note to avenge this foul deed if the opportunity presented itself."[40]

Over the next two days, elements of the 1st and 9th SS Panzer Divisions attempted to capture a bridge across the Salm River farther south in both the 505 and 508 sectors, but each attempt was repulsed and the bridges blown in the faces of the assaulting Germans. The fate of Kampfgruppe Peiper was sealed.

TO THE SOUTHWEST of the 2nd Battalion, 505th, elements of the 2nd SS Panzer Division overran the Baraque de Fraiture crossroads on the far right flank of the division on the evening of December 23. The road north to Werbomont was open as far as the village of Manhay. The U.S. 3rd Armored Division, responsible for the road, was unable to secure it. The division was threatened with an enemy panzer division in its rear.

BRITISH FIELD MARSHAL Bernard L. Montgomery, now commanding all forces north of the German breakthrough, arrived at the XVIII Airborne Corps command post in Werbomont that morning and ordered Ridgway to withdraw the 82nd Airborne Division to shorten its line, saying the division "could now withdraw with honor to itself and its units."[41] Montgomery told Ridgway that it was time to "sort out the battlefield and tidy up the lines. After all, gentlemen, you can't win a big victory without a tidy show."[42]

The 82nd Airborne Division, for the first time in its magnificent history, withdrew in the face of the enemy on the night of Christmas Eve to a line running southwest from near Trois Ponts to Vaux-Chavanne.

ON CHRISTMAS MORNING, Lieutenant Meyers and his 3rd Platoon, Company D troopers were dug in on a hill overlooking Trois Ponts, in an open pasture on both sides of a haystack. "It was a beautiful, clear day and the Army Air Corps was out in force. A fear of disclosing their location and inviting air attack caused the Germans to refrain from firing at us. We moved freely about our position. There was no turkey dinner, but we received ten-in-one rations—a welcome change after a constant diet of C and K rations. The ten-in-one was a large box that contained ten rations, or thirty meals for ten men. Unfortunately, the food in the ration could not be broken down into individual servings and eaten in a foxhole. It was necessary to cook or heat portions of the ration before dividing and serving it to the men. At the time of issue, [Sergeant Donald] Olds asked me if he could bring a few men to the haystack to eat after he had cooked the meal. I made another mistake. I approved his request.

"Around noon several flights of P-47 fighters came over and attacked the German positions to our front and to the front of the 30th Division on our left flank. We sat on the edges of our foxholes like spectators at a sporting event and cheered as our planes carried out their bombing and strafing runs. Other flights of P-47s came in. Instead of attacking the Germans, several flights attacked the 30th Division. I saw three fighters circling to our front, and suddenly they peeled off and made strafing runs on our position near the haystack, about fifty yards away from my hole. I stood up and waved at the pilots as they came in, but they took no notice. Normally, we would have had signal panels to display or colored smoke to mark our position. Because of our hasty departure from Suippes, we had no means of signaling the aircraft.

"They circled and on the second pass the lead aircraft dropped a bomb that landed near the haystack. The bomb exploded and obviously killed or wounded some of my men."[43]

Luckily, Private Voorhies P. "V. P." Dewailly was in his foxhole when the three P-47s made their bombing and strafing runs. "Suddenly, they began diving toward us and dropping five-hundred--pound bombs. They would dive, strafing us, then drop their bomb. My foxhole was about 125 feet from where the bomb hit [the troopers near the haystack]."[44]

Seeing his men hit, Lieutenant Meyers immediately left his foxhole and "ran forward across the open field toward the haystack as the second plane made its strafing run. I hit the ground midway and I could hear and feel the .50-caliber machine gun rounds striking the earth around me. Unharmed, I jumped to my feet, ran to the vicinity of the haystack, and jumped into a prone shelter occupied by one of my men. He was kneeling and I landed across his legs. The third plane finished its strafing pass and I decided to look around. I first turned my attention to the man in the hole with me. His head was a mass of pulp spread out on the ground next to the hole. I could see some of his teeth amid the gore. It was the remains of Private [First Class Edwin G.] Davis. Sergeant Olds was also dead. Private [John L.] Grant, severely wounded, died later. I crammed a mess kit spoon down Grant's throat to keep him from swallowing his tongue and gave him a shot of morphine. Several others arrived and helped evacuate the wounded."[45]

In addition to Davis, Olds, and Grant, Private Kenneth R. Craig, Private Bernard J. Schroeder, and Private Thomas H. Evans were also killed. Meyers was infuriated over the senseless loss of his men. "The P-47s had expended their ordnance and returned to base. I could only think of three pilots landing, going to the officer's club for dinner and a drink, and then spending the night between clean sheets in a warm, safe environment. I felt extreme guilt, anger, and frustration. I was guilty of allowing the men to gather, together near the haystack. I was angry because the ten-in-one rations contributed to the loss. Most of all, I was furious at the pilots who attacked us. A simple check of a compass and the terrain would have told them we were friendly. If the god of war had delivered the three pilots into my hands that day, they would have been dead men. My frustration came from my inability to do anything about it. I have had many enjoyable Christmas seasons since that day, but not one Christmas has gone by without my recalling that fateful day in December of '44."[46]

Private First Class Frank Bilich felt a deep personal loss as a result of the deaths. The "episode was tough for me to understand, especially since [Private Kenneth] Craig was the kindly soldier who gave me a lot of advice in that Quonset hut in Northern Ireland."[47]

The following day, December 26, several reconnaissance patrols were conducted to gather information regarding the enemy positions along the division's new front. When a Company F patrol became pinned down by two German machine guns, Technician Fifth Grade Chick Eitelman charged them firing his .30-caliber light machine gun from the hip as he advanced. He killed both enemy machine gun crews at close range with the deadly fire from his machine gun. Later the patrol entered a small village where it became engaged with a platoon sized German force. Eitelman again charged the most dangerous machine gun position firing his weapon on the run. He wiped out the crew, then raked the village with fire, allowing the patrol to withdraw, before he left his exposed position in the midst of the enemy. Eitelman was awarded the Silver Star for his actions.

Lieutenant Charles "Frankenstein" Qualls, who had recently transferred from D Company to Headquarters, 2nd Battalion, led a recon patrol to locate enemy snipers in buildings on the edge of nearby Trois Ponts. Lieutenant Qualls was the first man into each building as they cleared them room by room. When Qualls was fired on from a doorway of one building, he moved into it, spraying the room with a long deadly burst from his Thompson submachine gun, riddling three enemy soldiers who slumped to the floor—dead.

In the next building, Qualls was searching one of the rooms when one of his men was shot and wounded in the hallway. With hesitation, Lieutenant Qualls went to the aid of the trooper and was met by fire directly to his front. Qualls opened fire and killed two Germans before he was killed. Lieutenant Charles Qualls was posthumously awarded the Silver Star for his valor.

Later that day, Private First Class Dave Bowman was one of several D Company troopers "detailed to rid the building closest to our positions of any of the enemy that may be inside. The targeted building, the one nearest us, perhaps a hundred feet or more in length, sat on a concrete foundation several feet above the ground that extended approximately four feet in front of the building; thus creating a platform or deck that could be used as a walkway. The building was solid brick with no windows, only doorways with no doors, spaced about ten feet apart. I have no idea what their original purpose was, but one of them was now being used by the Germans as a shelter for snipers.

"Sometime after darkness fell, each of us was given an incendiary grenade and told to carry out the operation as instructed earlier: To stealthily creep along the walkway and post ourselves at the edge of our assigned doorways. Upon signal, the firing of a flare, we pull the pin and toss the grenade through the opening, then rush back to the assembly area. We were further cautioned that the grenades must be thrown sequentially—that is, the first thrown would be the furthest down, then on to the nearest so as to minimize the chances of anyone being hit by the residuals of the burning grenades that would certainly be flying out of the opening after they exploded. Since I was at the furthest end, it was incumbent that I throw mine first. But when I attempted to pull the pin it would not come out. Cursing, I again pinched the ends of the pin and again jerked on the ring. Still it did not budge. Desperately, I gave a couple of more yanks and finally it dislodged and the lever flew off. The grenade now armed, I tossed it through the opening and took off. By this time, however, the grenades further down the line were spewing out their burning fragments. Realizing there was nothing else I could do, I rushed by them as rapidly as I could as I smelled my heavy wool overcoat burning. Overcoat burned—but at least I emerged unscathed. Upon returning to the assembly point, an officer, the same one who admonished me about leaving my machine gun behind in Holland, looked at me and my smoldering coat, shook his head and scoffed, 'Fouled up again, didn't you Bowman,' as he put his hand on my shoulder and sent me on my way."[48]

A second tragedy struck Company D that evening when Sergeant Henry Jakiela went out to check on the company's outposts and was mistaken for the enemy and shot by one of his own men, a young replacement. Later that night, Private First Class Dave Bowman, along with three other Company D troopers, loaded the bodies of Jakiela and the men killed the previous day by the errant bombing onto a trailer for transport to the graves registration unit. These dead troopers had been their buddies. "When we arrived where they had been stacked, a jeep with a trailer was idling nearby. As callous as it may sound, we simply picked each up by the shoulders and feet and tossed them into the trailer—much as one would so many gunnysacks full of feed. One touching moment in this whole episode came when Jakiela's body began to roll off. [Corporal William] Bennett, his close friend, grabbed and repositioned him, at the same time saying in a soothing and casually intimate way, 'Hold on there, Jake.' The jeep then pulled off without a second glance from any of us."[49]

The next evening, Technician Fourth Grade Allan C. Barger, with Company D, finished digging a new slit trench and needed something to cover it. "I was walking across the frigid snow and wrestling with a bunch of old boards when I ran into Captain [George D.] Carlson with a couple of headquarters men, and since I didn't have the password, I just told him so and gave my name. That was O.K.—but for a second, I didn't know whether it would work.

"I was given instructions to pass a message to one of the BAR outposts, and since that soldier had just shot his own sergeant by mistake the night before, I advanced very cautiously to his position and didn't hesitate to holler to let him know I was approaching him. We knew each other fairly well.

"His sergeant was Henry Jakiela, who had just won a $1,000 savings bond in a raffle back at Suippes. He was well liked by all of us, too."[50]

During the next few days, the regiment rested and readied itself for the inevitable counteroffensive to drive the German Army back to its start line. During this period, Captain Taylor G. Smith, the 2nd Battalion executive officer, rotated to the United States on a thirty-day leave, replaced by Captain William R. Carpenter.

The First Army counteroffensive on the northern shoulder of the Bulge would commence on January 3, 1945. The 82nd Airborne Division plan for the attack consisted of a three-regiment assault with two regiments held in reserve. Even with the addition of the attached 517th Parachute Infantry Regiment and the 551st Parachute Infantry Battalion, the 82nd Airborne Division still didn't have its authorized strength. On the right flank the 325th Glider Infantry would seize the high ground of Heid-de-Heirlot and then push south to capture Amcomont. In the center, the 505th would take the high ground to its front including the villages of Noirfontaine on its right, Reharmont in the center, and Fosse on the left. The 517th Parachute Infantry Regiment with the 551st Parachute Infantry Battalion attached would attack on the left flank to capture Trois Ponts and the hamlets of St.-Jacques and Bergeval on the high ground to the south. Because the terrain was hilly and contained areas that were heavily wooded, British Field Marshal Montgomery insisted on the use of phase lines to prevent units from becoming isolated in front of the units to either side. The commanders of the 82nd were not happy with the phase line restrictions. They felt that once they broke the initial enemy line and got them on the run, they wanted to pursue them closely, so as not to give them an opportunity to recover.

The opposition in the 82nd Airborne Division sector would consist of the 62nd Volksgrendier Division. This division had been reconstituted in the autumn of 1944 from a cadre of veterans after being wiped out on the Eastern Front. This division had fought well at St.-Vith. Its strength was less than 10,000, with only two battalions in each of its three regiments. However, the 62nd possessed a full complement of artillery and heavy mortars.

On January 2, Lieutenant Rusty Hays transferred from Company F to D. It was also his birthday. That night, Hays prepared for the coming attack, scheduled to commence the following morning. "Each soldier took his overcoat and all his sleeping gear, rolled it in a bundle, and left it to be brought up at a later date after the attack. The idea was that we'd not be weighed down with this extra weight. The snow was about two feet deep and, the temperature about ten to twenty degrees below zero. While we were moving, the cold was not too bad. We were acclimated to the cold by that time. But it was impossible to sleep at night. We were already too lightly equipped for the weather we faced, and to drop what warm things we had and have to lie down in the snow to sleep was miserable.

"The night before our attack, I was faced with spending a miserable night in the snow in well below zero weather. Then, I remembered something I had read about when I was a boy. When I was growing up, I enjoyed reading Indian lore. One of the things I read about was how Indians managed to sleep warm when they were caught in the woods and had to spend the night. They had a technique of making a warm bed from fir, spruce, or pine branches. I decided to see if it would work for me. It took me an hour to prepare my bed, but it was well worth it. That night I slept soundly and warmly, thanks to the Indians."[51]

In order for the troopers to have mobility in the deep snow, the decision was made to have them leave blankets, bedrolls, and overcoats piled in fields, with the expectation of bringing the gear forward to the troopers after the assault.

CHAPTER 9

"One Of The Most Fearless"

At dawn on January 3, 1945, the American counteroffensive began in the midst of one to two-feet deep snow, fog, and an overcast sky. The German 62nd Volksgrenadier Division was dug in opposite of the 82nd Airborne Division.

Technician Fourth Grade Allan Barger, weighed down by a heavy SCR 300 radio and other gear struggled through the deep snow as Company D moved to the line of departure before dawn. "We started to walk and walk, endlessly through the night without having the least idea where we were going. We would get sore from walking and want to rest. We would get stiff from stopping because of the extreme cold, and want to move. Hour after hour.

"I kept repeating silently in my mind the Twenty-third Psalm . . .

"A little before eight o'clock in the morning of January the third of the new year, we finally worked our way down through some brush, and apparently we were facing east near a road and awaiting orders. I often thought this was a curious moment, as we stood around joking about this, even though we were uptight and fully aware that something big and dangerous was about to happen.

"I was reminded of a picture I used to study back in my school days with the title, 'Over the Top.' The soldiers were portrayed coming out of their trenches in World War I and heading into no man's land. As a mere boy, I used to wonder if I would have enough courage to do that. Well, now I would find out! I found there are times you do something whether you like it or not, even though fear is slicing through you, every minute in every vein in your body.

"We crossed a road to our front. I was staying close to Captain Carlson most of the time now, as I was his radioman to battalion. However, he ran across another road to our left flank near a 'Y' junction, telling me to stay where I was. He wasn't gone very long when he called me over. I ran over to where he was sitting—in a ditch—and slid over beside him.

"Then someone said, 'Hey! Barger, look what you just did!'

"I looked and a chill went up my spine, for I could see clearly in the light snow that my feet had slid right up against a small antipersonnel mine, and I had even left a layer of mushy snow up against it. I had been within a hair's breath of triggering it.

"Shortly after that, we moved eastward along this road, and it was easy to see there was a bloody battle going on just up to the front of us. Jeeps were hauling out one load after another of wounded and swiftly moving to our rear

199

"We proceeded down a narrow road through a little boggy draw, and started up a gentle slope on a small lane running between two clearly frozen meadows. Our battalion commander, Lieutenant Colonel Vandervoort, called Captain Carlson and our group over to his side and asked if we knew where F Company was. We didn't know and said so.

"So the colonel said he had sent them further up the lane into the edge of the woods to our west and asked if we would go check them out."[1]

The 2nd Battalion advanced south astride the road to Arbrefontaine, with Company F on the right, west of the road. The main objective in the Company F axis of advance was a group of farm buildings known as Noirfontaine. Sergeant Russ Brown, with Company F, led a 60mm mortar squad. "[Private First Class] Victor [G.] Saragosa had been in the 3rd Platoon mortar squad, but he was placed in my squad, because he was about the only one left in his squad.

"At the start of the attack, we rode on the tanks, until we were fired on. We jumped off the tank and some of the men had trouble crossing a ditch—the snow was so deep. I had the mortar, and Saragosa took it from me as we walked away from the tank. An 88 fired at the tank. Saragosa and I hit the ground—Saragosa was riddled with shrapnel and killed. My ears were ringing and I thought I was O.K. Someone said, 'Brown, you are bleeding.' I had a piece of shrapnel go through my ear, but that was all. I was O.K.

"I went into the edge of the woods and a German came out with his hands up and he handed me a folding trigger .22 pistol. It was so small I put it in my watch pocket.

"I saw Staff Sergeant Bonnie [G.] Wright lying on the side of the road with someone else. He was wounded [and later died]."[2]

Shortly after Company F dismounted, German tanks and self-propelled guns quickly knocked out two Sherman tanks and two M10 tank destroyers. Corporal Don McKeage was moving with the company headquarters group which "included a machine gun section from the 2nd Battalion, Headquarters Company; a total of nineteen men, led by Lieutenant [Harold E.] Case.

"Three platoons disappeared into the woods. We started up a fence row and figured we were behind one of our platoons. As we entered the woods, all hell broke loose. Two mortar shells hit with tree bursts right on our group. Sixteen of our men, including the complete machine gun section, went down—all wounded. Three of us were O.K.—Lieutenant Case, James [W.] Shuman, and myself. The Germans opened up with rifle fire. I had my rifle shot out of my hand. For some reason, the platoon was not where we figured."[3]

A Company E platoon, which was attached to Company F for the attack, became pinned down by machine gun and mortar fire in the vicinity where the Company F headquarters personnel had been struck down. While pinned down, a mortar shell landed in the midst of the platoon wounding a squad leader and blinding Technical Sergeant Irving Jacobs, the platoon sergeant. Jacobs, despite being blinded and still under heavy fire, directed his men in evacuating the eighteen wounded Company F headquarters troopers. Using his squad leader as his eyes and the voices of the troopers as his guide, he personally evacuated four of the wounded. He continued to refuse evacuation until he received a direct order from his platoon leader. Technical Sergeant Jacobs was later awarded the Silver Star for his gallantry.

Emerging from the wooded area, Company F crossed a snow covered field under fire, assaulted the Germans defending the Noirfontaine farm buildings, and captured the objective.

On the left, Company D moved south, east of the road, with Lieutenant Joe Meyers leading the 3rd Platoon. "Heavy mortar and artillery fire greeted us at the line of departure (LD). A short distance beyond the LD we forded a small stream and advanced into large, open, snow covered fields. The mortar and artillery fire was very heavy, and suddenly I felt a hot burning sensation in the fleshy part of my right upper arm. A medic cut away the layers of clothing [and] informed me I had a minor shrapnel wound.

"We continued to advance and arrived at a road junction where we halted briefly. Vandervoort joined [Captain George D.] Carlson and me. He wanted a patrol dispatched to contact the 3rd Battalion on our left. I volunteered to take the patrol, but Vandervoort wisely told me to send an NCO. After I dispatched the patrol, Carlson and I discussed the best route of advance. Directly to our front was a large, open field about one hundred fifty yards wide and three hundred yards long. A few yards inside the field, we saw a German antitank minefield hastily installed on top of the ground and covered by the new snow. It was not necessary to expose the entire company while crossing this open field. I recommended the 3rd Platoon cross the field, and that Carlson move the company along a covered route on the far side of the field. Carlson would have me in his sight all the way, and we could link up in the far woods. Carlson agreed. The 3rd Platoon crossed the field without losing a man.

"When we reached the woods at the far end of the field, we discovered several hastily installed booby traps and halted to disarm them. One of my BAR men, Private First Class James [D.] McKinley, flushed out and killed a couple of Germans. McKinley was a good soldier. His motto was, 'When it's too tough for everyone else, it's just right for me.' He lived up to it."[4]

Meanwhile, the rest of the company moved up the narrow, tree-lined lane. Vandervoort had told Captain Carlson that when they made contact with Company F, to radio him with the position. The SCR-300 radio operator for Company D was Technician Fourth Grade Allan Barger. "Just as we got to the position we expected to find F Company, we found them. But before we could even say a word on the radio, a shell struck right in our midst.

"I felt the left side of my face and my left shoulder go numb. And as I passed out, I remembered having been told in the case of such wounds, the portion damaged would turn numb. So of course, I thought the whole side of my face was removed along with a chunk of my shoulder. That meant I was finished. To myself I made the voiceless scream: 'I'm not ready to die!' It was as though I wanted to get my soul screwed on right before I left this planet.

"It was joyful surprise when I came to, and found all I had was a small, bloody hole in the top of my shoulder. A piece of shrapnel had gone through both my radio and musette bag shoulder straps and a thick layer of clothes. It lodged right next to my shoulder blade.

"As I looked around me I discovered a whole cluster of men wounded or dead on the floor of the forest. Captain Carlson was not only wounded in the leg, but Lieutenant Virgil Gould was lying on the ground with a hole in his knee. We were the lucky ones, for our operations sergeant, [Fred W.] Freddie Freeland, was mortally wounded by the same burst. The medics were pretty busy dressing our wounds and, of course, giving us shots."[5]

The D Company headquarters group was the second to be struck down, and the attack was just getting under way. Meanwhile, Lieutenant Meyers and his platoon were finishing disarming the booby traps. "A runner arrived and reported mortar fire had wounded both Carlson and [1st Sergeant John] Rabig, and had killed or wounded several other men. I assumed command and sent for [Lieutenant Lawrence M.] Price and [Lieutenant Marshall] Hughes. While they were coming, I contacted [Lieutenant] Harold Case, F Company commander, and informed him of our situation. When Price and Hughes arrived with the company radio, I notified battalion of our situation. I decided to continue the advance with three platoons in column, 3rd Platoon leading. Deployed platoons are difficult to control in dense woods, and, although mortar and artillery fire was extremely heavy, enemy resistance was spotty. The attack continued until shortly before dark, when we stopped and dug in for the night."[6]

Throughout the night of January 3, men suffered terribly from the cold, as the regiment's S-4 supply sections weren't able to bring up coats, bedrolls, blankets, or food because the evacuation of the wounded, bringing up ammunition and water, and moving artillery forward took priority over bringing the other items forward to the troopers. Logistics were severely limited by the lack of roads. There was only one leading south in the 505th axis of advance.

Most troopers were wearing only long johns or an olive drab wool sweater to supplement their cotton jumpsuits and jump boots. Freezing to death was a real danger. Most stayed awake in order to keep from freezing to death.

Troopers used just about every means at their disposal to get a little warmth that night. Private John Jackson, with Headquarters Company, 2nd Battalion, was a message center runner. "I spent most of the time standing behind a running tank so the exhaust would keep me warm. One night, I tore a sack into strips and lit them one by one in my foxhole to keep my feet from freezing."[7]

Snow continued to fall during the night, adding to the misery. Trench foot and frostbite began to take a toll on the officers and men, and that toll would increase with each day spent without overshoes and overcoats. The attack on January 3, had been the most costly in the history of the regiment and the division. But it had severely crippled the 62nd Volksgrenadier Division, which had lost almost two entire battalions, a third of its infantry strength, to the 505th.

Now, at dawn on January 4, men who had received little or nothing to eat and almost no sleep in order to keep from freezing to death, prepared to carry the attack forward yet again. The coming light of the dreary, overcast day would make these men drowsy as they struggled to advance through deep snow.

The 2nd Battalion encountered significant resistance in its zone of attack. The Germans were determined to hold on to the single north-south road to deny its use to the 505th, and to protect the primary route for supplying their own troops. The 2nd Battalion attacked toward Arbrefontaine. Corporal Don McKeage and Company F emerged from a wooded area and "started across the open field towards the German line—a fence row—maybe three hundred yards in front. We all walked out of the woods in line, firing forward. One of our sergeants, Vernon L. Francisco was killed when he mounted a tank destroyer to fire a .50-caliber machine gun at the Kraut line. When we reached the wooded fence row, many Krauts stood up with their hands in the air.

"As we moved on from this point, there was a curve in the road to the right. The tank destroyer, which had a 90mm gun, continued for another four hundred yards, where the road turned back to the left. Lieutenant Case and I walked up behind the tank destroyer. Just as we arrived, a German tank from behind us let go with an 88, right over our heads, and just missed the turret of our tank destroyer. Without hesitation, that 90mm swung over our heads, placing Case and me directly below the muzzle. I immediately knocked Case and myself to the ground, and the tank destroyer fired. Our tank destroyer had knocked out the Kraut tank to our left rear. We kept moving and finally came to the top of a hill, where we could see the town of Arbrefontaine around a big curve in the road, to our right front. Within a couple of minutes, a German Tiger tank caught us in his sight and knocked out our tank destroyer."[8]

Lieutenant Joe Meyers, commanding Company D, deployed his men in the woods on the east side of the road, and the company moved south. "Enemy mortar and artillery fire was intense. We were advancing through fairly dense woods, and every round was a tree burst. Shortly after we jumped off, I received word that [Lieutenant Marshall] Hughes was dead. Wounded by mortar fire and placed on a stretcher to await evacuation, he died when another round landed next to his stretcher. In the three days he was with us, I hardly got to know him.

"Ground resistance stiffened. The attached platoon of tanks moved up to support the attacking rifle companies. [Lieutenant] Russ Parker, now with Company F, was shot off the deck of an M4 tank while manning the tank's .50-caliber machine gun.

"About noon, we briefly broke out of the woods at a turn in the road and came under direct fire of some distant 88s. Unlike indirect-fire weapons, the direct-fire 88 got your attention immediately. You knew the gunner had you in his sights. If he could see you, he could hit you. One of the casualties of the 88s was Private Alfredo R. López, one of the 3rd Platoon's finest soldiers. A citizen of Ecuador, López volunteered for service in the U.S. Army while attending college in the States."[9]

Lieutenant Meyers and his men kept moving forward despite the 88mm and artillery fire. "We pressed on and in the late afternoon we seized the high ground overlooking the town of Arbrefontaine. As we approached the town, we came under fire from a lovely villa. I had two tanks supporting me. They answered the fire of a machine gun positioned behind open French doors on the villa's ground floor. The machine gun fell silent. When we were fifty yards away, a German officer stepped to the door, pistol in hand, and began to fire as us. Within seconds he was dead. We killed several of the enemy as they tried to escape out a side door. I received orders to halt and dig in for the night."[10]

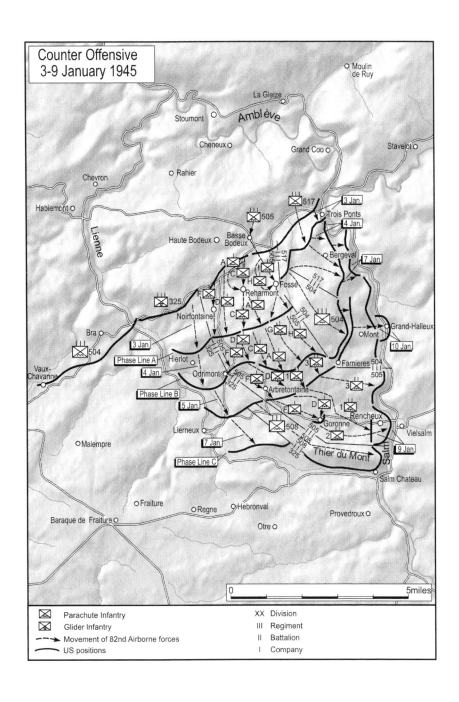

At the end of the day, Company D trooper, Private First Class Dave Bowman, and his assistant gunner set up their gun and flopped down in the snow—exhausted. "I was beginning to get comfortable—well, as comfortable as possible in two or three feet of snow at zero degrees—when I received word to report to company headquarters. I always hated such orders. Usually nothing good came of them. As I slogged my way over, a shell exploded near the headquarters, and activity there increased. I quickened my pace, and upon arrival saw Corporal [Edward J. 'Ozzie'] Olszewski lying on the ground with blood pouring from the area around his heart. The company clerk, Henry [J.] Matzelle, who was standing nearby, told me the blood had been spurting out like a miniature geyser. A captured German officer who had been standing by observing the whole thing, coldly mumbled, 'Kaput' and walked away.

"Oszewski dead—that was hard to take. He was one of the old timers, both in age and in the time spent with the 505. He was in his early thirties and came into the '05 at the beginning, at the Frying Pan area, and remained with us throughout. He was a stout, strongly-built mesomorph, whose only weakness was that he found it difficult to keep up on our frequent sprees of double-timing. One of the rare times he dropped out, I heard him bitterly moan, 'They can't make a race horse out of a work horse.' I do not recall his ever missing any combat at all—from wounds or from illness. Now, near the end of the war, he was killed."[11]

Late on the afternoon of January 4, the 62nd Volksgrenadier Division fell back to reestablish a main line of resistance on more favorable terrain. The following morning, Headquarters Company, 2nd Battalion's 81mm mortar platoon fired concentrations on the Germans holding Arbrefontaine in preparation for the battalion's push. Sergeant Joseph F. Gilhooly, who had set up a forward observation post near the outskirts of the town directed devastating fire on the German rear guard holding the town. German self-propelled guns, mortars, and artillery were directed against his position to neutralize his effective direction of the battalion's mortars. Despite being wounded, Gilhooly stayed at the forward observation post until the battalion jumped off. Sergeant Gilhooly moved forward with the lead skirmish line of troopers, stringing communications wire and continuing to adjust the 81mm mortar fire on the Germans firing from buildings and dug in positions. Sergeant Joseph Gilhooly would receive the Silver Star for his heroism.

The enemy rear guard pulled out of the town after a short fight in which Company F's last officer, Lieutenant Harold Case, was wounded. Don McKeage, who had entered the fighting as a corporal on December 18, was now the acting first sergeant and took temporary command of the company until Lieutenant John D. Phillips, the 2nd Battalion S-3, arrived to take command.

On January 6, the 505th troopers rested and ammunition, water, and food was brought up in preparation for the push the following day.

That evening, Lieutenant Joe Meyers, commanding Company D, reported to the 2nd Battalion command post to receive attack orders for the morning of January 7. "The battalion, reinforced by tanks and tank destroyers, would attack with E and F [Companies] along the Arbrefontaine-Goronne road that lay in a valley. D Company would make a secondary attack to seize the high ground north of Goronne. The success of the main attack, moving down the valley, depended upon the secondary attack seizing the high ground overlooking Goronne. Moreover, we were jumping off about two hours before dawn. In the initial phase, it was a night attack—a difficult operation to control over a distance of several thousand yards.

"I returned to the company, and I issued the attack order to my platoon leaders. We had a large, open area of about three hundred yards to negotiate before reaching the base of our objective, a very large, heavily wooded hill. I anticipated the Germans would defend along the wood line, but I could not be sure. We would advance in a column of platoons, with patrols to the front for security. I closed by instructing both platoon leaders to send runners to company headquarters."[12]

Before dawn the next morning, Meyers sent a runner to make sure that both of his platoon leaders were awake. "At the appointed time, company headquarters and the 1st Platoon saddled up and moved to the 2nd Platoon's position. I crossed the LD on time with the 1st Platoon. We advanced under cover of darkness over open, snow-covered fields for several hundred yards. Patrols checked out the edge of the wood line and reported the area was clear of enemy. We moved into a heavily wooded, cultivated pine forest with aligned trees tightly spaced in rows that ran at a tangent to our direction of advance. The darkness and the tree alignment made it extremely difficult to maintain an accurate compass heading through the dense woods. I abandoned the use of the compass in favor of moving uphill toward the high ground that was our objective. As we advanced uphill, we came upon a firebreak, where I found German communication wire, and I followed the wire uphill some five or six hundred yards. As we neared the top of the hill, we left the cultivated forest and entered a naturally wooded area. The point signaled a halt, and a messenger returned to tell me the point heard sounds of men snoring. I joined the point, only a few yards ahead, and listened. I could hear men snoring to our front, flanks and left rear.

"Using the men on the point, we organized two teams, one to work each side of the firebreak. The teams went from foxhole to foxhole awakening the sleeping German soldiers, disarming them and bringing them to the column where we passed them to the rear. It was a slow work, but all was going well. We had disarmed and captured about six or eight prisoners in this manner when a shot rang out at the rear of the column. One of our men was about half asleep on his feet. He looked up, saw a German POW, and in his confusion, shot him. All hell broke loose. We came under heavy small-arms fire from what appeared to me to be all directions. We managed to form what amounted to an elongated perimeter. The Germans to our rear must have panicked, for they withdrew, permitting the 2nd Platoon under First Sergeant [Thomas J.] Rogers to join us as first light broke. With Rogers on the left and [Lieutenant Lawrence] Price on the right, we pressed forward, clearing the area of enemy until we reached a second firebreak that ran at right angles to our direction of attack.

"At this firebreak we came under heavy machine gun and rifle fire and the fires of supporting mortars and artillery. Both Rogers and Price reported they were pinned down at the edge of the firebreak, a few yards from the defenders. I was only ten or twenty yards to their rear. By inspection, I was able to determine I was on my objective. The topographical crest lay only a few yards beyond the German position to our front.

"A lieutenant [Henry G. Coustillac] from the division AA battalion crawled up to me and reported he had a 57mm AT gun and crew with him. He reported his crew had attacked and destroyed a German machine gun to our rear on the way to our position. I was unable to reach the battalion on my radio, so the AA officer filled me in on the situation. He reported the battalion was held up in the valley by German infantry supported by two Tiger tanks. If we could seize the crest of the hill, he might be able to get a shot into the rear of one or both of the tanks. While all this was going on, we continued to exchange fires with the defenders at very close range. The AT officer returned to his crew, and minutes later I saw the slim figure of my battalion commander, Ben Vandervoort, crawling up the firebreak to my position. I briefed him on the situation, and I informed him I could muster a reserve of about ten men from my company headquarters, a mortar squad, and the AT gun crew. He said he had about six men (I assumed his driver, staff, and security) with him.

"He said, 'Give me about five minutes to get in position, then make a frontal assault with your platoons and company headquarters. I'll flank them with the battalion staff.'

"We carried out the assault as ordered. As we overran the position we received a heavy concentration of mortar fire. The AT officer was advancing a foot or two to my left, and [Donald E.] Harris, my runner, was immediately behind me. I saw an orange flash about five yards to my front.

"[Lieutenant Coustillac] threw his hand to his forehead and said, 'Joe, I'm hit.' He was dead when he hit the ground. Harris was on the ground behind me, severely wounded in both legs; I stood there feeling my body to see if I still was in one piece. Except for a multitude of tiny, needle-like fragment that sprayed my exposed face and hands, I was unharmed. A messenger arrived within minutes to tell me Vandervoort was wounded. I assume the same volley of mortar fire that killed the AT officer hit him. By the time I reorganized the company to protect against a possible counterattack, Vandervoort was gone, and I later learned he lost an eye."[13]

General Gavin "was out with the infantry when I heard that Colonel Vandervoort had been hit and that he was in an aid station in the town of Abrefontaine. When I got there, he was on stretcher in an ambulance. He had been hit in the eye by a shell fragment and apparently had lost one eye. I felt very bad about it, because just a day or two earlier we had been talking about bringing Vandervoort to division headquarters."[14]

Gavin and "the veterans among us believed that the chances of his luck running out were quite high and that we should make a change."[15]

In the valley below, Company F was having a tough time with German infantry and the two Tiger tanks as it attacked astride the road toward Goronne in the main attack. Lieutenant John Phillips, who had just assumed command of the company, led the fifty-six remaining troopers against vastly superior numbers of enemy troops.

When tank destroyers supporting Company D mistakenly opened fire on Company F troopers in the valley, Sergeant Phillip M. Lynch, instead of taking cover, rushed across an open field toward the tank destroyers waving his arms until the crews realized they were friendly troops and ceased fire. Sergeant Lynch's action no doubt saved lives of his fellow Company F troopers.

Sergeant Russ Brown was leading his Company F 60mm mortar squad as they "advanced to a small church and some trees. We saw two Tiger tanks. They were shelling the troops on our left flank and then they shelled us. We fell back and cut across a field. That was when 2nd Platoon mortar squad sergeant Phil Lynch was KIA [by an enemy mortar shell].[16] We went into a wooded area and stopped near the church."[17]

For his extraordinary bravery during the assault, Sergeant Phillip Lynch was posthumously awarded the Silver Star.

Sergeant Brown and Lieutenant George Essex decided to continue the advance by using the woods that lay on the far side of an open area as concealment from the two German tanks. "Lieutenant Essex asked Sergeant E. D. [Edward D.] Jones to send one man across an open field to the woods. He was shot when he got to the woods.

"Lieutenant Essex and the mortar squad, plus [Private First Class] Frank [R.] Rojas walked to the corner of the [same] woods, and four Germans came out—hands up. Lieutenant Essex went back; but my squad, with Rojas, went into the woods."[18]

Brown then led his squad through the woods, emerging on the far side. "In a field about two hundred yards ahead was a pile of straw, and up came a German—he shot [Private First Class] Lowell [C.] Schell. We all fired—Frank Rojas fired his bazooka. When we got to the pile of straw, the German was dead. He had a rifle with a scope. I took the rifle and gave it to someone. I had enough to carry with my Thompson.

"We went back to the woods and found [Kenneth T.] Ken Olsen wounded and [Private First Class] Charles [J.] Krka, who DOW [died of wound]. On the way into Goronne, Frank Rojas was killed."[19]

Sergeant R. A. Sandel, a squad leader with Headquarters Company, 2nd Battalion's light machine gun platoon was directing his men who were laying down a base of fire for Company F as it advanced when the squad's position took a direct hit by an enemy mortar shell. Sandel was hit in the face, neck, and hands, but despite his painful wounds, he carried his wounded troopers to comparative safety where he administered first aid. He then returned and directed another machine gun in support of the attack, inflicting heavy casualties on the German infantry. Sergeant R. A. Sandel was awarded an oak leaf cluster to the Silver Star he had previously received for valor.

Another Headquarters Company, 2nd Battalion squad leader, Corporal Ronald F. Adams, Sr., was covering the right rear flank of Company F during the attack. Leading his men forward, firing his machine gun from the waist, German automatic weapons concentrated intense fire on him until he was wounded and knocked to the ground. Adams rose up on one knee and continued to fire his machine gun until the German machine guns were knocked out. Too weak from the loss of blood, he continued to crawl forward to support the attack until he succumbed to his wounds. Sergeant Ronald Adams was posthumously awarded an oak leaf cluster to the Silver Star he was awarded for his actions in Holland during the assault on the Nijmegen bridges.

Meanwhile, Company D reached the crest of the hill as a Battery A, 80th Airborne Antiaircraft (Antitank) Battalion squad, led by Technician Fifth Grade Paul H. Schlupp manhandled a 57mm antitank gun over 100 yards in the deep snow and dense woods to bring it into position to support the battalion's attack.

Lieutenant Meyers reported the situation by radio to the 2nd Battalion command post. "I reported the AT squad was moving the 57mm gun in position for a shot at one of the Tigers. I was instructed not to fire, a TD was en route to my position. The TD arrived about two hours later with a captain in command. I pointed out both Tigers. The nearest one was in a ditch at the side of the road. The tank's hull was in defilade, its turret exposed. We were above the tank and to its right rear. The captain moved the TD into position. He placed the 57mm nearby, and he ordered both guns to bore sight before firing at the target. This accomplished, he ordered both crews to take cover in foxholes while he and one 57mm crewmember prepared to fire the two guns.

"As soon as the guns fired, the captain and the crewmember would take cover in nearby holes. The Tiger tank with its 88mm gun was a formidable opponent. If you missed a shot at a Tiger, you were in for big trouble. Earlier in the day, the regiment had lost several tanks and TDs to the two Tigers in the valley.

"A few minutes before the TD was scheduled to fire, a platoon of M4 tanks rolled in and reported to me. If the TD successfully eliminated the Tiger, I was to attack down the hill and seize Goronne. After I issued the necessary orders, the two antitank guns fired. After a minute or two, the captain and I inched forward and took a look. [The TD and the 57mm gun had each] scored a clean hit and disabled the Tiger. We observed the other Tiger withdrawing into Goronne and heading up the Thier-du-Mont, a large hill mass across the valley in the 508's sector.

"With the tanks in support, we immediately launched an assault down the hill. As we broke the military crest, we came upon a battery of horse-drawn artillery. The Germans were attempting to hitch up their teams to the howitzers and withdraw. At a range of about fifty yards, we engaged the battery with both tank and infantry weapons. It was a turkey shoot. The tanks engaged and disabled the howitzers, and we directed our fire at the men and the animals. It was a wild scene, horses rearing and plunging, tanks firing, and the men shouting as we overran the position, an aid station, and a nearby CP.

"During this assault, I saw my first and only enemy soldier killed with cold steel. One of my men jumped in a foxhole and landed on a German hiding in the bottom of the hole. The German probably wanted to surrender, but the trooper's blood was up. He pulled his trench knife and killed him with repeated blows. I estimated we took about fifty to seventy-five prisoners, including one German female nurse, plus horses, howitzers, individual weapons, etc. We didn't stop to count. We moved straight for Goronne. As we approached the town, the tank platoon leader got a report a Tiger was in town, and he refused to accompany us. We secured the town without meeting enemy resistance.

"The road into Goronne, a cobblestone street that branched off at right angles from the Arbrefontaine-Vielsalm road, climbed part way up the Thier-du-Mont. About a block off the main road, this street broadened to form a small plaza. Here a farmer and his two attractive young daughters greeted us and invited me to use their home as my CP. The house was a large, two-story structure with a barn attached. I accepted the invitation and we moved in after we set up our defensive position."[20]

The assault resulted in over two hundred German soldiers killed, wounded, or captured and an enemy company command post captured intact. The defeat was so demoralizing, the German regimental commander committed suicide. For his heroic leadership of Company F during the attack, Lieutenant John Phillips was awarded an oak leaf cluster as a second award of the Silver Star.

The 2nd Battalion's capture of Goronne came at a terrible cost—the loss of their much beloved commander, Lieutenant Colonel Vandervoort, whom many in the battalion thought invincible. One of Vandervoort's radio operators was Technician Fourth Grade Donald L. Brown. "I spent many hours and miles with Colonel Vandervoort—one of the most fearless people I have ever known. When shells were coming I would instinctively hit the ground, but he would be surveying the situation, standing."[21]

Private John Jackson, one of the battalion runners "felt a deep loss when Lieutenant Colonel Vandervoort was hit."[22]

Captain Lyle Putnam, who had treated him when he was brought into the 2nd Battalion aid station, felt that Vandervoort "was personally missed by each and every survivor when he was evacuated under protest during the Ardennes with an eye shot out and severe head wounds."[23]

Private First Class Don Lassen, who had served with Company E since Normandy, spoke for virtually everyone in the battalion when he stated, "The entire 2nd Battalion of the 505 respected and admired Colonel Vandy, and they would all have followed him through hell, which they did. And I can tell you that when Colonel Vandy got hit in the Battle of the Bulge, everyone in the battalion was concerned. Everyone loved Colonel Vandy."[24]

That afternoon, January 7, the 2nd Battalion executive officer, William R. Carpenter, recently promoted to major, replaced Vandervoort as commander. That same day, Lieutenant Bill Meddaugh, the Company E commander, was evacuated with pneumonia and replaced by Captain Charles L. Barnett.

Despite the loss of its great combat commander and inspirational leader, the 2nd Battalion fought on. On January 8, the 505th captured the high ground north of Rencheux, overlooking the Salm River, and established a roadblock between Goronne and Rencheux. During the attack, German infantry infiltrated back into abandoned holes and set up several machine guns to enfilade the exposed left flank of the 2nd Battalion assault. Lieutenant Arthur F. Draper, Jr., the platoon leader of the headquarters company light machine gun platoon, observed this and left his machine gunners to continue laying down suppressive fire for the attacking troopers. Then, under withering automatic weapons fire, Draper charged two of the positions and neutralized them, then tossed white phosphorous grenades into two other machine gun positions, destroying them. For his tremendous heroism in carrying out his one man attack, Lieutenant Draper was awarded the Silver Star.

The following day, the 2nd Battalion took Rencheux. Private First Class Earl Boling, promoted to staff sergeant the previous day, led the 1st Platoon of Company E. "The morning of the 9th of January, we again moved out—this time to take the village of Rencheux. Although the resistance in this area was considered light and mostly of the rear-guard type action of the Germans, I did lose another good man here. Private [William H.] Nealy was wounded just before we arrived at a row of houses, where we were to establish our defensive line. I secured an aid man for Private Nealy, who determined his wound was in the stomach and abdomen, passing into the body and apparently striking the spinal column.

"As he was unable to move his legs, or had no feeling in the lower body, the medic advised against moving him until the medical vehicle could arrive. I told Nealy I would return later, and proceeded to the line of houses where the platoon was placed in a defensive line, with a machine gun on the right flank and the BAR on the left flank. The rest of the few men left in the platoon were positioned in the houses facing the river, with orders that the men on the flanks were to be relieved periodically for a chance to [get] warm in the houses. While checking the houses, we found one lady still in the area. She spoke good English.

"I advised her to stay in the basement in case we received shellfire, and told her I was going to check on a wounded man. She gave me a quilt to cover him with, and I returned to Private Nealy's position. He was very cold, and apparently going into shock. I covered him with the quilt, and he asked me if I would mind praying with him. I took his hand and we said the Lord's Prayer together. At this time, a medical jeep arrived and he was placed on it. I wished him luck as he was taken away. The next day, I learned that he had died of wounds on the way to the clearing station."[25]

Later that day, a Company F patrol was pinned down by heavy mortar and machine gun, killing one and seriously wounding three. Private First Class Donald A. Doyle volunteered to cross open ground to go to their aid. As he crossed the field, a sniper's bullet struck him in the left shoulder, but despite the wound, Doyle continued on under fire and moved the three wounded men to safety where they could be evacuated. For his courageous actions, Private First Class Donald Doyle was awarded the Silver Star.

ON JANUARY 10, the U.S. 75th Infantry Division relieved the 82nd Airborne Division. The survivors of the previous week of combat were trucked to rest areas in small towns to the north. The 505 was sent to Theux, Belgium, where it was to rest and reorganize. The tired, dirty troopers were billeted in the homes of the town's citizens, who welcomed them.

So many of the "old men" who had survived Sicily, Salerno, Normandy, and Holland had been killed, seriously wounded, or evacuated with severe frostbite or trench foot. Those who were left felt almost alone. Lieutenant Joe Meyers mentally checked off the names and status of the Company D officers who had left France for Belgium less than a month prior: Captain George D. Carlson and Lieutenants Virgil Gould and Lawrence M. Price, wounded in action; Lieutenants Charles Qualls and Marshall Hughes, killed in action. Meyers was the only officer of the eight still on duty; although one of the company's officers, Lieutenant O. B. Carr, was on temporary duty with the pathfinders.

For the first time since leaving France on December 18, troopers took showers, were issued new clothes and jump boots, and received medical treatment for minor injuries and illnesses. Meyers and the others received their barracks bags, as they had finally caught up with the regiment. "I went upstairs where I had my first bath since leaving Suippes. A big copper bathtub, filled with hot water, was waiting. Soap and clean towels were nearby. It was heavenly. I dressed in clean clothes and for the first time in weeks, I felt like a human being.

"Our battalion mess operated nearby, and we ate three hot meals every day. The day following our arrival in Theux, the regimental officers assembled in the local theater to hear an address by General Gavin. It was a small group; we had not yet received replacements. From the outset, it was obvious Gavin thought he was talking to the officers of the 2nd Battalion, not the officers of the entire regiment. His mistake was understandable. Our ranks were very thin.

"On our third day in Theux, I arose at 06:30, dressed, and started downstairs, where I met General Gavin and Bill Ekman on the stairway. I reported to the general and he asked me what training I had scheduled for the day. I replied, 'None.' I was giving the men an opportunity to rest. He nodded and told me to report to General Swift, the assistant division commander, at a nearby road junction at 08:00 hours the following morning. Tanks would be at the site, and we would undergo tank-infantry training. I said nothing, but I boiled inside. What the hell was Gavin thinking? We had been fighting with tanks for the past three weeks. When I cooled off, I realized he was sending me a message: stop feeling sorry for yourself and your troops; get this show on the road; and there is still fighting to be done."[26]

The regiment reorganized—enlisted men were promoted to non-commissioned officers to replace those who were casualties. Changes in command were made as Captain Taylor Smith returned as 2nd Battalion executive officer. Captain William C. Martin replaced Lieutenant Meyers as Company D commander. Lieutenant O. B. Carr, returning from pathfinder duty, became the Company D executive officer. Captain Charles Barnett remained as the Company E commander. Lieutenant Rusty Hays returned from the hospital to command Company F.

As the regiment received replacements, new equipment and weapons, and winter clothing, it reorganized and conducted training in combined tank-infantry tactics to prepare for the upcoming operation. Additionally, training was conducted in the use of the German Panzerfaust, of which many had been captured in Holland and Belgium. Gavin felt the Panzerfaust was the only effective antitank weapon against the current German main battle tanks, the Mark V Panther and Mark VI Tiger II.

Just over two weeks after they arrived, the paratroopers of the 505 loaded into trucks and waved goodbye to the townspeople of Theux on the night of January 26, 1945 and were trucked along with the rest of the 82nd Airborne Division to the St.-Vith area. Units of the 505th PIR arrived at Born, Belgium, north of St.-Vith, between 4:00 a.m. to 7:10 a.m. on January 27, where they unloaded and marched to Montenau, Belgium.

The following morning, the division would pass through the lines of the U.S. 7th Armored Division and spearhead a drive eastward to pierce the fortifications of the Siegfried Line on the German border. The division's plan for the initial attack would be for two regiments abreast, the 325th Glider Infantry on the left and the 504th Parachute Infantry on the right, with the 505th following behind the 325th, and the 508th Parachute Infantry following behind the 504th. When the attacking regiments' momentum slowed, the trailing regiments would pass through to continue the drive.

That night, the troopers left their musette bags, overcoats, blankets, bedrolls, and sleeping bags in piles to be brought forward later. The troopers were now outfitted with long-john underwear, wool sweaters, gloves, and shoe pacs. Most wore white snow capes, pullovers, and bed sheets or mattress covers to serve as camouflage. However, they were facing weather and snow depths much worse than before.

AT 6:00 A.M. ON JANUARY 28, the division attacked eastward in knee-deep snow, surprising the Germans and capturing the Belgian towns of Wereth and Herresbach. The following morning, the 505th passed through the 325th pushing 2,000 yards northeast. During the attack, Company E became pinned down by intense enemy machine gun, rifle, and mortar fire from Germans manning a dug in strongpoint. Lieutenant Jack M. Bailey, one of the platoon leaders, advanced alone across 150 yards of open field in spite of intense enemy fire directed at him. He reached the enemy positions and began to move from hole to hole, tossing grenades and firing his Thompson submachine gun at the enemy soldiers. Lieutenant Bailey killed or captured twenty Germans and forced the remainder to flee to a nearby wooded area. Bailey signaled his platoon forward, then entered the woods and captured the remaining enemy soldiers. Lieutenant Bailey was later awarded the Silver Star for his heroism.

The 505th continued the advance, capturing the high ground 1,500 yards southwest of Honsfeld, Belgium. There, it established defensive positions and

sent out patrols to conduct reconnaissance and to maintain contact with the 1st
Infantry Division on the left.

On January 30, the 325th passed through the 505th positions, drove east to
capture Buchholtz, Belgium, then advanced to a railroad line running from
Losheim, Germany to Honsfeld.

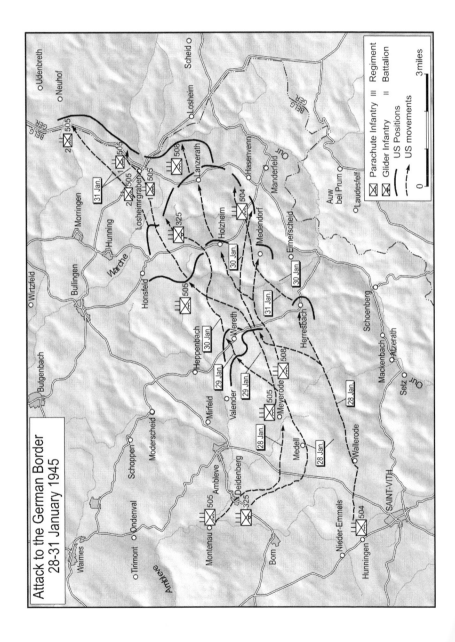

At 5:30 a.m. the next morning, the 505th passed through the 325th line. The 2nd Battalion, with Company D leading, moved in column east along a road toward its objective, a key road junction northwest of Losheimergraben, Germany. Lieutenant Joe Meyers was again the platoon leader of the 3rd Platoon. "Three 105mm self-propelled howitzers joined D Company in lieu of tanks. The personnel manning these SPs [self-propelled guns] were artillerymen, with no experience in tank-infantry operations. [Lieutenant John H.] Cobb's 1st Platoon and the attached SPs led off. [Lieutenant Albert W.] Short's 2nd Platoon followed, and I brought up the rear with the mortars. The XO normally moved at the rear of the column, so O. B. Carr and I walked together. It was pitch black as we advanced along a dirt road flanked by natural forests. Approximately fifteen minutes after we crossed the line of departure, an explosion occurred near the head of the column, and almost immediately a fire illuminated the area."[27]

Private Bill Slawson, a machine gunner, was riding on one of the self-propelled guns near the front of the column. "We hadn't gone very far when a sneaky Kraut tank up the road fired a round and hit the first [self-propelled gun] and it caught fire and lit up the whole woods. I jumped off the third [self-propelled gun]. The second [self-propelled gun] went past us after it turned around, like a bat out of hell. He missed us by inches, throwing snow all over and covering the boxes of machine gun ammo with snow.

"Captain [Bill] Martin, standing out in the middle of the road with his .45 in his hand, hollered, 'Slawson, get that machine gun in action.' We were probing in the snow for the machine gun ammo boxes. The Krauts were firing tracers at us from the woods. They were all around us. Finally, we located an ammo box, put the gun on a log, the tripod sunk in the snow. The cotton webbing belt was swollen with moisture and wouldn't feed in the gun, so we cut off [a] foot of webbing and finally got it loaded."[28]

The second self-propelled gun raced back through the D Company column, stopping ahead of Lieutenant Meyers. "Our troops had taken cover in the woods to either side of the road, but except for an occasional burst from a German machine gun, there was no sign of serious enemy opposition. After working his way forward and conferring with Martin, O. B. returned and informed me the attack had bogged down. He instructed me to go up the left side of the road and kick some tail, while he moved up the right side of the road. As I worked my way forward, the reason for our lack of progress became clear. The troops were taking advantage of this opportunity to get some rest. I located a squad leader who informed me a rocket launcher team was attempting to get into position to fire on the German gun that knocked out our SP. There was sporadic firing, and in a short time a messenger returned with the news the rocket launcher team had knocked out a Panther tank. The skirmish appeared to be over, and I headed for the Panther. When I arrived, I found [James A.] 'Baby' Donlon inside the tank, attempting to start the vehicle. Donlon, a rocket launcher gunner, had fired a round at the tank and hit the vehicle's armor-plated skirt. Apparently, the crew thought the round had disabled the vehicle, and they bailed out of a perfectly good tank. In a few minutes, Donlon had the tank running, and he drove it up and down the road before disabling both the gun and the engine. It was about first light when we moved out."[29]

When Private Paul R. Brandt, a replacement, joined Company E on January 31, he "saw about twenty guys there—so I asked a stupid question—where are the other platoons? The company then had only thirty-four men."[30]

The regiment maintained its position the next day, February 1. It conducted reconnaissance patrols to the Siegfried Line and contact patrols with the 508th PIR on the right and the 1st Infantry Division on the left.

At around 7:00 a.m., near the crossroads that was its objective, the 2nd Battalion ran into a strong enemy force backed by four self-propelled guns, which knocked out the lead tank moving with Company F. The 2nd Battalion deployed as the other tanks and self-propelled guns moved up, then attacked and overran the German force, capturing the road junction.

That afternoon, the 505th received an order to advance northeast to be in position to attack the Siegfried Line the following day. The 2nd Battalion captured the high ground opposite of the small hamlet of Neuhof.

On February 2, the 325th assaulted the Siegfried Line at Neuhof and Udenbreth, Germany, on the left, while the 504th attacked east and captured the Hertesrott Heights. The 505th attacked southeasterly on the right flank of the 504th, driving as much as four thousand yards against very light opposition, with the left flank reaching the Siegfried Line defenses.

On the morning of February 3, strong German counterattacks were repulsed with heavy enemy casualties and the 505th resumed the attack southeastwardly. It was relieved later that day and trucked to Vielsalm, Belgium. There, the regiment, now at about one-third strength, was billeted at Salmchâteau, just south of Vielsalm. From February 4 to 6, the remainder of the 82nd Airborne Division was relieved in place and trucked to the Vielsalm area.

ON FEBRUARY 6, the 505th Regimental Combat Team, designated Task Force "A," commanded by the assistant division commander, Colonel Ira P. Swift, was trucked thirty miles north to the vicinity to Vossenack, Germany, in the Hürtgen Forest, approximately twenty miles south of Aachen, Germany, where it relieved elements of the 8th Infantry Division the next evening.

The Hürtgen Forest had proven to be a meat grinder, crippling a number of U.S. Army divisions the previous fall. It was by this time a scene of complete destruction, caused by artillery, tank, and mortar fire—with much of the forest now just splintered tree trunks, the ground churned with thousands of craters, and towns in rubble.

On February 8, the 505th jumped off southeast of Vossenack, advancing 2,500 yards southeastward to Kommerscheidt, Germany, against mostly sporadic artillery fire and minefields, resulting in few casualties. This took the regiment through the Kall River valley, nicknamed "Death Valley"—the site of the destruction of much of the 112th Infantry Regiment, 28th Infantry Division the previous November.

The 28th Infantry Division had been a Pennsylvania National Guard unit that had been federalized for the war effort. The sight of so many bodies that had lied unburied during the winter was particularly painful for Sergeant Russ Brown, with Company F. "I was from Pennsylvania, and it made me sick to see the 28th soldiers lying all around."[31]

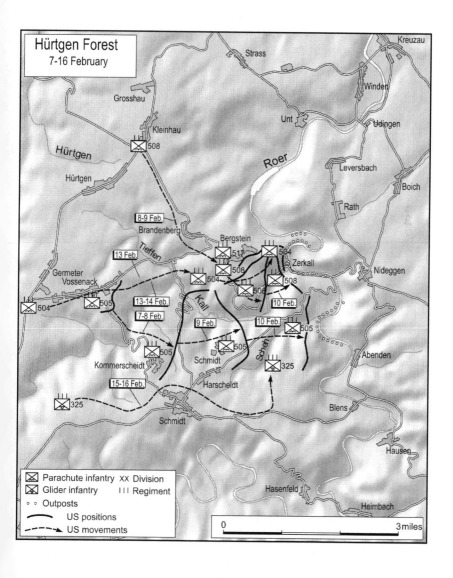

Hürtgen Forest
7-16 February

The following day, February 9, the 82nd Airborne Division attacked eastward with the final objective of reaching the western shore of the Roer River upriver from the Schwammenauel Dam. Then the division was to conduct an assault river crossing above site of the dam. The 505th advanced against light artillery fire and upon reaching its objective, sent reconnaissance patrols forward that evening that found no enemy in front of the regiment.

Moving out in the predawn darkness of February 10, the regiment captured the high ground west of the river before first light. Outpost lines were established along the west bank to prevent enemy infiltration across the river. The troopers manning these outposts were relieved during darkness every night.

On February 11, the 2nd Battalion's 81mm mortar platoon's observation post, which was 300 yards in front of the battalion's lines, came under a fierce artillery fire, severing the field telephone wires to the platoon. At the observation post, Private First Class Joseph L. Melahn, a wireman with Headquarters Company, 2nd Battalion, didn't wait for an order, and moved out under the intense artillery and small arms fire to repair the wire, which he was successful in doing in time for the platoon to complete a fire mission. Before he could return to the cover of the observation post, he was struck by a direct hit from an artillery shell, killing him instantly. Private First Class Melahn was posthumously awarded the Silver Star for his courage and sacrifice.

THE 505TH remained in this position until the night of February 18, when elements of the 9th Infantry Division relieved the regiment and the rest of the 82nd Airborne Division. The 505th was trucked to Walheim, Germany, near Aachen, where it spent the night. The next morning, the regiment was trucked to the train station at Aachen, where it departed by rail for the Rheims, France area. The Suippes barracks had been taken over by an army hospital, so the 505th was billeted in tents nearby.

The remnants of the regiment arrived in France exhausted and in need of new equipment and replacements. Staff Sergeant Earl Bowling, with Company E, was released from the hospital at the end of February and was shocked when he rejoined the regiment. "There were few of the original men of the regiment left—and even the first replacements of the EGB units who had joined as replacements in Africa were mostly gone. With the number of killed in action, wounded, reclassified and not returned to duty, and missing in action, the ranks of the men with three and four combat jumps were growing ever thinner."[32]

Sergeant Paul Nunan returning from a thirty-day furlough to the United States found the Company D tents. "I walked around the company area for ten or fifteen minutes before I saw anybody I knew."[33]

Passes were issued to the officers and men and everyone was given a few days of rest. Meanwhile, replacements were brought in, many directly from the United States, where most had just graduated from parachute school.

Those wounded in Holland and Belgium returning from hospitals, brought some cohesion back to their respective companies. However, the personnel makeup of most of the rifle companies was almost unrecognizable from those who had jumped in Holland less than six months earlier. Most companies were led by new officers, and many enlisted men were now non-coms.

The 505th began training once more to rebuild unit cohesion. The veterans, tired of the repetitive training they knew by heart, helped the young replacements learn the tricks and techniques that would keep them alive and insure success in combat.

ON MARCH 30, 1945, the 82nd Airborne Division was attached to the U.S. Fifteenth Army and ordered to move to a location southwest of Bonn, Germany, to patrol the west bank of the Rhine River, opposite German forces trapped in the Ruhr pocket. On the morning of April 2, eight trains and numerous motorized convoys carrying the division's artillery and antitank units began the journey by rail and truck to Germany. That evening and all of the following day, trains carrying the division unloaded at a single rail siding at Stolberg, Germany, with completion shortly before 12:00 a.m. on April 4.

The 82nd Airborne Division relieved the U.S. 86th Infantry Division on the night of April 3-4. The division's sector included the city of Cologne and an area which extended eight miles north and thirteen miles south—a total frontage of about thirty-two miles. The 505th sector extended from just south of Cologne to just north of Bonn. The regiment set up positions fronting the Rhine in factories, homes, and commercial buildings, with listening posts along the river, manned only at night. Any movement observed by the enemy brought artillery, mortar, and 20mm antiaircraft fire from across the river.

Technician Fifth Grade William F. Borda was a new replacement with F Company, which occupied a row of houses a few hundred yards from the river. "Sam [C.] Formicola, [Robert M.] Bob Burdick, [Kenneth E.] Ken Stillings, and I had a .30-caliber machine gun on the third floor, looking out on the river. We could see the Krauts in trenches on their side."[34]

Aggressive patrolling was conducted across the Rhine River to capture prisoners for interrogation in order to determine enemy intentions. The patrols suffered some casualties, mostly from enemy minefields planted along the eastern shore and by drowning. Staff Sergeant Earl Boling, with Company E, was told that patrols across the Rhine would begin on the night of April 5-6. "Our company sent a patrol out the first night, which upon landing ran into heavy enemy fire. In trying to find cover, they ran into a minefield, resulting in two deaths [Sergeant Frankie B. Ensley and Private First Class Francis H. Markwood]."[35]

The two remaining members of the patrol, Lieutenant Howard E. Jensen and Private First Class Jim Keenan, tried to get back across the river the next morning. Lieutenant Jim Coyle, the Company E executive officer, away from company headquarters the night the patrol was conducted, found out the next evening what had occurred. "Jensen and Private First Class Jim Keenan were trying to get back to our lines, but it had turned light before they could get organized for the return. They were caught by enemy fire on the return trip.

They had jumped out of the kayak to avoid the fire, but Jensen was shot in the head and Keenan had to swim the rest of the way to our side.

"The next night, Major Carpenter, the new battalion CO, had ordered another patrol to check for the body of the man who was killed. I don't know if they wanted the body recovered or if they thought the man might still be alive. They had observed the body with high-powered artillery binoculars during the day without any sign of life as far as I could see. The patrol was assigned to Lieutenant [Clifford J.] John O'Dea, an officer who had just joined the company. I was on the bank with several men when O'Dea and one other man left in a kayak. They had only been gone about fifteen minutes when a terrific explosion lit up the sky on the other side. It had to be a Teller mine. We waited to see if anyone would come back from the patrol. In another twenty minutes, the man who had gone over with O'Dea came running along the bank in a state of shock. He said O'Dea had stepped out of the kayak in the dark and had apparently tripped a mine. Without any discussion, Major Carpenter and Captain [Charles] Barnett got into a nearby kayak and started for the other side. I didn't understand this move—it was no place for a battalion and company commander.

"They had just about gotten out of sight on the river when I heard what I was sure was the kayak overturned. There was some splashing, but no other sound. I immediately stripped to my shorts and started to swim out to them. Carpenter's jeep driver came in after me. As I swam out, I heard their first cries for help and swam toward the sound. Before I got to them, the cries for help stopped. I called to them, but got no reply. When I got to about where I thought they might have overturned, I dove down a few times, but realized it was useless in the pitch dark.

"I also discovered that the current in the river was now much stronger than it had been nearer the shore, and that I was caught in it. I did not realize this at first, until I saw a large boat or barge go close by me in the dark at a fairly rapid clip. My first thought was, 'What is this boat doing going up the river in the dark?' I knew I was disoriented, but had enough sense to finally realize that the boat was sunk and stationary. It was I who was moving rapidly down the river!

"It was pitch black. I couldn't see the shore, but I knew if I kept the current coming from my left, I could swim to the bank on our side of the river. I finally reached the bank on our side and then thought of another problem. I did not know how far down the river I had been swept. I had no way of knowing what unit I might encounter. All I had on were my shorts and dog-tags. All I needed was to have some trigger-happy green guy see me come out of the river, think I was a German coming from the other side, and shoot without challenging me. I had barely climbed up on the river bank when I was challenged. I gave the countersign and my name and unit. I had been challenged by Staff Sergeant [Louis] Yarchak, one of the old veterans of F Company, who had gone back to the States [on furlough] in my group.

"Yarchak took me to the F Company CP, got me a blanket, and I got on the phone to Captain T. G. Smith, the battalion executive officer. I told him what had happened and that I knew Carpenter and Barnett had drowned. I told him that I would be willing to go across the river just before dawn to look for O'Dea when it got light—but I was not about to go stumbling around in a minefield in the dark. Captain Smith immediately told me that Colonel Ekman, the regimental commander, had already been told that Carpenter, Barnett, and I were missing, and that no one was going to go across the river until further orders.

"The next day, Colonel Ekman came to our company CP. He was furious over the loss of five men, including a battalion commander. He ordered me to write up a complete report and forward it to him at regimental headquarters. He then told me that I would take over as company commander. Then he broke my heart by telling me that it would only be temporary—that I didn't have enough seniority to keep it."[36]

THE U.S. 13TH ARMORED DIVISION, advancing north along the eastern side of the Rhine River, captured the territory across the river from the 505th, eliminating the need to cover the west bank. The 505th assembled in battalion areas on April 14, preparatory to occupation duties. On April 17, the 505th moved to the vicinity of Bruhl, a rural town a short distance from Bonn.

Lieutenant Joe Meyers had replaced Lieutenant O. B. Carr as Company D executive officer while the regiment was at Salmchâteau, Belgium, when Carr received orders to report for pathfinder training again. Meyers received a briefing before the move. "Rumors abounded of the formation of stay-behind groups of resistance, called 'Werewolves.' Our mission was to patrol a large assigned area and secure it against possible 'Werewolf' attacks. D Company used a village schoolhouse as its CP and billets. As executive officer, I planned and supervised the execution of the company patrol plan. At my request, [Captain] Bill Martin ordered the village mayor to requisition and deliver to us several serviceable bicycles for use by our patrols.

"The mayor selected the poorest machines for our use. The defective bikes broke down, making it difficult to cover all of our assigned patrol area. I repeatedly urged Martin to lay the law down to the mayor and insist on the delivery of better machines. For some reason, Bill was reluctant to follow this advice. On the other hand, he was quick to find fault with the patrolling. One afternoon, the matter came to a head. In response to a critical remark, I informed Bill that until he 'got off his ass and put some heat on the mayor,' I couldn't properly execute the patrol plan. Hot words ensued. Earlier in the day, Special Services had delivered recreational gear that included boxing gloves. Bill, a former Army boxer, invited me outside to put on the gloves, and I accepted his invitation.

"At the supply room, Bill and I learned the boxing gloves were [checked] out. We walked into the schoolyard where a large group watched two men spar. When the match ended, Bill asked if anyone objected to the two of us putting on the gloves. Delighted at the prospect of seeing their CO and XO square off in the ring, the men quickly designated seconds, appointed a referee, and named a timekeeper. We stripped to the waist, put on the gloves, and made ready for individual combat. Bill was stocky and thick-set. We were about the same weight; however, I was several years younger, three inches taller, and I had a reach advantage. The referee called time and the match started. Speck McKenna's boxing lessons stood me in good stead. I had a stiff, punishing left jab and I knew to follow it with a right cross. We fought two rounds before Bill suggested we quit. He did not lay a glove on me and he got a free boxing lesson. Bill showed no signs of holding a grudge. In fact, he treated me with more respect, and in later years, when he commanded a battalion, he asked me to join his staff.

"The following day, the 2nd Battalion moved to Bonn, the future capital of West Germany. Again, our mission was to neutralize a potential 'Werewolf' threat. We were to conduct a house-to-house, building-to-building, search of the city for illegal weapons, explosives, etc. We carried out this search in a manner designed to convince the local population that we meant business. After dividing the city into sectors, the sectors to be searched were sealed off. The first day, I led a team that searched the Bonn city hall and its adjoining air raid shelter. The shelter, which rose several stories above ground, was also a flak tower. There were four or five underground levels. The regional air defense CP occupied one of these underground floors. At the lower levels, we discovered room after room filled with oil paintings and other art objects. I reported this to the U.S. military government authorities.

"The following day we searched residences and business establishments near the center of town. We were to search everything and to break into locked rooms, cabinets, etcetera. Initially, almost every dwelling or shop had a locked door with a 'lost key.' After we shot a few locks, the owners got the message. Lost keys, they claimed not to have seen in years, suddenly appeared. While searching a basement under a shop, we came across the find of the operation—a cellar full of wine and other spirits. The owners were nervous, and I was certain they would move the liquor as soon as we departed. Two men were posted atop a nearby building where they could observe the shop. After dark, several civilians moved the booty to another cellar several blocks away. My lookouts noted the new location and reported it to me. I borrowed a 2 1/2-ton truck and the next morning we backed up to the door where the cache was stored, loaded the spirits, and drove away."[37]

IN APRIL, Supreme Headquarters Allied Expeditionary Force (SHAEF), concerned about a possible Soviet occupation of Denmark, ordered the British Second Army to cross the Elbe River and drive to the Baltic Sea, to prevent the Soviet Union's Red Army from turning north into Denmark.

Speed was essential, so SHAEF attached Ridgway's XVIII Airborne Corps, consisting of the U.S. 8th Infantry Division, the U.S. 7th Armored Division, the 82nd Airborne Division, and the British 6th Airborne Division, to the British Second Army and assigned it to carry out the operation.

On April 23, the division was alerted for possible movement then, received orders to move by rail to the Elbe River, northeast of Hanover, Germany. On

April 26, the 505th moved northeast by rail to a staging area at the town of Bleckede, Germany on the Elbe River. Lieutenant Joe Meyers was playing pinochle with several other troopers in one of the 40 & 8 boxcars as the train moved north. "The weather was warm and the right boxcar door was open. Some men slept in improvised shelter tent hammocks suspended between rings installed to tether horses. Other men slept on the floor. A few men cooked meals on small gasoline stoves, while still other troopers sat with their feet dangling out the door. We played cards on two C-ration boxes covered with a GI blanket. One of the men sitting in the door announced our train was approaching the new Franklin D. Roosevelt Memorial Bridge over the Rhine River. The bridge, a large wooden structure, was high above the stream, and its western approach was sixty or seventy feet above the surrounding terrain. Several men displayed an interest and moved to the door to get a better view. Our boxcar began to bounce around and someone remarked on the rough tracks. At this point, another man shouted out, 'Rough tracks, hell! We're off the tracks!'

"The boxcar began turning on its right side. No one had to tell these troopers it was time to bail out. With few exceptions, they cleared the boxcar in seconds. Seated at the rearmost of the car, I was one of the exceptions. Ammunition, mortars, machine guns, and rations stacked against the car's back wall came down on me when the engineer applied the emergency brakes. After the boxcar was on its side, I freed myself, discovered I was alone, and crawled to the door. The train was still moving and the ground flashed by a foot or two below the open door. After positioning my body parallel to the door, I rolled out of the boxcar and on to the ground.

"My timing was perfect. The only rail switch in sight struck me squarely in the back. The boxcars were speeding by a foot or two above my head and they provided me the incentive I needed to get clear of danger. I had no feeling in my legs, so I used my hands and arms to pull my body clear. Finally, I got sideways to the slope, let gravity take over, and rolled down the embankment until I reached the bottom some sixty or seventy feet below.

"One of the platoon medics gave me a shot of morphine and loaded me on a stretcher. That is the last I remember. I awoke in the enlisted men's ward of a field hospital near München-Gladbach, Germany."[38] The troopers on the derailed cars were loaded on other boxcars, the derailed cars unhooked, and the journey continued uneventfully.

Private First Class Dominick Di Battista was a BAR man with Company E. "On the train ride, which took more than a day, the rumors were flying hot and heavy, and as is usually the case, one rumor always proves to be pretty much fact."[39]

On the night of April 28–29, the lead element, the division reconnaissance platoon, arrived at Bleckede and sent three patrols across the Elbe River to probe enemy defenses along the river. Only one patrol encountered stiff opposition and reported it to division headquarters.

The trains carrying the 1st and 2nd Battalions arrived in Bleckede in the predawn hours of April 29. Only a few officers and men in the regiment knew the mission—make an assault crossing of the Elbe River. Most troopers thought it would be more occupation duty.

After disembarking from the train at Bleckede, Private First Class Di Battista moved out with his squad. "We were assigned billets in the various houses around the town and our non-coms were called to company headquarters to get all the info on the company's part it was to play in the operation. Indeed it turned out that we were to cross the Elbe River the next morning at 1:00 a.m. and keep going until we met up with the Russian troops who were coming west toward us."[40]

Di Battista and the other troopers "thought we were getting a raw deal. You could sense that the war was on its last legs and I'd be a liar if I didn't say that we were all watching out for our own skins."[41]

It was especially hard for the "old men" of the 505, many of whom had made four combat jumps, fought in five previous campaigns, and been wounded one or more times. Many felt their luck would run out—and they would be killed, seriously wounded, or drown during the closing days of the war.

A number of the troopers dug up wine and liquor buried in the backyards of the houses, hidden by the owners prior to their evacuation. Many were in various stages of intoxication when the operation began.

The plan called for the 2nd Battalion to cross on the left, with the 1st Battalion on its right. Two companies from each battalion would cross in the first wave. Engineers would ferry the boats back for the second wave, consisting of the remaining rifle companies and headquarters companies of each battalion. In addition, other engineers were assigned to clear minefields. The attached regimental demolition platoon would deal with obstacles and pillboxes. Company D would cross on the left flank, with Company E on its right to the south. The operation would commence at 1:00 a.m. on the morning of April 30.

As darkness approached, Technician Fifth Grade Bill Borda, with Company F, waited anxiously for the boats to arrive. "It rained, snowed, and sleeted while we were waiting for the assault boats. Sergeant [Stephen] Steve Epps, a real leader—a 'follow me men' type—was about 'half in the bag,' having dug up a batch of Holland gin."[42]

Lieutenant Jim Coyle received orders that his 1st Platoon would lead Company E across. "My main concern was that with our inexperience in river crossings, could we keep the platoon and, for that matter, the company together? The Elbe was with the spring flood, at least 150 yards across in our area, with a swift-running current. I was praying that we would all land together so we could organize on the other side. We were told that we would have a large concentration of artillery fire for support prior to our crossing at 2000 hours. We were to move our boats into the water under cover of the artillery. We were not informed of the kind of resistance we would receive from the enemy on the other side when we landed.

"Shortly after dark, we organized the company and moved down to the area chosen for embarking. We spread the men out in the area and waited for the trucks to arrive with the boats and the engineers who were to man them. When 2000 hours arrived, the artillery commenced firing. It was the greatest barrage that I had seen. Large-caliber guns fired for at least one-half hour, and 40mm antiaircraft Bofors placed direct fire like machine guns on the opposite bank. The problem was that our assault boats had not arrived by the time the artillery ceased!

"It became very quiet. Then a drizzle of rain began, which lasted for the next two hours, while the men stood around in the pitch dark, waiting for the boats. For the first time in the war, I had a feeling of dread about an operation. The element of surprise was gone with the artillery barrage. With that amount of artillery preparation, the enemy would know that an attack was coming. I had visions of the company stepping out of the boats and into a minefield as had happened to the patrols across the Rhine only a few weeks before. Waiting for those boats in the rain was very nerve wracking.

"The boats finally arrived. I can't remember how many hours behind schedule they were. I don't know what kinds of boats I expected, but I was unpleasantly surprised to see that each boat could carry about eight men at most with one engineer per boat. We were going to do the paddling. We unloaded the boats from the trucks, assigned the men per boat, and carried them down the bank to the water."[43]

Shortly before 1:00 a.m., on the left flank, Company D began the crossing. The troopers in Technician Fourth Grade Allan Barger's boat initially had difficulty rowing together. "At first, since we had never practiced doing this, we started to zigzag clumsily for a bit. Then Captain Martin, who was kneeling just in front of me in the middle of the boat, started giving the paddlers a cadence. That did it. We began to move evenly across the silvery body of flowing water. And so did the rest of the company. We were in the lead.

"As we approached the shore, I saw the distant bank as a foreboding silhouette. I kept sucking in my guts anticipating machine gun fire opening up on us any minute. This could have been a disaster. But before we knew it, we were coming up to a small boat landing and we stepped out onto some dry floats. Still, we kept expecting the enemy to open up on us, but nothing happened as we walked to shore. We didn't even get our feet wet! We walked up a pathway and worked ourselves over in the darkness to an empty old barn and went inside to wait for the others to catch up to us."[44]

To the right of D Company, Lieutenant Jim Coyle's Company E boats had similar difficulties. "We pushed off and I headed the lead boat to the outlet of the little bay toward the river. Just before we were about to leave the protection of the inlet and enter the river proper, I heard a lot of shouting behind me. I looked around to see that only a couple of boats were following me. I couldn't imagine how it had happened (we had briefed the men on the size of the river), but I could see that the rest of the company had paddled across the inlet and with the best of spirit, including rebel yells, was assaulting the opposite bank of the inlet. I put our boats ashore and went back along the bank to stop the premature landing. I started yelling as I approached them, because it occurred to me that if they thought they were on the other side of the Elbe, they might think I was the enemy coming at them. I told them that they hadn't crossed the river yet, and we finally got the company reorganized and headed out toward the river.

"By this time, the rain had stopped and a fairly bright moon had come out. This was a mixed blessing. We could see the other boats to stay organized during the crossing, but the Germans could see us coming, too.

"As we crossed the river, we were able to stay in a column despite the current. When we approached the enemy side, I was waiting for the enemy to open fire, but none came. Our boat pulled in near a small jetty and we landed. One of the men told me that he heard Germans talking in a building on a small dock. I told him to ignore it. If they were enemy soldiers, they were not going to fire on us, or they would have done it before we landed. They could be mopped up later. The 1st Platoon quickly spread out into a mini beachhead, and the rest of the company followed us ashore. I could hardly believe that after all of my fears and all that had gone wrong, there was no minefield, no enemy in sight, and we were ashore without losing a boat or a man. We quickly got the company organized and started moving inland."[45]

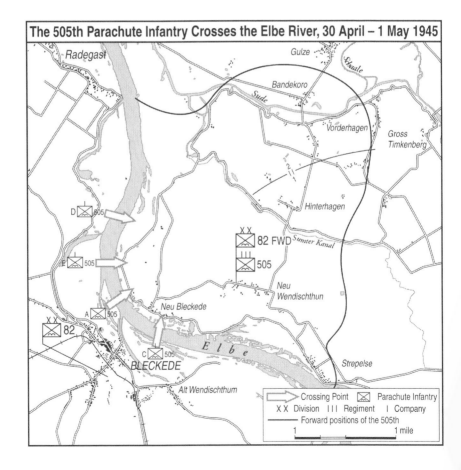

The 505th Parachute Infantry Crosses the Elbe River, 30 April – 1 May 1945

The lack of enemy resistance on the far shore surprised Company E trooper, Staff Sergeant Earl Boling. "I guess some of the Germans had figured it was too late in the war to die for a lost cause. However, a bit later, we were getting more action from machine guns and 20mm flak guns fired from the depressed position to cover the fields in a sweeping field of fire. But these were being knocked out, their crews captured, and started to the rear as prisoners, with a token guard to keep them moving."[46]

After Companies D and E landed, the engineers brought the boats back to the west bank, where Company F loaded into them and rowed across. Technician Fifth Grade Bill Borda's boat also struck the sandbar. Everyone jumped out, pulled it to the other side, and continued rowing. "Going across was a real chore. When we neared the far shore, Steve [Epps] stood up, said, 'Follow me, men,' stepped out and went under, but popped up almost immediately. I grabbed his pack and held him up until he could stand, and then we all moved forward. We were supposed to cross two phase lines, but we were beyond four of them by 10:00 a.m. and [encountered] little opposition."[47]

The paratroopers advanced rapidly against light resistance, overrunning many Germans asleep in their foxholes and hiding in houses and woods. Most chose not to die for Hitler. By dark, the regiment dug in for the night, having established a large bridgehead.

At 5:52 a.m. on May 1, the 505th attacked eastward another nine miles against light resistance, reaching its objective, the Correnzien Forest by mid afternoon. That same morning, German radio in Berlin announced the news of Hitler's death.

The 325th Glider Infantry Regiment arrived on May 1, and passed through the 505th's lines to continue the attack the following morning. The following day, the division assigned the 505th control of two camps established near the towns of Dellien and Zeetze to handle displaced persons (DPs) and German POWs.

At 10:00 p.m. that night, General Gavin accepted the unconditional surrender of the German 21st Army. The following day, the 82nd Airborne Division began the overwhelming task of processing an estimated 144,000 prisoners, another 10,000 freed Allied prisoners of war, and uncounted displaced persons.

Sergeant Russ Brown, with Company F, watched the spectacle of masses of German soldiers moving along the road and gathered in fields on both sides. "The German army had very many horses to pull the guns and other equipment. They were hoping to cross the Elbe River and be in the American zone. They did not want to be in the Russian zone.

"I talked with a young German who said, 'If you go fight the Russians, my men will join you.'

"I said, 'The Russians are our allies.'"[48]

Troopers took German army vehicles for personal use, including motorcycles, convertible-topped Kubelwagens, and staff cars. Suddenly, the regiment was "mechanized."

When the Wöbbelin concentration camp was discovered near Ludwigslust, many 505th officers and men visited it, personally witnessing the atrocities of the Third Reich. General Gavin ordered the leading citizens of Ludwigslust to dig graves for two hundred of the inmates in the park in front of the Palace of the Grand Duke of Mecklenburg, which was a part of the town square. Gavin required all of the townspeople and a group of captured German Army officers to attend the funeral on May 7. The nearby towns of Hagenow and Schwerin held similar funerals for two hundred at each location the following day.

During the early hours of May 7, at SHAEF headquarters in Rheims, France, the Germans signed documents agreeing to the unconditional surrender of all German forces to the Allied nations. General Eisenhower sent the following telegram to the Combined Allied Chiefs of Staffs: "The mission of this Allied Force was fulfilled at 02:41 hours, local time, May 7, 1945. Eisenhower"[49]

The surrender of all German forces took effect at 11:01 a.m. on May 8, 1945. It had been a long, costly struggle.

EPILOGUE

"He Was A True Warrior"

There is no doubt that Lieutenant Colonel Vandervoort's leadership and courage had been responsible in large measure for the success of the 2nd Battalion, 505th during the fierce fighting in Normandy, Holland, and Belgium.

The loss of his left eye forced Vandervoort to retire from the army in 1946 at the rank of full colonel. Like many career military men no longer able to serve because of serious wounds, Vandervoort joined the Central Intelligence Agency. As chief of station in South Korea during the Korean War, he was under cover as a U.S. Army colonel in charge of the Joint Advisory Commission Korea (JACK), the CIA's own cover organization for its operations in Korea. He was in charge of operations to insert and extract agents into North Korea as well as raids conducted to sabotage the lines of communications of the Chinese army.

Vandervoort later served as a CIA advisor in Vietnam during the early stages of America's involvement.

In 1990, the U.S. Army Command and General Staff College's Center for Army Leadership selected one officer at the rank of colonel or below from each of America's wars from the Revolution to Vietnam (except two for the Civil War—one for the Confederacy and one for the Federal armies and two for World War II—one for the Air Corps and one for the ground forces) as the outstanding combat commander. The ground forces officer selected as the "Outstanding Battle Commander of World War II" was Lieutenant Colonel Vandervoort.

No less an authority than General Gavin stated that Vandervoort "was probably the best battalion commander I had."[1] General Ridgway called Vandervoort "one of the bravest, toughest battle commanders I ever knew."[2]

Colonel Vandervoort's combat leadership had been a powerful example for young officers and NCOs to emulate. Bob Hughart had served as an enlisted man with Company F. "Our officers were up front all the time. They led the way and we followed—none of this couple of blocks behind, telling some sergeant, 'Take your squad and go this way' and his corporal to take his men and go down another street. We lost a lot of good men that way, because they were up front and saying, 'Follow me.' We'd follow them into hell and back."[3]

Vandervoort believed that the key to the unsurpassed combat record of the 505th had been a "mutual faith" between the officers and NCOs and the enlisted men they led. "No regiment in the European Theater put in as many man-to-man close-combat hours and had as many of its original members survive the war. They came home alive because they fought hard and well to do their jobs.

229

Concern for their own safety was secondary. That was not heroics. It was professionalism. They teamed together to make a 'lucky' regiment that never lost a battle. They were magnificent and fun to be with. All of us are very proud of our regiment.

"The older paratroopers of the 1940s won't fade away. Their mutual faith and competitive spirit lives today with the airborne. And the next time America goes for broke they will be there, as invisible pathfinders, to help today's troopers scramble off the broken plays that always have, and always will, come with the airborne territory."[4]

Vandervoort continued to inspire those who had served with him long after the end of World War II. James J. "Joe" Meyers had risen from an assistant platoon leader to company commander with Company D while serving under Vandervoort and eventually retired at the rank of colonel. "During my thirty years of service, I hope I was able to instill in the young troopers who served under me some of the outstanding traits of character and leadership I observed in Colonel Vandervoort. He was a true warrior."[5]

NOTES

Chapter 1 "Tough and Intelligent"
1. Benjamin H. Vandervoort, "Drop Zone Europe," p. 1.
2. Russell W. Brown, response to author's questionnaire.
3. James M. Gavin, *On To Berlin*, Viking Press, 1978, pp. 3–4.
4. Ibid, p. 4.
5. Frank P. Woosley, memoirs, courtesy of Frank P. Woosley.
6. Ibid, p. 4.
7. Ibid.
8. David V. Bowman, "Memoirs of a Machine Gunner," courtesy of David V. Bowman, pp. 8–9.
9. Irvin W. Seelye, response to author's questionnaire.
10. David V. Bowman, "Memoirs of a Machine Gunner," courtesy of David V. Bowman, p. 11.
11. The James M. Gavin Papers, Personal Diaries, Box 8—Folder "Diary Passages, Apr-Dec 1943," courtesy of the U.S. Army Military History Institute.
12. David V. Bowman, "Memoirs of a Machine Gunner," courtesy of David V. Bowman, p. 41.
13. Irvin W. Seelye, response to author's questionnaire.
14. Berge Avadanian, response to author's questionnaire.
15. Otis L. Sampson, "Time Out For Combat," unpublished manuscript, p. 2–3.
16. Vandervoort, "Drop Zone Europe," p. 2.
17. Gavin, *On To Berlin*, p. 24.
18. Ibid, pp. 24–25.
19. Ibid, pp. 25–26.
20. Vandervoort, "Drop Zone Europe," p. 2.
21. Mark J. Alexander, "Personal Memories of Sicily," courtesy of Mark J. Alexander, p. 2.
22. Berge Avadanian, response to author's questionnaire.
23. Irvin W. Seelye, response to author's questionnaire.
24. David V. Bowman, "Memoirs of a Machine Gunner," courtesy of David V. Bowman, pp. 14–15.
25. Russell W. Brown, response to author's questionnaire.
26. James J. Coyle, written account, "Echoes of the Warriors," compiled by George Jacobus, pp. 59–60.
27. Alexander, "Sicily," p. 2.
28. Ibid., pp. 2–3.
29. Captain John D. Rice, recommendation, awards file, Lieutenant John D. Sprinkle, National Archives, Record Group 338, Stack 290, Seventh Army awards, Box 20, Sprinkle DSC file.
30. Ibid., p. 3.

31. James J. Coyle, written account, "Echoes of the Warriors," compiled by George Jacobus, p. 60.
32. "82nd Airborne Division In Sicily And Italy, Part II – Sicily," courtesy of the 82nd Airborne Division War Memorial Museum, p. 25.
33. Ibid.
34. James M. Gavin, *On To Berlin*, p. 29.
35. Ibid.
36. Alfred W. Ireland, as quoted in, Patrick K. O'Donnell, *Beyond Valor*, The Free Press, 2001, p. 46.
37. Benjamin H. Vandervoort, as quoted in, Samuel W. Mitcham, Jr., and Friedrich Von Stauffenberg, *The Battle of Sicily*, Stackpole, 1991, p. 126.
38. Mark J. Alexander, "Personal Memories of Sicily" (Revision 7-20-2002), p. 6.
39. Vandervoort, "Drop Zone Europe." pp. 3–4.
40. Mark J. Alexander, "Italy—1943," courtesy of Mark J. Alexander, pp. 2–3.
41. Spencer F. Wurst and Gayle Wurst, *Descending from the Clouds*, Casemate, 2004, p. 85.
42. Alexander, "Italy," p. 3.
43. Wurst and Wurst, *Descending from the Clouds*, pp. 85–86.
44. Victor M. Schmidt, in *Echoes of the Warriors*, comp. and ed. by Jacobus, n.p., 1992, pp. 198–199.
45. Berge Avadanian, response to author's questionnaire.
46. Alexander, "Italy," p. 3.
47. Russell W. Brown, response to author's questionnaire.
48. Dr. Daryle E. Whitfield, interview with author.
49. Brown, questionnaire.
50. Wurst and Wurst, *Descending from the Clouds*, pp. 88–89.
51. Julius D. Axman, as quoted in Otis L. Sampson, "Time Out For Combat," unpublished manuscript, pp. 131–132.
52. Edward B. Carpus, as quoted in Otis L. Sampson, "Time Out For Combat," unpublished manuscript, p. 133.
53. Earl W. Boling, written account in, *Echoes of the Warriors*, 1992, p. 109.
54. John W. Keller, written account in, *Echoes of the Warriors*, 1992, p. 191.
55. Axman, in "Time Out For Combat," p. 132.
56. Otis L. Sampson, *Time Out For Combat*, Booksurge, 2004, pp. 103–104.
57. Ibid., p. 104.
58. Ibid., pp. 105–106.
59. Jack L. Francis, as quoted in Otis L. Sampson, "Time Out For Combat," unpublished manuscript, p. 133.
60. Talton W. Long, as quoted in Otis L. Sampson, "Time Out For Combat," unpublished manuscript, pp. 138–139.
61. Sampson, *Time Out For Combat*, p. 107.
62. Long, in "Time Out For Combat," p. 139.
63. Alexander, "Italy," p. 5.
64. Dr. Robert Franco, letter to Al Ireland, April 19, 1999.

65. Alexander, "Italy," pp. 5–6.
66. Earl W. Boling, as quoted in, *Echoes of the Warriors*, compiled and edited by George Jacobus, n. p., 1992, pp. 111–112.

Chapter 2 "He Was Pushing Everybody"
1. Frank A. Bilich, interview with author.
2. James J. Coyle, in *Echoes of the Warriors*, p. 65.
3. Bilich, interview.
4. Ibid.
5. Irvin W. Seelye, in *Echoes of the Warriors*, p. 265.
6. Brown, questionnaire.
7. Bilich, interview.
8. Frank A. Bilich, as quoted in, Deryk Wills, *Put On Your Boots and Parachutes!*, 1992, p. 56.
9. Bilich, interview.
10. Ibid.
11. John H. Rabig, in *Put On Your Boots and Parachutes!*, p. 56.
12. Berge Avadanian, response to author's questionnaire.
13. "82nd Airborne Division Action in Normandy, France June—July 1944," Section II – Narrative, p. 2.
14. Matthew B. Ridgway, Foreward, *Ready*, Allen Langdon, Western Newspaper Publishing Company, Inc., p. XI
15. Hubert S. Bass, letter to Cornelius Ryan, March 20, 1959, courtesy of the Cornelius Ryan Collection, Alden Library, Ohio University.
16. Coyle, in *Echoes of the Warriors*, p. 66.
17. Roy O. King, response to author's questionnaire.
18. Cullen E. Clark, Jr., written account, courtesy of the Cornelius Ryan Collection, Alden Library, Ohio University.
19. Vandervoort, "Drop Zone Europe," p. 3.
20. Dr. Lyle B. Putnam, questionnaire, courtesy of the Cornelius Ryan Collection, Alden Library, Ohio University.
21. Kenneth E. Russell, oral history transcript, courtesy of the Eisenhower Center.
22. Ibid.
23. Dennis G. O'Loughlin, "Fierce Individualists—US Paratroopers in WWII," 1977, courtesy of Frank P. Woosley, pp. 187, 188–189.
24. John W. Keller, letter to Cornelius Ryan, March 7, 1959, courtesy of the Cornelius Ryan Collection, Alden Library, Ohio University.
25. Buffalo Boy Canoe, questionnaire, courtesy of the Cornelius Ryan Collection, Alden Library, Ohio University.
26. Bass to Ryan, March 20, 1959.
27. Ibid.
28. Anthony J. DeMayo, questionnaire, courtesy of the Cornelius Ryan Collection, Alden Library, Ohio University.

Chapter 3 "Well, Let's Go!"
1. Benjamin H. Vandervoort, written account, courtesy of the Cornelius Ryan Collection, Alden Library, Ohio University, p. 1.
2. Daryle E. Whitfield, interview with author.
3. Anthony J. DeMayo, written account, courtesy of the Cornelius Ryan Collection, Alden Library, Ohio University, p. 4.
4. Hubert S. Bass letter to Cornelius Ryan, March 20, 1959, courtesy of the Cornelius Ryan Collection, Alden Library, Ohio University.
5. Vandervoort, written account, p. 1.
6. William J. Meddaugh, questionnaire, courtesy of the Cornelius Ryan Collection, Alden Library, Ohio University.
7. Bass to Ryan, March 20, 1959.
8. Vandervoort, written account, p. 1.
9. James J. Coyle, as quoted in, *Echoes of the Warriors*, compiled and edited by George Jacobus, n. p., 1992, p. 261.
10. John W. Keller, letter to Cornelius Ryan, March 7, 1959, courtesy of the Ryan Collection, Alden Library, Ohio University.
11. Cullen E. Clark, Jr., written account, courtesy of the Ryan Collection, Alden Library, Ohio University, pp. 2–3.
12. George Jacobus, in *Echoes of the Warriors*, pp. 239–240.
13. Otis L. Sampson, *Time Out For Combat*, Booksurge, 2004, p. 191.
14. Julius Eisner, interview with author.
15. Lieutenant Colonel Clyde R. Russell, letter to Cornelius Ryan, March 17, 1959, courtesy of the Ryan Collection, Alden Library, Ohio University.
16. Ramond Paris, as quoted in, Russell Miller, *Nothing Less Than Victory*, Quill, 1998, p. 261.
17. Kenneth E. Russell, oral history transcript, courtesy of the Eisenhower Center.
18. Whitfield, interview.
19. Ibid.
20. "D-Day Participant Survived By Feigning Death," Fayetteville Observer, May 16, 1969, Section B, p. 1.
21. Paris, in *Nothing Less Than Victory*, pp. 261–262.
22. Russell, oral history.
23. Whitfield, interview.
24. Bass to Ryan, March 20, 1959.
25. Ibid.
26. Vandervoort, written account, p. 2.
27. Roy O. King, written account, courtesy of Roy O. King.
28. Ibid.
29. Paul D. Nunan, interview with author.
30. Charles H. Miller, oral history transcript, courtesy of the Eisenhower Center.
31. Donald E. Ellis, interview with author.
32. Robert M. Robinson, questionnaire, courtesy of the Cornelius Ryan Collection, Alden Library, Ohio University.

33. Robert H. Dumke, as quoted in, "Ottawans recall WWII days as parachutists," The Daily Times, Ottawa, Illinois.
34. Sampson, *Time Out For Combat*, p. 192.
35. Dr. Lyle B. Putnam, questionnaire, courtesy of the Cornelius Ryan Collection, Alden Library, Ohio University, p. 2.
36. John M. Steele, questionnaire, courtesy of the Cornelius Ryan Collection, Alden Library, Ohio University.
37. Lieutenant Colonel Benjamin H. Vandervoort, as quoted in, "Debriefing Conference – Operation Neptune," courtesy of the 82nd Airborne Division War Memorial Museum, p. 2.
38. Dr. Lyle B. Putnam, as quoted in, Michel DeTrez, *The Way We Were: Colonel Ben Vandervoort*, D-Day Publishing, 2004, p. 40.
39. Vandervoort, written account, p. 1.
40. Milton E. Schlesener, letter to Frank Vanderbilt, courtesy of Mrs. Frankie James.
41. Ibid.
42. Gerald R. Weed, interview with author.
43. Vandervoort, in Michel DeTrez, *The Way We Were*, p. 36.
44. Benjamin H. Vandervoort, as quoted in, Deryk Wills, *Put On Your Boots and Parachutes!*, 1992, p. 74.
45. Sampson, *Time Out For Combat*, p. 193.
46. Robert R. Hughart, response to author's questionnaire.
47. Ibid.
48. Vandervoort, written account, p. 1.
49. Russell to Ryan.
50. Ibid.
51. Putnam, questionnaire.
52. W. A. Jones, interview with author.
53. Reverend George B. Wood, questionnaire, courtesy of the Cornelius Ryan Collection, Alden Library, Ohio University, p. 3.
54. Ibid.
55. Ibid.
56. Charles E. Sammon, letter to Cornelius Ryan, March 21, 1959, courtesy of the Cornelius Ryan Collection, Alden Library, Ohio University.
57. Clark, written account.
58. Weed, interview.
59. Vandervoort, written account, pp. 1–2.
60. Ibid., p. 2.
61. Theodore L. Peterson, letter to Cornelius Ryan, March 22, 1959, courtesy of the Cornelius Ryan Collection, Alden Library, Ohio University.
62. Weed, interview.
63. Ibid.
64. Sampson, *Time Out For Combat*, p. 195.
65. Peterson to Ryan, March 22, 1959.
66. Stanley W. Kotlarz, interview with author.

67. Sampson, *Time Out For Combat*, p. 196.

68. Peterson to Ryan, March 22, 1959.

69. Kotlarz, interview.

70. Weed, interview.

71. Ibid.

72. Ibid.

73. Vandervoort, written account, p. 2.

Chapter 4 "On One Leg And A Crutch"

1. Benjamin H. Vandervoort, "Waverly Wray, Ste.-Mére-Église, Normandy – June 7, 1944," courtesy of Lieutenant General Jack Norton, p. 1.

2. Frank A. Bilich, interview with author.

3. Captain Taylor G. Smith, statement, awards file, Lieutenant Waverly W. Wray, National Archives, Record Group 338, Stack 290, First Army awards, Box 37, Wray DSC file.

4. Charles E. Sammon, letter to Cornelius Ryan, March 21, 1959, courtesy of the Cornelius Ryan Collection, Alden Library, Ohio University.

5. Floyd West, Jr., letter to Walter J. Turnbull, Jr.

6. Stanley W. Kotlarz, interview with author.

7. Floyd West, Jr., letter to Mr. Walter J. Turnbull, Jr., April 14, 1947, courtesy of Mrs. Frankie James.

8. Irvin W. Seelye, response to author's questionnaire.

9. Vandervoort, "Waverly Wray," pp. 1–2.

10. David V. Bowman, "Memoirs of a Machine Gunner," courtesy of David V. Bowman, pp. 41–42.

11. Vandervoort, "Waverly Wray," pp. 2–3.

12. Thomas J. McClean, sworn statement supporting Medal of Honor resubmission for Waverly Wray, March 1, 1984, courtesy of Lieutenant General John Norton.

13. Frank Silanskis, sworn statement supporting Medal of Honor resubmission for Waverly Wray, March 5, 1984, courtesy of Lieutenant General John Norton.

14. Paul D. Nunan, sworn statement supporting Medal of Honor resubmission for Waverly Wray, March 2, 1984, courtesy of Lieutenant General John Norton.

15. Ibid.

16. Charles H. Miller, oral history transcript, courtesy of the Eisenhower Center.

17. Vandervoort, "Waverly Wray," pp. 3–4.

18. James Elmo Jones, oral history transcript, courtesy of the Eisenhower Center.

19. Benjamin H. Vandervoort, letter to Clay Blair, December 18, 1983.

20. James J. Coyle, in *Echoes of the Warriors*, compiled and edited by George Jacobus, n. p. 1992, p. 263.

21. Earl W. Boling, in *Echoes of the Warriors*, p. 125.

22. Coyle, in *Echoes of the Warriors*, p. 263.

23. Otis L. Sampson, *Time Out For Combat*, Booksurge, 2004, p. 203.

24. Jones, oral history.

25. Benjamin H. Vandervoort, written account, courtesy of the Cornelius Ryan Collection, Alden Library, Ohio University, p. 6.

26. Otis L. Sampson, "Time Out For Combat," unpublished manuscript, pp. 215–216.

27. Frank P. Woosley, in "Time Out For Combat," unpublished manuscript, p. 224.

28. Coyle, in *Echoes of the Warriors*, p. 263.

29. Woosely, in *Time Out For Combat*, p. 209.

30. Coyle, in *Echoes of the Warriors*, pp. 263–264.

31. Sampson, *Time Out For Combat*, p. 203.

32. Boling, in *Echoes of the Warriors*, p. 125.

33. John W. Keller, letter to Cornelius Ryan, March 7, 1959, courtesy of the Cornelius Ryan Collection, Alden Library, Ohio University.

34. Coyle, in *Echoes of the Warriors*, p. 264.

35. Sampson, *Time Out For Combat*, p. 203.

36. Woosley in *Time Out For Combat*, p. 209.

37. Sampson, in *Time Out For Combat*, pp. 204–205.

38. Coyle, in *Echoes of the Warriors*, p. 264.

39. Sampson, *Time Out For Combat*, p. 205.

40. Keller to Ryan, March 7, 1959.

41. Coyle, in *Echoes of the Warriors*, p. 264.

42. Benjamin H. Vandervoort, written account, p. 6.

43. Benjamin H. Vandervoort, "Drop Zone Europe," p. 4.

44. Benjamin H. Vandervoort, "Testimonial," supporting Medal of Honor resubmission for Waverly Wray, courtesy of Lieutenant General John Norton.

45. Vandervoort, 'Waverly Wray," p. 4.

46. General James M. Gavin, as quoted in Allen L. Langdon, *Ready: The History of the 505th, 82nd Airborne Division*, Western Newspaper Publishing Company, 1986, p. 64.

47. Lieutenant Colonel William E. Ekman, statement, awards file, Lieutenant Colonel Benjamin H. Vandervoort, National Archives, Record Group 338, Stack 290, First Army awards, Box 34, Vandervoort DSC file.

48. Eldon M. Clark, interview with author.

49. Reverend George B. Wood, questionnaire, courtesy of the Cornelius Ryan Collection, Alden Library, Ohio University.

50. Leonard M. Skolek, written account, courtesy of Leonard M. Skolek.

51. Russell W. Brown, response to author's questionnaire.

52. Allen Langdon states in *Ready* on page 74 that there were forty paratroopers at Neuville-au-Plain. The unit history, June 1944, of the 746th Tank Battalion states, "The flanking platoon in their movement reached Neuville au Plain, seized the town, liberating 19 American paratroopers from the 82nd A/B Div., taking 60 prisoners. In radioing back as to instructions as to disposition of the prisoners, Lt. Rainer, platoon leader, inquired as to possibility of bringing back a quantity of what he called 'fine saddle horses' which he was loath to leave in their present situation. Being refused permission, the horses were turned loose, prisoners taken aboard the tanks, and the column returned to bivouac at St. Martin after the town had been taken over by friendly infantry. The task force closed in bivouac at 2300." http://www.geocities.com/viajero43081/history.htm
53. Bilich, interview.
54. Benjamin H. Vandervoort, questionnaire, courtesy of the Cornelius Ryan Collection, Alden Library, Ohio University.
55. Hubert S. Bass, letter to Cornelius Ryan, March 20, 1959, courtesy of the Cornelius Ryan Collection, Alden Library, Ohio University.
56. Spencer F. Wurst and Gayle Wurst, *Descending from the Clouds*, Casemate, 2004, p. 135.
57. Sampson, *Time Out For Combat*, pp. 213–214.
58. Mark J. Alexander, "Thirty-four Days in Normandy in 1944," courtesy of Mark J. Alexander, p. 4.
59. Frank P. Woosley, written account, courtesy of Frank P. Woosley.
60. Seelye, questionnaire.
61. Woosley, written account.
62. Ibid.
63. David V. Bowman, response to author's questionnaire.
64. Wilton H. Johnson, response to author's questionnaire.
65. Roy O. King, response to author's questionnaire.
66. Boling, in *Echoes of the Warriors*, p. 127.
67. Ibid., pp. 127–128.
68. James V. Rodier, response to author's questionnaire.
69. Wurst and Wurst, *Descending from the Clouds*, p. 148.
70. Wurst and Wurst, *Descending from the Clouds*, pp. 148–149.
71. Ibid, p. 148.
72. Omar N. Bradley, in *Ready*, p. 80.
73. Matthew B. Ridgway, in Ibid.
74. Paul D. Nunan, interview with author.
75. Victor M. Schmidt, in *Echoes of the Warriors*, pp. 284–285.
76. Brown, questionnaire.
77. Wurst and Wurst, *Descending from the Clouds*, p. 149.
78. Boling, in *Echoes of the Warriors*, p. 129.
79. Ibid.
80. Donald D. Lassen, email to author, November 20, 2007.
81. Wurst and Wurst, *Descending from the Clouds*, pp. 150–151.

82. Clark, interview.
83. Wurst and Wurst, *Descending from the Clouds*, p. 157.
84. Bass to Ryan, March 20, 1959.
85. Bilich, interview.
86. Ibid.
87. Robert M. Robinson, courtesy of the Cornelius Ryan Collection, Alden Library, Ohio University.

Chapter 5 "The Best Damn Soldiers In The War"
1. Frank A. Bilich, interview with author.
2. Dr. Lyle B. Putnam, questionnaire, courtesy of the Ryan Collection, Alden Library, Ohio University.
3. First Lieutenant Claiborne Cooperider, interview, 97th General Hospital, courtesy of the National Archives.
4. Benjamin H. Vandervoort, "Drop Zone Europe," pp. 1–2.
5. Vandervoort, "Drop Zone Europe," p. 6.
6. Spencer F. Wurst and Gayle Wurst, *Descending From the Clouds*, Casemate, 2004, p. 166.
7. Wurst and Wurst, *Descending From the Clouds*, pp. 165–166.
8. James J. Meyers, "Proud To Be, Memoirs of Colonel James J. Meyers," courtesy of the 82nd Airborne Division War Memorial Museum and Mrs. James J. Meyers, p. 76.
9. Ibid., pp. 76–78, 81.
10. The James M. Gavin Papers, Personal Diaries, Box 8, Folder – "Diary Passages," courtesy of the US Army Military History Institute.
11. HQ 82nd Airborne Division, APO 469, US Army, 11 September 1944, "Order of Battle Summary."
12. Captain Jack Tallerday, "Operations of the 505th Parachute Infantry Regiment (82nd Airborne Division) in the Airborne Landing and Battle of Groesbeek and Nijmegen, Holland 17–25 September 1944, (Rhineland Campaign), (Personal Experience of a Company Commander)," Infantry School, 1948-1949, courtesy of the Donovan Research Library, Fort Benning, Georgia, p. 11.
13. Ibid.
14. Ibid.
15. William J. Meddaugh, as quoted in, *Echoes of the Warriors*, compiled and edited by George Jacobus, n. p. 1992, pp. 353–356.
16. Meddaugh, in *Echoes of the Warriors*, p. 356.
17. Dennis G. O'Loughlin, "Fierce Individualists—US Paratroopers in WWII," unpublished manuscript 1977, courtesy of Frank P. Woosley, pp. 238–239.
18. Meddaugh, in *Echoes of the Warriors*, p. 356.
19. Ibid., pp. 356–357.
20. William R. Hays, Jr., "A Paratrooper in WWII," courtesy of the William R. Hays, Jr. family, p. 9.
21. Meyers, "Proud To Be," p. 84.

22. Michael A. Brilla, questionnaire, courtesy of the Ryan Collection, Alden Library, Ohio University.
23. Meddaugh, in *Echoes of the Warriors*, p. 357.
24. Robert Franco, as quoted in, Deryk Wills, *Put On Your Boots And Parachutes!*, 1992, p. 127.
25. Frank A. Bilich, letter to Al Ireland, June 5, 1998, courtesy of the 82nd Airborne Division War Memorial Museum.
26. Bilich, interview.
27. Meddaugh, in *Echoes of the Warriors*, pp. 357–358.
28. Dr. Daniel B. McIlvoy, Jr., letter to Clarence F. Montgomery, October 31, 1960, courtesy of the Cornelius Ryan Collection, Alden Library, Ohio University.
29. Paul D. Nunan, written account, courtesy of the Cornelius Ryan Collection, Alden Library, Ohio University.
30. McIlvoy to Montgomery, October 31, 1960.
31. James J. Coyle, in *Echoes of the Warriors*, p. 318.
32. Lieutenant Jack P. Carroll, interview, 160th General Hospital, courtesy of the National Archives.
33. Robert R. Hughart, questionnaire, courtesy of the Cornelius Ryan Collection, Alden Library, Ohio University.
34. Russell W. Brown, response to author's questionnaire.
35. Wurst and Wurst, *Descending From the Clouds*, p. 172.
36. Hays, "A Paratrooper in WWII," p. 10.
37. Hughart, questionnaire.
38. Benjamin H. Vandervoort, in *Echoes of the Warriors*, p. 360.
39. Ibid., p. 359.

Chapter 6 "You Fired Fast And Straight"
1. Benjamin H. Vandervoort, "Nijmegen Bridge," courtesy of the U.S. Army Center of Military History.
2. James J. Smith, in *Echoes of the Warriors*, p. 349.
3. Donald D. Lassen, email to author, November 20, 2007.
4. John H. Rabig, as quoted in Deryk Wills, *Put On Your Boots And Parachutes!*, 1992, p. 132.
5. Smith, in *Echoes of the Warriors*, p. 349.
6. Donald D. Lassen, email to author, November 20, 2007.
7. Vandervoort, "Nijmegen Bridge."
8. James E. Keenan, questionnaire, courtesy of the Ryan Collection, Alden Library, Ohio University.
9. Vandervoort, "Nijmegen Bridge."
10. James J. Meyers, "Proud To Be, Memoirs of Colonel James J. Meyers," courtesy of the 82nd Airborne Division War Memorial Museum and Mrs. James J. Meyers, p. 89.
11. Rabig, in *Put On Your Boots And Parachutes!*, p. 132.
12. Paul D. Nunan, in *Put On Your Boots And Parachutes!*, p. 132.

13. Gerald R. Weed, interview with author.

14. Meyers, "Proud To Be," p. 89.

15. Roy O. King, response to author's questionnaire.

16. David V. Bowman, "Memoirs of a Machine Gunner," courtesy of David V. Bowman, p. 42.

17. Ibid., pp. 42–43.

18. Meyers, "Proud To Be," p. 89.

19. Donald E. Ellis, interview with author.

20. Ibid.

21. Ibid.

22. Julius Eisner, interview with author.

23. Ibid.

24. Bowman, "Memoirs of a Machine Gunner," p. 43.

25. Eisner, interview.

26. Bowman, "Memoirs of a Machine Gunner," p. 43.

27. Frank Aguerrebere, letter to author.

28. Ibid.

29. Bowman, "Memoirs of a Machine Gunner," p. 45.

30. Aguerrebere to author.

31. Bowman, "Memoirs of a Machine Gunner," p. 45.

32. Meyers, "Proud To Be," pp. 89–90.

33. Frank Bilich, letter to author, June 4, 2003

34. Paul D. Nunan, written account, courtesy of the Ryan Collection, Alden Library, Ohio University.

35. Ibid.

36. Nunan, in *Put On Your Boots And Parachutes!*, p. 132.

37. Vandervoort, "Nijmegen Bridge."

38. Frank A. Bilich, in *Put On Your Boots And Parachutes!*, p. 129.

39. Ibid., pp. 129–130.

40. Vandervoort, "Nijmegen Bridge."

41. Otis L. Sampson, in *Echoes of the Warriors*, p. 341.

42. Smith, in *Echoes of the Warriors*, pp. 349–350.

43. Coyle, in *Echoes of the Warriors*, p. 319.

44. Earl W. Boling, in *Echoes of the Warriors*, p. 135.

45. Coyle, in *Echoes of the Warriors*, p. 319.

46. Boling, in *Echoes of the Warriors*, p. 135.

47. Coyle, in *Echoes of the Warriors*, p. 320.

48. Boling, in *Echoes of the Warriors*, p. 136.

49. Captain John D. Phillips, Jr., "Operations of the 3d Platoon, Company E, 505th Parachute Infantry Regiment (82d Airborne Division) in the Seizure of the Nijmegen Bridge, 19 – 20 September 1944. (Operation of the 1st Allied Airborne Army in the Invasion of Holland), (Rhineland Campaign), (Personal Experience of a Platoon Leader), Infantry School, 1947-1948, courtesy of the Donovan Research Library, Fort Benning, Georgia, p. 13.

50. Coyle, in *Echoes of the Warriors*, p. 320.

51. Vandervoort, "Nijmegen Bridge."
52. Coyle, in *Echoes of the Warriors*, p. 320.
53. Otis L. Sampson, *Time Out For Combat*, Booksurge, 2004, p. 260.
54. Coyle, in *Echoes of the Warriors*, p. 320.
55. Boling, in *Echoes of the Warriors*, p. 136.
56. Smith, in *Echoes of the Warriors*, p. 350.
57. Coyle, in *Echoes of the Warriors*, pp. 320–321.
58. Sampson, *Time Out For Combat*, p. 260.
59. Carl Beck, in *Put On Your Boots And Parachutes!*, p. 127.
60. Coyle, in *Echoes of the Warriors*, p. 321.
61. Ibid., p. 320.
62. Phillips, "Operations of the 3d Platoon, Company E," pp. 13–14.
63. William R. Hays, Jr., "A Paratrooper in WWII," courtesy of the William R. Hays, Jr. family, p. 11.
64. Spencer F. Wurst and Gayle Wurst, *Descending from the Clouds*, Casemate, 2004, p. 179.
65. First Lieutenant Claiborne Cooperider, interview, 97th General Hospital, courtesy of the National Archives.
66. Vandervoort, "Nijmegen Bridge."
67. Cooperider, interview.
68. Russell W. Brown, response to author's questionnaire.
69. Hays, "A Paratrooper in WWII," p. 12.
70. Wurst and Wurst, *Descending from the Clouds*, pp. 180–181.
71. Hays, "A Paratrooper in WWII," p. 12.
72. Wurst and Wurst, *Descending from the Clouds*, pp. 181–182.
73. Hays, "A Paratrooper in WWII," p. 12.
74. Jack P. Carroll, questionnaire, courtesy of the Ryan Collection, Alden Library, Ohio University.
75. Vandervoort, "Nijmegen Bridge."
76. Coyle, in *Echoes of the Warriors*, pp. 321–322.
77. Phillips, "Operations of the 3d Platoon, Company E," p. 14.
78. Ibid., pp. 14–16.
79. Ibid., p. 16.
80. Donald D. Lassen, questionnaire, courtesy of the Ryan Collection, Alden Library, Ohio University.
81. Donald D. Lassen, email to author, November 20, 2007.
82. Meyers, "Proud To Be," p. 90.
83. Sampson, in *Echoes of the Warriors*, p. 342.
84. James M. Gavin, *On To Berlin*, Viking Press, 1978, p. 170.
85. Ibid.
86. George Chatterton, in Cornelius Ryan, *A Bridge Too Far*, Simon and Schuster, 1974, pp. 432–433.
87. James M. Gavin, in *A Bridge Too Far*, p. 433.
88. Frederick M. Browning, in *A Bridge Too Far*, p. 433.
89. Vandervoort, "Nijmegen Bridge."

90. Boling, in *Echoes of the Warriors*, p. 137.
91. Bilich, *Put On Your Boots And Parachutes!*, p. 130.

Chapter 7 "No Quarter Combat"
1. James J. Meyers, "Proud to Be," courtesy of the 82nd Airborne Division War Memorial Museum and Mrs. James J. Meyers, p. 93.
2. James J. Smith, as quoted in, *Echoes of the Warriors*, compiled and edited by George Jacobus, n. p. 1992, p. 350.
3. Captain John D. Phillips, Jr., "Operations of the 3d Platoon, Company E, 505th Parachute Infantry Regiment (82d Airborne Division) in the Seizure of the Nijmegen Bridge, 19 – 20 September 1944. (Operation of the 1st Allied Airborne Army in the Invasion of Holland), (Rhineland Campaign), (Personal Experience of a Platoon Leader), Infantry School, 1947-1948, courtesy of the Donovan Research Library, Fort Benning, Georgia, pp. 16–18.
4. Benjamin H. Vandervoort, "Nijmegen Bridge," courtesy of the U.S. Army Center of Military History.
5. Wayne W. Galvin, questionnaire, courtesy of the Ryan Collection, Alden Library, Ohio University.
6. James J. Coyle, in *Echoes of the Warriors*, p. 322.
7. Earl W. Boling, in *Echoes of the Warriors*, p. 138.
8. Coyle, in *Echoes of the Warriors*, p. 322.
9. Boling, in *Echoes of the Warriors*, pp. 138–139.
10. Coyle, in *Echoes of the Warriors*, p. 322.
11. William J. Meddaugh, written account, courtesy of William J. Meddaugh.
12. Phillips, "Operations of the 3d Platoon, Company E," p. 18.
13. Jack P. Carroll, questionnaire, courtesy of the Ryan Collection, Alden Library, Ohio University.
14. William R. Hays, Jr., "A Paratrooper in WWII," courtesy of the William R. Hays, Jr. family, pp. 13–14.
15. Wurst, Spencer F. and Wurst, Gayle, *Descending from the Clouds*, Casemate Publishing, 2004, p. 186.
16. Ibid, p. 187.
17. Hays, "A Paratrooper in WWII," p. 14.
18. Vandervoort, "Nijmegen Bridge."
19. Wurst and Wurst, *Descending from the Clouds*, p. 189.
20. W. A. Jones, interview with author.
21. Wurst and Wurst, *Descending from the Clouds*, p. 189.
22. Jones, interview.
23. Hays, "A Paratrooper in WWII," p. 14.
24. Benjamin H. Vandervoort, as quoted in, Michel DeTrez, *The Way We Were, Lieutenant Colonel Ben Vandervoort*, D-Day Publishing, 2004, p. 73.
25. Vandervoort, in *Echoes of the Warriors*, p. 365.
26. Galvin, questionnaire.
27. Vandervoort, in *The Way We Were*, p. 73.
28. Robert R. Hughart, response to author's questionnaire.

29. James T. Steed, questionnaire, courtesy of the Ryan Collection, Alden Library, Ohio University.

30. Ibid.

31. Smith, in *Echoes of the Warriors*, p. 351.

32. Clyde F. Knox, questionnaire, courtesy of the Ryan Collection, Alden Library, Ohio University.

33. James E. Keenan, questionnaire, courtesy of the Cornelius Ryan Collection, Alden Library, Ohio University.

34. Donald D. Lassen, email to author, November 20, 2007.

35. Vandervoort, "Nijmegen Bridge."

36. Hays, "A Paratrooper in WWII," pp. 14–15.

37. Wurst and Wurst, *Descending from the Clouds*, p. 190.

38. Jones, interview.

39. Wurst and Wurst, *Descending from the Clouds*, p. 190.

40. Jones, interview.

41. Wurst and Wurst, *Descending from the Clouds*, pp. 190–191.

42. Vandervoort, "Nijmegen Bridge."

43. Wurst and Wurst, *Descending from the Clouds*, p. 191.

44. Ibid.

45. Hughart, questionnaire.

46. Kenneth Russell, letter to author, May 27, 2003.

47. Michael A. Brilla, questionnaire, Cornelius Ryan Collection, Alden Library, Ohio University.

48. Hughart, questionnaire.

49. Galvin, questionnaire.

50. Vandervoort, "Nijmegen Bridge."

51. Heinz Harmel, as quoted in Cornelius Ryan, *A Bridge Too Far*, Simon and Schuster, 1974, p. 473.

52. Ibid., p. 473.

53. Ibid., pp. 473-474.

54. Donald W. McKeage, written account, courtesy of Donald W. McKeage.

55. Ibid.

56. Meyers, "Proud to Be," p. 93.

57. British General Sir Miles Dempsey, as quoted in Gavin, *On To Berlin*, p. 185.

58. Meyers, "Proud to Be," pp. 93–94.

59. David V. Bowman, "Memoirs of a Machine Gunner," courtesy of David V. Bowman, p. 41.

60. Boling, in *Echoes of the Warriors*, pp. 142–143.

61. Meyers, "Proud to Be," pp. 96–97.

62. Ibid., p. 94.

63. Ibid., pp. 97–98.

64. Hays, "A Paratrooper in WWII," p. 18.

Chapter 8 "We Had Never Retreated"

1. William E. Slawson, written account, courtesy of William E. Slawson.
2. William R. Hays, Jr., "A Paratrooper in WWII," courtesy of the William R. Hays, Jr. family, pp. 18–19.
3. John R. Jackson, response to author's questionnaire.
4. James V. Rodier, response to author's questionnaire.
5. Colonel William E. Ekman, interview by Captain K. W. Hechler, courtesy of Colonel Mike Ekman, p. 1.
6. Malcolm Neel, memoirs, courtesy of Bob Burns.
7. "The Story of the 82nd Airborne Division in the Battle of the Belgian Bulge, in the Siegfried Line, and the Roer River," Section II—The Division Commander's Report, p. 1
8. Wilton H. Johnson, response to author's questionnaire.
9. Hays, "A Paratrooper in WWII," p. 20.
10. Ibid.
11. William J. Meddaugh, written account, courtesy of William J. Meddaugh.
12. Benjamin H. Vandervoort, as quoted in, *Echoes of the Warriors*, compiled and edited by George Jacobus, n. p. 1992, p. 399.
13. Ibid.
14. Meddaugh, written account.
15. Vandervoort, in *Echoes of the Warriors*, p. 401.
16. Meddaugh, written account.
17. Julius D. Axman, response to author's questionnaire.
18. Vandervoort, in *Echoes of the Warriors*, pp. 400–401.
19. Virgil D. Gould, interview with author.
20. James J. Meyers, "Proud To Be, Memoirs of Colonel James J. Meyers," courtesy of the 82nd Airborne Division War Memorial Museum, and Mrs. James J. Meyers, pp. 104–106.
21. Meddaugh, written account.
22. Julius D. Axman, response to author's questionnaire.
23. Ibid.
24. Vandervoort, in *Echoes of the Warriors*, pp. 401–402.
25. Edward W. Arndt, in *Echoes of the Warriors*, p. 417.
26. Meddaugh, written account.
27. Vandervoort, in *Echoes of the Warriors*, p. 402.
28. Hays, "A Paratrooper in WW II," p. 21.
29. Donald W. McKeage, written account, courtesy of Donald W. McKeage.
30. Vandervoort, in *Echoes of the Warriors*, pp. 402–403.
31. Arndt in *Echoes of the Warriors*, p. 417.
32. Ibid., pp. 417–418.
33. Dennis G. O'Loughlin, "Fierce Individualists," unpublished manuscript, pp. 309—310.
34. Meddaugh, written account.
35. Vandervoort, in *Echoes of the Warriors*, pp. 403–404.
36. Donald W. McKeage, response to author's questionnaire.

37. Vandervoort, in *Echoes of the Warriors*, p. 405.

38. Meddaugh, written account.

39. Meyers, "Proud To Be," p. 106.

40. Ibid.

41. Field Marshal Bernard L. Montgomery, as quoted in, Clay Blair, *Ridgway's Paratroopers*, Dial Press, 1985, p. 468.

42. Ibid., p. 448.

43. Meyers, "Proud To Be," p. 108.

44. V. P. Dewailly, written account, courtesy of V. P. Dewailly.

45. Meyers, "Proud To Be," p. 108.

46. Ibid, pp. 108–109.

47. Frank A. Bilich, letter to Al Ireland, June 5, 1998, courtesy of the 82nd Airborne Division War Memorial Museum.

48. Ibid, pp. 53–54.

49. David V. Bowman, "Memoirs of a Machine Gunner," courtesy of David V. Bowman, p. 53.

50. Allan C. Barger, "War and People," 2001, p. 117.

51. Hays, "A Paratrooper in WWII," p. 24.

Chapter 9 "One Of The Most Fearless"

1. Allan C. Barger, "War and People," pp. 119–121.

2. Russell W. Brown, response to author's questionnaire.

3. Donald W. McKeage, "Battle of the Bulge," courtesy of Donald McKeage.

4. James J. Meyers, "Proud To Be, Memoirs of Colonel James J. Meyers," courtesy of the 82nd Airborne Division War Memorial Museum, and Mrs. James J. Meyers, p. 111.

5. Barger, "People and War," pp. 121–122.

6. Meyers, "Proud To Be," p. 111.

7. John R. Jackson, response to author's questionnaire.

8. McKeage, "Battle of the Bulge."

9. Meyers, "Proud To Be," p. 112.

10. Ibid., p. 112.

11. David V. Bowman, "Memoirs of a Machine Gunner," courtesy of David V. Bowman, pp. 58–59.

12. Meyers, "Proud To Be," p. 113.

13. Ibid, pp. 113–115.

14. James M. Gavin, *On To Berlin*, Viking Press, 1978, p. 253.

15. Ibid.

16. Died of wounds January 13, 1945.

17. Brown, questionnaire.

18. Ibid.

19. Ibid.

20. Meyers, "Proud To Be," pp. 115–116.

21. Donald L. Brown, letter to Don W. McKeage, March 29, 1995, courtesy of the 82nd Airborne Division War Memorial Museum.

22. Jackson, questionnaire.
23. Dr. Lyle B. Putnam, questionnaire, courtesy of the Cornelius Ryan Archive, Alden Library, Ohio University.
24. Donald D. Lassen, email to author, November 19, 2007.
25. Earl W. Boling, in *Echoes of the Warriors*, compiled and edited by George Jacobus, n. p, 1992, pp. 149–150.
26. Meyers, "Proud To Be," p. 118.
27. Ibid., p. 123.
28. William E. Slawson, written account, courtesy of William E. Slawson.
29. Meyers, "Proud To Be," p. 123.
30. Paul R. Brandt, response to author's questionnaire.
31. Russell W. Brown, response to author's questionnaire.
32. Boling, in *Echoes of the Warriors*, p. 152.
33. Paul D. Nunan, interview with author.
34. William F. Borda, response to author's questionnaire.
35. Boling, in *Echoes of the Warriors*, p. 153.
36. James J. Coyle, in *Echoes of the Warriors*, pp. 326–328.
37. Meyers, "Proud To Be," p. 131–132.
38. Ibid., p. 132.
39. Dominick Di Battista, letter to Cornelius Ryan, April 6, 1964, courtesy of the Cornelius Ryan Collection, Alden Library, Ohio University.
40. Ibid.
41. Ibid.
42. Borda, questionnaire.
43. Coyle, in *Echoes of the Warriors*, pp. 330–331.
44. Barger, "War and People," 2001, p. 132.
45. Coyle, in *Echoes of the Warriors*, p. 331.
46. Boling, in *Echoes of the Warriors*, p. 155.
47. Borda, questionnaire.
48. Brown, questionnaire.
49. Stephen E. Ambrose, *The Victors*, Simon and Schuster, 1998, p. 344

Epilogue "He Was A True Warrior"
1. Lieutenant General James M. Gavin, letter to William Breuer, September 1, 1982, Gavin Papers, U.S. Military History Institute.
2. Matthew B. Ridgway and Harold H. Martin, *Soldier: The Memoirs of Matthew B. Ridgway*, Greenwood Publishing Group, 1974, p. 7.
3. Robert R. Hughart, oral history transcript, courtesy of the Eisenhower Center.
4. Benjamin H. Vandervoort, "Drop Zone Europe," p. 10.
5. James J. Meyers, "Proud To Be, Memoirs of Colonel James J. Meyers," courtesy of the 82nd Airborne Division War Memorial Museum, and Mrs. James J. Meyers, p. 115.

BIBLIOGRAPHY

Published Sources

Ambrose, Stephen E., *The Victors*, Simon and Schuster, 1998.

Blair, Clay, Ridgway's Paratroopers, Dial Press, 1985.

DeTrez Michel, *The Way We Were, Colonel Ben Vandervoort*, D-Day Publishing, 2004.

Dougdale, J., *Panzer Divisions, Panzergrenadier Divisions, Panzer Brigades of the Army and Waffen SS in the West, Autumn 1944-Februray 1945, Ardennes and Nordwind*, Galago Publishing, 2000.

Gavin, James M., *On To Berlin*, Viking Press, 1978.

Kershaw, Robert J., *It Never Snows in September*, Sarpedon, 2001.

Langdon, Allen, *Ready*, Western Newspaper Publishing Co., 1986.

MacDonald, Charles B., *The U.S. Army in World War II: The Siegfried Line Campaign*, Office of the Chief of Military History, US Army.

Margry, Karel, Editor, *Operation Market-Garden Then and Now*, Battle of Britain International Limited, 2002.

Marshall, S. L. A., *Night Drop*, Little, Brown and Company, 1962.

Miller, Russell, *Nothing Less Than Victory*, Quill, 1998.

Mitcham, Samuel W., Jr., and Friedrich Von Stauffenberg, *The Battle of Sicily*, Stackpole, 1991.

Nordyke, Phil, *All American All The Way*, Zenith Press, 2005.

Nordyke, Phil, *Four Stars of Valor*, Zenith Press, 2006.

Patrick K. O'Donnell, *Beyond Valor*, The Free Press, 2001.

Pallud, Jean Paul, *Battle of the Bulge Then and Now*, Battle of Britain International Limited, 1999.

Ridgway, Matthew B., and Martin, Harold H., *Soldier: The Memoirs of Matthew B. Ridgway*, Greenwood Press, 1956.

Ruppenthal, Major Roland G., *Utah Beach to Cherbourg*, US Army Center of Military History, 1994.

Ryan, Cornelius, *A Bridge Too Far*, Simon and Schuster, 1974.

Sampson, Otis L., *Time Out for Combat*, Booksurge, 2004.

Saunders, Tim, *Nijmegen*, Leo Cooper, 2001.

Thuring, G., *Roll of Honor 82nd Airborne Division World War II*, The Liberation Museum, Groesbeek, Holland, 1997.

Thuring, G.; van den Bergh, F.; Zwaaf, L.; Thuring, J.; *Waal Crossing*, The Liberation Museum, Groesbeek, Holland, 1992.

Thuring, G.; Langdon, A.; *Yes, We Shall and Will Return 505th Parachute Infantry*, The Liberation Museum, Groesbeek, Holland, 1994.

Warren, Dr. John C., *Airborne Operations in World War II, European Theater – USAF Historical Studyies: No. 97*, MA/AH Publishing, 1956.

Wills, Deryk, *Put On Your Boots And Parachutes!"* Deryk Wills, 1992.

Wurst, Spencer F. and Wurst, Gayle, *Descending from the Clouds*, Casemate Publishing, 2004.

Articles

Steele, John M., "D-Day Participant Survived By Feigning Death," *Fayetteville Observer*, May 16, 1969.

Unpublished Diaries, Sworn Statements, Letters, Emails, Written Accounts, Memoirs, and Manuscripts

Aguerrebere, Frank, letter to author, not dated.

Alexander, Mark J., "Italy – 1943," Mark J. Alexander.

Alexander, Mark J., "Personal Memories of Sicily", Mark J. Alexander.

Alexander, Mark J., "Thirty-four Days in Normandy in 1944," Mark J. Alexander.

Barger, Allan C., "People and War," 2001, Allan C. Barger.

Bass, Hubert S., letter to Cornelius Ryan, March 20, 1959, Cornelius Ryan Collection, Alden Library, Ohio University.

Bilich, Frank A., letter to Alfred W. Ireland, June 5, 1998, 82nd Airborne Division War Memorial Museum.

Bilich, Frank A., letter to author, June 4, 2003.

Bowman, David V., "Memoirs of a Machine Gunner," David V. Bowman.

Brown, Donald L., letter to Donald W. McKeage, March 29, 1995, 82nd Airborne Division War Memorial Museum.

Cornelius Ryan Collection, Alden Library, Ohio University, written accounts from the following veterans:

Cullen E. Clark, Jr.
Anthony J. DeMayo
James M. Gavin
Paul D. Nunan
Benjamin H. Vandervoort

Dewailly, Voohies P., written account, courtesy of Voorhies P. Dewailly.

Di Battista, Dominick, letter to Cornelius Ryan, April 6, 1964, Cornelius Ryan Collection, Alden Library, Ohio University.

Echoes of the Warriors, compiled and edited by George Jacobus, 1992.

Ekman, Lieutenant Colonel William E., recommendation, awards file, Lieutenant Colonel Benjamin H. Vandervoort, National Archives.

Franco, Dr. Robert, letter to Alfred W. Ireland, April 19, 1999, 82nd Airborne Division War Memorial Museum.

Gavin, Lieutenant General James M., letter to William Breuer, September 1, 1982, Gavin Papers, U.S. Military History Institute.

Hays, William R. Jr., "A Paratrooper in WWII," William R. Hays, Jr. family.

Herkness, Frank G., Army Services Experiences Questionnaire Continuation Sheet, U.S. Army Military History Institute.

John W. Keller, letter to Cornelius Ryan, March 7, 1959, Cornelius Ryan Collection, Alden Library, Ohio University.

King, Roy O., written account, Roy O. King.

Lassen, Donald D., email to author, November 20, 2007, Donald D. Lassen

Matzelle, Henry J., written account, Mrs. Frankie James.

McClean, Thomas J., sworn statement supporting Medal of Honor resubmission for Waverly Wray, March 1, 1984, Lieutenant General John Norton.

McIlvoy, Dr. Daniel B., Jr., letter to Clarence F. Montgomery, October 31, 1960, Cornelius Ryan Collection, Alden Library, Ohio University.

McKeage, Donald W., "Battle of the Bulge," Donald W. McKeage.

McKeage, Donald W., written account, Donald W. McKeage.

Meddaugh, William J., written account, William J. Meddaugh.

Meyers, James J., "Proud To Be, Memoirs of Colonel James J. Meyers," Mrs. James J. Meyers and the 82nd Airborne Division War Memorial Museum.

Neel, Malcolm, memoirs, Robert Burns.

Nunan, Paul D., sworn statement supporting Medal of Honor resubmission for Waverly Wray, March 2, 1984, Lieutenant General John Norton.

O'Loughlin, Dennis G., "Fierce Individualists," 1977, Frank P. Woosley.

Peterson, Theodore L., letter to Cornelius Ryan, March 22, 1959, Cornelius Ryan Collection, Alden Library, Ohio University.

Rice, Captain John D., recommendation, awards file, Lieutenant John D. Sprinkle, National Archives

Russell, Lieutenant Colonel Clyde R., letter to Cornelius Ryan, March 17, 1959, Cornelius Ryan Collection, Alden Library, Ohio University.
.
Russell, Kenneth E., letter to author, May 27, 2003.

Sammon, Charles E., letter to Cornelius Ryan, March 21, 1959, Cornelius Ryan Collection, Alden Library, Ohio University.

Sampson, Otis L., "Time Out For Combat," unpublished manuscript.

Schlesener, Milton E., letter to Frank Vanderbilt, Mrs. Frankie James.

Silanskis, Frank V., sworn statement supporting Medal of Honor resubmission for Waverly Wray, March 5, 1984, Lieutenant General John Norton.

Skolek, Leonard M., written account, Leonard M. Skolek.

Slawson, William E., written account, William E. Slawson.

Smith, Captain Taylor G., statement, awards file, Lieutenant Waverly W. Wray, National Archives.

The James M. Gavin Papers, Personal Diaries, Box 8, U.S. Army Center of Military History.

Vandervoort, Benjamin H., "Drop Zone Europe," Army Heritage and Education Center.

Vandervoort, Benjamin H., "Nijmegen Bridge," U.S. Army Center of Military History.

Vandervoort, Benjamin H., "Testimonial,"supporting Medal of Honor resubmission for Waverly Wray, March 1, 1984, Lieutenant General John Norton.

Vandervoort, Benjamin H., "Waverly Wray, Ste.-Mére-Église, Normandy—June 7, 1944," Lieutenant General (U.S. Army Retired) John Norton.

Walberg, Gordon A., *Static Line*, February 1989.

West, Floyd Jr., letter to Mr. Walter J. Turnbull, Jr., April 14, 1947, Mrs. Frankie James.

Woosley, Frank P., memoirs, Frank P. Woosley.

Wurst, Spencer F., unpublished manuscript.

Responses by Veterans to Questionnaires

Cornelius Ryan Collection, Alden Library, Ohio University, questionnaires with the following veterans:

Michael A. Brilla
Buffalo Boy Canoe
Jack P. Carroll
Anthony J. DeMayo
William E. Ekman
Wayne W. Galvin
Robert R. Hughart
James E. Keenan
Clyde F. Knox

Donald D. Lassen
William J. Meddaugh
Paul D. Nunan
Dr. Lyle B. Putnam
Robert M. Robinson
James T. Steed
John M. Steele
Benjamin H. Vandervoort
Reverend George B. Wood

Author's questionnaires with the following veterans:

Berge Avadanian Berge Avadanian
Julius D. Axman
William F. Borda
David V. Bowman
Paul R. Brandt
Russell W. Brown
Robert R. Hughart

John R. Jackson
Wilton H. Johnson
Roy O. King
Donald W. McKeage
James V. Rodier
Irvin W. Seelye

U.S. Military Documents, After Action Reports, Studies, Monographs, Statements, and Combat Interviews

"82nd Airborne Division In Sicily And Italy," 82nd Airborne Division War Memorial Museum.

82nd Airborne Division, "World War II Casualties, Decorations, Citations,"
82nd Airborne Division War Memorial Museum.

Combat Interviews, Operation Market-Garden, Cornelius Ryan Collection,
Alden Library, Ohio University.

Copies of Distinguished Service Cross citations and Presidential Unit citations,
82nd Airborne Division War Memorial Museum.

Copies of Distinguished Service Cross citations, maps, photos, and after-action
reports, Cornelius Ryan Collection, Alden Library, Ohio University.

"Debriefing Conference—Operation Neptune," 13 August 1944, 82nd Airborne
Division War Memorial Museum.

G-2 Reports, Normandy, 82nd Airborne Division War Memorial Museum.

Gavin, Major General James M., letter to Capt. John C. Westover, July 25,
1945, courtesy of the 82nd Airborne Division War Memorial Museum.

Headquarters IX Troop Carrier Command, "Operation Market, Air Invasion of
Holland," Cornelius Ryan Collection, Alden Library, Ohio University.

HQ 82nd Airborne Division, APO 469, US Army, 11 September 1944, "Order
of Battle Summary," Cornelius Ryan Collection, Alden Library, Ohio
University.

Marshall, S. L. A. Colonel, "Regimental Unit Study Number 6, "The Capture of
Ste.-Mére-Église, An Action by 505th Infantry Regiment of the 82nd Airborne
Division," History Section, European Theater of Operations.

"Operation Market, A Graphic History of the 82nd Airborne Division," 82nd
Airborne Division War Memorial Museum.

"Operation Market-Garden," after-action report, 82nd Airborne Division,
National Archives.

"'Operation Neptune,' 82nd Airborne Division Action in Normandy, France,"
82nd Airborne Division War Memorial Museum.

Orders and Reports for Operation Market, Cornelius Ryan Collection, Alden
Library, Ohio University.

"S-3 Journal, 505th Parachute Infantry Regiment, October 1944 – 16 June
1945," John Fielder and U.S. Military History Institute.

Supreme Headquarters Allied Expeditionary Force, Office of Assistant Chief of Staff, G-2, "Weekly Intelligence Summary, For Week ending 16 September 1944," Cornelius Ryan Collection, Alden Library, Ohio University.

Tallerday, Captain Jack, "Operations of the 505th Parachute Infantry Regiment (82nd Airborne Division) in the Airborne Landing and Battle of Groesbeek and Nijmegen, Holland 17–25 September 1944, (Rhineland Campaign), (Personal Experience of a Company Commander)," Infantry School, 1948-1949, Donovan Research Library, Fort Benning, Georgia.

"The Story of the 82nd Airborne Division in the Battle of the Belgian Bulge, in the Siegfried Line, and of the Roer River," 82nd Airborne Division War Memorial Museum.

Taped Interviews and Oral Histories, Interview and Oral History Transcripts

Carroll, First Lieutenant Jack P. Carroll, 160th General Hospital, National Archives.

Copperider, First Lieutenant Claiborne, interview, 97th General Hospital, National Archives.

Eisenhower Center, oral history transcripts of the following veterans:

Robert R. Hughart
James Elmo Jones
Charles H. Miller
Kenneth E. Russell
John R. Taylor

Ekman, Colonel William E., interview with Captain K. W. Hechler, Colonel Mike Ekman.

Ekman, Colonel William E., interview with Colonel Mike Ekman, Colonel Mike Ekman.

Gavin, James M., interview, Cornelius Ryan Collection, Alden Library, Ohio University.

Interviews with author with the following veterans:

Frank A. Bilich   Julius Eisner
Eldon M. Clark   Donald E. Ellis

Virgil D. Gould
W. A. Jones
Stanley W. Kotlarz

Paul D. Nunan
Gerald R. Weed
Dr. Daryle E. Whitfield

Phillips, Captain John D., Jr., "Operations of the 3d Platoon, Company E, 505th Parachute Infantry Regiment (82d Airborne Division) in the Seizure of the Nijmegen Bridge, 19 – 20 September 1944. (Operation of the 1st Allied Airborne Army in the Invasion of Holland), (Rhineland Campaign), (Personal Experience of a Platoon Leader)," Infantry School, 1947-1948, courtesy of the Donovan Research Library, Fort Benning, Georgia.

Ridgway, Matthew B., oral history, Part 2, U.S. Army Military History Institute.

Internet Web Pages

Cole, Hugh M. *The Ardennes: Battle of the Bulge*, US Army Center of Military History, 1990, **http://www.army.mil/cmh-pg/books/wwii/7-8/7-8_cont.htm**

Fifth Army Historical Section, Salerno: American Operations From the Beaches to the Volturno (9 September-6 October 1943*), US Army Center of Military History, 1990,* **http://www.army.mil/cmh-pg/books/wwii/salerno/sal-fm.htm**

Research of the armored strength of the Hermann Göring Panzer Division during the Sicily Campaign, **http://www.feldgrau.net/phpBB2/index.php**

Research of the composition of German units in the Cotentin Peninsula at the beginning of the Normandy invasion, **http://web.telia.com/~u18313395/normandy/gerob/infdiv/91id.html**

Roll of Honor of 82nd Airborne Division, **http://www.ww2-airborne.us/division/82_overview.html**

Unit History of the US 746th Tank Battalion in Normandy, **http://www.geocities.com/viajero43081/history.htm**

INDEX TO MAPS

MAP 1   North Africa 13

MAP 2   Planned Air Route of the 505th RCT from Kairouan to Sicily 16

MAP 3   Sicily, 11 July 1943 22

MAP 4   Airborne Plan, 82nd and 101st Airborne Divisions, 6 June 1944 ...45

MAP 5   Invasion Routes to Normandy, 5–6 June 1944 49

MAP 6   505th PIR Drop Pattern, 6 June 1944 54

MAP 7   Ste.-Mére-Église, 6 June 1944 62

MAP 8   Ste.-Mére-Église, 7 June 1944 77

MAP 9   Montebourg Station and Le Ham, 8–11 June 1944 92

Map 10   505th RCT Drive to St.-Sauveur-le-Vicomte, 15–18 June 1944 94

MAP 11   505th RCT Hill 131 and Hill 95, 1–4 July 1944 104

MAP 12   Operation Market Garden, Zones of Operation 111

MAP 13   Holland, 17 September 1944 112

MAP 14   Nijmegen, 19 September 1944 127

MAP 15   Nijmegen, 20 September 1944 158

MAP 16   Movement of the 82nd to Werbomont 178

MAP 17   Salm River Defense, 21–24 December 1944 180

MAP 18   Trois Ponts, Belgium 187

MAP 19   Counter Offensive, 3–9 January 1945 204

MAP 20   Attack to the German Border, 28–31 January 1945 214

MAP 21   Hürtgen Forest, 7–16 February 1945 217

MAP 22 The 505th Crossing of the Elbe River, 30 April–1 May 1945 226

INDEX

Aa River, Holland, 109
Aachen, Germany, 216, 218
Adair, Gen. Allan, 124, 148, 159
Adams Sr., Cpl. Ronald F., 151, 209
Aguerrebere, Pvt. Frank, 131, 171
Aguirre, Pvt. Alfonso R., 141
Alabama Area, 9, 10
Alexander, Lt. Col. Mark J., 15, 19, 21, 23, 26, 28, 29, 31, 36-37, 38, 93
Allen, Cpl. Lewis D., 79
Amblève River, Belgium, 181, 182
Amcomont, Belgium, 197
Amsterdam, Holland, 109
Antwerp, Belgium, 184
Anzio, Italy, 110
Appleby, Cpl. Sam J., 85, 87
Arbrefontaine, Belgium, 200, 203, 205, 210
Arkwright, Brig. Gen. H. R., 37
Arndt, PFC Edward W., 162, 187, 188, 190, 191
Arnhem, Holland, 109, 110, 113, 121, 122, 123, 148
Arnone, Italy, 28, 31, 32, 36
Atchley, Pvt. John E., 75
August, Cpl. Francis J., 30
Auther, Cpl. Kenneth W., 78
Autrand, Lt. Vernon L., 147
Avadanian, Pvt. Berge, 17, 19, 30, 43
Avellino, Italy, 27
Axman, Sgt. Julius D., 32, 33, 183, 185, 186
Bailey, Lt. Jack N., 183, 213
Baldwin, PFC Richard R., 192
Bandienville, France, 87
Baraque de Fraiture, Belgium, 194
Barger, T/4 Allan C., 197, 199-200, 201-202, 225
Barnett, Capt. Charles L., 210, 212, 220, 221
Bartley, S/Sgt. Jack M., 14
Barton, Gen. Raymond O., 79, 80
Bartunek, Sgt. Edward G., 32
Bass, Capt. Hubert S., 44, 48, 51, 57, 91, 103, 119
Basse-Bodeux, Belgium, 179, 181
Bastogne, Belgium, 178
Batcheller, Lt. Col. Herbert F., 37, 43
Batesville, Mississippi, 75
Bay of Salerno, 27
Baynes, Pvt. John J., 159
Beck Private Carl A., 39, 137, 139
Belfast, Northern Ireland, 39
Bellice, Sicily, 26
Bennett, Cpl. William, 197
Bergeval, Belgium, 197
Berlin, Germany, 227

Beuzeville-la-Bastille, France, 44
Biazzo Ridge, Sicily, 24, 25
Bilich, PFC Frank A., 39-40, 41-42, 72, 90, 103, 105, 118, 132, 135, 151, 195
Bittrich, Gen. Wilhelm, 167
Blanchard, Ernest R., 56
Blankenberg, Holland, 120
Blankenship, PFC Charles P., 47, 56, 63
Bleckede, Germany, 223, 224
Bois de Limors, France, 101, 102
Boling, S/Sgt. Earl W., 33, 38, 82, 84, 96-97, 99-100, 136, 137, 139, 150-151, 154, 172, 211, 218, 219, 227
Bonn, Germany, 219, 221, 222
Born, Belgium, 213
Borda, T/5 William F., 219, 224, 227
Bowman, PFC David V., 11-12, 17, 20, 75, 95, 129, 130-131, 171, 196-197, 205
Bradgate Park, England, 41
Bradley, Gen. Omar N., 97, 98, 108
Brandt, Pvt. Paul R., 216
British Military Units
I Airborne Corps, 108
1st Airborne Division, 108, 109, 122, 123, 149, 170
Second Army, 109, 122, 169, 170, 222
6th Airborne Division, 222
23rd Armoured Brigade, 28, 37
XXX Corps, 109, 148
130th Brigade, 173
Glider Pilot Regiment, 149
Guards Armoured Division, 122, 124, 126, 135, 149
Grenadier Guards Regiment, 128, 139, 153, 156, 163, 165, 166
1st Grenadier Guards Battalion
No. 2 Company, 124
2nd Grenadier Guards Battalion
No. 3 Squadron, 124
SAS Phantom Detachment, 110
Brereton, Gen. Lewis H., 109
Brilla, Pvt. Michael A., 116, 166
Brown, T/4 Donald L., 210
Brown, PFC Horace H., 60
Brown, Melvin P., 42
Brown, S/Sgt. Russell W. Brown, 9, 20, 31, 41, 90, 99, 121, 142, 200, 208, 217, 227
Browning, Gen. Frederick, 108, 109, 148, 149
Bruhl, Germany, 221
Bryant Jr., Pvt. H. T., 56, 63
Buchholtz, Belgium, 214
Buffalo Boy, S/Sgt. Herbert J., 132, 133, 184, 185
Burdge, Pvt. John W., 35, 96, 186

258

Burdick, Robert M., 219
Burke, Cpl. Thomas J., 32, 35, 38, 70, 84, 154, 155
Byrd, PFC Thomas B., 95
Cadish, Lt. Harold O., 56
Camp Billy Mitchell, Alabama, 9
Camp Edwards, Massachusetts, 12
Camp Hoffman, North Carolina, 11
Camp Quorn, England, 41, 105, 106
Canoe, T/Sgt. Buffalo Boy, 48
Capuccini airfield, Italy, 28
Carlson, Capt. George D., 174, 197, 200, 201, 202, 212
Carnes, PFC Vernon D., 161
Carpenter, Maj. William R., 197, 210, 220, 221
Carpus, Cpl. Edward B., 32
Carr Jr., Lt. Oliver B., "O. B.", 72, 89, 106, 132, 133, 134, 173, 174, 212, 215, 221
Correnzien Forest, Germany, 227
Carroll, Lt. Jack P., 120, 144, 157, 160
Casablanca, French Morocco, 12
Case, Lt. Harold E., 170, 189, 200, 202, 203, 205
Central Intelligence Agency, 229
Chattahoochee River, 9, 10
Chatterton, Col. George, 149
Chef-du-Pont, France, 44, 81
Cheneux, Belgium 184
Cherbourg, France, 44, 63, 101
Chestertown, Maryland, 8
Chicago, Illinois, 39
Citizen Military Training Corps, 8
Clark Jr., Sgt. Cullen E., 45, 52-53, 66-67
Clark, Sgt. Eldon M., 89, 102
Clark, Sgt. George A., 53
Clark, Brig. Gen. Hal, 14
Clark, Gen. Mark, 14, 27
Cliff, Lt. John C., 74
Cobb, Lt. John H., 215
Collins, Gen. Lawton, 80, 87
Cologne, Germany, 219
Comly, Pvt. David D., 35
Connell, Lt. Ivey K., 21
Cookstown, Northern Ireland, 39
Cooper, Lt. John L., 172, 185
Cooper, Pvt. Robert H., 162
Cooperider, Lt. Claiborne, 105, 141, 142
Corti, John P., 98
Costa Rica, 9
Cotentin Peninsula, France, 43, 44, 50, 53, 97
Cottesmore airfield, England, 8, 44, 47, 113
Cotton's Fish Camp, 9, 10, 42
Coustillac, Lt. Henry G., 207
Coventry, England, 48
Coyle, Lt. James J., 20-21, 23, 40, 44, 52, 59, 70, 81, 82, 83, 84-85, 86, 87, 120, 136-
137, 138, 139-140, 145-146, 148, 153-155, 219-220, 224-226
Craig, Pvt. Kenneth R., 195
Crouse, Cpl. Richard, 154
Custer, Maj. Gen. George A. Custer, 108
Davis, PFC Allen B., 89
Davis, PFC Edwin G., 195
Dellien, Germany, 227
DeMayo, PFC Anthony J., 48, 50
Dempsey, Gen. Sir Miles, 169
Dewailly, Pvt. Voorhies P., 195
Di Battista, PFC Dominick, 223, 224
Dippolito, PFC Dominic J., 174
Distinguished Service Cross, 21, 74, 75, 87, 88, 168, 190
Dodd, Lt. John H., 41, 142, 161
Doerfler, Lt. Eugene A., 19, 81, 82, 83, 84, 87, 104, 186
Dommel River, Holland, 109
Donlon, James A., 215
Douve River, France, 43, 44, 95, 97, 98, 99, 10
Doyle, PFC Donald A., 211
Draper Jr., Lt. Arthur F., 211
Dumke, PFC Robert H., 58
Dunnegan, Pvt. Harold V., 60
Durbin, PFC Samuel D., 186
Durst, Cpl. John, 102
Eastern Force, 124, 125, 128, 135
Ede, Holland, 113
Eindhoven, Holland, 109
Eisenhower, Gen. Dwight D., 27, 108, 228
Eisner, Cpl. Julius, 54, 129, 130, 176
Eitelman, T/5 Chick, 195-196
Ekman, Col. William E., 43, 60, 88-89, 93, 107, 112, 113, 116, 177-178, 189, 212, 221
Elbe River, Germany, 222, 223, 224, 225, 227
Elizondo, Pvt. Joe, 146
Ellingson, T/5 Lloyd G., 165
Ellis, PFC Donald E., 58, 130
Emerick, Pvt. Ulysses S., 171
Ensley, Sgt. Frankie B., 219
Epps, Sgt. Stephen, 224, 227
Escaut River, Belgium, 108
Essex, Lt. George, 208
Ètienville, France, 44, 95
Euling, SS Capt. Karl-Heinz, 122, 165
Evans, Pvt. Thomas H., 195
Failaise, France, 108
Fauville, France, 66, 81
Fields, Lt. John J., 186
Flynn, Jack S., 67
Folkingham airfield, England, 113
Formicola, Sam C., 219
Forsythe, Wesley A., 148
Fort Benjamin Harrison, Indiana, 8
Fort Benning, Georgia, 9, 193

Parachute School, 8, 9
Fort Bragg, North Carolina, 11, 12
Fort Hayes, Ohio, 8
Fort Yates, North Dakota, 132
Fosse, Belgium, 197
Fotovich, PFC George, 118
Francis, Cpl. Jack, 33, 35
Francisco, Sgt. Vernon L., 161, 203
Franco, Capt. Robert, 37, 118
Freeland, Cpl. Fred W., 21
Gagne, Pvt. Camille E., 161
Galvin, Pvt. Wayne W., 153, 161, 16
Garlick, Pvt. Harry, 174
Garrett, PFC Louis H., 30
Gasport, New York, 8
Gavin, Maj. Gen. James M., 9, 10, 11, 14, 15,
    17-19, 23, 24, 25, 26, 28, 37, 88, 107,
    108, 109, 110, 123, 148-149, 169, 179,
    207, 212, 213, 227, 229
Gela, Sicily, 14, 20, 24
Gennep, Holland, 110, 170
German Military Units
1st SS Panzer Division, 184, 186, 193
1st SS Panzer Grenadier Regiment, 184
Panzerjäger Abteilung 1, 184
Panzer Artillery Regiment 1
Abteilung 1, 184
II SS Panzer Corps, 167
2nd SS Panzer Division, 194
Sixth SS Panzer Army
Seventh Army Sturm Battalion, 72, 74, 81
9th SS Panzer Division, 122, 193
9th SS Reconnaissance Battalion, 122, 145,
    163
10th SS Panzer Division, 121, 122, 123, 166
15th Panzer Grenadier Division, 27
21st Army, 227
62nd Volsgrenadier Division, 198, 199, 202,
    205
91st Air Landing Division, 43, 71
1058th Grenadier Regiment, 89
1st Battalion, 72, 76, 79, 81, 87, 135
2nd Battalion, 72, 81, 87
3rd Battalion, 66
Infantry Gun Company, 55
406th Division, 122
572nd Heavy Flak Battalion
4th Company, 122
709th Antitank Battalion, 72, 81
795th Georgian Battalion, 81
Herman Göring Panzer Division, 23, 27
1st Herman Göring Panzer Grenadier
Regiment, 23
2nd Company, 504th Schwere Panzer
Abteilung, 23
Herman Göring Training Regiment, 122
Kampfgrupper Euling, 122

Kampfgruppe Hansen, 184
Kampfgruppe Links, 23
Kampfgrupper Melitz, 122
Kampfgruppe Peiper, 184, 193
Kampfgrupper Runge, 122
Gilhooly, Sgt. Joseph F., 205
Gill, Pvt. John L., 154
Goulburn, Lt. Col. Edward H., 127, 159, 166
Goronne, Belgium, 205, 206, 209, 210, 211
Gould, Lt. Virgil D., 184, 185, 202, 212
Grand-Halleux, Belgium, 181
Grant, Pvt. John L., 195
Grave, Holland, 109
Graves, Lee G., 46
Gray, Maj. James A., 9, 15
Gregory, Sgt. Arthur L., 31, 160
Groesbeek, Holland, 109, 110, 113, 116, 119,
    121, 122, 124, 142, 169, 170, 171, 172,
    173
Guatemala, 9
Hable, PFC Earl H., 137, 139, 188, 191
Hagan, Maj. William J., 24
Hagenow, Germany, 228
Haggard, Pvt. John O., 102
Hall, Pvt. William L., 159
Hanover, Germany, 222
Harden Jr., Lt. Col. Harrison B., 14, 23
Harmel, Gen. Heinz, 166, 167
Harris, Donald E., 207
Harris, Capt. William J., 44, 138
Hart, Pvt. Alvin E., 32
Hayes Jr., Lt. William R. "Rusty", 116, 121,
    140-141, 143, 157, 159, 160, 163, 164,
    174-175, 176-177, 179-181, 189, 198,
    213
Haynes, PFC William R., 42, 95, 129
Hebein, PFC Fred J., 66, 100, 147, 156, 160,
    162, 187
Heid-de-Heirlot, Belgium, 197
Heller, Pvt. Leland C., 134
Herman Jr., Pvt. Jacob T., 129, 147
Herresbach, Belgium, 213
Hertesrott Heights, Germany, 216
Heumen, Holland, 120
Hicks Jr., Cpl. Howard W., 79
Hill 20, France, 81
Hill 30, France, 66
Hill 71, France, 43
Hill 81.8, Holland, 120
Hill 82, France, 43
Hill 110, France, 43
Hill 131, France, 102, 103
Hill, PFC Jack, 86
Hodge, Cpl. William E., 100
Hodges, Gen. Courtney, 179, 181
Holcomb, Lt. Joseph W., 159, 160
Honduras, 9

Honsfeld, Belgium, 213, 214
Horrocks, Gen. Brian G., 148, 149
Hudson, PFC Dale C., 101
Hughart, PFC Robert R., 61, 120, 121-122, 161, 165, 166, 229
Hughes, Lt. Marshall, 202, 203, 212
Hungerford, Pvt. Kenneth V. "Mickey", 153, 162, 165
Hunner Park, Nijmegen, Holland, 122, 123, 137, 138, 145, 156, 157, 158, 159, 160, 162, 163, 165, 166
Hupfer Lt. Col. C. G., 87
Hürtgen Forest, Germany, 216
Ireland, Capt. Alfred W., 15, 17, 19, 23, 24, 25
Italian Military Units
4th Livorno Division, 27
54th Napoli Division, 27
206th Coastal Division, 27
Jackson, Pvt. John R., 177, 179, 202, 210
Jacobs, T/Sgt. Irving, 200
Jacobus, Pvt. George R., 53
Jakiela, Sgt. Henry, 197
Janney, Lt. Richard M., 30
Jensen, Lt. Howard E., 183, 185, 219
Johnson, Richard L., 191
Johnson, Capt. William H., 14
Johnson, Cpl. Wilton H., 95
Joint Advisory Commission Korea, 229
Jones, Sgt. Edward D., 208
Jones, Sgt. James Elmo, 79, 80, 83
Jones, Cpl. William A. "W. A.", 63, 160, 164
Joster, Sgt. Roy, 115, 116
Kacyainski, Lt. Edward, 14
Kairouan, Tunisia, 15, 20, 27
Kall River, Germany, 216
Kamp, Holland, 116
Keenan, PFC James E., 100, 126-127, 162, 219
Keller, Pvt. John W., 33, 47-48, 52, 84, 86, 139, 150
Kelly, Cpl. James I., 70
Kiekberg Woods, Holland, 170, 171
King, Cpl. Roy O. King, 45, 57, 96, 129
Klee, Lt. Kurt B., 21
Knox, PFC Clyde F., 30, 162
Kommerscheidt, Germany, 216
Korean War, 229
Kotlarz, PFC Stanley W., 41, 70, 71, 74
Kouns, Lt. Col. Charles W., 14
Krause, Lt. Col. Edward C. "Cannonball", 24, 61, 80
Krayenhof Park, Nijmegen Holland, 132
Krka, PFC, Charless J., 208
Krueger, Howard R., 163
La Bonneville, France, 95
La Fiere, France, 44
La Gleize, Belgium, 184
La Haye-du-Puits, France, 102, 103

La Tour, Belgium, 181, 182, 184, 193
Lankford, Jules, 186
Lassen, Pvt. Donald D., 100, 125, 147, 163, 210
Le Ham, France, 93, 94
Leicester, England, 41, 43
Lent, Holland, 122, 166
Les Forges, France, 66
Les Rosiers, France, 95
Long, Capt. Talton W. "Woody", 31, 33, 35, 36, 37
López, Pvt. Alfredo R., 203
Lord, Cpl. Richard J., 129, 131
Loshheim, Germany, 215
Losheimergraben, Germany, 215
Loughborough, England, 41
Lough Neagh, Northern Ireland, 40
Lucero, Pvt. Gasper, 10
Ludwigslust, Germany, 228
Lynch, Sgt. Phillip M., 208
Maas River, Holland, 109, 110, 112
Maas-Waal Canal, Holland, 109, 110, 113, 116, 120, 149, 171
Malay, Pvt. Francis L., 32
Malden, Holland, 149
Manhay, Belgium, 194
Marienboom Girls' School, Nijmegen, Holland, 109
Marina di Ragusa, Sicily, 21, 23, 27
Markwood, PFC Francis H., 219
Martin, Capt. William C., 212, 215, 221, 222, 225
Matisick, T/5 Alexander J., 79
Matzelle, Henry J., 205
Mauldin, Bill, 28
McCarthy, George R., 67, 191
McClean, Lt. Thomas J., 72, 76, 78, 80, 81, 82, 84, 85, 87, 96, 106, 107, 118, 152, 171, 173
McCleary, Cpl. Max D., 159
McGrew, Cpl. Ralph H., 93
McIlvoy, Maj. Daniel B., 119
McKeage, Cpl. Donald W., 167, 189, 192-193, 200, 203, 205
McKinley, PFC James D., 201
McMandon, Pvt. William T., 135, 151
McPhee, Pvt. John D., 95
McRoberts, Capt. Neal L., 31
Meddaugh, Lt. William J., 51, 113-119, 136, 155, 173, 181, 182, 183, 185, 188, 189, 192, 193, 210
Mediterranean Sea, 19
Melahn, PFC Joseph L., 218
Merderet River, France, 44, 51, 90, 94, 95
Meyers, Lt. James J. "Joe", 106-108, 116, 128-129, 131-132, 147-148, 152, 168, 169-170, 173, 174, 185, 193, 194-195, 201,

202, 203, 205-207, 209-210, 212, 215-216, 221-222, 223, 230
Michaud, Pvt. Thomas J., 19
Michelman, Lt. Isaac, 60, 106, 128, 129, 132, 147
Miller, PFC Charles H., 58, 78-79, 132
Molenberg, Holland, 119
Montebourg Station, France, 89, 90, 93
Montenau, Belgium, 213
Montgomery, Field Marshal Bernard L., 109, 194, 198
Mook, Holland, 109, 112, 120, 170, 171
Muller, William A., 147
München-Gladbach, Germany, 223
Murphy, Audie, 134
Murphy, Sgt. Edward F., 168, 185
Naples, Italy, 27, 28, 29, 30, 37, 39
Nealy, Pvt. William H., 96, 97, 211
Neel, PFC Malcolm, 178
Neuberger, Pvt. William H., 70
Neuhof, Germany, 216
Neuville-au-Plain, France, 44, 59, 60, 67, 68, 69, 72, 74, 75, 87, 89, 90
Nicaragua, 9
Niepling, Larry, 164
Nijmegen, Holland, 109, 110, 113, 119, 120, 121, 122, 123, 124, 125, 126, 127, 141, 145, 148, 149, 152, 153, 155, 156, 167, 168, 169, 170, 171, 174, 190
Niland, Sgt. Robert J., 41, 60, 70, 90
Noirfontaine, Belgium, 197, 201
Northern Ireland, 39, 40, 41
Norton, Capt. John "Jack", 21, 60, 97
Nowinski, PFC Frank J., 31
Nunan, S/Sgt. Paul D., 57-58, 78, 89, 98, 119, 128, 132-134, 135, 218
Nurse, Pvt. Robert E., 162
O'Dea, Lt. Clifford J. "John", 220
O'Loughlin, PFC Dennis G., 36, 47, 115, 156, 191-192
Olds, Sgt. Donald H., 168, 169, 170, 194, 195
Olsen, Kenneth T., 208
Olszewski, Cpl. Edward J., 107, 205
Omaha Beach, France, 101
Oosterhout, Holland, 123
Operation Avalanche, 27
Operation Husky, 14, 15, 17
Operation Market Garden, 109, 119, 170
Operation Overlord, 8
Operation Pirate, 15
Oujda, French Morocco, 12, 14, 15
Over Asselt, Holland, 110
Pack, Pvt. Elmer, 95
Pack, T/5 Hubert G., 91
Packard, Lt. David L., 32, 37, 85
Paestum, Italy, 27
Pagalotis, George A., 164

Paris, France, 44
Paris, Raymond, 55-56
Parker, Lt. Russell E., 106, 132, 133, 203
Patton, Gen. George S., 14, 108
Payne, Lt. Houston, 83
Peddicord, Lt. Roper R., 52, 53, 66, 67
Peiper, Obersturmbahnführer Joachim, 184
Peterman, Pvt. Harold E., 142
Peterson, Lt. Theodore L. "Pete", 37, 69-70, 71, 75, 82, 83, 87, 113
Phenix City, Alabama, 9, 10, 42
Phillips Jr., Lt. John D., 138, 140, 146-147, 152-153, 155-156, 205, 208
Pickels, Cpl. Harry G., 34, 83
Polish 1st Independent Parachute Brigade, 109
Popilsky, PFC Ben N., 32, 146, 150, 154
Porter, S/Sgt. John C., 146
Prairies Marécageuses, France, 43
Presidential Unit Citation, 168
Price, Lt. Lawrence M., 173, 202, 206, 207, 212
Pritchard, PFC Norman M., 98
Pryzborowski, PFC Edward T., 146, 162, 163
Psaki, Lt. Nicholas J., 156, 161
Purcell, Cpl. George H., 79
Putman, Cpl. Clifford W., 155, 162, 167, 182
Putnam, Capt. Lyle B., 46, 59, 60, 63, 89, 105, 172, 210
Quorndon, England, 41, 105
Qualls, Lt. Charles K., 106, 167, 196, 212
Rabig, 1st Sgt. John H., 39, 42-43, 88, 90, 103, 106, 125, 128, 202
Raff, Col. Edson, 79, 81
Rajca, PFC Joseph J., 131
Rajner, PFC George J., 103
Raub, Pvt. Edwin L., 118
Ray, Sgt. John P., 56
Razumich, 1st Sgt. John R., 40
Reed Jr., Lt. William W., 188
Reharmont, Belgium, 197
Reichswald, Germany, 110
Reinhold, SS Maj. Leo, 123
Rencheux, Belgium, 181, 211
Rheims, France, 218, 228
Rhine River, Germany, 109, 170, 219, 221, 223, 225
Rice, Capt. John D. "Casey", 21, 31, 40
Rickerd, Pvt. Clyde M., 100, 136, 139
Ridgway, Maj. Gen. Matthew B., 11, 14, 15, 26, 27, 44, 60, 79, 81, 97, 98, 107, 108, 194, 222, 229
Robinson, Sgt. Peter, 166, 167
Robinson, PFC Robert M., 58, 103, 132, 134
Rodier, PFC James V., 97, 177
Roer River, Germany, 218
Rogers, 1st Sgt. Thomas J., 206, 207
Rojas, PFC Frank R., 208

Rome, Italy, 27
Rosen, Capt. Robert H., 108, 156, 158, 159
Russell, Capt. Clyde R., 23, 37, 40, 44, 45, 54, 61, 81, 82, 93, 108
Russell, Cpl. Jerome B., 190
Russell, Pvt. Kenneth E., 46-47, 55, 56-57, 165
Salerno, Italy, 8, 28, 47
Salmchâteau, Belgium, 216, 221
Salm River, Belgium, 181, 182, 183, 184, 193, 211
Sammon, Lt. Charles E., 63-66, 189
Sampson, S/Sgt. Otis L., 17, 33-36, 53, 59, 61, 69, 70-71, 73, 82, 83, 84, 85-86, 91, 120, 136, 138-139, 148, 156
Sandel, Sgt. R. A., 208
Santa Margherita, Sicily, 26
Saragosa, PFC Victor G., 200
Savell, Lt. William H., 160
Sayre, Capt. Edwin M., 31
Schell, PFC Lowell C., 208
Schlesener, Sgt. Milton E., 60, 168
Schlupp, T/5 Paul H., 209
Schmees, Lt. William E., 44, 177
Schmidt, Sgt. Victor M., 29-30, 99
Schneider, Pvt. Frank, 41
Schroeder, Pvt. Bernard J., 195
Schwammenauel Dam, Germany, 218
Schwerin, Germany, 228
Sebastian, PFC Julius A., 70
Seelye, PFC Irvin W. "Turk", 12, 17, 19, 41, 74, 93
Seine River, France, 108
Short, Lt. Albert W., 215
Shuman, James W., 200
Siegfried Line, Germany 213, 216
Silanskis, Pvt. Frank V. "Barney", 78, 131
Sink, Capt. Robert F. Sink, 9
Sionshof Hotel, 124
Skolek, Pvt. Leonard M., 41, 89-90
Slaverio, Pvt. John P., 60
Slavin, Edward A., 32
Slawson, Pvt. William E., 176, 215
Slugai, Pvt. Frank S., 133
Smith, Lt. James J. "J. J.", 48, 51, 57, 79, 80, 83, 108, 117, 124, 125, 136, 139, 146, 148, 152, 155, 161, 173
Smith, Capt. Taylor G. "T. G.", 44, 72-73, 75, 78, 88, 103, 107, 108, 128, 134, 135, 173, 174, 188, 190, 197, 212, 220, 221
Smith, S/Sgt. William, 82
Smithson, Cpl. Raymond D., 70
Sonnenburg, Pvt. George R., 193
Sorrento Mountains, Italy, 27
Spa, Belgium, 179
Spanhoe airfield, England, 44, 47
Sprinkle, Lt. John D., 21
St. Canisuis College, Nijemegn, Holland, 109

St.-Jacques, Belgium, 197
St. Lo, France, 108
St.-Martin-de-Varreville, 80
St. Oedenrode, Holland, 109
St.-Sauveur-le-Vicomte, France, 43, 95, 97, 99, 100, 101, 102, 103
St.-Vith, Belgium, 179, 213
Stavelot, Belgium, 179
Steed, Sgt. James T., 161
Steele, Pvt. John M., 55, 56, 59
Stein, Capt. Lester, 19
Ste.-Mère-Église, France, 44, 50, 51, 53, 55, 57, 59, 60, 61, 63, 66, 67, 68, 69, 71, 72, 73, 74, 75, 79, 80, 81, 82, 83, 86, 89, 104, 105
Stillings, Kenneth E., 219
Stiner, Pvt. Gordon M., 191
Stolberg, Germany, 219
Strawberry Hill, Northern Ireland, 40
Suippes, France, 176, 178, 179, 197, 212, 218
Supreme Headquarters Allied Expeditionary Force (SHEAF), 108, 222, 228
Sweeney, Lt. Alexander F., 65
Swift, Col. Ira P., 181, 188, 189, 212, 216
Syrene, S/Sgt. Irving N., 171
Taylor, Cpl. Stokes M., 190
Theux, Belgium, 212, 213
Thier-du-Mont, Belgium, 209, 210
Thompson, Lt. Col. Tommy, 19
Thompson, Sgt. Tommy, 10, 42
Tlapa, Pvt. Ladislaw, 56
Tournai, Belgium, 108
Trapani, Sicily, 26
Trieber, PFC Douglas J., 142
Trois Ponts, Belgium, 181, 182, 183, 184, 186, 188, 189, 190, 192, 193, 194, 196, 197
Trotman, Pvt. Paul C., 162
Tucker, Col. Reuben H., 14, 149, 156
Tumminello, Sicily, 26
Turnbull, Lt. Turner B., 60, 61, 67, 68, 69, 70, 71, 74, 75, 90, 106
Tuttle, Sgt. Roy M., 172, 173
Udenbreth, Germany, 216
United States Army Units
First Allied Airborne Army, 109
First Army, 179, 181, 197
1st Infantry Division, 14, 20, 24, 214, 216
1st Special Service Force, 176
3rd Armored Division, 194
4th Infantry Division, 44, 67, 79, 81, 83
8th Infantry Regiment, 81, 82, 83
1st Battalion, 81
2nd Battalion, 81, 82
12th Infantry Regiment, 80, 81, 82
Third Army, 108
Fifth Army, 14, 27
V Corps, 179

5th Infantry Division
10th Infantry Regiment, 8
7th Armored Division, 213, 222
Seventh Army, 14
VII Corps, 44, 80, 87, 90, 97, 101, 179
8th Infantry Division, 216, 222
9th Infantry Division, 101, 218
11th Infantry Regiment, 8
13th Armored Division, 221
Fifteenth Army, 219
17th Airborne Division, 108
XVIII Airborne Corps, 108, 194, 222
28th Infantry Division, 217
112th Infantry Regiment, 216
30th Infantry Division, 184, 194
39th Infantry Division, 26
45th Infantry Division, 14, 23, 24, 25, 27
180th Infantry Regiment, 24
Company L, 24
51st Engineer Combat Battalion
Company C, 181
75th Infantry Division, 212
79th Infantry Division, 102
80th Airborne Antiaircraft (Antitank)
Battalion, 112
Battery A, 74, 110, 178, 186, 209
Battery C, 99
82nd Airborne Division, 11, 14, 15, 24, 26, 27,
    28, 39, 43, 44, 46, 47, 48, 50, 57, 61, 79,
    102, 104, 108, 109, 110, 122, 135, 149,
    169, 171, 175, 176, 178, 179, 180, 181,
    194, 197, 198, 199, 213, 216, 218, 219,
    222, 227
82nd Airborne Reconnaissance Platoon, 110
82nd Airborne Signal Company, 14, 110
307th Airborne Engineer Battalion, 110
Company A, 110, 112
Company B, 14, 24, 44, 110, 183
Company C, 110
Company D, 110
Headquarters and Headquarters Company, 110
307th Airborne Medical Company, 14
325th Glider Infantry Regiment, 95, 112, 170,
    171, 197, 213, 214, 215, 216, 227
2nd Battalion, 90, 94
376th Parachute Field Artillery Battalion, 110
456th Parachute Field Artillery Battalion, 14,
    23, 25, 93, 94, 112
Battery C, 44, 188
504th Parachute Infantry Regiment, 14, 26, 27,
    110, 113, 120, 149, 156, 166, 173, 213,
    216
3rd Battalion, 14, 159, 167
504th Regimental Combat Team, 26
505th Parachute Infantry Regiment, 9, 11, 12,
    24, 27, 37, 39, 41, 43, 44, 45, 46, 48, 50,
    59, 60, 66, 87, 90, 91, 94, 95, 97, 99, 101,

102, 104, 110, 112, 113, 116, 135, 170,
    173, 176, 177, 178, 179, 181, 189, 193,
    194, 197, 202, 205, 210, 212, 213, 214,
    215, 216, 218, 219, 221, 223, 224, 227,
    228, 229
Headquarters and Headquarters Company, 30,
    37, 44, 47, 113
1st Battalion, 14, 28, 29, 37, 44, 47, 90, 93, 97,
    102, 103, 110, 112, 121, 170, 173, 181,
    223, 224
Company A, 31, 36, 37, 79
Company B, 79, 83
Headquarters Company, 79
2nd Battalion, 8, 9, 15, 19, 26, 27, 28, 29, 37,
    39, 40, 41, 43, 44, 46, 47, 50, 52, 57, 59,
    61, 63, 75, 79, 81, 83, 89, 90, 93, 94, 96,
    97, 101, 102, 103, 104, 105, 106, 108,
    110, 113, 115, 116, 119, 120, 122, 123,
    141, 145, 150, 153, 156, 167, 168, 169,
    170, 171, 173, 177, 181, 182, 188, 197,
    200, 202, 209, 210, 211, 212, 215, 216,
    218, 222, 223, 224, 229
Company D, 10, 11, 12, 17, 20, 21, 31, 37, 40,
    41, 42, 44, 45, 48, 54, 57, 58, 60, 61, 67,
    71, 72, 74, 75, 76, 78, 79, 80, 81, 82, 84,
    85, 87, 88, 89, 90, 93, 95, 96, 98, 101,
    102, 103, 106, 107, 108, 116, 117, 118,
    124, 128, 134, 135, 144, 147, 151, 152,
    167, 169, 171, 173, 174, 176, 182, 183,
    184, 185, 193, 194, 196, 197, 198, 201,
    202, 203, 205, 208, 209, 212, 215, 218,
    221, 224, 225, 227, 230
Company E, 10, 12, 17, 19, 20, 23, 29, 32, 33,
    36, 37, 38, 39, 40, 44, 47, 48, 50, 51, 52,
    53, 54, 59, 61, 66, 67, 68, 69, 71, 75, 81,
    82, 83, 84, 87, 91, 93, 96, 98, 99, 100,
    103, 108, 113, 115, 118, 119, 124, 125,
    136, 140, 144, 145, 146, 148, 150, 151,
    152, 153, 155, 156, 157, 159, 160, 161,
    162, 167, 168, 172, 173, 181, 182, 183,
    185, 186, 188, 189, 190, 192, 193, 194,
    200, 205, 210, 211, 213, 216, 218, 219,
    223, 224, 225, 227
Company F, 9, 20, 28, 29, 31, 32, 36, 37, 39,
    41, 44, 48, 50, 51, 55, 56, 57, 59, 61, 63,
    90, 91, 93, 98, 99, 100, 101, 103, 105,
    108, 116, 117, 120, 121, 124, 125, 140,
    142, 144, 153, 156, 157, 159, 160, 161,
    162, 163, 165, 166, 167, 170, 174, 176-
    177, 179, 182, 183, 189, 192, 195, 198,
    200, 201, 202, 203, 205, 206, 208, 210,
    211, 213, 216, 217, 219, 220, 224, 227,
    229
Headquarters and Headquarters Company, 17,
    19, 31, 44, 58, 63, 73, 79, 95, 97, 103,
    105, 124, 128, 132, 134, 141, 147, 151,

156, 159, 160, 162, 172, 177, 179, 182,
188, 192, 200, 202, 205, 208, 209, 218
3rd Battalion, 24, 25, 28, 44, 47, 57, 59, 60, 61,
80, 90, 101, 102, 110, 113, 116, 121, 170,
171, 173, 174, 181, 201
Company G, 24, 79
Company H, 25, 75
505th Regimental Combat Team, 14, 17, 26,
216
507th Parachute Infantry Regiment, 43, 51, 57,
95
508th Parachute Infantry Regiment, 43, 51,
101, 110, 177, 181, 189, 193, 213, 216
1st Battalion, 43, 121, 122
86th Infantry Division, 219
90th Infantry Division, 4
101st Airborne Division, 46, 56, 57, 61, 75, 93,
108, 109, 179
501st Parachute Infantry Battalion, 8, 9
Company B, 9
502nd Parachute Infantry Regiment
2nd Battalion, 57
506th Parachute Infantry Regiment, 9
106th Infantry Division, 179
517th Parachute Infantry Regiment, 197
551st Parachute Infantry Battalion, 197
746th Tank Battalion, 83, 87
Company A, 96
United States Army Air Corps Units
Eighth Air Force, 113
IX Troop Carrier Command, 108
50th Troop Carrier Wing, 110
52nd Troop Carrier Wing, 14, 110
Urquhart, Gen. Robert F., 149
USS Monterey, 12
USS Nevada, 71
Utah Beach, France, 43, 44, 66, 104
The Valkhof, Nijmegen, Holland, 123, 153,
163, 164
Van Fleet, Col. James, 81
Vandervoort, Lt. Col. Benjamin H. 8, 9, 11, 15,
17, 18, 19, 23, 24, 26, 27, 37, 38, 40, 41,
44, 46, 50, 51, 52, 57, 59-60, 61, 63, 68,
69, 71, 72, 73, 74, 75-76, 79, 81, 83, 87-
88, 90, 96, 97, 98, 99, 103, 104, 105, 106,
116, 119, 121, 122, 123, 124, 125, 126,
127, 135, 136, 138, 140, 141-142, 144-
145, 150, 153, 156, 157, 159, 160, 161,
163, 164, 165, 166, 169, 174, 175, 181-
184, 186, 188, 189-190, 192, 193, 200,
201, 207, 210, 229-230
Varenquebec, France, 102
Varvakis, PFC Charles R., 160, 162, 187, 188,
191
Vaux-Chavanne, Belgium, 194
Vechel, Holland, 109
Vielsalm, Belgium, 210, 216

Villa Belvoir, Nijmegen Holland, 122, 123,
137, 140
Villa Literno, Italy, 28, 29
Volturno River, Italy, 28, 31, 37
Vossenack, Germany, 216
Waal River, Holland, 109, 110, 121, 122, 124,
145, 149, 156, 159, 165, 167, 168, 170,
173
Walas, Lt. John, 181, 182, 185, 190
Walberg, Cpl. Gordon, 190-191
Walheim, Germany, 218
Wanne, Belgium, 184
Washington College, 8
Watts, Pvt. Roy L., 34
Wechsler, Lt. Ben L., 24
Weed, Sgt. Gerald R. "Jerry", 60-61, 67, 69,
71, 128, 131, 184, 185
Werboment, Belgium, 179, 185, 194
Wereth, Belgium, 213
Wertich, Lt. Jake L., 186, 190
West Jr., S/Sgt. Floyd, 74
Western Force, 124, 125, 128
Whitfield, PFC Daryle E., 31, 50, 55, 57
Wienecke, Col. Robert H., 177
Wilhelmina Canal, Holland, 109
Williams, Pvt. Jack C., 159
Wilson, Lt. William T., 21
Wöbbelin Concentration Camp, Germany, 228
Wood, Capt. George B., 37, 63, 89
Wood, Pvt. George M., 150
Woosley, Lt. Frank W., 10, 11, 82, 83-84, 85,
93
Worcester, Massachusetts, 30
Wray, Lt. Waverly W., 10, 17, 20, 21, 23, 72,
73, 75, 76, 78, 79, 87, 88, 104, 106, 128,
129, 130, 131, 135, 168
Wright, S/Sgt. Bonnie G., 200
Wurst, S/Sgt. Spencer F., 28, 29, 32, 63, 91,
98, 99, 100-101, 103, 105-106, 121, 141,
143-144, 157-158, 160, 163-164, 165
Wyngaert, Pvt. Julius A., 79
Yarchak, S/Sgt. Louis, 220
Yeatts, Maj. George, 87
Zahurance, PFC Paul V., 189
Zais, Lt. Melvin, 9
Zeetze, Germany, 227
Ziemski, Cpl. George S., 141
Zon, Holland, 109
Zuid Willems Vaart Canal, Holland, 109

Made in the USA
Lexington, KY
16 November 2012